Large Scale Machine Learning with Python

Learn to build powerful machine learning models quickly and deploy large-scale predictive applications

Bastiaan Sjardin

Luca Massaron

Alberto Boschetti

[PACKT] open source ✳
PUBLISHING   community experience distilled

BIRMINGHAM - MUMBAI

Large Scale Machine Learning with Python

First published: July 2016

Production reference: 1270716

Published by Packt Publishing Ltd.
Livery Place
35 Livery Street
Birmingham B3 2PB, UK.

ISBN 978-1-78588-721-5

www.packtpub.com

Credits

Authors
Bastiaan Sjardin
Luca Massaron
Alberto Boschetti

Reviewers
Oleg Okun
Kai Londenberg

Commissioning Editor
Akram Hussain

Acquisition Editor
Sonali Vernekar

Content Development Editor
Sumeet Sawant

Technical Editor
Manthan Raja

Copy Editor
Tasneem Fatehi

Project Coordinator
Shweta H Birwatkar

Proofreader
Safis Editing

Indexer
Mariammal Chettiyar

Graphics
Disha Haria
Kirk D'Penha

Production Coordinator
Arvindkumar Gupta

Cover Work
Arvindkumar Gupta

About the Authors

Bastiaan Sjardin is a data scientist and founder with a background in artificial intelligence and mathematics. He has a MSc degree in cognitive science obtained at the University of Leiden together with on campus courses at Massachusetts Institute of Technology (MIT). In the past 5 years, he has worked on a wide range of data science and artificial intelligence projects. He is a frequent community TA at Coursera in the social network analysis course from the University of Michigan and the practical machine learning course from Johns Hopkins University. His programming languages of choice are Python and R. Currently, he is the cofounder of Quandbee (http://www.quandbee.com/), a company providing machine learning and artificial intelligence applications at scale.

Luca Massaron is a data scientist and marketing research director who is specialized in multivariate statistical analysis, machine learning, and customer insight, with over a decade of experience in solving real-world problems and generating value for stakeholders by applying reasoning, statistics, data mining, and algorithms. From being a pioneer of Web audience analysis in Italy to achieving the rank of a top ten Kaggler, he has always been very passionate about everything regarding data and its analysis, and also about demonstrating the potential of data-driven knowledge discovery to both experts and non-experts. Favoring simplicity over unnecessary sophistication, he believes that a lot can be achieved in data science just by doing the essentials.

I would like to thank Yukiko and Amelia for their continued support, help, and loving patience.

Alberto Boschetti is a data scientist with expertise in signal processing and statistics. He holds a PhD in telecommunication engineering and currently lives and works in London. In his work projects, he faces challenges that span from natural language processing (NLP) and machine learning to distributed processing. He is very passionate about his job and always tries to stay updated about the latest developments in data science technologies, attending meet-ups, conferences, and other events.

About the Reviewer

Oleg Okun is a machine learning expert and an author/editor of four books, numerous journal articles, and conference papers. He has been working for more than a quarter of a century. During this time, Oleg was employed in both academia and industry in his mother country, Belarus, and abroad (Finland, Sweden, and Germany). His work experience includes document image analysis, fingerprint biometrics, bioinformatics, online/offline marketing analytics, and credit-scoring analytics. He is interested in all aspects of distributed machine learning and the Internet of Things. Oleg currently lives and works in Hamburg, Germany, and is about to start a new job as a chief architect of intelligent systems. His favorite programming languages are Python, R, and Scala.

> I would like to express my deepest gratitude to my parents for everything that they have done for me.

Kai Londenberg is a data science and big data expert with many years of professional experience. Currently, he is working as a data scientist at the Volkswagen Data Lab. Before that, he had the pleasure of being the lead data scientist at Searchmetrics, where Luca Massaron was a member of his team. Kai enjoys working with cutting-edge technologies, and while he is a pragmatic machine learning practitioner and software developer at work, he always enjoys staying up-to-date with the latest technologies and research in machine learning, AI, and related fields. You can find him on LinkedIn at `https://www.linkedin.com/in/kailondenberg`.

www.PacktPub.com

eBooks, discount offers, and more

Did you know that Packt offers eBook versions of every book published, with PDF and ePub files available? You can upgrade to the eBook version at www.PacktPub.com and as a print book customer, you are entitled to a discount on the eBook copy. Get in touch with us at customercare@packtpub.com for more details.

At www.PacktPub.com, you can also read a collection of free technical articles, sign up for a range of free newsletters and receive exclusive discounts and offers on Packt books and eBooks.

https://www2.packtpub.com/books/subscription/packtlib

Do you need instant solutions to your IT questions? PacktLib is Packt's online digital book library. Here, you can search, access, and read Packt's entire library of books.

Why subscribe?

- Fully searchable across every book published by Packt
- Copy and paste, print, and bookmark content
- On demand and accessible via a web browser

Table of Contents

Preface

"The nice thing about having a brain is that one can learn, that ignorance can be supplanted by knowledge, and that small bits of knowledge can gradually pile up into substantial heaps."

– Douglas Hofstadter

Machine learning is often referred to as *the part of artificial intelligence that actually works*. Its aim is to find a function based on an existing set of data (training set) in order to predict outcomes of a previously unseen dataset (test set) with the highest possible correctness. This occurs either in the form of labels and classes (classification problems) or in the form of a continuous value (regression problems). Tangible examples of machine learning in real-life applications range from predicting future stock prices to classifying the gender of an author from a set of documents. Throughout this book, the most important machine learning concepts, together with methods suitable for larger datasets, will be made clear to the reader, thanks to practical examples in Python. We will look at supervised learning (classification & regression), as well as unsupervised learning (such as Principal Component Analysis (PCA), clustering, and topic modeling) that have been found to be applicable to larger datasets.

Large IT corporations such as Google, Facebook, and Uber have generated a lot of buzz by claiming that they successfully applied such machine learning methods at a large scale. With the onset and availability of big data, the demand for scalable machine learning solutions has grown exponentially and many other companies and individuals have started aspiring to ripe the fruits of hidden correlations in big datasets. Unfortunately, most learning algorithms don't scale well, straining CPUs and memory either on a desktop computer or on a larger computing cluster. During these times, even if *big data* has passed the peak of hype, scalable machine learning solutions are not plentiful.

Frankly, we still need to work around a lot of bottlenecks even with datasets we would hardly categorize as *big data* (think of datasets up to 2GB or even smaller). The mission of this book is to provide methods (and sometimes unconventional ones) to apply the most powerful open source machine learning methods at a larger scale, without the need for expensive enterprise solutions or large computing clusters. Throughout this book, we will use Python and some other readily available solutions that integrate well in scalable machine learning pipelines. Reading the book is a journey that will redefine what you knew about machine learning, setting you on the starting blocks of real big data analysis.

What this book covers

Chapter 1, First Steps to Scalability, sets the problem of scalable machine learning under the right perspective and familiarizes you with the tools that we will be using in this book.

Chapter 2, Scalable Learning in Scikit-learn, discusses strategies for stochastic gradient descent (SGD) where we mitigate memory consumption; it is based on the theme of *out-of-core* learning. We will also deal with data preparation techniques that can deal with a variety of data, such as the hashing trick.

Chapter 3, Fast-Learning SVMs, covers streaming algorithms that are capable of discovering non-linearity in the form of support vector machines. We will present alternatives to Scikit-learn, such as LIBLINEAR and Vowpal Wabbit, which, although operating as external shell commands, can be easily wrapped and directed by Python scripts.

Chapter 4, Neural Networks and Deep Learning, provides useful tactics for applying deep neural networks within the Theano framework together with large-scale applications with H2O. Even though it is a hot topic, it can be quite a challenge to apply it successfully, let alone provide scalable solutions. We will also resort to unsupervised pre-training with autoencoders with the theanets package.

Chapter 5, Deep Learning with TensorFlow, covers interesting deep learning techniques together with an online method for neural networks. Although TensorFlow is only in its infancy, the framework provides elegant machine learning solutions. We will also utilize Keras Convolutional Neural Networks capabilities within the TensorFlow environment.

Chapter 6, Classification and Regression Trees at Scale, explains scalable solutions for random forest, gradient boosting, and XGboost. CART, an acronym for classification and regression trees, is a machine learning method usually applied in the framework of ensemble methods. We will also provide examples of a large-scale application using H2O.

Chapter 7, Unsupervised Learning at Scale, dives into unsupervised learning, as we will cover PCA, cluster analysis, and topic modeling using the right approach for scaling them up.

Chapter 8, Distributed Environments – Hadoop and Spark, teaches us how to set up Spark within a virtual machine environment, shifting from a single machine to a computational network paradigm. As Python can easily glue and power up our efforts on a cluster of machines, it becomes a piece of cake to leverage the power of a Hadoop cluster.

Chapter 9, Practical Machine Learning with Spark, gets into action with Spark, teaching all the essentials for starting immediately to manipulate data and build predictive models on large datasets.

What you need for this book

The execution of the code examples provided in this book requires an installation of Python 2.7 or higher versions on macOS, Linux, or Microsoft Windows.

The examples throughout the book will make frequent use of Python's essential libraries, such as SciPy, NumPy, Scikit-learn, and StatsModels, and to a minor extent, matplotlib and pandas, for scientific and statistical computing. We will also make use of an out-of-core cloud computing application called H2O.

This book is highly dependent on Jupyter and its Notebooks powered by the Python kernel. We will use its most recent version, 4.1, for this book.

The first chapter will provide you with all the step-by-step instructions and some useful tips to set up your Python environment, these core libraries, and all the necessary tools.

Who this book is for

This book is suitable for aspiring and actual data science practitioners, developers, and everyone who intends to work with large and complex datasets. We strive to make this book as accessible as possible to a wider audience. Yet, considering that the topics in this book are quite advanced, it is recommended, but not strictly compulsory, that readers are familiar with basic machine learning concept such as classification and regression, error minimizing functions, and cross validation.

We also assume some experience with Python, Jupyter Notebooks, and command-line execution together with a reasonable level of mathematical knowledge to grasp the concepts behind the various large solutions we propose. The text is written in a style that programmers of other languages (R, Java, and MATLAB) can follow. Ideally, it is highly suitable for (but not limited to) a data scientist familiar with machine learning and interested in leveraging Python, in respect to other languages such as R or MATLAB, because of its computational, memory, and I/O capabilities.

Conventions

In this book, you will find a number of text styles that distinguish between different kinds of information. Here are some examples of these styles and an explanation of their meaning.

Code words in text, database table names, folder names, filenames, file extensions, pathnames, dummy URLs, user input, and Twitter handles are shown as follows: "When inspecting the linear model, first check the coef_ attribute."

A block of code is set as follows:

```
from sklearn import datasets
iris = datasets.load_iris()
```

Since we will be using Jupyter Notebooks along most of the examples, expect to have always an input (marked as In:) and often an output (marked Out:) from the cell containing the block of code. On your computer you have just to input the code after the In: and check if results correspond to the Out: content:

```
In: clf.fit(X, y)
Out: SVC(C=1.0, cache_size=200, class_weight=None, coef0=0.0,
    degree=3, gamma=0.0, kernel='rbf', max_iter=-1, probability=False,
    random_state=None, shrinking=True, tol=0.001, verbose=False)
```

When a command should be given in the terminal command line, you'll find the command with the prefix $>, otherwise, if it's for the Python REPL it will be preceded by >>>:

```
$>python
```

```
>>> import sys
```

```
>>> print sys.version_info
```

New terms and **important words** are shown in bold. Words that you see on the screen, for example, in menus or dialog boxes, appear in the text like this: "As a rule, you just have to type the code after **In:** in your cells and run it."

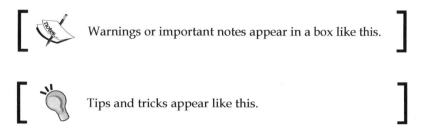

Warnings or important notes appear in a box like this.

Tips and tricks appear like this.

Reader feedback

Feedback from our readers is always welcome. Let us know what you think about this book—what you liked or disliked. Reader feedback is important for us as it helps us develop titles that you will really get the most out of.

To send us general feedback, simply e-mail feedback@packtpub.com, and mention the book's title in the subject of your message.

If there is a topic that you have expertise in and you are interested in either writing or contributing to a book, see our author guide at www.packtpub.com/authors.

Customer support

Now that you are the proud owner of a Packt book, we have a number of things to help you to get the most from your purchase.

Downloading the example code

You can download the example code files for this book from your account at http://www.packtpub.com. If you purchased this book elsewhere, you can visit http://www.packtpub.com/support and register to have the files e-mailed directly to you.

You can download the code files by following these steps:

1. Log in or register to our website using your e-mail address and password.
2. Hover the mouse pointer on the **SUPPORT** tab at the top.
3. Click on **Code Downloads & Errata**.
4. Enter the name of the book in the **Search** box.
5. Select the book for which you're looking to download the code files.
6. Choose from the drop-down menu where you purchased this book from.
7. Click on **Code Download**.

You can also download the code files by clicking on the **Code Files** button on the book's webpage at the Packt Publishing website. This page can be accessed by entering the book's name in the **Search** box. Please note that you need to be logged into your Packt account.

Once the file is downloaded, please make sure that you unzip or extract the folder using the latest version of:

- WinRAR / 7-Zip for Windows
- Zipeg / iZip / UnRarX for Mac
- 7-Zip / PeaZip for Linux

The code bundle for the book is also hosted on GitHub at `https://github.com/PacktPublishing/Large-Scale-Machine-Learning-With-Python`.We also have other code bundles from our rich catalog of books and videos available at `https://github.com/PacktPublishing/`. Check them out!

 On Github, you will also find Vowpal Wabbit executables for Windows.

Downloading the color images of this book

We also provide you with a PDF file that has color images of the screenshots/diagrams used in this book. The color images will help you better understand the changes in the output. You can download this file from `https://www.packtpub.com/sites/default/files/downloads/LargeScaleMachineLearningWithPython_ColorImages.pdf`.

Errata

Although we have taken every care to ensure the accuracy of our content, mistakes do happen. If you find a mistake in one of our books—maybe a mistake in the text or the code—we would be grateful if you could report this to us. By doing so, you can save other readers from frustration and help us improve subsequent versions of this book. If you find any errata, please report them by visiting `http://www.packtpub.com/submit-errata`, selecting your book, clicking on the **Errata Submission Form** link, and entering the details of your errata. Once your errata are verified, your submission will be accepted and the errata will be uploaded to our website or added to any list of existing errata under the Errata section of that title.

To view the previously submitted errata, go to `https://www.packtpub.com/books/content/support` and enter the name of the book in the search field. The required information will appear under the **Errata** section.

Piracy

Piracy of copyrighted material on the Internet is an ongoing problem across all media. At Packt, we take the protection of our copyright and licenses very seriously. If you come across any illegal copies of our works in any form on the Internet, please provide us with the location address or website name immediately so that we can pursue a remedy.

Please contact us at `copyright@packtpub.com` with a link to the suspected pirated material.

We appreciate your help in protecting our authors and our ability to bring you valuable content.

Questions

If you have a problem with any aspect of this book, you can contact us at `questions@packtpub.com`, and we will do our best to address the problem.

1
First Steps to Scalability

Welcome to this book on scalable machine learning with Python.

In this chapter, we will discuss how to learn effectively from big data with Python and how it can be possible using your single machine or a cluster of other machines, which you can get, for instance, from **Amazon Web Services** (**AWS**) or the Google Cloud Platform.

In the book, we will be using Python's implementation of machine learning algorithms that are scalable. This means that they can work with a large amount of data and do not crash because of memory constraints. They also take a reasonable amount of time, which is something manageable for a data science prototype and also deployment in production. Chapters are organized around solutions (such as streaming data), algorithms (such as neural networks or ensemble of trees), and frameworks (such as Hadoop or Spark). We will also provide you with some basic reminders about the machine learning algorithms and explain how to make them scalable and suitable to problems with massive datasets.

Given such premises as a start, you'll need to learn the basics (so as to figure out the perspective under which this book has been written) and set up all your basic tools to start reading the chapters immediately.

In this chapter, we will introduce you to the following topics:

- What scalability actually means
- What bottlenecks you should pay attention to when dealing with data
- What kind of problems this book will help you solve
- How to use Python to analyze datasets at scale effectively
- How to set up your machine quickly to execute the examples presented in this book

Let's start this journey together around scalable solutions with Python!

Explaining scalability in detail

Even if the hype now is about big data, large datasets existed long before the term itself had been coined. Large collections of texts, DNA sequences, and vast amounts of data from radio telescopes have always represented a challenge for scientists and data analysts. As most machine learning algorithms have a computational complexity of $O(n^2)$ or even $O(n^3)$, where n is the number of training instances, the challenge from massive datasets has been previously faced by data scientists and analysts by resorting to data algorithms that could be more efficient. A machine learning algorithm is deemed scalable when it can work after an appropriate setup, in case of large datasets. A dataset can be large because of a large number of cases or variables, or because of both, but a scalable algorithm can deal with it in an efficient way as its running time increases almost linearly accordingly to the size of the problem. Therefore, it is just a matter of exchanging 1:1 more time (or more computational power) with more data. Instead, a machine learning algorithm doesn't scale if it's faced with large amounts of data; it simply stops working or operates with a running time that increases in a nonlinear way, for instance, exponentially, thus making learning unfeasible.

The introduction of cheap data storage, a large RAM, and multiprocessor CPU dramatically changed everything, increasing the ability of single laptops to analyze large amounts of data. Another big game changer arrived on the scene in the past years, shifting the attention from single powerful machines to clusters of commodity computers (cheaper, easily available machines). This big change has been the introduction of **MapReduce** and the open source framework Apache Hadoop with its **Hadoop Distributed File System** (**HDFS**) and, in general, of parallel computation on networks of computers.

In order to figure out how both of these changes deeply and positively affected your capabilities of solving your large scale problems, we should first start from what actually prevented you (and still prevents, depending on how massive is your problem) from analyzing large datasets.

No matter what your problem is, you will eventually find out that you cannot analyze your data because of any of these limits:

- Computing affecting the time taken to execute the analysis
- I/O affecting how much of your data you can take from storage to memory in a time unit
- Memory affecting how much large data you can process at a time

Your computer has limitations that will determine if you can learn from your data and how long it will take before you hit a wall. Computing limitations occur in many intensive calculations, I/O problems will bottleneck your prompt access to data, and finally memory limitations can constraint you to take on only a part of your data, thus limiting the kind of matrix computations that you may have access to or the precision or even exactness of your estimations.

Each of these hardware limitations will also affect you differently in severity with regard to the data you are analyzing:

- Tall data, which is characterized by a large number of cases
- Wide data, which is characterized by a large number of features
- Tall and wide data, which has a large number of both cases and features
- Sparse data, which is characterized by a large number of zero entries or entries that could be transformed into zeros (that is, the data matrix may be tall and/or wide but informative, but not all the matrix entries have informative value)

Finally, it comes down to the algorithm that you are going to use in order to learn from the data. Each algorithm has its own characteristics, being able to map data using a solution differently affected by bias or variance. Therefore, with respect to your problem that, so far, you solved by machine learning, you considered, based on experience or empirical tests, that certain algorithms may work better than others did. With large scale problems, you have to add other and different considerations when deciding on the algorithm:

- How complex your algorithm is; that is, if the number of rows and columns in your data affects the number of computations in a linear or nonlinear way. Most machine learning solutions are based on algorithms of quadratic or cubic complexity, thus strongly limiting their applicability to big data.

- How many parameters your model has; here, it's not just a problem of variance of the estimates (overfitting), but of the time it may take to compute them all.

- If the optimization processes are parallelizable; that is, can you easily split the computations across multiple nodes or CPU cores, or do you have to rely on a single, sequential, optimization process?

- Should the algorithm learn from all the data at once or can you use single examples or small batches of data instead?

If you cross-evaluate hardware limitations with data characteristics and these kind of algorithms, you'll get a host of possible problematic combinations that can prevent you from getting results from large scale analysis. From a practical point of view, all the problematic combinations can be solved by three approaches:

- Scaling up, that is, improving performances on a single machine by software or hardware modifications (more memory, faster CPU, faster storage disk, and using GPUs)

- Scaling out, that is, distributing the computation (and the performances) across multiple machines leveraging outside resources, namely other storage disks and other CPUs (or GPUs)

- Scaling up and out, that is, taking the best of the scaling up and out solutions together

Making large scale examples

Some motivating examples may make things clearer and more memorable for you. Let's take two simple examples:

- Being able to predict the **click-through rate (CTR)** can help you earn quite a lot these days when Internet advertising is so widespread, diffused, and eating large shares of traditional media communication

- Being able to propose the right information to your customers, when they are searching the products and services offered by your site, could really enhance your chances to sell if you can guess what to put at the top of their results

In both cases, we have quite large datasets as they are produced by users' interactions on the Internet.

Depending on the business that we have in mind (we can imagine some big players here), we are clearly talking of millions of data points per day in both our examples. In the advertising case, data is certainly tall, being a continuous stream of information as the most recent data, more representative of markets and consumers, replaces the older one. In the search engine case, data is wide, being enriched by the feature provided by the results you offered to your customers: for instance, if you are in the travels business, you will have quite a lot of features about hotels, locations, and services offered.

Clearly, scalability is an issue for both these problems:

- You have to learn from data that is growing every day and you have to learn fast because as you are learning, new data keeps arriving. Yet, you have to deal with data that clearly cannot fit in memory because the matrix is too tall or too large.

- You frequently need to update your machine learning model in order to accommodate new data. You need an algorithm that can process the information in a timely manner. $O(n^2)$ or $O(n^3)$ complexities could be impossible for you to handle because of the data quantity; you need some algorithm that can work with lower complexity (such as $O(n)$) or by dividing the data so that n will be much, much smaller.

- You have to be able to predict fast because the predictions have to be delivered only to new customers. Again, the complexity of your algorithm does matter.

The scalability problem can be solved in one or multiple ways:

- Scaling up by reducing the dimensionality of the problem; for instance, in the case of the search engine, by effectively selecting the relevant features to be used

- Scaling up using the right algorithm; for instance, in the case of advertising data, there are appropriate algorithms to learn effectively from streams

- Scaling out the learning process by leveraging multiple machines

- Scaling up the deployment process using multiprocessing and vectorization on a single server effectively

In this book, we will point out for you what kind of practical problems can be solved by each one of the solutions or algorithms proposed. It will become automatic for you to connect a particular constraint in time and execution (CPU, memory, or I/O) to the most suitable solution among the ones that we propose.

Introducing Python

As our treatise will depend on Python—our open source language of choice for this book—we have to stop for a brief moment and present the language before clarifying how Python can easily help you scale up and out with your massive data problem.

Created in 1991 as a general-purpose, interpreted, object-oriented language, Python has slowly and steadily conquered the scientific community and grown into a mature ecosystem of specialized packages for data processing and analysis. It allows you to have uncountable and fast experimentations, easy theory developments, and prompt deployments of scientific applications.

As a machine learning practitioner, you will find using Python interesting for various reasons:

- It offers a large, mature system of packages for data analysis and machine learning. It guarantees that you will get all that you may need in the course of a data analysis, and sometimes even more.

- It is very versatile. No matter what your programming background or style is (object-oriented or procedural), you will enjoy programming with Python.

- If you don't know it yet but you know other languages such as C/C++ or Java well, then it is very simple to learn and use. After you grasp the basics, there's no other better way to learn more than by immediately starting with the coding.

- It is cross-platform; your solutions will work perfectly and smoothly on Windows, Linux, and macOS systems. You won't have to worry about portability.

- Although interpreted, it is undoubtedly fast compared to other mainstream data analysis languages such as R and MATLAB (though it is not comparable to C, Java, and the newly emerged Julia language).

- It can work with in-memory big data because of its minimal memory footprint and excellent memory management. The memory garbage collector will often save the day when you load, transform, dice, slice, save, or discard data using the various iterations and reiterations of data wrangling.

 If you are not already an expert (and actually we require some basic knowledge of Python in order to be able to make the most out of this book), you can read everything about the language and find the basic installations files directly from the Python foundations at https://www.python.org/.

Scale up with Python

Python is an interpreted language; it runs the reading of your script from memory and executes it during runtime, thus accessing the necessary resources (files, objects in memory, and so on). Apart from being interpreted, another important aspect to take into consideration when using Python for data analysis and machine learning is that Python is single-threaded. Being single-threaded means that any Python program is executed sequentially from the start to the end of the script and that Python cannot take advantage of the extra processing power offered by the multiple threads and processors likely present in your computer (most computers nowadays are multicore).

Given such a situation, scaling up using Python can be achieved by different strategies:

- Compiling Python scripts in order to achieve more speed of execution. Though easily possible using, for instance, **PyPy**—a **Just-in-Time (JIT)** compiler that can be found at http://pypy.org/, we actually didn't resort to such a solution in our book because it requires writing algorithms in Python from scratch.

- Using Python as a wrapping language; thus putting together the operations executed by Python with the execution of external libraries and programs, some capable of multicore processing. In our book, you will find many examples of this when we call specialized libraries such as the **Library for Support Vector Machines (LIBSVM)** or programs such as **Vowpal Wabbit (VW)**, **XGBoost**, or **H2O** in order to execute machine learning activities.

- Effectively using vectorization techniques, that is, special libraries for matrix computations. This can be achieved using **NumPy** or **pandas**, both using computations from GPUs. GPUs are just like multicore CPUs, each one with their own memory and ability to process calculations in parallel (you can figure out that they have multiple tiny cores). Especially when working with neural networks, vectorization techniques based on GPUs can speed up computations incredibly. However, GPUs have their own limitations; first of all, their available memory has a certain I/O in passing your data to their memory and getting the results back to your CPU, and they require parallel programming via a special API, such as **CUDA** for NVIDIA-manufactured GPUs (so you have to install the appropriate drivers and programs).

- Reducing a large problem into chunks and solving each chunk one at a time in-memory (divide and conquer algorithms). This leads to the partitioning or subsampling of data from memory or disk and managing approximate solutions of your machine learning problem, which is quite effective. It is important to notice that both partitioning and subsampling can operate for cases and features (and both). If the original data is kept on a disk storage, I/O constraints will become quite determinant of the resulting performances.

- Effectively leveraging both multiprocessing and multithreading, depending on the learning algorithm that you will be using. Some algorithms will naturally be able to split their operations into parallel ones. In such cases, the only constraint will be your CPU's and your memory (as your data will have to be replicated for every parallel worker that you will be using). Some other algorithms will instead take advantage of multithreading, thus managing more operations at the same time on the same memory blocks.

Scale out with Python

Scaling out solutions simply involve connecting together multiple machines into a cluster. As you connect the machines (scaling out), you can also scale up each one of them using configurations that are more powerful (thus augmenting CPU, memory, and I/O), applying the techniques we mentioned in the previous paragraph and enhancing their performances.

By connecting multiple machines, you can leverage their computational power in a parallel fashion. Your data will be distributed across multiple storage disks/memory, limiting I/O transfers by having each machine work only on its available data (that is, its own storage disk or RAM memory).

In our book, this translates into using outside resources effectively by means of the following:

- The H2O framework
- The Hadoop framework and its components, such as HDFS, MapReduce, and **Yet Another Resource Negotiator (YARN)**
- The Spark framework on top of Hadoop

Each of these frameworks will be controlled by Python (for instance, Spark by its Python interface named pySpark).

Python for large scale machine learning

Given the availability of many useful packages for machine learning and the fact that it is a programming language quite popular among data scientists, Python is our language of choice for all the code presented in this book.

In this book, when necessary, we will provide further instructions in order to install any further necessary library or tool. Here, we will instead start installing the basics, that is, the Python language and the most frequently used packages for computations and machine learning.

Choosing between Python 2 and Python 3

Before starting, it is important to know that there are two main branches of Python: versions 2 and 3. As many core functionalities have changed, scripts built for one version are sometimes incompatible with the other one (they won't work without raising errors and warnings). Although the third version is the newest, the older one is still the most used version in the scientific area and the default version for many operative systems (mainly for compatibility in upgrades). When version 3 was released (in 2008), most scientific packages weren't ready so the scientific community stuck with the previous version. Fortunately, since then, almost all packages have been updated leaving just a few (see `http://py3readiness.org` for a compatibility overview) as orphans of Python 3 compatibility.

In spite of the recent growth in popularity of Python 3 (which, we shouldn't forget, is the future of Python), Python 2 is still widely used among data scientists and data analysts. Moreover, for a long time Python 2 has been the default Python installation (for instance, on Ubuntu), so it is the most likely version that most of the readers should have ready at hand. For all these reasons, we will adopt Python 2 for this book. It is not merely *love for the old technologies*, it is just a practical choice in order to make *Large Scale Machine Learning with Python* accessible to the largest audience:

- The Python 2 code will immediately address the existing audience of data experts.

- Python 3 users will find it very easy to convert our scripts in order to work under their favored Python version because the code we wrote is easily convertible and we will provide a Python 3 version of all our scripts and notebooks, freely downloadable from the Packt website.

In case you need to understand the differences between Python 2 and Python 3 in depth, we suggest reading this web page about writing Python 2-3 compatible code:

`http://python-future.org/compatible_idioms.html`

From **Python-Future**, you may also find reading about how to convert Python 2 code to Python 3 useful:

`http://python-future.org/automatic_conversion.html`

Installing Python

As the first step, we are going to create a working environment for data science that you can use to replicate and test the examples in the book and prototype your own large solutions.

No matter in what language you are going to develop your application, Python will gift you with an easy time getting your data, building your model from it, and extracting the right parameters you need to make your predictions in a production environment.

Python is an open source, object-oriented, cross-platform programming language that, compared with its direct competitors (for instance, C/C++ and Java), produces very concise and readable code. It allows you to build a working software prototype in a very short time and tests, maintains, and scales it in the future. It has become the most used language in the data scientist's toolbox because, in the end, it is a general-purpose language turned very flexible thanks to a large variety of available packages that can easily and rapidly help you solve a wide spectrum of both common and niche problems.

Step-by-step installation

If you have never used Python (but this doesn't mean that you may not already have it installed on your machine), you need to first download the installer from the main website of the project, `https://www.python.org/downloads/` (remember, we're using version 3), and then install it on your local machine.

This section provides you with full control over what can be installed on your machine. This is very useful when you are going to use Python as both your prototyping and production language. Furthermore, it could help you keep track of the packages' versions that you are using. Anyway, be warned that a step-by-step installation really takes time and effort. Instead, installing a ready-made scientific distribution will lessen the burden of installation procedures and it may be well-suited to first start and learn because it can save you quite a lot of time, though it will install a large number of packages (that for the most part you won't maybe ever use) on your computer all at once. Therefore, if you want to start immediately and don't want to bother much about controlling your installation, just skip this part and proceed to the next section, *Scientific distributions*.

Being a multiplatform programming language, you'll find installers for computers that either run on Windows or Linux-/Unix-like operating systems. Remember that some Linux distributions (such as Ubuntu) already have Python 2 packed in the repository, which makes the installation process even easier.

1. Open a Python shell, type `python` in the terminal, or click on the Python icon.

2. Then, to test the installation, run the following code in the Python interactive shell or its **Read-Eval-Print Loop** (**REPL**) interface provided by Python's standard IDE or other solutions such as Spyder or PyCharm:

```
>>> import sys
>>> print sys.version
```

If a syntax error has been raised, it means that you are running Python 2 instead of Python 3. If you don't experience an error and you can read that your Python version is 3.4.x or 3.5.x (at the time of writing, the latest version is 3.5.2), then congratulations for running the version of Python that we elected for this book.

To clarify, when a command is given in the terminal command line, we prefix the command with $. Otherwise, if it's for the Python REPL, it's preceded by `>>>`.

The installation of packages

Depending on your system and past installations, Python may not come bundled with all that you need unless you have installed a distribution (which, on the other hand, usually is stuffed with much more than you may need).

To install any packages that you need, you can use either the `pip` or `easy_install` commands; however, `easy_install` is going to be dropped in the future and **pip** has important advantages over it.

pip is a tool to install Python packages directly accessing the Internet and picking them from the **Python Package Index** (`https://pypi.python.org/pypi`). **PyPI** is a repository containing third-party open source packages, which are constantly maintained and stored in the repository by their authors.

It is preferable to install everything using `pip` because of the following reasons:

- It is the preferred package manager for Python and starting with Python 2.7.9 and Python 3.4, it is included by default with the Python binary installers

- It provides an uninstall functionality

- It rolls back and leaves your system clear if, for whatever reason, the package installation fails

The pip command runs in the command line and makes the process of installation, upgrade, and removal of Python packages a breeze.

As we mentioned, if you're running at least Python 2.7.9 or Python 3.4, the pip command should already be there. To assure which tools have been installed on your local machine, directly test with the following command if any error is raised:

```
$ pip -V
```

In some Linux and Mac installations, Python 3 and not Python 2 being installed, the command may be present as pip3, so if you receive an error when looking for pip, try running the following command:

```
$ pip3 -V
```

If this is the case, remember that pip3 is suitable only to install packages on Python 3. As we are working with Python 2 in the book (unless you decide to use the most recent Python 3.4), pip should always be your choice to install packages.

Alternatively, you can also test whether the old easy_install command is available:

```
$ easy_install --version
```

> Using easy_install in spite of pip and its advantages makes sense if you are working on Windows because pip will not install binary packages; therefore, if you are experiencing unexpected difficulties installing a package, easy_install can save your day.

If your test ends with an error, you really need to install pip from scratch (and in doing so, also easy_install at the same time).

To install pip, simply follow the instructions given at https://pip.pypa.io/en/stable/installing/. The safest way is to download the get-pip.py script from https://bootstrap.pypa.io/get-pip.py and then run it using the following:

```
$ python get-pip.py
```

By the way, the script will also install the setup tool from https://pypi.python.org/pypi/setuptools, which contains easy_install.

As an alternative, if you are running a Debian/Ubuntu Unix-like system, then a fast shortcut would be to install everything using apt-get:

```
$ sudo apt-get install python3-pip
```

After checking this basic requirement, you're now ready to install all the packages that you need in order to run the examples provided in this book. To install a generic <pk> package, you just need to run the following command:

```
$ pip install <pk>
```

Alternatively, if you prefer to use easy_install, you can also run the following command:

```
$ easy_install <pk>
```

After this, the <pk> package and all its dependencies will be downloaded and installed.

If you're not sure whether a library has been installed or not, just try to import a module in it. If the Python interpreter raises an **ImportError** error, it can be concluded that the package has not been installed.

Let's take an example. This is what happens when the NumPy library has been installed:

```
>>> import numpy
```

This is what happens if it's not installed:

```
>>> import numpy
Traceback (most recent call last):
File "<stdin>", line 1, in <module>
ImportError: No module named numpy
```

In the latter case, before importing it, you'll need to install it through pip or easy_install.

Take care that you don't confuse packages with modules. With pip, you install a package; in Python, you import a module. Sometimes, the package and module have the same name, but in many cases, they don't match. For example, the **sklearn** module is included in the package named **Scikit-learn**.

Package upgrades

More often than not, you will find yourself in a situation where you have to upgrade a package because the new version is either required by a dependency or has additional features that you would like to use. To do so, first check the version of the library that you have installed by glancing at the __version__ attribute, as shown in the following example using the NumPy package:

```
>>> import numpy
>>> numpy.__version__  # 2 underscores before and after
'1.9.0'
```

Now, if you want to update it to a newer release, say precisely the 1.9.2 version, you can run the following command from the command line:

```
$ pip install -U numpy==1.9.2
```

Alternatively (but we do not recommend it unless it proves necessary), you can also use the following command:

```
$ easy_install --upgrade numpy==1.9.2
```

Finally, if you're just interested in upgrading it to the latest available version, simply run the following command:

```
$ pip install -U numpy
```

You can also run the easy_install alternative:

```
$ easy_install --upgrade numpy
```

Scientific distributions

As you've read so far, creating a working environment is a time-consuming operation for a data scientist. You first need to install Python and then, one by one, you can install all the libraries that you will need. (Sometimes, the installation procedures may not go as smoothly as you'd hoped for earlier.)

If you want to save time and effort and want to ensure that you have a fully working Python environment that is ready to use, you can just download, install, and use the scientific Python distribution. Apart from Python, they also include a variety of preinstalled packages, and sometimes they even have additional tools and an IDE setup for your usage. A few of them are very well-known among data scientists, and in the sections that follow, you will find some of the key features for two of these packages that we found most useful and practical.

To immediately focus on the contents of the book, we suggest that you first promptly download and install a scientific distribution, such as **Anaconda** (which is the most complete one around, in our opinion), and decide to fully uninstall the distribution and set up Python alone after practicing the examples in the book, which can be accompanied by just the packages you need for your projects.

Again, if possible, download and install the version containing Python 3.

The first package that we would recommend you to try is Anaconda (`https://www.continuum.io/downloads`), which is a Python distribution offered by Continuum Analytics that includes nearly 200 packages, including NumPy, SciPy, pandas, IPython, matplotlib, Scikit-learn, and StatsModels. It's a cross-platform distribution that can be installed on machines with other existing Python distributions and versions, and its base version is free. Additional add-ons that contain advanced features are charged separately. Anaconda introduces **conda**, a binary package manager, as a command-line tool to manage your package installations. As stated on its website, Anaconda's goal is to provide enterprise-ready Python distribution for large-scale processing, predictive analytics and scientific computing. As for Python version 2.7, we recommend the Anaconda distribution 4.0.0. (In order to have a look at the packages installed with Anaconda, you can have a look at the list at `https://docs.continuum.io/anaconda/pkg-docs`.)

As a second suggestion, if you are working on Windows and you desire a portable distribution, **WinPython** (`http://winpython.sourceforge.net/`) could be a quite interesting alternative (sorry, no Linux or MacOS versions). WinPython is also a free, open source Python distribution maintained by the community. It is also designed with scientists in mind, and it includes many essential packages such as NumPy, SciPy, matplotlib, and IPython (basically the same as Anaconda's). It also includes **Spyder** as an IDE, which can be helpful if you have experience using the MATLAB language and interface. Its crucial advantage is that it is portable (you can put it in any directory or even in a USB flash drive), so you can have different versions present on your computer, move a version from a Windows computer to another, and you can easily replace an older version with a newer one just by replacing its directory. When you run WinPython or its shell, it will automatically set all the environment variables necessary to run Python as if it were regularly installed and registered on your system.

At the time of writing, Python 2.7 was the most recent distribution prepared on October 2015 with the release 2.7.10; since then, WinPython has published only updates of the Python 3 version of the distribution. After installing the distribution on your system, you may need to update some of the key packages necessary for the examples present in this book.

Introducing Jupyter/IPython

IPython was initiated in 2001 as a free project by Fernando Perez, addressing a lack in the Python stack for scientific investigations using a user-programming interface that could incorporate the scientific approach (mainly experimenting and interactively discovering) in the process of software development.

A scientific approach implies the fast experimentation of different hypotheses in a reproducible fashion (as does the data exploration and analysis task in data science), and when using IPython, you will be able to implement an explorative, iterative, and trial-and-error research strategy more naturally during your code writing.

Recently, a large part of the IPython project has moved to a new one called **Jupyter**. This new project extends the potential usability of the original IPython interface to a wide range of programming languages. (For a complete list, visit `https://github.com/ipython/ipython/wiki/IPython-kernels-for-other-languages`.)

Thanks to the powerful idea of kernels, programs that run the user's code are communicated by the frontend interface and provide feedback on the results of the executed code to the interface itself; you can use the same interface and interactive programming style, no matter what language you are developing in.

Jupyter (IPython is the zero kernel, the original starting one) can be simply described as a tool for interactive tasks operable by a console or web-based notebook, which offers special commands that help developers better understand and build the code that is being currently written.

Contrary to an IDE, which is built around the idea of writing a script, running it afterward and evaluating its results, Jupyter lets you write your code in chunks named **cells**, run each of them sequentially, and evaluate the results of each one separately, examining both textual and graphic outputs. Besides graphical integration, it provides you with further help, thanks to customizable commands, a rich history (in the JSON format), and computational parallelism for an enhanced performance when dealing with heavy numeric computations.

Such an approach is also particularly fruitful for the tasks involving developing code based on data as it automatically accomplishes the often neglected duty of documenting and illustrating how data analysis has been done, its premises and assumptions, and its intermediate and final results. If a part of your job is to also present your work and persuade internal or external stakeholders to the project, Jupyter can really do the magic of storytelling for you with few additional efforts. There are many examples on `https://github.com/ipython/ipython/wiki/A-gallery-of-interesting-IPython-Notebooks`, some of which you may find inspiring for your work as we did.

Actually, we have to confess that keeping a clean, up-to-date Jupyter Notebook has saved us uncountable times when meetings with managers/stakeholders have suddenly popped up, requiring us to hastily present the state of our work.

In short, Jupyter offers you the following features:

- Seeing intermediate (debugging) results for each step of the analysis
- Running only some sections (or cells) of the code
- Storing intermediate results in the JSON format and having the ability to do version control on them
- Presenting your work (this will be a combination of text, code, and images), sharing it via the Jupyter Notebook Viewer service (http://nbviewer. jupyter.org/), and easily exporting it to HTML, PDF, or even slideshows

Jupyter is our favored choice throughout this book, and it is used to clearly and effectively illustrate storytelling operations with scripts and data and their consequent results.

Though we strongly recommend using Jupyter, if you are using an REPL or IDE, you can use the same instructions and expect identical results (except for print formats and extensions of the returned results).

If you do not have Jupyter installed on your system, you can promptly set it up using the following command:

```
$ pip install jupyter
```

 You can find complete instructions about the Jupyter installation (covering different operating systems) at http://jupyter. readthedocs.io/en/latest/install.html.

If you already have Jupyter installed, it should be upgraded to at least version 4.1.

After installation, you can immediately start using Jupyter, calling it from the command line:

```
$ jupyter notebook
```

Once the Jupyter instance has opened in the browser, click on the **New** button, and in the Notebooks section, choose **Python 2** (other kernels may be present in the section, depending on what you installed):

At this point, your new empty notebook will look like the following screenshot and you can start entering the commands in the cells:

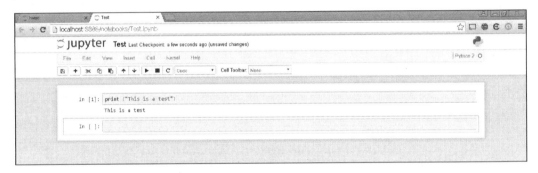

For instance, you may start typing the following in the cell:

```
In: print ("This is a test")
```

After writing in cells, you just press the play button (below the **Cell** tab) to run it and obtain an output. Then, another cell will appear for your input. As you are writing in a cell, if you press the plus button on the above menu bar, you will get a new cell, and you can move from a cell to another using the arrows on the menu.

Most of the other functions are quite intuitive and we invite you to try them. In order to know better how Jupyter works, you may use a quick-start guide such as http://jupyter-notebook-beginner-guide.readthedocs.io/en/latest/ or you can get a book specialized in Jupyter functionalities.

For a complete treatise of the full range of Jupyter functionalities when running the IPython kernel, refer to the following two Packt Publishing books:

- *IPython Interactive Computing and Visualization Cookbook* by *Cyrille Rossant, Packt Publishing*, September 25, 2014
- *Learning IPython for Interactive Computing and Data Visualization* by *Cyrille Rossant, Packt Publishing*, April 25, 2013

For our illustrative purposes, just consider that every Jupyter block of instructions has a numbered input statement and an output one, so you will find the code presented in this book structured in to two blocks—at least when the output is not trivial at all—otherwise, just expect only the input part:

```
In:  <the code you have to enter>
Out: <the output you should get>
```

As a rule, you just have to type the code after **In:** in your cells and run it. You can then compare your output with the output that we provide using **Out:** followed by the output that we actually obtained on our computers when we tested the code.

Python packages

The packages that we are going to introduce in the present paragraph will be frequently used in the book. If you are not using a scientific distribution, we offer you a walkthrough on what versions you should decide on and how to install them quickly and successfully.

NumPy

NumPy, which is Travis Oliphant's creation, is at the core of every analytical solution in the Python language. It provides the user with multidimensional arrays along with a large set of functions to operate multiple mathematical operations on these arrays. Arrays are blocks of data arranged along multiple dimensions, which implement mathematical vectors and matrices. Arrays are useful not just to store data, but also for fast matrix operations (vectorization), which are indispensable when you wish to solve ad hoc data science problems.

- Website: http://www.numpy.org/
- Version at the time of writing: 1.11.1
- Suggested install command:

```
$ pip install numpy
```

As a convention that is largely adopted by the Python community, when importing NumPy, it is suggested that you alias it as np:

```
import numpy as np
```

SciPy

An original project by Travis Oliphant, Pearu Peterson, and Eric Jones, SciPy completes NumPy's functionalities, offering a larger variety of scientific algorithms for linear algebra, sparse matrices, signal and image processing, optimization, fast Fourier transformation, and much more.

- Website: http://www.scipy.org/
- Version at the time of writing: 0.17.1
- Suggested install command:

  ```
  $ pip install scipy
  ```

Pandas

Pandas deals with everything that NumPy and SciPy cannot do. In particular, thanks to its specific object data structures, DataFrames, and Series, it allows the handling of complex tables of data of different types (something that NumPy's arrays cannot) and time series. Thanks to Wes McKinney's creation, you will be able to easily and smoothly load data from a variety of sources, and then slice, dice, handle missing elements, add, rename, aggregate, reshape, and finally visualize it at your will.

- Website: http://pandas.pydata.org/
- Version at the time of writing: 0.18.0
- Suggested install command:

  ```
  $ pip install pandas
  ```

 Conventionally, pandas is imported as pd:

```
import pandas as pd
```

Scikit-learn

Started as part of SciKits (SciPy Toolkits), Scikit-learn is the core of data science operations in Python. It offers all that you may need in terms of data preprocessing, supervised and unsupervised learning, model selection, validation, and error metrics. Expect us to talk at length about this package throughout the book.

Scikit-learn started in 2007 as a Google Summer of Code project by David Cournapeau. Since 2013, it has been taken over by the researchers at Inria (French Institute for Research in Computer Science and Automation).

Scikit-learn offers modules for data processing (`sklearn.preprocessing` and `sklearn.feature_extraction`), model selection and validation (`sklearn.cross_validation`, `sklearn.grid_search`, and `sklearn.metrics`), and a complete set of methods (`sklearn.linear_model`) in which the target value, being a number or probability, is expected to be a linear combination of the input variables.

- Website: `http://scikit-learn.org/stable/`
- Version at the time of writing: 0.17.1
- Suggested install command:

  ```
  $ pip install scikit-learn
  ```

 Note that the imported module is named `sklearn`.

The matplotlib package

Originally developed by John Hunter, matplotlib is the library containing all the building blocks to create quality plots from arrays and visualize them interactively.

You can find all the MATLAB-like plotting frameworks inside the PyLab module.

- Website: `http://matplotlib.org/`
- Version at the time of writing: 1.5.1
- Suggested install command:

  ```
  $ pip install matplotlib
  ```

You can simply import just what you need for your visualization purposes:

```
import matplotlib as mpl
from matplotlib import pyplot as plt
```

Gensim

Gensim, programmed by Radim Řehůřek, is an open source package suitable to analyze large textual collections by the usage of parallel distributable online algorithms. Among advanced functionalities, it implements **Latent Semantic Analysis (LSA)**, topic modeling by **Latent Dirichlet Allocation (LDA)**, and Google's **word2vec**, a powerful algorithm to transform texts into vector features to be used in supervised and unsupervised machine learning.

- Website: `http://radimrehurek.com/gensim/`
- Version at the time of writing: 0.13.1
- Suggested install command:

```
$ pip install gensim
```

H2O

H2O is an open source framework for big data analysis created by the start-up **H2O.ai** (previously named as 0xdata). It is usable by R, Python, Scala, and Java programming languages. H2O easily allows using a standalone machine (leveraging multiprocessing) or Hadoop cluster (for example, a cluster in an AWS environment), thus helping you scale up and out.

- Website: `http://www.h2o.ai`
- Version at the time of writing: 3.8.3.3

In order to install the package, you first have to download and install Java on your system, (You need to have **Java Development Kit (JDK)** 1.8 installed as H2O is Java-based.) then you can refer to the online instructions provided at `http://www.h2o.ai/download/h2o/python`.

We can overview all the installation steps together in the following lines.

You can install both H2O and its Python API, as we have been using in our book, by the following instructions:

```
$ pip install -U requests
$ pip install -U tabulate
$ pip install -U future
$ pip install -U six
```

These steps will install the required packages, and then we can install the framework, taking care to remove any previous installation:

```
$ pip uninstall h2o
$ pip install h2o
```

In order to have installed the same version as we have in our book, you can change the last `pip install` command with the following:

```
$ pip install http://h2o-release.s3.amazonaws.com/h2o/rel-turin/3/Python/
h2o-3.8.3.3-py2.py3-none-any.whl
```

If you run into problems, please visit the H2O Google groups page, where you can get help with your problems:

```
https://groups.google.com/forum/#!forum/h2ostream
```

XGBoost

XGBoost is a scalable, portable, and distributed gradient boosting library (a tree ensemble machine learning algorithm). It is available for Python, R, Java, Scala, Julia, and C++ and it can work on a single machine (leveraging multithreading), both in Hadoop and Spark clusters.

- Website: `https://xgboost.readthedocs.io/en/latest/`
- Version at the time of writing: 0.4

Detailed instructions to install XGBoost on your system can be found at `https://github.com/dmlc/xgboost/blob/master/doc/build.md`.

The installation of XGBoost on both Linux and Mac OS is quite straightforward, whereas it is a little bit trickier for Windows users. For this reason, we provide specific installations steps to have XGBoost working on Windows:

1. First of all, download and install **Git for Windows** (`https://git-for-windows.github.io/`).

2. Then you need a **Minimalist GNU for Windows (MinGW)** compiler present on your system. You can download it from `http://www.mingw.org/` according to the characteristics of your system.

3. From the command line, execute the following:

   ```
   $ git clone --recursive https://github.com/dmlc/xgboost
   $ cd xgboost
   $ git submodule init
   $ git submodule update
   ```

4. Then, from the command line, copy the configuration for 64-bit systems to be the default one:

```
$ copy make\mingw64.mk config.mk
```

Alternatively, you can copy the plain 32-bit version:

```
$ copy make\mingw.mk config.mk
```

5. After copying the configuration file, you can run the compiler, setting it to use four threads in order to speed up the compiling procedure:

```
$ make -j4
```

6. Finally, if the compiler completed its work without errors, you can install the package in your Python by executing the following commands:

```
$ cd python-package
$ python setup.py install
```

Theano

Theano is a Python library that allows you to define, optimize, and evaluate mathematical expressions involving multidimensional arrays efficiently. Basically, it provides you with all the building blocks that you need to create deep neural networks.

- Website: http://deeplearning.net/software/theano/
- Release at the time of writing: 0.8.2

The installation of Theano should be straightforward as it is now a package on PyPI:

```
$ pip install Theano
```

If you want the most updated version of the package, you can get them with GitHub cloning:

```
$ git clone git://github.com/Theano/Theano.git
```

Then you can proceed with the direct Python installation:

```
$ cd Theano
$ python setup.py install
```

To test your installation, you can run the following from the shell/CMD and verify the reports:

```
$ pip install nose
$ pip install nose-parameterized
$ nosetests theano
```

If you are working on a Windows OS and the previous instructions don't work, you can try these steps:

1. Install TDM-GCC x64 (http://tdm-gcc.tdragon.net/).

2. Open the Anaconda command prompt and execute the following:

    ```
    $ conda update conda
    $ conda update -all
    $ conda install mingw libpython
    $ pip install git+git://github.com/Theano/Theano.git
    ```

> Theano needs libpython, which isn't compatible yet with version 3.5, so if your Windows installation is not working, that could be the likely cause.

In addition, Theano's website provides some information to Windows users that could support you when everything else fails:

http://deeplearning.net/software/theano/install_windows.html

An important requirement for Theano to scale out on GPUs is to install NVIDIA **CUDA** drivers and SDK for code generation and execution on GPU. If you do not know too much about the CUDA Toolkit, you can actually start from this web page in order to understand more about the technology being used:

https://developer.nvidia.com/cuda-toolkit

Therefore, if your computer owns an NVIDIA GPU, you can find all the necessary instructions in order to install CUDA using this tutorial page from NVIDIA itself:

http://docs.nvidia.com/cuda/cuda-quick-start-guide/index.html#axzz4A8augxYy

TensorFlow

Just like Theano, **TensorFlow** is another open source software library for numerical computation using data flow graphs instead of just arrays. Nodes in such a graph represent mathematical operations, whereas the graph edges represent the multidimensional data arrays (the so-called tensors) moved between the nodes. Originally, Google researchers, being part of the Google Brain Team, developed TensorFlow and recently they made it open source for the public.

- Website: `https://github.com/tensorflow/tensorflow`
- Release at the time of writing: 0.8.0

For the installation of TensorFlow on your computer, follow the instructions found at the following link:

`https://github.com/tensorflow/tensorflow/blob/master/tensorflow/g3doc/get_started/os_setup.md`

Windows support is not present at the moment but it is in the current roadmap:

`https://github.com/tensorflow/tensorflow/blob/master/tensorflow/g3doc/resources/roadmap.md`

For Windows users, a good compromise could be to run the package on a Linux-based virtual machine or Docker machine. (The preceding OS set-up page offers directions to do so.)

The sknn library

The **sknn** library (for extensions, **scikit-neuralnetwork**) is a wrapper for Pylearn2, helping you to implement deep neural networks without requiring you to become an expert on Theano. As a bonus, the library is compatible with the Scikit-learn API.

- Website: `https://scikit-neuralnetwork.readthedocs.io/en/latest/`
- Release at the time of publication: 0.7
- To install the library, just use the following command:

```
$ pip install scikit-neuralnetwork
```

Optionally, if you want to take advantage of the most advanced features such as convolution, pooling, or upscaling, you have to complete the installation as follows:

```
$ pip install -r https://raw.githubusercontent.com/aigamedev/scikit-
neuralnetwork/master/requirements.txt
```

After installation, you also have to execute the following:

```
$ git clone https://github.com/aigamedev/scikit-neuralnetwork.git

$ cd scikit-neuralnetwork

$ python setup.py develop
```

As seen for XGBoost, this will make the sknn package available in your Python installation.

Theanets

The **theanets** package is a deep learning and neural network toolkit written in Python and uses Theano to accelerate computations. Just as with sknn, it tries to make it easier to interface with Theano functionalities in order to create deep learning models.

- Website: https://github.com/lmjohns3/theanets
- Version at the time of writing: 0.7.3
- Suggested installation procedure:
  ```
  $ pip install theanets
  ```

You can also download the current version from GitHub and install the package directly in Python:

```
$ git clone https://github.com/lmjohns3/theanets
$ cd theanets
$ python setup.py develop
```

Keras

Keras is a minimalist, highly modular neural networks library written in Python and capable of running on top of either TensorFlow or Theano.

- Website: http://keras.io/
- Version at the time of writing: 1.0.5
- Suggested installation from PyPI:
  ```
  $ pip install keras
  ```

You can also install the latest available version (advisable as the package is in continuous development) using the following command:

```
$ pip install git+git://github.com/fchollet/keras.git
```

Other useful packages to install on your system

Concluding this long tour of the many packages that you will see in action among the pages of this book, we close with three simple, yet quite useful, packages, that need little presentation but need to be installed on your system: **memory profiler**, **climate**, and **NeuroLab**.

Memory profiler is a package monitoring memory usage by a process. It also helps dissecting memory consumption by a specific Python script, line by line. It can be installed as follows:

```
$ pip install -U memory_profiler
```

Climate just consists of some basic command-line utilities for Python. It can be promptly installed as follows:

```
$ pip install climate
```

Finally, NeuroLab is a very basic neural network package loosely based on the **Neural Network Toolbox (NNT)** in MATLAB. It is based on NumPy and SciPy, not Theano; consequently, do not expect astonishing performances but know that it is a good learning toolbox. It can be easily installed as follows:

```
$ pip install neurolab
```

Summary

In this introductory chapter, we have illustrated the different ways in which we can make machine learning algorithms scalable using Python (scale up and scale out techniques). We also proposed some motivating examples and set the stage for the book by illustrating how to install Python on your machine. In particular, we introduced you to Jupyter and covered all the most important packages that will be used in this book.

In the next chapter, we will dive into discussing how stochastic gradient descent can help you deal with massive datasets by leveraging I/O on a single machine. Basically, we will cover different ways of streaming data from large files or data repositories and feed it into a basic learning algorithm. You will be amazed at how simple solutions can be effective, and you will discover that even your desktop computer can easily crunch big data.

2
Scalable Learning in Scikit-learn

Loading a dataset into memory, preparing a data matrix, training a machine learning algorithm, and testing its generalization capabilities using out-of-sample observations are often not such a big deal given the quite powerful and yet affordable computers of this day and age. However, more and more frequently, the scale of the data to be elaborated is so huge that loading it into the core memory of your computer is not possible and, even if manageable, the result is intractable both in terms of data management and machine learning.

Alternative viable strategies beyond the core memory processing are possible: splitting the data into samples, using parallelism, and finally learning in small batches or by single instances. The present chapter will focus on the out-of-the-box solution that the Scikit-learn package offers: the streaming of mini batches of instances (our observations) from data storage and the incremental learning based on them. Such a solution is called out-of-core learning.

To treat the data by working on manageable chunks and learning incrementally is a great idea. However, when you try to implement it, it can also prove challenging because of the limitations in the available learning algorithms and streaming data in a flow will require you to think differently in terms of data management and feature extraction. Beyond presenting the Scikit-learn functionalities for out-of-core learning, we will also strive to present you with Python solutions for apparently daunting problems you can face when forced to observe only small portions of your data at a time.

In this chapter, we will cover the following topics:

- The way out-of-core learning is implemented in Scikit-learn
- Effectively managing streams of data using the hashing trick
- The nuts and bolts of stochastic learning
- Implementing data science with online learning
- Unsupervised transformations of streams of data

Out-of-core learning

Out-of-core learning refers to a set of algorithms working with data that cannot fit into the memory of a single computer, but that can easily fit into some data storage such as a local hard disk or web repository. Your available RAM, the core memory on your single machine, may indeed range from a few gigabytes (sometimes 2 GB, more commonly 4 GB, but we assume that you have 2 GB at maximum) up to 256 GB on large server machines. Large servers are like the ones you can get on cloud computing services such as Amazon **Elastic Compute Cloud** (EC2), whereas your storage capabilities can easily exceed terabytes of capacity using just an external drive (most likely about 1 TB but it can reach up to 4 TB).

As machine learning is based on globally reducing a cost function, many algorithms initially have been thought to work using all the available data and having access to it at each iteration of the optimization process. This is particularly true for all algorithms based on statistical learning that exploit matrix calculus, for instance, inverting matrices, but also algorithms based on greedy search need to have an evaluation on as much data as is possible before taking the next step. Therefore, the most common out-of-the-box regression-like algorithms (weighted linear combinations of features) update their coefficients trying to minimize the pooled error of the entire dataset. In a similar way, being so sensible to the noise present in the dataset, decision trees have to decide on the best splits based on all the data available in order to find an optimum solution.

If data cannot fit in the core memory of the computer in such a situation, you don't have many possible solutions. You can increase the available memory (depending on the limitations of the motherboard; after that, you will have to turn to distributed systems such as Hadoop and Spark, a solution we'll mention in the last chapters of the book) or simply reduce your dataset in order to have it fit the memory.

If your data is sparse, that is, you have many zero values in your dataset, you can transform your dense matrix into a sparse one. This is typical with textual data with many columns because each one is a word but with few values representing word counts because single documents usually display a limited selection of words. Sometimes, using sparse matrices can solve the problem allowing you to both load and process other quite large datasets, but this not a panacea (sorry, no free lunch, that is, there is no solution that can fit all problems) because some data matrices, though sparse, can have daunting sizes.

In such a situation, you can always try to reduce your dataset by cutting the number of instances or limiting the number of features, thus reducing the dimensions of the dataset matrix and its occupied area in-memory. Reducing the size of the dataset, by picking only a part of the observations, is a solution called subsampling (or simply sampling). Subsampling is not wrong per se but it has serious drawbacks and it is necessary to keep them in mind before deciding the course of analysis.

Subsampling as a viable option

When you subsample, you are actually discarding part of your informational richness and you cannot be so sure that you are only discarding redundant, not so useful observations. Actually, some hidden gems can be found only by considering all the data. Though computationally appealing—because subsampling just requires a random generator to tell you if you should pick an instance or not—by picking a subsampled dataset, you really risk limiting the capabilities of your algorithm to learn the rules and associations in your data in a complete way. In the bias-variance tradeoff, subsampling causes variance inflation of the predictions because estimates will be more uncertain due to random noise or outlying observations in your data.

In a world of big data, the algorithm with more quality data wins because it can learn more ways to relate predictions to predictors than other models with less (or more noisy) data. Consequently, subsampling, though acceptable as a solution, can impose a limit on the results of your machine learning activities because of less precise predictions and more variance of the estimates.

Subsampling limitations can be somehow overcome by learning multiple models on multiple subsamples of the data and then finally ensembling all the solutions or stacking the results of all the models together, thus creating a reduced data matrix for further training. This procedure is known as Bagging. (You actually compress the features in this way, thus reducing the space of your data in memory.) We will explore ensembling and stacking in a later chapter and discover how they can actually reduce the variance of estimates inflated by subsampling.

As an alternative, instead of cutting the instances, we could cut the features, but again, we will incur the problem that we need to build a model from the data in order to test what features we can select, so we still have to build a model with data that cannot fit in-memory.

Optimizing one instance at a time

Having realized that subsampling, though always viable, is not an optimal solution, we have to evaluate a different approach and out-of-core actually doesn't require you to give up observations or features. It just takes a bit longer to train a model, requiring more iterations and data transfer from your storage to your computer memory. We immediately provide a first intuition of how an out-of-core learning process works.

Let's start from the learning, which is a process where we try to map the unknown function expressing a response (a number or outcome that is a regression or classification problem) with respect to the available data. Learning is possible by fitting the internal coefficients of the learning algorithm trying to achieve the best fit on the data available that is minimizing a cost function, a measure that tells us how good our approximation is. Boiled down to basics, we are talking of an optimization process.

Different optimization algorithms, just like gradient descent, are processes able to work on any volume of data. They work at deriving a gradient for optimization (a direction in the optimization process) and they have the learning algorithm adapt its parameters in order to follow the gradient.

In the specific case of gradient descent, after a certain number of iterations, if the problem can be solved and there are no other problems such as a too high learning rate, the gradient should become so small that we can stop the optimization process. At the end of the process, we can be confident to have found a solution that is the optimum one (because it is a global optimum though sometimes it may be a local minimum, if the function to approximate is not convex).

As the directionality, dictated by the gradient, can be taken based on any volume of examples, it can also be taken on a single instance. Taking the gradient on a single instance requires a small learning rate, but in the end, the process can arrive at the same optimization as a gradient descent taken on the full data. In the end, all our algorithm needs is a direction to orientate correctly the learning process on its fitting the data available. Learning such a direction from a single case randomly taken from the data is therefore perfectly doable:

- We can obtain the same results as if we were working on all our data at one time, though the optimization path may turn a bit rough; if the majority of your observations point to an optimum direction, the algorithm will take that one. The only issue will be to correctly tune the correct parameters of the learning process and pass over the data multiple times in order to be sure for the optimization to complete as this learning procedure is much slower than working with all the data available.

- We don't have any particular issue in managing to keep a single instance in our core memory, leaving the bulk of the data out of it. Other issues may arise from moving the data by single examples from its repository to our core memory. Scalability is assured because the time it takes to process the data is linear; the time cost of using an instance more is always the same, no matter the total number of instances we have to process.

The approach of fitting a learning algorithm on a single instance or a subset of data fitting to memory at a time is called online learning and the gradient descent taken based on such single observations is called stochastic gradient descent. As previously suggested, online learning is an out-of-core technique and adopted by many learning algorithms in Scikit-learn.

Building an out-of-core learning system

We will illustrate the inner workings of a stochastic gradient descent in the next few paragraphs, offering more details and reasoning about it. Now knowing how it is possible to learn out-of-core (thanks to the stochastic gradient descent) allows us to depict with higher clarity what we should do to make it work on our computer.

You can partition your activity into different tasks:

1. Prepare your data repository access to stream the data instance by instance. This activity may require you to randomize the order of the data rows before fetching data to your computer in order to remove any information that ordering may bring about.

2. Do some data surveying first, maybe on a portion of all the data (for instance, the first ten thousand rows), trying to figure out if the arriving instances are consistent in their number of features, type of data, presence or lack of data values, minimum and maximum values for each variable, and mean and median. Find out the range or class of the target variable.

3. Prepare each received data row into a fixed format that can be accepted by the learning algorithm (a dense or sparse vector). At this stage, you can perform any basic transformation, turning categorical features into numeric ones, for instance, or having numeric features interact by themselves by a cross-product of the features themselves.

4. After randomizing the order of examples (as mentioned by the first point), establish a validation procedure using a systematic holdout or a holdout after a certain number of observations.

5. Tune hyperparameters by repeatedly streaming the data or working on small samples of it. This is also the right time to do some feature engineering (using unsupervised learning and special transformation functions such as kernel approximations) and leverage regularization and feature selection.

6. Build your final model using the data that you reserved for the training and ideally test the efficacy of the model on completely new data.

As a first step, we will discuss how to prepare your data and then easily create a stream suitable for online learning, leveraging useful functions from Python packages such as pandas and Scikit-learn.

Streaming data from sources

Some data is really streaming through your computer when you have a generative process that transmits data, which you can process on the fly or just discard, but not recall afterward unless you have stored it away in some data archival repository somewhere. It is like dragging water from a flowing river—the river keeps on flowing but you can filter and process all the water as it goes. It's a completely different strategy from processing all the data at once, which is more like putting all the water in a dam (an analogy for working with all the data in-memory).

As an example of streaming, we could quote the data flow produced instant by instant by a sensor or, even more simply, a Twitter streamline of tweets. Generally, the main sources of data streams are as follows:

- Environment sensors measuring temperature, pressure, and humidity
- GPS tracking sensors recording the location (latitude/longitude)
- Satellites recording image data

- Surveillance videos and sound records
- Web traffic

However, you won't often work on real streams of data but on static records left stored in a repository or file. In such cases, a stream can be recreated according to certain criteria, for example, extracting sequentially or randomly a single record at a time. If, for instance, our data is contained in a TXT or CSV file, all we need to do is fetch a single row of the file at a time and pass it to the learning algorithm.

For the examples in the present and following chapter, we will be working on files stored on your local hard disk and prepare the Python code necessary for its extraction as a stream. We won't use a toy dataset but we won't clutter your local hard drive with too much data for tests and demonstrations.

Datasets to try the real thing yourself

Since 1987, at **University of California, Irvine (UCI)**, the **UCI Machine Learning Repository** has been hosted, which is a large repository of datasets for the empirical testing of machine learning algorithms by the machine learning community. At the time of writing this, the repository contains about 350 datasets from very different domains and purposes, from supervised regression and classification to unsupervised tasks. You can have a look at the available dataset at `https://archive.ics.uci.edu/ml/`.

From our side, we have selected a few datasets that will turn useful throughout the book, proposing challenging problems to you with an unusual, but still manageable, 2 GB RAM computer and a high number of rows or columns:

Dataset name	Dataset URL	Type of problem	Rows and columns
Bike-sharing dataset	`https://archive.ics.uci.edu/ml/datasets/Bike+Sharing+Dataset`	Regression	17389, 16
BlogFeedback dataset	`https://archive.ics.uci.edu/ml/datasets/BlogFeedback`	Regression	60021, 281
Buzz in social media dataset	`https://archive.ics.uci.edu/ml/datasets/Buzz+in+social+media+`	Regression and classification	140000, 77
Census-Income (KDD) dataset	`https://archive.ics.uci.edu/ml/datasets/Census-Income+%28KDD%29`	Classification with missing data	299285, 40

Dataset name	Dataset URL	Type of problem	Rows and columns
Covertype dataset	`https://archive.ics.uci.edu/ml/datasets/Covertype`	Classification	581012, 54
KDD Cup 1999 dataset	`https://archive.ics.uci.edu/ml/datasets/KDD+Cup+1999+Data`	Classification	4000000, 42

In order to download and use the dataset from the UCI repository, you have to go to the page dedicated to the dataset and follow the link under the title: **Download: Data Folder**. We have prepared some scripts for automatic downloading of the data that will be placed exactly in the directory that you are working with in Python, thus rendering the data access easier.

Here are some functions that we have prepared and will recall throughout the chapters when we need to download any of the datasets from UCI:

```
In: import urllib2 # import urllib.request as urllib2 in Python3
import requests, io, os, StringIO
import numpy as np
import tarfile, zipfile, gzip

def unzip_from_UCI(UCI_url, dest=''):
    """
    Downloads and unpacks datasets from UCI in zip format
    """
    response = requests.get(UCI_url)
    compressed_file = io.BytesIO(response.content)
    z = zipfile.ZipFile(compressed_file)
    print ('Extracting in %s' %  os.getcwd()+'\\'+dest)
    for name in z.namelist():
        if '.csv' in name:
            print ('\tunzipping %s' %name)
            z.extract(name, path=os.getcwd()+'\\'+dest)

def gzip_from_UCI(UCI_url, dest=''):
    """
    Downloads and unpacks datasets from UCI in gzip format
    """
    response = urllib2.urlopen(UCI_url)
    compressed_file = io.BytesIO(response.read())
    decompressed_file = gzip.GzipFile(fileobj=compressed_file)
    filename = UCI_url.split('/')[-1][:-3]
    with open(os.getcwd()+'\\'+filename, 'wb') as outfile:
        outfile.write(decompressed_file.read())
```

```
    print ('File %s decompressed' % filename)

def targzip_from_UCI(UCI_url, dest='.'):
    """
    Downloads and unpacks datasets from UCI in tar.gz format
    """
    response = urllib2.urlopen(UCI_url)
    compressed_file = StringIO.StringIO(response.read())
    tar = tarfile.open(mode="r:gz", fileobj = compressed_file)
    tar.extractall(path=dest)
    datasets = tar.getnames()
    for dataset in datasets:
        size = os.path.getsize(dest+'\\'+dataset)
        print ('File %s is %i bytes' % (dataset,size))
    tar.close()

def load_matrix(UCI_url):
    """
    Downloads datasets from UCI in matrix form
    """
    return np.loadtxt(urllib2.urlopen(UCI_url))
```

Downloading the example code

Detailed steps to download the code bundle are mentioned in the Preface of this book. Please have a look.

The code bundle for the book is also hosted on GitHub at https://github.com/PacktPublishing/Large-Scale-Machine-Learning-With-Python. We also have other code bundles from our rich catalog of books and videos available at https://github.com/PacktPublishing/. Check them out!

The functions are just convenient wrappers built around various packages working with compressed data such as tarfile, zipfile, and gzip. The file is opened using the urllib2 module, which generates a handle to the remote system and allows the sequential transmission of data and being stored in memory as a string (StringIO) or in binary mode (BytesIO) from the io module—a module devoted to stream handling (https://docs.python.org/2/library/io.html). After being stored in memory, it is recalled just as a file would be from functions specialized in deflating the compressed files from disk.

The four provided functions should conveniently help you download the datasets quickly, no matter if they are zipped, tarred, gzipped, or just plain text in matrix form, avoiding the hassle of manual downloading and extraction operations.

The first example – streaming the bike-sharing dataset

As the first example, we will be working with the bike-sharing dataset. The dataset comprises of two CSV files containing the hourly and daily count of bikes rented in the years between 2011 and 2012 within the Capital Bike-share system in Washington D.C., USA. The data features the corresponding weather and seasonal information regarding the day of rental. The dataset is connected with a publication by *Fanaee-T, Hadi, and Gama, Joao, Event labeling combining ensemble detectors and background knowledge, Progress in Artificial Intelligence (2013): pp. 1-15, Springer Berlin Heidelberg.*

Our first target will be to save the dataset on the local hard disk using the convenient wrapper functions defined just a few paragraphs earlier:

```
In: UCI_url = 'https://archive.ics.uci.edu/ml/machine-learning-
databases/00275/Bike-Sharing-Dataset.zip'
unzip_from_UCI(UCI_url, dest='bikesharing')

Out: Extracting in C:\scisoft\WinPython-64bit-2.7.9.4\notebooks\
bikesharing
    unzipping day.csv
    unzipping hour.csv
```

If run successfully, the code will indicate in what directory the CSV files have been saved and print the names of both the unzipped files.

At this point, having saved the information on a physical device, we will write a script constituting the core of our out-of-core learning system, providing the data streaming from the file. We will first use the csv library, offering us a double choice: to recover the data as a list or Python dictionary. We will start with a list:

```
In: import os, csv
local_path = os.getcwd()
source = 'bikesharing\\hour.csv'
SEP = ',' # We define this for being able to easily change it as
required by the file
with open(local_path+'\\'+source, 'rb') as R:
    iterator = csv.reader(R, delimiter=SEP)
    for n, row in enumerate(iterator):
        if n==0:
            header = row
        else:
            # DATA PROCESSING placeholder
            # MACHINE LEARNING placeholder
            pass
```

```
        print ('Total rows: %i' % (n+1))
        print ('Header: %s' % ', '.join(header))
        print ('Sample values: %s' % ', '.join(row))
```

```
Out: Total rows: 17380
Header: instant, dteday, season, yr, mnth, hr, holiday, weekday,
workingday, weathersit, temp, atemp, hum, windspeed, casual,
registered, cnt
Sample values: 17379, 2012-12-31, 1, 1, 12, 23, 0, 1, 1, 1, 0.26,
0.2727, 0.65, 0.1343, 12, 37, 49
```

The output will report to us how many rows have been read, the content of the header—the first row of the CSV file (stored in a list)—and the content of a row (for convenience, we printed the last seen one). The `csv.reader` function creates an `iterator` that, thanks to a `for` loop, will release each row of the file one by one. Note that we have placed two remarks internally in the code snippet, pointing out where, throughout the chapter, we will place the other code to handle data preprocessing and machine learning.

Features in this case have to be handled using a positional approach, which is indexing the position of the label in the header. This can be a slight nuisance if you have to manipulate your features extensively. A solution could be to use `csv.DictReader` that produces a Python dictionary as an output (which is unordered but the features may be easily recalled by their labels):

```
In: with open(local_path+'\\'+source, 'rb') as R:
        iterator = csv.DictReader(R, delimiter=SEP)
        for n, row in enumerate(iterator):
            # DATA PROCESSING placeholder
            # MACHINE LEARNING placeholder
            pass
        print ('Total rows: %i' % (n+1))
        print ('Sample values: %s' % str(row))
```

```
Out: Total rows: 17379
Sample values: {'mnth': '12', 'cnt': '49', 'holiday': '0', 'instant':
'17379', 'temp': '0.26', 'dteday': '2012-12-31', 'hr': '23', 'season':
'1', 'registered': '37', 'windspeed': '0.1343', 'atemp': '0.2727',
'workingday': '1', 'weathersit': '1', 'weekday': '1', 'hum': '0.65',
'yr': '1', 'casual': '12'}
```

Using pandas I/O tools

As an alternative to the csv module, we can use pandas' read_csv function. Such a function, specialized in uploading CSV files, is part of quite a large range of functions devoted to input/output on different file formats, as specified by the pandas documentation at http://pandas.pydata.org/pandas-docs/stable/io.html.

The great advantages of using pandas I/O functions are as follows:

- You can keep your code consistent if you change your source type, that is, you need to redefine just the streaming iterator

- You can access a large number of different formats such as CSV, plain TXT, HDF, JSON, and SQL query for a specific database

- The data is streamed into chunks of the desired size as DataFrame data structures so that you can access the features in a positional way or by recalling their label, thanks to .loc, .iloc, .ix methods typical of slicing and dicing in a pandas dataframe

Here is an example using the same approach as before, this time built around pandas' read_csv function:

```
In: import pandas as pd
CHUNK_SIZE = 1000
with open(local_path+'\\'+source, 'rb') as R:
    iterator = pd.read_csv(R, chunksize=CHUNK_SIZE)
    for n, data_chunk in enumerate(iterator):
        print ('Size of uploaded chunk: %i instances, %i features' %
(data_chunk.shape))
            # DATA PROCESSING placeholder
            # MACHINE LEARNING placeholder
            pass
    print ('Sample values: \n%s' % str(data_chunk.iloc[0]))


Out:
Size of uploaded chunk: 2379 instances, 17 features
Size of uploaded chunk: 2379 instances, 17 features
Size of uploaded chunk: 2379 instances, 17 features
Size of uploaded chunk: 2379 instances, 17 features
Size of uploaded chunk: 2379 instances, 17 features
Size of uploaded chunk: 2379 instances, 17 features
Size of uploaded chunk: 2379 instances, 17 features
Sample values:
instant                 15001
```

```
dteday           2012-09-22
season                    3
yr                        1
mnth                      9
hr                        5
holiday                   0
weekday                   6
workingday                0
weathersit                1
temp                   0.56
atemp                0.5303
hum                    0.83
windspeed            0.3284
casual                    2
registered               15
cnt                      17
Name: 0, dtype: object
```

Here, it is very important to notice that the iterator is instantiated by specifying a chunk size, that is, the number of rows the iterator has to return at every iteration. The `chunksize` parameter can assume values from 1 to any value, though clearly the size of the mini-batch (the chunk retrieved) is strictly connected to your available memory to store and manipulate it in the following preprocessing phase.

Bringing larger chunks into memory offers an advantage only in terms of disk access. Smaller chunks require multiple access to the disk and, depending on the characteristics of your physical storage, a longer time to pass through the data. Nevertheless, from a machine learning point of view, smaller or larger chunks make little difference for Scikit-learn out-of-core functions as they learn taking into account only one instance at a time, making them truly linear in computational cost.

Working with databases

As an example of the flexibility of the pandas I/O tools, we will provide a further example using a SQLite3 database where data is streamed from a simple query, chunk by chunk. The example is not proposed for just a didactical use. Working with a large data store in databases can indeed bring advantages from the disk space and processing time point of view.

Data arranged into tables in a SQL database can be normalized, thus removing redundancies and repetitions and saving disk storage. Database normalization is a way to arrange columns and tables in a database in a way to reduce their dimensions without losing any information. Often, this is accomplished by splitting tables and recoding repeated data into keys. Moreover, a relational database, being optimized on memory and operations and multiprocessing, can speed up and anticipate part of those preprocessing activities otherwise dealt within the Python scripting.

Using Python, SQLite (http://www.sqlite.org) is a good default choice because of the following reasons:

- It is open source
- It can handle large amounts of data (theoretically up to 140 TB per database, though it is unlikely to see any SQLite application dealing with such amounts of data)
- It operates on macOS and both Linux and Windows 32- and 64-bit environments
- It does not require any server infrastructure or particular installation (zero configuration) as all the data is stored in a single file on disk
- It can be easily extended using Python code to be turned into a stored procedure

Moreover, the Python standard library includes a sqlite3 module providing all the functions to create a database from scratch and work with it.

In our example, we will first upload the CSV file containing the bike-sharing dataset on both a daily and hourly basis to a SQLite database and then we will stream from it as we did from a CSV file. The database uploading code that we provide can be reusable throughout the book and for your own applications, not being tied to the specific example we provide (you just have to change the input and output parameters, that's all):

```
In : import os, sys
import sqlite3, csv,glob

SEP = ','

def define_field(s):
    try:
        int(s)
        return 'integer'
    except ValueError:
        try:
```

```
                float(s)
                return 'real'
        except:
                return 'text'


def create_sqlite_db(db='database.sqlite', file_pattern=''):
    conn = sqlite3.connect(db)
    conn.text_factory = str  # allows utf-8 data to be stored

    c = conn.cursor()

    # traverse the directory and process each .csv file useful for
building the db
    target_files = glob.glob(file_pattern)

    print ('Creating %i table(s) into %s from file(s): %s' %
(len(target_files), db, ', '.join(target_files)))

    for k,csvfile in enumerate(target_files):
        # remove the path and extension and use what's left as a table
name
        tablename = os.path.splitext(os.path.basename(csvfile))[0]

        with open(csvfile, "rb") as f:
            reader = csv.reader(f, delimiter=SEP)

            f.seek(0)
            for n,row in enumerate(reader):
                if n==11:
                    types = map(define_field,row)
                else:
                    if n>11:
                        break

            f.seek(0)
            for n,row in enumerate(reader):
                if n==0:

                    sql = "DROP TABLE IF EXISTS %s" % tablename
                    c.execute(sql)
                    sql = "CREATE TABLE %s (%s)" % (tablename,\
                            ", ".join([ "%s %s" % (col, ct) \
for col, ct  in zip(row, types)]))
                    print ('%i) %s' % (k+1,sql))
```

```
                    c.execute(sql)

                    # Creating indexes for faster joins on long
strings
                    for column in row:
                        if column.endswith("_ID_hash"):
                            index = "%s__%s" % \
( tablename, column )
                            sql = "CREATE INDEX %s on %s (%s)" % \
( index, tablename, column )
                            c.execute(sql)

                    insertsql = "INSERT INTO %s VALUES (%s)" %
(tablename,
                        ", ".join([ "?" for column in row ]))

                    rowlen = len(row)
                else:
                    # raise an error if there are rows that don't have
the right number of fields
                    if len(row) == rowlen:
                        c.execute(insertsql, row)
                    else:
                        print ('Error at line %i in file %s') %
(n,csvfile)
                        raise ValueError('Houston, we\'ve had a
problem at row %i' % n)

            conn.commit()
            print ('* Inserted %i rows' % n)

    c.close()
    conn.close()
```

The script provides a valid database name and pattern to locate the files that you want to import (wildcards such as * are accepted) and creates from scratch a new database and table that you need, filling them afterwards with all the data available:

```
In: create_sqlite_db(db='bikesharing.sqlite', file_
pattern='bikesharing\\*.csv')

Out: Creating 2 table(s) into bikesharing.sqlite from file(s):
bikesharing\day.csv, bikesharing\hour.csv
```

```
1) CREATE TABLE day (instant integer, dteday text, season integer, yr
integer, mnth integer, holiday integer, weekday integer, workingday
integer, weathersit integer, temp real, atemp real, hum real,
windspeed real, casual integer, registered integer, cnt integer)
* Inserted 731 rows
2) CREATE TABLE hour (instant integer, dteday text, season integer, yr
integer, mnth integer, hr integer, holiday integer, weekday integer,
workingday integer, weathersit integer, temp real, atemp real, hum
real, windspeed real, casual integer, registered integer, cnt integer)
* Inserted 17379 rows
```

The script also reports the data types for the created fields and number of rows, so it is quite easy to verify that everything has gone smoothly during the importation. Now it is easy to stream from the database. In our example, we will create an inner join between the hour and day tables and extract data on an hourly base with information about the total rentals of the day:

```
In: import os, sqlite3
import pandas as pd

DB_NAME = 'bikesharing.sqlite'
DIR_PATH = os.getcwd()
CHUNK_SIZE = 2500

conn = sqlite3.connect(DIR_PATH+'\\'+DB_NAME)
conn.text_factory = str  # allows utf-8 data to be stored
sql = "SELECT H.*, D.cnt AS day_cnt FROM hour AS H INNER JOIN day as D
ON (H.dteday = D.dteday)"
DB_stream = pd.io.sql.read_sql(sql, conn, chunksize=CHUNK_SIZE)
for j,data_chunk in enumerate(DB_stream):
    print ('Chunk %i -' % (j+1)),
    print ('Size of uploaded chunk: %i instances, %i features' %
(data_chunk.shape))
    # DATA PROCESSING placeholder
    # MACHINE LEARNING placeholder


Out:
Chunk 1 - Size of uploaded chunk: 2500 instances, 18 features
Chunk 2 - Size of uploaded chunk: 2500 instances, 18 features
Chunk 3 - Size of uploaded chunk: 2500 instances, 18 features
Chunk 4 - Size of uploaded chunk: 2500 instances, 18 features
Chunk 5 - Size of uploaded chunk: 2500 instances, 18 features
Chunk 6 - Size of uploaded chunk: 2500 instances, 18 features
Chunk 7 - Size of uploaded chunk: 2379 instances, 18 features
```

If you need to speed up the streaming, you just have to optimize the database, first of all building the right indexes for the relational query that you intend to use.

 `conn.text_factory = str` is a very important part of the script; it allows UTF-8 data to be stored. If such a command is ignored, you may experience strange errors when inputting data.

Paying attention to the ordering of instances

As a concluding remark for the streaming data topic, we have to warn you about the fact that, when streaming, you are actually including hidden information in your learning process because of the order of the examples you are basing your learning on.

In fact, online learners optimize their parameters based on each instance that they evaluate. Each instance will lead the learner toward a certain direction in the optimization process. Globally, the learner should take the right optimization direction, given a large enough number of evaluated instances. However, if the learner is instead trained by biased observations (for instance, observations ordered by time or grouped in a meaningful way), the algorithm will also learn the bias. Something can be done during training in order to not remember previously seen instances, but some bias will be introduced anyway. If you are learning time series—the response to the flow of time often being part of the model—such a bias is quite useful, but in most other cases, it acts as some kind of overfitting and translates into a certain lack of generalization in the final model.

If your data has some kind of ordering which you don't want to be learned by the machine learning algorithm (such as an ID order), as a cautionary measure, you can shuffle its rows before streaming the data and obtain a random order more suitable for online stochastic learning.

The fastest way, and the one occupying less space on disk, is to stream the dataset in memory and shrink it by compression. In most cases, but not all, this will work thanks to the compression algorithm applied and the relative sparsity and redundancy of the data that you are using for the training. In the cases where it doesn't work, you have to shuffle the data directly on the disk implying more disk space consumption.

Here, we first present a fast way to shuffle in-memory, thanks to the `zlib` package that can rapidly compress the rows into memory, and the `shuffle` function from the `random` module:

```
In: import zlib
from random import shuffle

def ram_shuffle(filename_in, filename_out, header=True):
    with open(filename_in, 'rb') as f:
        zlines = [zlib.compress(line, 9) for line in f]
        if header:
            first_row = zlines.pop(0)
    shuffle(zlines)
    with open(filename_out, 'wb') as f:
        if header:
            f.write(zlib.decompress(first_row))
        for zline in zlines:
            f.write(zlib.decompress(zline))

import os

local_path = os.getcwd()
source = 'bikesharing\\hour.csv'
ram_shuffle(filename_in=local_path+'\\'+source, \
                filename_out=local_path+'\\bikesharing\\shuffled_
hour.csv', header=True)
```

For Unix users, the `sort` command, which can be easily used with a single invocation (the `-R` parameter), shuffles huge amounts of text files very easily and much more efficiently than any Python implementation. It can be combined with decompression and compression steps using pipes.

So something like the following command should do the trick:

```
zcat sorted.gz | sort -R | gzip - > shuffled.gz
```

In case the RAM is not enough to store all the compressed data, the only viable solution is to operate on the file as it is on the disk itself. The following snippet of code defines a function that will repeatedly split your file into increasingly smaller files, shuffle them internally, and arrange them again randomly in a larger file. The result is not a perfect random rearrangement, but the rows are scattered around enough to destroy any previous order that could influence online learning:

```
In: from random import shuffle
import pandas as pd
```

```
import numpy as np
import os

def disk_shuffle(filename_in, filename_out, header=True, iterations =
3, CHUNK_SIZE = 2500, SEP=','):
    for i in range(iterations):
        with open(filename_in, 'rb') as R:
            iterator = pd.read_csv(R, chunksize=CHUNK_SIZE)
            for n, df in enumerate(iterator):
                if n==0 and header:
                    header_cols =SEP.join(df.columns)+'\n'
                df.iloc[np.random.permutation(len(df))].to_
csv(str(n)+'_chunk.csv', index=False, header=False, sep=SEP)
        ordering = list(range(0,n+1))
        shuffle(ordering)
        with open(filename_out, 'wb') as W:
            if header:
                W.write(header_cols)
            for f in ordering:
                with open(str(f)+'_chunk.csv', 'r') as R:
                    for line in R:
                        W.write(line)
                os.remove(str(f)+'_chunk.csv')
        filename_in = filename_out
        CHUNK_SIZE = int(CHUNK_SIZE / 2)

import os

local_path = os.getcwd()
source = 'bikesharing\\hour.csv'
disk_shuffle(filename_in=local_path+'\\'+source, \
                filename_out=local_path+'\\bikesharing\\shuffled_
hour.csv', header=True)
```

Stochastic learning

Having defined the streaming process, it is now time to glance at the learning process as it is the learning and its specific needs that determine the best way to handle data and transform it in the preprocessing phase.

Online learning, contrary to batch learning, works with a larger number of iterations and gets directions from each single instance at a time, thus allowing a more erratic learning procedure than an optimization made on a batch, which immediately tends to get the right direction expressed from the data as a whole.

Batch gradient descent

The core algorithm for machine learning, gradient descent, is therefore revisited in order to adapt to online learning. When working on batch data, gradient descent can minimize the cost function of a linear regression analysis using much less computations than statistical algorithms. The complexity of gradient descent ranks in the order $O(n*p)$, making learning regression coefficients feasible even in the occurrence of a large n (which stands for the number of observations) and large p (number of variables). It also works perfectly when highly correlated or even identical features are present in the training data.

Everything is based on a simple optimization method: the set of parameters is changed through multiple iterations in a way that it gradually converges to the optimal solution starting from a random one. Gradient descent is a theoretically well-understood optimization method with known convergence guarantees for certain problems such as regression ones. Nevertheless, let's start with the following image representing a complex mapping (typical of neural networks) between the values that the parameters can take (representing the hypothesis space) and result in terms of minimization of the cost function:

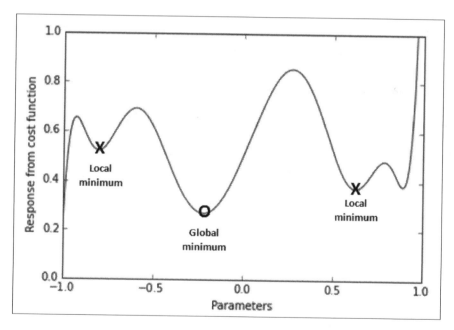

Using a figurative example, gradient descent resembles walking blindfolded around mountains. If you want to descend to the lowest valley without being able to see the path, you can just proceed by taking the direction that you feel is going downhill; try it for a while, then stop, feel the terrain again, and then proceed toward where you feel it is going downhill, and so on, again and again. If you keep on heading toward where the surface descends, you will finally arrive at a point when you cannot descend anymore because the terrain is flat. Hopefully, at that point, you should have reached your destination.

Using such a method, you need to perform the following actions:

- Decide the starting point. This is usually achieved by an initial random guess of the parameters of your function (multiple restarts will ensure that the initialization won't cause the algorithm to reach a local optimum because of an unlucky initial setting).

- Be able to feel the terrain, that is, be able to tell when it goes down. In mathematical terms, this means that you should be able to take the derivative of your actual parameterized function with respect to your target variable, that is, the partial derivative of the cost function that you are optimizing. Note that the gradient descent works on all of your data, trying to optimize the predictions from all your instances at once.

- Decide how long you should follow the direction dictated by the derivative. In mathematical terms, this corresponds to a weight (usually called alpha) to decide how much you should change your parameters at every step of the optimization. This aspect can be considered as the learning factor because it points out how much you should learn from the data at each optimization step. As with any other hyperparameter, the best value of alpha can be determined by performance evaluation on a validation set.

- Determine when to stop, given a too marginal improvement of the cost function with respect to the previous step. In such a sense, you also should be able to notice when something goes wrong and you are not going in the right direction maybe because you are using too large an alpha for the learning. This is actually a matter of *momentum*, that is, the speed at which the algorithm converges toward the optimum. It is just like throwing a ball down a mountainside: it just rolls over small dents in the surface, but if its speed is too high, it won't stop at the right point. Thus, if alpha is set correctly, the momentum will naturally slow down as the algorithm is approaching the optimum as shown in the following image in the right panel. However, if it is not set properly, it will just jump over the global optimum and report further errors to be minimized, as depicted in the following image on the right panel, when the optimization process causes parameters to jump across different values without achieving the required error minimization:

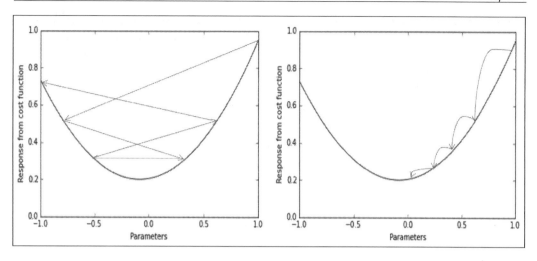

In order to better depict what happens with gradient descent, let's take the example of a linear regression whose parameters are optimized by such a procedure.

We start from the cost function J given the vector of weights w:

$$J(w) = \frac{1}{2n} \sum (Xw - y)^2$$

The matrix-vector multiplication Xw between the training data matrix X and the vector of coefficients w represents the predictions from the linear model, whose deviance from the response y is squared, then summed, and finally divided by two times n, the number of instances.

Initially, the vector w could be instantiated using random numbers taken from the standardized normal distribution whose mean is zero and standard deviation is the unit. (Actually, initialization can be done in a lot of different ways, all working equally well to approximate linear regression whose cost function is bowl-shaped and has a unique minimum.) This allows our algorithm to start somewhere along the optimization path and could effectively speed up the convergence of the process. As we are optimizing a linear regression, initialization shouldn't cause much trouble to the algorithm (at worst, a wrong start will just slow it down). Instead, when we are using gradient descent in order to optimize different machine learning algorithms such as neural networks, we risk being stuck because of a wrong initialization. This will happen if, for instance, the initial w is just filled with zero values (the risk is getting stuck on a perfectly symmetric hilltop, where no directionality can immediately bring an optimization better than any other). This can happen with optimization processes that have multiple local minima, too.

Given the starting random coefficients vector w, we can immediately calculate the cost function $J(w)$ and determine the initial direction for each single coefficient by subtracting from each a portion alpha (a, the learning rate) of the partial derivative of the cost function, as explicated by the following formula:

$$w_j = w_j - \alpha \frac{\partial}{\partial w} J(w)$$

This can be better conveyed after solving the partial derivative, as follows:

$$w_j = w_j - \alpha \frac{1}{n} \sum (Xw - y)x_j$$

Noticeably, the update is done on each singular coefficient (wj) given its feature vector xj, but based on all the predictions at once (hence the summation).

After iterating over all the coefficients in w, the coefficients' update will be completed and the optimization may restart again by calculating the partial derivative and updating the w vector.

An interesting characteristic of the process is that the update will be less and less as the w vector approaches the optimal configuration. Therefore, the process could stop when the change induced in w, with respect to the previous operation, is small. Anyway, it is true that we have decreasing updates when alpha, the learning rate, is set to the right size. In fact, if its value is too large, it may cause the optimization to detour and fail, causing—in some cases—a complete divergence of the process and the impossibility to converge finally to a solution. In fact, the optimization will tend to overshoot the target and actually get farther away from it.

At the other end, too small an alpha value will not only move the optimization process toward its target too slowly, but it may also be easily stuck somewhere in a local minima. This is especially true with regard to more complex algorithms, just like neural networks. As for linear regression and its classification counterpart, logistic regression, because the optimization curve is bowl-shaped, just like a concave curve, it features a single minimum and no local minima at all.

In the implementation that we illustrated, alpha is a fixed constant (a fixed learning rate gradient descent). As alpha plays such an important role in converging to an optimal solution, different strategies have been devised for it to start larger and shrink as the optimization goes on. We will discuss such different approaches when examining the Scikit-learn implementation.

Stochastic gradient descent

The version of the gradient descent seen so far is known as full batch gradient descent and works by optimizing the error of the entire dataset, and thus needs it in-memory. The out-of-core versions are the **stochastic gradient descent (SGD)** and mini batch gradient descent.

Here, the formulation stays exactly the same, but for the update; the update is done for a single instance at a time, thus allowing us to leave the core data in its storage and take just a single observation in-memory:

$$w_j = w_j - \alpha(x_j w - y)x_j$$

The core idea is that, if the instances are picked randomly without particular biases, the optimization will move on average toward the target cost minimization. That explains why we discussed how to remove any ordering from a stream and making it as random as possible. For instance, in the bike-sharing example, if you have stochastic gradient descent learn the patterns of the early season first, then focus on the summer, then on the fall, and so on, depending on the season when the optimization is stopped, the model will be tuned to predict one season better than the others because most of the recent examples are from that season. In a stochastic gradient descent optimization, when data is **independent and identically distributed (i.i.d.)**, convergence to the global minimum is guaranteed. Practically, i.i.d. means that your examples should have no sequential order or distribution but should be proposed to the algorithm as if picked randomly from your available ones.

The Scikit-learn SGD implementation

A good number of online learning algorithms can be found in the Scikit-learn package. Not all machine learning algorithms have an online counterpart, but the list is interesting and steadily growing. As for supervised learning, we can divide available learners into classifiers and regressors and enumerate them.

As classifiers, we can mention the following:

- `sklearn.naive_bayes.MultinomialNB`
- `sklearn.naive_bayes.BernoulliNB`
- `sklearn.linear_model.Perceptron`
- `sklearn.linear_model.PassiveAggressiveClassifier`
- `sklearn.linear_model.SGDClassifier`

As regressors, we have two options:

- `sklearn.linear_model.PassiveAggressiveRegressor`
- `sklearn.linear_model.SGDRegressor`

They all can learn incrementally, updating themselves instance by instance; though only `SGDClassifier` and `SGDRegressor` are based on the stochastic gradient descent optimization that we previously described, and they are the main topics of this chapter. The SGD learners are optimal for all large-scale problems as their complexity is bound to $O(k*n*p)$, where k is the number of passes over the data, n is the number of instances, and p is the number of features (naturally non-zero features if we are working with sparse matrices): a perfectly linear time learner, taking more time exactly in proportion to the number of examples shown.

Other online algorithms will be used as a comparative benchmark. Moreover, all algorithms have the usage of the same API in common, based on the `partial_fit` method for online learning and mini-batch (when you stream larger chunks rather than a single instance). Sharing the same API makes all these learning techniques interchangeable in your learning frame.

Contrary to the fit method, which uses all the available data for its immediate optimization, `partial_fit` operates a partial optimization based on each of the single instances passed. Even if a dataset is passed to the `partial_fit` method, the algorithm won't process the entire batch but for its single elements, making the complexity of the learning operations indeed linear. Moreover, a learner, after `partial_fit`, can be perpetually updated by subsequent `partial_fit` calls, making it perfect for online learning from continuous streams of data.

When classifying, the only caveat is that at the first initialization, it is necessary to know how many classes we are going to learn and how they are labeled. This can be done using the classes parameter, pointing out a list of the numeric values labels. This requires to be explored beforehand, streaming through the data in order to record the labels of the problem and also taking notice of their distribution in case they are unbalanced — a class is numerically too large or too small with respect to the others (but the Scikit-learn implementation offers a way to automatically handle the problem). If the target variable is numeric, it is still useful to know its distribution, but this is not necessary to successfully run the learner.

In Scikit-learn, we have two implementations—one for classification problems (SGDClassifier) and one for regression ones (SGDRegressor). The classification implementation can handle multiclass problems using the **one-vs-all (OVA)** strategy. This strategy implies that, given k classes, k models are built, one for each class against all the instances of other classes, therefore creating k binary classifications. This will produce k sets of coefficients and k vectors of predictions and their probability. In the end, based on the emitted probability of each class compared against the other, the classification is assigned to the class with the highest probability. If we need to give actual probabilities for the multinomial distribution, we can simply normalize the results by dividing by their sum. (This is what is happening in a softmax layer in a neural network, which we will see in the following chapters.)

Both classification and regression SGD implementations in Scikit-learn feature different loss functions (the cost function, the core of the stochastic gradient descent optimization).

For classification, expressed by the loss parameter, we can rely on the following:

- loss='log': Classical logistic regression
- loss='hinge': Softmargin, that is, a linear support vector machine
- loss='modified_huber': A smoothed hinge loss

For regression, we have three loss functions:

- loss='squared_loss': **Ordinary least squares (OLS)** for linear regression
- loss='huber': Huber loss for robust regression against outliers
- loss='epsilon_insensitive': A linear support vector regression

We will present some examples using the classical statistical loss functions, which are logistic loss and OLS. Hinge loss and **support vector machines (SVMs)** will be discussed in the next chapter, a detailed introduction about their functioning being necessary.

As a reminder (so that you won't have to go and consult any other supplementary machine learning book), if we define the regression function as h and its predictions are given by $h(X)$ because X is the matrix of features, then the following is the suitable formulation:

$$y \approx h(X) = \beta X + \beta_0$$

Consequently, the OLS cost function to be minimized is as follows:

$$\frac{1}{2n} * \sum (h(X) - y)^2$$

In logistic regression, having a transformation of the binary outcome *0/1* into an odds ratio, пy being the probability of a positive outcome, the formula is as follows:

$$y \approx h(X) = \frac{1}{1 + e^{\beta X + \beta_0}}$$

The logistic cost function, consequently, is defined as follows:

$$-\frac{1}{n} * \sum \left[y * \ln\big(h(X)\big) + (1-y) * \ln\big(1 - h(X)\big) \right]$$

Defining SGD learning parameters

To define SGD parameters in Scikit-learn, both in classification and regression problems (so that they are valid for both `SGDClassifier` and `SGDRegressor`), we have to make clear how to deal with some important parameters necessary for a correct learning when you cannot evaluate all the data at once.

The first one is `n_iter`, which defines the number of iterations through the data. Initially set to 5, it has been empirically shown that it should be tuned in order for the learner, given the other default parameters, to see around `10^6` examples; therefore a good solution to set it would be `n_iter = np.ceil(10**6 / n)`, where *n* is the number of instances. Noticeably, `n_iter` only works with in-memory datasets, so it acts only when you operate by the fit method but not with `partial_fit`. In reality, `partial_fit` will reiterate over the same data just if you restream it in your procedure and the right number of iterations of restreams is something to be tested along the learning procedure itself, being influenced by the type of data. In the next chapter, we will illustrate hyperparameter optimization and the right number of passes will be discussed.

It might make sense to reshuffle the data after each complete pass over all of the data when doing mini-batch learning.

`shuffle` is a parameter required if you want to shuffle your data. It refers to the mini-batch present in-memory and not to out-of-core data ordering. It also works with `partial_fit` but its effect in such a case is very limited. Always set it to True, but for data to be passed in chunks, shuffle your data out-of-core, as we described before.

`warm_start` is another parameter that works with the fit method because it remembers the previous fit coefficients (but not the learning rate if it has been dynamically modified). If you are using the `partial_fit` method, the algorithm will remember the previously learned coefficients and the state of the learning rate schedule.

The `average` parameter triggers a computational trick that, at a certain instance, starts averaging new coefficients with older ones allowing a faster convergence. It can be set to `True` or an integer value indicating from what instance it will start averaging.

Last, but not least, we have `learning_rate` and its related parameters, `eta0` and `power_t`. The `learning_rate` parameter implies how each observed instance impacts on the optimization process. When presenting SGD from a theoretical point of view, we presented constant rate learning, which can be replicated setting `learning_rate='constant'`.

However, other options are present, letting the eta η (called the learning rate in Scikit-learn and defined at time t) gradually decrease. In classification, the solution proposed is `learning_rate='optimal'`, given by the following formulation:

$$\eta^t = \frac{1}{\alpha_{t0} + \alpha_t}$$

Here, t is the time steps, given by the number of instances multiplied by iterations, and $t0$ is a value heuristically chosen because of the studies by Léon Bottou, whose version of the *Stochastic Gradient SVM* has heavily influenced the SGD Scikit-learn implementation (`http://leon.bottou.org/projects/sgd`). The clear advantage of such a learning strategy is that learning decreases as more examples are seen, avoiding sudden perturbations of the optimization given by unusual values. Clearly, this strategy is also out-of-the-box, meaning that you don't have much to do with it.

In regression, the suggested learning fading is given by this formulation, corresponding to `learning_rate= 'invscaling'`:

$$\eta^t = \frac{eta_0}{t^{power\_t}}$$

Here, `eta0` and `power_t` are hyperparameters to be optimized by an optimization search (they are initially set to `0` and `0.5`). Noticeably, using the `invscaling` learning rate, SGD will start with a lower learning rate, less than the optimal rate one, and it will decrease more slowly, being a bit more adaptable during learning.

Feature management with data streams

Data streams pose the problem that you cannot evaluate as you would do when working on a complete in-memory dataset. For a correct and optimal approach to feed your SGD out-of-core algorithm, you first have to survey the data (by taking a chuck of the initial instances of the file, for example) and find out the type of data you have at hand.

We distinguish among the following types of data:

- Quantitative values
- Categorical values encoded with integer numbers
- Unstructured categorical values expressed in textual form

When data is quantitative, it could just be fed to the SGD learner but for the fact that the algorithm is quite sensitive to feature scaling; that is, you have to bring all the quantitative features into the same range of values or the learning process won't converge easily and correctly. Possible scaling strategies are converting all the values in the range [0,1], [-1,1] or standardizing the variable by centering its mean to zero and converting its variance to the unit. We don't have particular suggestions for the choice of the scaling strategy, but converting in the range [0,1] works particularly well if you are dealing with a sparse matrix and most of your values are zero.

As for in-memory learning, when transforming variables on the training set, you have to take notice of the values that you used (Basically, you need to get minimum, maximum, mean, and standard deviation of each feature.) and reuse them in the test set in order to achieve consistent results.

Given the fact that you are streaming data and it isn't possible to upload all the data in-memory, you have to calculate them by passing through all the data or at least a part of it (sampling is always a viable solution). The situation of working with an ephemeral stream (a stream you cannot replicate) poses even more challenging problems; in fact, you have to constantly keep trace of the values that you keep on receiving.

If sampling just requires you to calculate your statistics on a chunk of n instances (under the assumption that your stream has no particular order), calculating statistics on the fly requires you to record the right measures.

For minimum and maximum, you need to store a variable each for every quantitative feature. Starting from the very first value, which you will store as your initial minimum and maximum, for each new value that you will receive from the stream you will have to confront it with the previously recorded minimum and maximum values. If the new instance is out of the previous range of values, you just update your variable accordingly.

In addition, the average doesn't pose any particular problems because you just need to keep a sum of the values seen and a count of the instances. As for variance, you need to recall that the textbook formulation is as follows:

$$\sigma^2 = \frac{1}{n}\sum(x - \mu)^2$$

Noticeably, you need to know the mean μ, which you are also just learning incrementally from the stream. However, the formulation can be explicated as follows:

$$\sigma^2 = \frac{1}{n}\left(\sum x^2 - \frac{(\sum x)^2}{n}\right)$$

As you are just recording the number n of instances and a summation of x values, you just need to store another variable, which is the summation of values of x squared, and you will have all the ingredients for the recipe.

As an example, using the bike-sharing dataset, we can calculate the running mean, standard deviation, and range reporting the final result and plot how such stats changed as data was streamed from disk:

```
In: import os, csv
local_path = os.getcwd()
source = 'bikesharing\\hour.csv'
SEP=','
running_mean = list()
running_std = list()
with open(local_path+'\\'+source, 'rb') as R:
    iterator = csv.DictReader(R, delimiter=SEP)
    x = 0.0
    x_squared = 0.0
    for n, row in enumerate(iterator):
        temp = float(row['temp'])
        if n == 0:
            max_x, min_x = temp, temp
        else:
            max_x, min_x = max(temp, max_x),min(temp, min_x)
        x += temp
        x_squared += temp**2
        running_mean.append(x / (n+1))
        running_std.append(((x_squared - (x**2)/(n+1))/(n+1))**0.5)
        # DATA PROCESSING placeholder
        # MACHINE LEARNING placeholder
        pass
    print ('Total rows: %i' % (n+1))
    print ('Feature \'temp\': mean=%0.3f, max=%0.3f, min=%0.3f,\
sd=%0.3f' % (running_mean[-1], max_x, min_x, running_std[-1]))

Out: Total rows: 17379
Feature 'temp': mean=0.497, max=1.000, min=0.020, sd=0.193
```

In a few moments, the data will be streamed from the source and key figures relative to the `temp` feature will be recorded as a running estimation of the mean and standard deviation is calculated and stored in two separated lists.

By plotting the values present in the lists, we can examine how much the estimates fluctuated with respect to the final figures and get an idea about how many instances are required before getting a stable mean and standard deviation estimate:

```
In: import matplotlib.pyplot as plt
%matplotlib inline
plt.plot(running_mean,'r-', label='mean')
plt.plot(running_std,'b-', label='standard deviation')
plt.ylim(0.0,0.6)
plt.xlabel('Number of training examples')
plt.ylabel('Value')
plt.legend(loc='lower right', numpoints= 1)
plt.show()
```

If you previously processed the original bike-sharing dataset, you will obtain a plot where clearly there is a trend in the data (due to temporal ordering, because the temperature naturally varies with seasons):

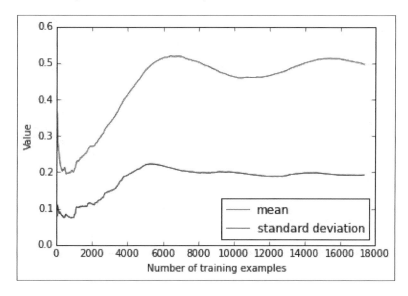

On the contrary, if we had used the shuffled version of the dataset as a source, the `shuffled_hour.csv` file, we could have obtained a couple of much more stable and quickly converging estimates. Consequently, we would have learned an approximate but more reliable estimate of the mean and standard deviation observing fewer instances from the stream:

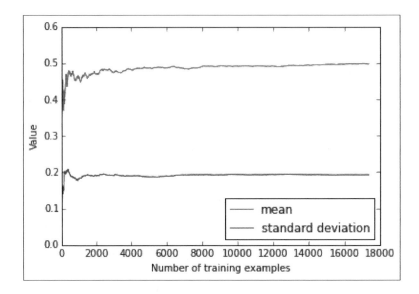

The difference in the two charts reminds us of the importance of randomizing the order of the observations. Even learning simple descriptive statistics can be influenced heavily by trends in the data; consequently, we have to pay more attention when learning complex models by SGD.

Describing the target

In addition, the target variable also needs to be explored before starting. We need, in fact, to be sure about what values it assumes, if categorical, and figure out if it is unbalanced when in classes or has a skewed distribution when a number.

If we are learning a numeric response, we can adopt the same strategy shown previously for the features, whereas for classes, a Python dictionary keeping a count of classes (the keys) and their frequencies (the values) will suffice.

As an example, we will download a dataset for classification, the **Forest Covertype** data.

For a fast download and preparation of the data, we will use the `gzip_from_UCI` function as defined in the *Datasets to try the real thing yourself* section of the present chapter:

```
In: UCI_url = 'https://archive.ics.uci.edu/ml/machine-learning-
databases/covtype/covtype.data.gz'
gzip_from_UCI(UCI_url)
```

In case of problems in running the code, or if you prefer to prepare the file by yourself, just go to the UCI website, download the dataset, and unpack it on the directory where Python is currently working:

```
https://archive.ics.uci.edu/ml/machine-learning-databases/covtype/
```

Once the data is available on disk, we can scan through the 581,012 instances, converting the last value of each row, representative of the class that we should estimate, to its corresponding forest cover type:

```
In: import os, csv
local_path = os.getcwd()
source = 'covtype.data'
SEP=','
forest_type = {1:"Spruce/Fir", 2:"Lodgepole Pine", \
               3:"Ponderosa Pine", 4:"Cottonwood/Willow",\
               5:"Aspen", 6:"Douglas-fir", 7:"Krummholz"}
forest_type_count = {value:0 for value in forest_type.values()}
forest_type_count['Other'] = 0
lodgepole_pine = 0
spruce = 0
proportions = list()
with open(local_path+'\\'+source, 'rb') as R:
    iterator = csv.reader(R, delimiter=SEP)
    for n, row in enumerate(iterator):
        response = int(row[-1]) # The response is the last value
        try:
            forest_type_count[forest_type[response]] +=1
            if response == 1:
                spruce += 1
            elif response == 2:
                lodgepole_pine +=1
            if n % 10000 == 0:
                proportions.append([spruce/float(n+1),\
                lodgepole_pine/float(n+1)])
        except:
            forest_type_count['Other'] += 1
    print ('Total rows: %i' % (n+1))
```

```
print ('Frequency of classes:')
for ftype, freq in sorted([(t,v) for t,v \
    in forest_type_count.iteritems()], key = \
    lambda x: x[1], reverse=True):
        print ("%-18s: %6i %04.1f%%" % \
               (ftype, freq, freq*100/float(n+1)))
```

```
Out: Total rows: 581012
Frequency of classes:
Lodgepole Pine     : 283301 48.8%
Spruce/Fir         : 211840 36.5%
Ponderosa Pine     :  35754 06.2%
Krummholz          :  20510 03.5%
Douglas-fir        :  17367 03.0%
Aspen              :   9493 01.6%
Cottonwood/Willow  :   2747 00.5%
Other              :      0 00.0%
```

The output displays that two classes, `Lodgepole Pine` and `Spruce/Fir`, account for most observations. If examples are shuffled appropriately in the stream, the SGD will appropriately learn the correct a-priori distribution and consequently adjust its probability emission (a-posteriori probability).

If, contrary to our present case, your objective is not classification accuracy but increasing the **receiver operating characteristic (ROC) area under the curve (AUC)** or f1-score (error functions that can be used for evaluation; for an overview, you can directly consult the Scikit-learn documentation at `http://scikit-learn.org/stable/modules/model_evaluation.html` regarding a classification model trained on imbalanced data, and then the provided information can help you balance the weights using the `class_weight` parameter when defining `SGDClassifier` or `sample_weight` when partially fitting the model. Both change the impact of the observed instance by overweighting or underweighting it. In both ways, operating these two parameters will change the a-priori distribution. Weighting classes and instances will be discussed in the next chapter.

Before proceeding to training and working with classes, we can check whether the proportion of classes is always consistent in order to convey the correct a-priori probability to the SGD:

```
import matplotlib.pyplot as plt
import numpy as np
%matplotlib inline
proportions = np.array(proportions)
plt.plot(proportions[:,0],'r-', label='Spruce/Fir')
plt.plot(proportions[:,1],'b-', label='Lodgepole Pine')
```

```
plt.ylim(0.0,0.8)
plt.xlabel('Training examples (unit=10000)')
plt.ylabel('%')
plt.legend(loc='lower right', numpoints= 1)
plt.show()
```

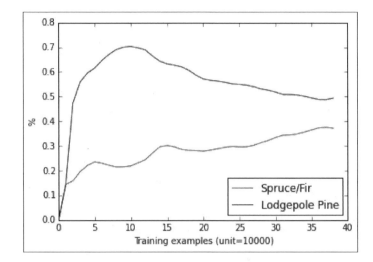

In the previous figure, you can notice how the percentage of examples change as we progress streaming the data in the existing order. A shuffle is really necessary, in this case, if we want a stochastic online algorithm to learn correctly from data.

Actually, the proportions are changeable; this dataset has some kind of ordering, maybe a geographic one, that should be corrected by shuffling the data or we will risk overestimating or underestimating certain classes with respect to others.

The hashing trick

If, among your features, there are categories (encoded in values or left in textual form), things can get a bit trickier. Normally, in batch learning, you would one-hot encode the categories and get as many new binary features as categories that you have. Unfortunately, in a stream, you do not know in advance how many categories you will deal with, and not even by sampling can you be sure of their number because rare categories may appear really late in the stream or require a too large sample to be discovered. You will have to first stream all the data and take a record of every category that appears. Anyway, streams can be ephemeral and sometimes the number of classes can be so large that they cannot be stored in-memory. The online advertising data is such an example because of its high volumes that are difficult to store away and because the stream cannot be passed over more than once. Moreover, advertising data is quite varied and features change constantly.

Working with texts makes the problem even more strikingly evident because you cannot anticipate what kind of word could be part of the text that you will be analyzing. In a bag-of-words model—where for each text the present words are counted and their frequency value pasted in an element in the feature vector specific to each word—you should be able to map each word to an index in advance. Even if you can manage this, you'll always have to handle the situation when an unknown word (therefore never mapped before) will pop up during testing or when the predictor is in production. Marginally, it should also be added that, being a spoken language, dictionaries made of hundreds of thousands or even millions of different terms are not unusual at all.

To recap, if you can handle knowing in advance the classes in your features, you can deal with them using the one-hot encoder from Scikit-learn (http://Scikit-learn. org/stable/modules/generated/sklearn.preprocessing.OneHotEncoder. html). We actually won't illustrate it here but basically the approach is not at all different from what you would apply when working with batch learning. What we want to illustrate to you is when you cannot really apply one-hot encoding.

There is a solution called the hashing trick because it is based on the hash function and can deal with both text and categorical variables in integer or string form. It can also work with categorical variables mixed with numeric values from quantitative features. The core problem with one-hot encoding is that it assigns a position to a value in the feature vector after having mapped its feature to that position. The hashing trick can univocally map a value to its position without any prior need to evaluate the feature because it leverages the core characteristic of a hashing function—to transform a value or string into an integer value deterministically.

Therefore, the only necessary preparation before applying it is creating a sparse vector large enough to represent the complexity of the data (potentially containing from $2^{**}19$ to $2^{**}30$ elements, depending on the available memory, bus architecture of your computer, and type of hash function that you are using). If you are working on some text, you'll also need a tokenizer, that is, a function that will split your text into single words and removes punctuation.

A simple toy example will make this clear. We will be using two specialized functions from the Scikit-learn package: `HashingVectorizer`, a transformer based on the hashing trick that works on textual data, and `FeatureHasher`, which is another transformer, specialized in converting a data row expressed as a Python dictionary to a sparse vector of features.

As the first example, we will turn a phrase into a vector:

```
In: from sklearn.feature_extraction.text import HashingVectorizer
h = HashingVectorizer(n_features=1000, binary=True, norm=None)
sparse_vector = h.transform(['A simple toy example will make clear how
it works.'])
print(sparse_vector)

Out:
   (0, 61)         1.0
   (0, 271)        1.0
   (0, 287)        1.0
   (0, 452)        1.0
   (0, 462)        1.0
   (0, 539)        1.0
   (0, 605)        1.0
   (0, 726)        1.0
   (0, 918)        1.0
```

The resulting vector has unit values only at certain indexes, pointing out an association between a token in the phrase (a word) and a certain position in the vector. Unfortunately, the association cannot be reversed unless we map the hash value for each token in an external Python dictionary. Though possible, such a mapping would be indeed memory consuming because dictionaries can prove large, in the range of millions of items or even more, depending on the language and topics. Actually, we do not need to keep such tracking because hash functions guarantee to always produce the same index from the same token.

A real problem with the hashing trick is the eventuality of a collision, which happens when two different tokens are associated to the same index. This is a rare but possible occurrence when working with large dictionaries of words. On the other hand, in a model composed of millions of coefficients, there are very few that are influential. Consequently, if a collision happens, probably it will involve two unimportant tokens. When using the hashing trick, probability is on your side because with a large enough output vector (for instance, the number of elements is above 2^{24}), though collisions are always possible, it will be highly unlikely that they will involve important elements of the model.

The hashing trick can be applied to normal feature vectors, especially when there are categorical variables. Here is an example with `FeatureHasher`:

```
In: from sklearn.feature_extraction import FeatureHasher
h = FeatureHasher(n_features=1000, non_negative=True)
example_row = {'numeric feature':3, 'another numeric feature':2,
'Categorical feature = 3':1, 'f1*f2*f3':1*2*3}
print (example_row)

Out: {'another numeric feature': 2, 'f1*f2*f3': 6, 'numeric feature':
3, 'Categorical feature = 3': 1}
```

If your Python dictionary contains the feature names for numeric values and a composition of feature name and value for any categorical variable, the dictionary's values will be mapped using the hashed index of the keys creating a one-hot encoded feature vector, ready to be learned by an SGD algorithm:

```
In: print (h.transform([example_row]))
Out:
  (0, 16)        2.0
  (0, 373)       1.0
  (0, 884)       6.0
  (0, 945)       3.0
```

Other basic transformations

As we have drawn the example from our data storage, apart from turning categorical features into numeric ones, another transformation can be applied in order to have the learning algorithm increase its predictive power. Transformations can be applied to features by a function (by applying a square root, logarithm, or other transformation function) or by operations on groups of features.

In the next chapter, we will propose detailed examples regarding polynomial expansion and random kitchen-sink methods. In the present chapter, we will anticipate how to create quadratic features by nested iterations. Quadratic features are usually created when creating polynomial expansions and their aim is to intercept how predictive features interact between them; this can influence the response in the target variable in an unexpected way.

As an example to intuitively clarify why quadratic features can matter in modeling a target response, let's explain the case of the effect of two medicines on a patient. In fact, it could be that each medicine is effective, more or less, against the disease we are fighting against. Anyway, the two medicines are made up of different components that, when ingested together by the patient, tend to nullify each other's effect. In such a case, though both medicines are effective, but together they do not work at all because of their negative interaction.

In such a sense, interactions between features can be found among a large variety of features, not just in medicine, and it is critical to find out the most significant one in order for our model to work better in predicting its target. If we are not aware that certain features interact with respect to our problem, our only choice is to systematically test them all and have our model retain the ones that work better.

In the following simple example, a vector named v, an example we imagine has been just streamed in-memory in order to be learned is transformed into another vector vv where the original features of v are accompanied by the results of their multiplicative interactions (every feature is multiplied once by all the others). Given the larger number of features, the learning algorithm will be fed using the vv vector in place of the original v vector in order to achieve a better fit of the data:

```
In: import numpy as np
v = np.array([1, 2, 3, 4, 5, 6, 7, 8, 9, 10])
vv = np.hstack((v, [v[i]*v[j] for i in range(len(v)) for j in
range(i+1, len(v))]))
print vv

Out:[ 1  2  3  4  5  6  7  8  9 10  2  3  4  5  6  7  8  9 10  6  8 10
 12 14 16 18 20 12 15 18 21 24 27 30 20 24 28 32 36 40 30 35 40 45 50
 42 48 54 60 56 63 70 72 80 90]
```

Similar transformations, or even more complex ones, can be generated on the fly as the examples stream to the learning algorithm, exploiting the fact that the data batch is small (sometimes reduced to single examples) and expanding the number of features of so a few examples can feasibly be achieved in-memory. In the following chapter, we will explore more examples of such transformations and their successful integration into the learning pipeline.

Testing and validation in a stream

We have withheld showing full examples of training after introducing SGD because we need to introduce how to test and validate in a stream. Using batch learning, testing, and cross-validating is a matter of randomizing the order of the observations, slicing the dataset into folds and taking a precise fold as a test set, or systematically taking all the folds in turn to test your algorithm's learning capabilities.

Streams cannot be kept in-memory, so on the basis that the following instances are already randomized, the best solution is to take validation instances after the stream has unfolded for a while or systematically use a precise, replicable pattern in the data stream.

An out-of-sample approach on part of a stream is actually comparable to a test sample and can be successfully accomplished only knowing in advance the length of the stream. For continuous streams, it is still possible but implies stopping the learning definitely once the test instances start. This method is called a holdout after *n* strategy.

A cross-validation type of approach is possible using a systematic and replicable sampling of validation instances. After having defined a starting buffer, an instance is picked for validation every *n* times. Such an instance is not used for the training but for testing purposes. This method is called a periodic holdout strategy every *n* times.

As validation is done on a single instance base, a global performance measure is calculated, averaging all the error measures collected so far within the same pass over the data or in a window-like fashion, using the most recent set of *k* measures, where *k* is a number of tests that you think is validly representative.

As a matter of fact, during the first pass, all instances are actually unseen to the learning algorithm. It is therefore useful to test the algorithm as it receives cases to learn, verifying its response on an observation before learning it. This approach is called progressive validation.

Trying SGD in action

As a conclusion of the present chapter, we will implement two examples: one for classification based on the Forest Covertype data and one for regression based on the bike-sharing dataset. We will see how to put into practice the previous insights on response and feature distributions and how to use the best validation strategy for each problem.

Starting with the classification problem, there are two noticeable aspects to consider. Being a multiclass problem, first of all we noticed that there is some kind of ordering in the database and distribution of classes along the stream of instances. As an initial step, we will shuffle the data using the `ram_shuffle` function defined during the chapter in the *Paying attention to the ordering of instances* section:

```
In: import os
local_path = os.getcwd()
source = 'covtype.data'
ram_shuffle(filename_in=local_path+'\\'+source, \
            filename_out=local_path+'\\shuffled_covtype.data', \
            header=False)
```

As we are zipping the rows in-memory and shuffling them without much disk usage, we can quickly obtain a new working file. The following code will train `SGDClassifier` with log loss (equivalent to a logistic regression) so that it leverages our previous knowledge of the classes present in the dataset. The `forest_type` list contains all the codes of the classes and it is passed every time (though just one, the first, would suffice) to the `partial_fit` method of the SGD learner.

For validation purposes, we define a cold start at `200.000` observed cases. At every ten instances, one will be left out of training and used for validation. This schema allows reproducibility even if we are going to pass over the data multiple times; at every pass, the same instances will be left out as an out-of-sample test, allowing the creation of a validation curve to test the effect of multiple passes over the same data.

The holdout schema is accompanied by a progressive validation, too. So each case after the cold start is evaluated before being fed to the training. Although progressive validation provides an interesting feedback, such an approach will work only for the first pass; in fact after the initial pass, all the observations (but the ones in the holdout schema) will become in-sample instances. In our example, we are going to make only one pass.

As a reminder, the dataset has `581.012` instances and it may prove a bit long to stream and model with SGD (it is quite a large-scale problem for a single computer). Though we placed a limiter to observe just `250.000` instances, still allow your computer to run for about 15-20 minutes before expecting results:

```
In: import csv, time
import numpy as np
from sklearn.linear_model import SGDClassifier
source = 'shuffled_covtype.data'
SEP=','
forest_type = [t+1 for t in range(7)]
```

```
SGD = SGDClassifier(loss='log', penalty=None, random_state=1,
average=True)
accuracy = 0
holdout_count = 0
prog_accuracy = 0
prog_count = 0
cold_start = 200000
k_holdout = 10
with open(local_path+'\\'+source, 'rb') as R:
    iterator = csv.reader(R, delimiter=SEP)
    for n, row in enumerate(iterator):
        if n > 250000: # Reducing the running time of the experiment
            break
        # DATA PROCESSING
        response = np.array([int(row[-1])]) # The response is the last
value
        features = np.array(map(float,row[:-1])).reshape(1,-1)
        # MACHINE LEARNING
        if (n+1) >= cold_start and (n+1-cold_start) % k_holdout==0:
            if int(SGD.predict(features))==response[0]:
                accuracy += 1
            holdout_count += 1
            if (n+1-cold_start) % 25000 == 0 and (n+1) > cold_start:
                print '%s holdout accuracy: %0.3f' % (time.
strftime('%X'), accuracy / float(holdout_count))
        else:
            # PROGRESSIVE VALIDATION
            if (n+1) >= cold_start:
                if int(SGD.predict(features))==response[0]:
                    prog_accuracy += 1
                prog_count += 1
                if n % 25000 == 0 and n > cold_start:
                    print '%s progressive accuracy: %0.3f' % (time.
strftime('%X'), prog_accuracy / float(prog_count))
            # LEARNING PHASE
            SGD.partial_fit(features, response, classes=forest_type)
print '%s FINAL holdout accuracy: %0.3f' % (time.strftime('%X'),
accuracy / ((n+1-cold_start) / float(k_holdout)))
print '%s FINAL progressive accuracy: %0.3f' % (time.strftime('%X'),
prog_accuracy / float(prog_count))

Out:
18:45:10 holdout accuracy: 0.627
18:45:10 progressive accuracy: 0.613
```

```
18:45:59 holdout accuracy: 0.621
18:45:59 progressive accuracy: 0.617
18:45:59 FINAL holdout accuracy: 0.621
18:45:59 FINAL progressive accuracy: 0.617
```

As the second example, we will try to predict the number of shared bicycles in Washington based on a series of weather and time information. Given the historical order of the dataset, we do not shuffle it and treat the problem as a time series one. Our validation strategy is to test the results after having seen a certain number of examples in order to replicate the uncertainities to forecast from that moment of time onward.

It is also interesting to notice that some of the features are categorical, so we applied the `FeatureHasher` class from Scikit-learn in order to represent having the categories recorded in a dictionary as a joint string made up of the variable name and category code. The value assigned in the dictionary for each of these keys is one in order to resemble a binary variable in the sparse vector that the hashing trick will be creating:

```
In: import csv, time, os
import numpy as np
from sklearn.linear_model import SGDRegressor
from sklearn.feature_extraction import FeatureHasher
source = '\\bikesharing\\hour.csv'
local_path = os.getcwd()
SEP=','
def apply_log(x): return np.log(float(x)+1)
def apply_exp(x): return np.exp(float(x))-1
SGD = SGDRegressor(loss='squared_loss', penalty=None, random_state=1,
average=True)
h = FeatureHasher(non_negative=True)
val_rmse = 0
val_rmsle = 0
predictions_start = 16000
with open(local_path+'\\'+source, 'rb') as R:
    iterator = csv.DictReader(R, delimiter=SEP)
    for n, row in enumerate(iterator):
        # DATA PROCESSING
        target = np.array([apply_log(row['cnt'])])
        features = {k+'_'+v:1 for k,v in row.iteritems() \
        if k in ['holiday','hr','mnth','season', \
            'weathersit','weekday','workingday','yr']}
        numeric_features = {k:float(v) for k,v in \
            row.iteritems() if k in ['hum', 'temp', '\
            atemp', 'windspeed']}
```

```
            features.update(numeric_features)
            hashed_features = h.transform([features])
            # MACHINE LEARNING
            if (n+1) >= predictions_start:
                # HOLDOUT AFTER N PHASE
                predicted = SGD.predict(hashed_features)
                val_rmse += (apply_exp(predicted) \
                    - apply_exp(target))**2
                val_rmsle += (predicted - target)**2
                if (n-predictions_start+1) % 250 == 0 \
                    and (n+1) > predictions_start:
                        print '%s holdout RMSE: %0.3f' \
                            % (time.strftime('%X'), (val_rmse \
                            / float(n-predictions_start+1))**0.5),
                        print 'holdout RMSLE: %0.3f' % ((val_rmsle \
/ float(n-predictions_start+1))**0.5)
            else:
                # LEARNING PHASE
                SGD.partial_fit(hashed_features, target)

print '%s FINAL holdout RMSE: %0.3f' % \
(time.strftime('%X'), (val_rmse \
    / float(n-predictions_start+1))**0.5)
print '%s FINAL holdout RMSLE: %0.3f' % \
(time.strftime('%X'), (val_rmsle \
    / float(n-predictions_start+1))**0.5)


Out:
18:02:54 holdout RMSE: 281.065 holdout RMSLE: 1.899
18:02:54 holdout RMSE: 254.958 holdout RMSLE: 1.800
18:02:54 holdout RMSE: 255.456 holdout RMSLE: 1.798
18:52:54 holdout RMSE: 254.563 holdout RMSLE: 1.818
18:52:54 holdout RMSE: 239.740 holdout RMSLE: 1.737
18:52:54 FINAL holdout RMSE: 229.274
18:52:54 FINAL holdout RMSLE: 1.678
```

Summary

In this chapter, we have seen how learning is possible out-of-core by streaming data, no matter how big it is, from a text file or database on your hard disk. These methods certainly apply to much bigger datasets than the examples that we used to demonstrate them (which actually could be solved in-memory using non-average, powerful hardware).

We also explained the core algorithm that makes out-of-core learning possible—SGD—and we examined its strength and weakness, emphasizing the necessity of streams to be really stochastic (which means in a random order) to be really effective, unless the order is part of the learning objectives. In particular, we introduced the Scikit-learn implementation of SGD, limiting our focus to the linear and logistic regression loss functions.

Finally, we discussed data preparation, introduced the hashing trick and validation strategies for streams, and wrapped up the acquired knowledge on SGD fitting two different models—classification and regression.

In the next chapter, we will keep on enriching our out-of-core capabilities by figuring out how to enable non-linearity in our learning schema and hinge loss for support vector machines. We will also present alternatives to Scikit-learn, such as **Liblinear**, **Vowpal Wabbit**, and **StreamSVM**. Although operating as external shell commands, all of them could be easily wrapped and controlled by Python scripts.

3
Fast SVM Implementations

Having experimented with online-style learning in the previous chapter, you may have been surprised by its simplicity yet effectiveness and scalability in comparison to batch learning. In spite of learning just one example at a time, SGD can approximate the results well as if all the data resides in the core memory and you were using a batch algorithm. All you need is that your stream be indeed stochastic (there are no trends in data) and that the learner is tuned well to the problem (the learning rate is often the key parameter to be fixed).

Anyway, examining such achievements closely, the results are still just comparable to batch linear models but not to learners that are more sophisticated and characterized by higher variance than bias, such as SVMs, neural networks, or bagging and boosting ensembles of decision trees.

For certain problems, such as tall and wide but sparse data, just linear combinations may be enough according to the observation that a simple algorithm with more data often wins over more complex ones trained on less data. Yet, even using linear models and by resorting to explicitly mapping existing features into higher-dimensionality ones (using different order of interactions, polynomial expansions, and kernel approximations), we can accelerate and improve the learning of complex nonlinear relationships between the response and features.

In this chapter, we will therefore first introduce linear SVMs as a machine learning algorithm alternative to linear models, powered by a different approach to the problem of learning from data. Then, we will demonstrate how we can create richer features from the existing ones in order to solve our machine learning tasks in a better way when facing large scale data, especially tall data (that is, datasets having many cases to learn from).

In summary, in this chapter, we will cover the following topics:

- Introducing SVMs and providing you with the basic concepts and math formulas to figure out how they work

- Proposing SGD with hinge loss as a viable solution for large scale tasks that uses the same optimization approach as the batch SVM

- Suggesting nonlinear approximations to accompany SGD

- Offering an overview of other large scale online solutions besides SGD algorithm made available by Scikit-learn

Datasets to experiment with on your own

As in the previous chapter, we will be using datasets from the UCI Machine Learning Repository, in particular the bike-sharing dataset (a regression problem) and Forest Covertype Data (a multiclass classification problem).

If you have not done so before or if you need to download both the datasets again, you will need a couple of functions defined in the *Datasets to try the real thing yourself* section of *Chapter 2, Scalable Learning in Scikit-learn*. The needed functions are `unzip_from_UCI` and `gzip_from_UCI`. Both have a Python connect to the UCI repository; download a compressed file and unzip it in the working Python directory. If you call the functions from an IPython cell, you will find the necessary new directories and files exactly where IPython will look for them.

In case the functions do not work for you, never mind; we will provide you with the link for a direct download. After that, all you will have to do is unpack the data in the current working Python directory, which you can discover by running the following command on your Python interface (IPython or any IDE):

```
In: import os
print "Current directory is: \"%s\"" % (os.getcwd())

Out: Current directory is: "C:\scisoft\WinPython-64bit-2.7.9.4\
notebooks\Packt - Large Scale"
```

The bike-sharing dataset

The dataset comprises of two files in CSV format containing the hourly and daily count of bikes rented in the years between 2011 and 2012 within the Capital bike-share system in Washington D.C., USA. As a reminder, the data features the corresponding weather and seasonal information regarding the day of the rental.

The following code snippet will save the dataset on the local hard disk using the convenient `unzip_from_UCI` wrapper function:

```
In: UCI_url = 'https://archive.ics.uci.edu/ml/machine-learning-
databases/00275/Bike-Sharing-Dataset.zip'
unzip_from_UCI(UCI_url, dest='bikesharing')

Out: Extracting in C:\scisoft\WinPython-64bit-2.7.9.4\notebooks\
bikesharing
    unzipping day.csv
    unzipping hour.csv
```

If run successfully, the code will indicate in what directory the CSV files have been saved and print the names of both the unzipped files. If unsuccessful, just download the file from `https://archive.ics.uci.edu/ml/machine-learning-databases/00275/Bike-Sharing-Dataset.zip` and unzip the two files, `day.csv` and `hour.csv`, in a directory named `bikesharing` that you previously created in your Python working directory.

The covertype dataset

Donated by Jock A. Blackard, Dr. Denis J. Dean, Dr. Charles W. Anderson, and the Colorado State University, the covertype dataset contains 581,012 examples and a series of 54 cartographic variables, ranging from elevation to soil type, expected to be able to predict the forest cover type, which comprises seven kinds (so this is a multiclass problem). In order to assure comparability with academic studies on the same data, instructions recommend using the first 11,340 records for the training, the next 3,780 records for validation, and finally the remaining 565,892 records as test examples:

```
In: UCI_url = 'https://archive.ics.uci.edu/ml/machine-learning-
databases/covtype/covtype.data.gz'
gzip_from_UCI(UCI_url)
```

In case of problems in running the code or if you prefer to prepare the file by yourself, just go to the UCI website, download the dataset from `https://archive.ics.uci.edu/ml/machine-learning-databases/covtype/covtype.data.gz`, and unpack it into the directory that Python is currently working on.

Support Vector Machines

Support Vector Machines (SVMs) are a set of supervised learning techniques for classification and regression (and also for outlier detection), which is quite versatile as it can fit both linear and nonlinear models thanks to the availability of special functions — kernel functions. The specialty of such kernel functions is to be able to map the input features into a new, more complex feature vector using a limited amount of computations. Kernel functions nonlinearly recombine the original features, making possible the mapping of the response by very complex functions. In such a sense, SVMs are comparable to neural networks as universal approximators, and thus can boast a similar predictive power in many problems.

Contrary to the linear models seen in the previous chapter, SVMs started as a method to solve classification problems, not regression ones.

SVMs were invented at the AT&T laboratories in the '90s by the mathematician, Vladimir Vapnik, and computer scientist, Corinna Cortes (but there are also many other contributors that worked with Vapnik on the algorithm). In essence, an SVM strives to solve a classification problem by finding a particular hyperplane separating the classes in the feature space. Such a particular hyperplane has to be characterized as being the one with the largest separating margin between the boundaries of the classes (the margin is to be intended as the gap, the space between the classes themselves, empty of any example).

Such intuition implies two consequences:

- Empirically, SVMs try to minimize the test error by finding a solution in the training set that is exactly in the middle of the observed classes, thus the solution is clearly computational (it is an optimization based on quadratic programming — https://en.wikipedia.org/wiki/Quadratic_programming).

- As the solution is based on just the boundaries of the classes as set by the adjoining examples (called the support vectors), the other examples can be ignored, making the technique insensible to outliers and less memory-intensive than methods based on matrix inversion such as linear models.

Given such a general overview on the algorithm, we will be spending a few pages pointing out the key formulations that characterize SVMs. Although a complete and detailed explanation of the method is beyond the scope of this book, sketching how it works can indeed help figure out what is happening under the hood of the technique and provide the foundation to understand how it can be made scalable to big data.

Historically, SVMs were thought as *hard-margin* classifiers, just like the perceptron. In fact, SVMs were initially set trying to find two hyperplanes separating the classes whose reciprocal distance was the maximum possible. Such an approach worked perfectly with linearly-separable synthetic data. Anyway, in the hard-margin version, when an SVM faced nonlinearly separable data, it could only succeed using nonlinear transformations of the features. However, they were always deemed to fail when misclassification errors were due to noise in data instead of non-linearity.

For such a reason, softmargins were introduced by means of a cost function that took into account how serious the error was (as hard margins kept track only if an error occurred), thus allowing a certain tolerance to misclassified cases whose error was not too big because they were placed next to the separating hyperplane.

Since the introduction of softmargins, SVMs also became able to withstand non-separability caused by noise. Softmargins were simply introduced by building the cost function around a slack variable that approximates the number of misclassified examples. Such a slack variable is also called the empirical risk (the risk of making a wrong classification as seen from the training data point of view).

In mathematical formulations, given a matrix dataset X of n examples and m features and a response vector expressing the belonging to a class in terms of +1 (belonging) and -1 (not belonging), a binary classification SVM strives to minimize the following cost function:

$$\frac{\lambda}{2}\|w^2\| + \left[\frac{1}{n}\sum_{i=1}^{n}\max\left(0, 1 - y(wX + b)\right)\right]$$

In the preceding function, w is the vector of coefficients that expresses the separating hyperplane together with the bias b, representing the offset from the origin. There is also lambda ($\lambda >= 0$), which is the regularization parameter.

For a better understanding of how the cost function works, it is necessary to divide it into two parts. The first part is the regularization term:

$$\frac{\lambda}{2}\|w^2\|$$

The regularization term is contrasting the minimization process when the vector w assumes high values. The second term is called the loss term or slack variable, and actually is the core of the SVM minimization procedure:

$$\frac{1}{n}\sum_{i=1}^{n} \max\left(0, 1 - y(wX + b)\right)$$

The loss term outputs an approximate value of misclassification errors. In fact, the summation will tend to add a unit value for each classification error, whose total divided by n, the number of examples, will provide an approximate proportion of the classification error.

Often, as in the Scikit-learn implementation, the lambda is removed from the regularization term and replaced by a misclassification parameter C multiplying the loss term:

$$\frac{1}{2}\|w^2\| + C\left[\sum_{i=1}^{n} \max\left(0, 1 - y(wX + b)\right)\right]$$

The relation between the previous parameter lambda and the new C is as follows:

$$\lambda = \frac{1}{nC}$$

It is just a matter of conventions, as the change from the parameter lambda to C on the optimization's formula doesn't imply different results.

The impact of the loss term is mediated by a hyperparameter C. High values of C impose a high penalization on errors, thus forcing the SVM to try to correctly classify all the training examples. Consequently, larger C values tend to force the margin to be tighter and take into consideration fewer support vectors. Such a reduction of the margin translates into an increased bias and reduced variance.

This leads us to specify the role of certain observations with respect to others; in fact, we define as support vectors those examples that are misclassified or not classified with confidence as they are inside the margin (noisy observations that make class separation impossible). Optimization is possible taking into account only such examples, making SVM a memory-efficient technique indeed:

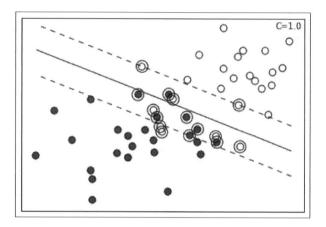

In the preceding visualization, you can notice the projection of two groups of points (blue and white) on two feature dimensions. An SVM solution with the C hyperparameter set to 1.0 can easily discover a separating line (in the plot represented as the continuous line), though there are some misclassified cases on both sides. In addition, the margin can be visualized (defined by the two dashed lines), being identifiable thanks to the support vectors of the respective class further from the separating line. In the chart, support vectors are marked by an external circle and you can actually notice that some support vectors are outside the margin; this is because they are misclassified cases and the SVM has to keep track of them for optimization purposes as their error is considered in the loss term:

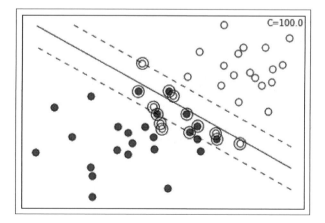

Increasing the C value, the margin tends to restrict as the SVM is taking into account fewer support vectors in the optimization process. Consequently, the slope of the separating line also changes.

On the contrary, smaller C values tend to relax the margin, thus increasing the variance. Extremely small C values can even lead the SVM to consider all the example points inside the margin. Smaller C values are ideal when there are many noisy examples. Such a setting forces the SVM to ignore many misclassified examples in the definition of the margin (Errors are weighted less, so they are tolerated more when searching for the maximum margin.):

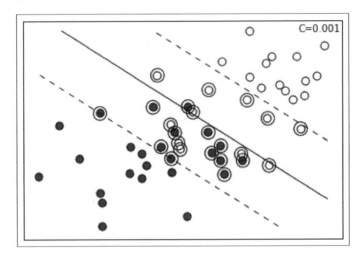

Continuing on the previous visual example, if we decrease the hyperparameter C, the margin actually expands because the number of the support vectors increases. Consequently, the margin being different, SVM resolves for a different separating line. There is no C value that can be deemed correct before being tested on data; the right value always has to be empirically found by cross-validation. By far, C is considered the most important hyperparameter in an SVM, to be set after deciding what kernel function to use.

Kernel functions instead map the original features into a higher-dimensional space by combining them in a nonlinear way. In such a way, apparently non-separable groups in the original feature space may turn separable in a higher-dimensional representation. Such a projection doesn't need too complex computations in spite of the fact that the process of explicitly transforming the original feature values into new ones can generate a potential explosion in the number of the features when projecting to high dimensionalities. Instead of doing such cumbersome computations, kernel functions can be simply plugged into the decision function, thus replacing the original dot product between the features and coefficient vector and obtaining the same optimization result as the explicit mapping would have had. (Such plugging is called the kernel trick because it is really a mathematical trick.)

Standard kernel functions are linear functions (implying no transformations), polynomial functions, **radial basis functions** (**RBF**), and sigmoid functions. To provide an idea, the RBF function can be expressed as follows:

$$K(x_i, x) = \exp\left(-\|x_i - x\|^2/2\sigma\right)$$

Basically, RBF and the other kernels just plug themselves directly into a variant of the previously seen function to be minimized. The previously seen optimization function is called the primal formulation whereas the analogous re-expression is called the dual formulation:

$$f(x) = \sum_{i=1}^{n} \alpha_i \, y_i K(x_i, x) + b$$

Though passing from the primal to the dual formulation is quite challenging without a mathematical demonstration, it is important to grasp that the kernel trick, given a kernel function that compares the examples by couples, is just a matter of a limited number of calculations with respect to the infinite dimensional feature space that it can unfold. Such a kernel trick renders the algorithm so particularly effective (comparable to neural networks) with respect to quite complex problems such as image recognition or textual classification:

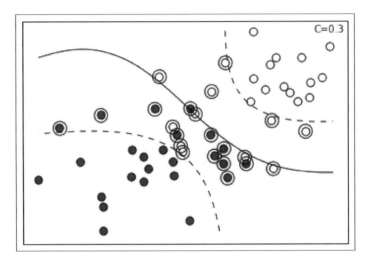

For instance, the preceding SVM solution is possible thanks to a sigmoid kernel, whereas the following one is due to an RBF one:

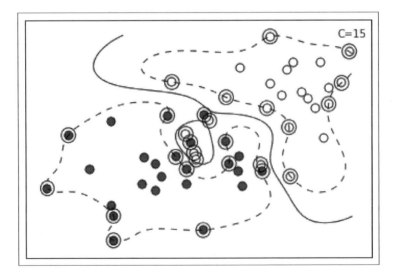

As visually noticeable, the RBF kernel allows quite complex definitions of the margin, even splitting it into multiple parts (and an enclave is noticeable in the preceding example).

The formulation of the RBF kernel is as follows:

$$k(x_i, x_j) = \exp\left(-\gamma \|x_i - x_j\|^2\right)$$

Gamma is a hyperparameter for you to define a-priori. The kernel transformation creates some sort of classification bubbles around the support vectors, thus allowing the definition of very complex boundary shapes by merging the bubbles themselves.

The formulation of the sigmoid kernel is as follows:

$$k(x_i, x_j) = \tanh\left(\gamma \langle x_i x_j \rangle^2 + r\right)$$

Here, apart from gamma, r should be also chosen for the best result.

Clearly, solutions based on sigmoid, RBF, and polynomial, (Yes, it implicitly does the polynomial expansion that we will talk about in the following paragraphs.) kernels present more variance than the bias of the estimates, thus requiring a severe validation when deciding their adoption. Though an SVM is resistant to overfitting, it is not certainly immune to it.

Support vector regression is related to support vector classification. It varies just for the notation (more similar to a linear regression, using betas instead of a vector w of coefficients) and loss function:

$$\sum_{j=1}^{m} \beta_j^2 + C \sum_{i=1}^{n} L_\epsilon \left(y_i - \hat{y}_i\right)$$

Noticeably, the only significant difference is the loss function L-epsilon, which is insensitive to errors (thus not computing them) if examples are within a certain distance epsilon from the regression hyperplane. The minimization of such a cost function optimizes the result for a regression problem, outputting values and not classes.

Hinge loss and its variants

As concluding remarks about the inner nuts and bolts of an SVM, remember that the cost function at the core of the algorithm is the hinge loss:

$$loss(y, \hat{y}) = \max(0, 1 - y\hat{y})$$

As seen before, $\hat{y}$ is expressed as the summation of the dot product of X and coefficient vector w with the bias b:

$$\hat{y} = wX + b$$

Reminiscent of the *perceptron*, such a loss function penalizes errors linearly, expressing an error when the example is classified on the wrong side of the margin, proportional to its distance from the margin itself. Though convex, having the disadvantage of not being differentiable everywhere, it is sometimes replaced by always differentiable variants such as the squared hinge loss (also called L2 loss whereas L1 loss is the hinge loss):

$$L2\_loss(y, \hat{y}) = \max(0, 1 - y\hat{y})^2$$

Another variant is the Huber loss, which is a quadratic function when the error is equal or below a certain threshold value h but a linear function otherwise. Such an approach mixes L1 and L2 variants of the hinge loss based on the error and it is an alternative quite resistant to outliers as larger error values are not squared, thus requiring fewer adjustments by the learning SVM. Huber loss is also an alternative to log loss (linear models) because it is faster to calculate and able to provide estimates of class probabilities (the hinge loss does not have such a capability).

From a practical point of view, there are no particular reports that Huber loss or L2 hinge loss can consistently perform better than hinge loss. In the end, the choice of a cost function just boils down to testing the available functions with respect to every different learning problem. (According to the principle of the no-free-lunch theorem, in machine learning, there are no solutions suitable for all the problems.)

Understanding the Scikit-learn SVM implementation

Scikit-learn offers an implementation of SVM using two C++ libraries (with a C API to interface with other languages) developed at the National Taiwan University, **A Library for Support Vector Machines (LIBSVM)** for SVM classification and regression (http://www.csie.ntu.edu.tw/~cjlin/libsvm/) and LIBLINEAR for classification problems using linear methods on large and sparse datasets (http://www.csie.ntu.edu.tw/~cjlin/liblinear/). Having both the libraries free to use, quite fast in computations, and already tested in quite a number of other solutions, all Scikit-learn implementations in the sklearn.svm module rely on one or the other, (The Perceptron and LogisticRegression classes also make use of them, by the way.) making Python just a convenient wrapper.

On the other hand, SGDClassifier and SGDRegressor use a different implementation as neither LIBSVM nor LIBLINEAR have an online implementation, both being batch learning tools. In fact, when operating, both LIBSVM and LIBLINEAR perform the best when allocated a suitable memory for kernel operations via the cache_size parameter.

The implementations for classification are as follows:

Class	Purpose	Hyperparameters
sklearn.svm.SVC	The LIBSVM implementation for binary and multiclass linear and kernel classification	C, kernel, degree, gamma
sklearn.svm.NuSVC	same as above	nu, kernel, degree, gamma
sklearn.svm. OneClassSVM	Unsupervised detection of outliers	nu, kernel, degree, gamma
sklearn.svm.LinearSVC	Based on LIBLINEAR, it is a binary and multiclass linear classifier	Penalty, loss, C

As for regression, the solutions are as follows:

Class	Purpose	Hyperparameters
sklearn.svm.SVR	The LIBSVM implementation for regression	C, kernel, degree, gamma, epsilon
sklearn.svm.NuSVR	same as above	nu, C, kernel, degree, gamma

As you can see, there are quite a few hyperparameters to be tuned for each version, making SVMs good learners when using default parameters and excellent ones when properly tuned by cross-validation, using `GridSearchCV` from the `grid_search` module in Scikit-learn.

As a golden rule, some parameters influence the result more and so should be fixed beforehand, others being dependent on their values. According to such an empirical rule, you have to correctly set the following parameters (ordered by rank of importance):

- `C`: This is the penalty value that we discussed before. Decreasing it makes the margin larger, thus ignoring more noise but also making for more computations. A best value can be normally looked for in the `np.logspace(-3, 3, 7)` range.

- `kernel`: This is the non-linearity workhorse because an SVM can be set to `linear`, `poly`, `rbf`, `sigmoid`, or a custom kernel (for experts!). The widely used one is certainly `rbf`.

- `degree`: This works with `kernel='poly'`, signaling the dimensionality of the polynomial expansion. It is ignored by other kernels. Usually, values from 2-5 work the best.

- `gamma`: This is a coefficient for `'rbf'`, `'poly'`, and `'sigmoid'`; high values tend to fit data in a better way. The suggested grid search range is `np.logspace(-3, 3, 7)`.

- `nu`: This is for regression and classification with `nuSVR` and `nuSVC`; this parameter approximates the training points that are not classified with confidence, misclassified points, and correct points inside or on the margin. It should be a number in the range [0,1] as it is a proportion relative to your training set. In the end, it acts as C with high proportions enlarging the margin.

- `epsilon`: This parameter specifies how much error an SVR is going to accept by defining an epsilon large range where no penalty is associated with respect to the true value of the point. The suggested search range is `np.insert(np.logspace(-4, 2, 7),0,[0])`.

- `penalty`, `loss` and `dual`: For LinearSVC, these parameters accept the `('l1','squared_hinge',False)`, `('l2','hinge',True)`, `('l2','squared_hinge',True)`, and `('l2','squared_hinge',False)` combinations. The `('l2','hinge',True)` combination is equivalent to the `SVC(kernel='linear')` learner.

As an example for basic classification and regression using SVC and SVR from Scikit-learn's `sklearn.svm` module, we will work with the Iris and Boston datasets, a couple of popular toy datasets (http://scikit-learn.org/stable/datasets/).

First, we will load the Iris dataset:

```
In: from sklearn import datasets
iris = datasets.load_iris()
X_i, y_i = iris.data, iris.target
```

Then, we will fit an SVC with an RBF kernel (C and gamma were chosen on the basis of other known examples in Scikit-learn) and test the results using the `cross_val_score` function:

```
from sklearn.svm import SVC
from sklearn.cross_validation import cross_val_score
import numpy as np
h_class = SVC(kernel='rbf', C=1.0, gamma=0.7, random_state=101)
scores = cross_val_score(h_class, X_i, y_i, cv=20, scoring='accuracy')
print 'Accuracy: %0.3f' % np.mean(scores)

Output: Accuracy: 0.969
```

The fitted model can provide you with an index pointing out what are the support vectors among your training examples:

```
In: h_class.fit(X_i,y_i)
print h_class.support_

Out: [ 13  14  15  22  24  41  44  50  52  56  60  62  63  66  68  70
 72  76  77  83  84  85  98 100 106 110 114 117 118 119 121 123 126 127
129 131 133 134 138 141 146 149]
```

Here is a graphical representation of the support vectors selected by the SVC for the Iris dataset, represented with color decision boundaries (we tested a discrete grid of values in order to be able to project for each area of the chart what class the model will predict):

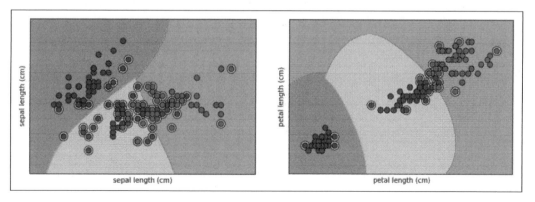

If you are interested in replicating the same charts, you can have a look and tweak this code snippet from `http://scikit-learn.org/stable/auto_examples/svm/plot_iris.html`.

To test an SVM regressor, we decided to try SVR with the Boston dataset. First, we upload the dataset in the core memory and then we randomize the ordering of examples as, noticeably, such a dataset is actually ordered in a subtle fashion, thus making results from not order-randomized cross-validation invalid:

```
In: import numpy as np
from sklearn.datasets import load_boston
from sklearn.preprocessing import StandardScaler
scaler = StandardScaler()
boston = load_boston()
shuffled = np.random.permutation(boston.target.size)
X_b = scaler.fit_transform(boston.data[shuffled,:])
y_b = boston.target[shuffled]
```

 Due to the fact that we used the `permutation` function from the random module in the NumPy package, you may obtain a differently shuffled dataset and consequently a slightly different cross-validated score from the following test. Moreover, the features having different scales, it is a good practice to standardize the features so that they will have zero-centered mean and unit variance. Especially when using SVM with kernels, standardization is indeed crucial.

Finally, we can fit the SVR model (we decided on some C, gamma, and epsilon parameters that we know work fine) and, using cross-validation, we evaluate it by the root mean squared error:

```
In: from sklearn.svm import SVR
from sklearn.cross_validation import cross_val_score
h_regr = SVR(kernel='rbf', C=20.0, gamma=0.001, epsilon=1.0)
scores = cross_val_score(h_regr, X_b, y_b, cv=20, scoring='mean_
squared_error')
print 'Mean Squared Error: %0.3f' % abs(np.mean(scores))

Out: Mean Squared Error: 28.087
```

Pursuing nonlinear SVMs by subsampling

SVMs have quite a few advantages over other machine learning algorithms:

- They can handle majority of the supervised problems such as regression, classification, and anomaly detection, though they are actually best at binary classification.

- They provide a good handling of noisy data and outliers and they tend to overfit less as they only work with support vectors.

- They work fine with wide datasets (more features than examples); though, as with other machine learning algorithms, an SVM would gain both from dimensionality reduction and feature selection.

As drawbacks, we have to mention the following:

- They provide just estimates, but no probabilities unless you run some time-consuming and computationally-intensive probability calibration by means of Platt scaling

- They scale super-linearly with the number of examples

In particular, the last drawback puts a strong limitation on the usage of SVMs for large datasets. The optimization algorithm at the core of this learning technique—quadratic programming—scales in the Scikit-learn implementation between *O(number of feature * number of samples^2)* and *O(number of feature * number of samples^3)*, a complexity that seriously limits the operability of the algorithm to datasets that are under 10^4 number of cases.

Again, as seen in the last chapter, there are just a few options when you give a batch algorithm and too much data: subsampling, parallelization, and out-of-core learning by streaming. Subsampling and parallelization are seldom quoted as the best solutions, streaming being the favored approach to implement SVMs with large-scale problems.

However, though less used, subsampling is quite easy to implement leveraging reservoir sampling, which can produce random samples rapidly from streams derived from datasets and infinite online streams. By subsampling, you can produce multiple SVM models, whose results can be averaged for better results. The predictions from multiple SVM models can even be stacked, thus creating a new dataset, and used to build a new model fusing the predictive capabilities of all, which will be described in *Chapter 6, Classification and Regression Trees at Scale*.

Reservoir sampling is an algorithm for randomly choosing a sample from a stream without having prior knowledge of how long the stream is. In fact, every observation in the stream has the same probability of being chosen. Initialized with a sample taken from the first observations in the stream, each element in the sample can be replaced at any moment by the example in the stream according to a probability proportional to the number of elements streamed up so far. So, for instance, when the *i-th* element of the stream arrives, it has a probability of being inserted in place of a random element in the sample. Such an insertion probability is equivalent to the sample dimension divided by *i*; therefore, it is progressively decreasing with respect to the stream length. If the stream is infinite, stopping at any time assures that the sample is representative of the elements seen so far.

In our example, we draw two random, mutually exclusive samples from the stream — one to train and one to test. We will extract such samples from the Covertype database, using the original ordered file. (As we will stream all the data before taking the sample, the random sampling won't be affected by the ordering.) We decided on a training sample of 5,000 examples, a number that should scale well on most desktop computers. As for the test set, we will be using 20,000 examples:

```
In: from random import seed, randint
SAMPLE_COUNT = 5000
TEST_COUNT   = 20000
seed(0) # allows repeatable results
sample = list()
test_sample = list()
for index, line in enumerate(open('covtype.data','rb')):
    if index < SAMPLE_COUNT:
        sample.append(line)
    else:
        r = randint(0, index)
        if r < SAMPLE_COUNT:
            sample[r] = line
        else:
            k = randint(0, index)
            if k < TEST_COUNT:
                if len(test_sample) < TEST_COUNT:
                    test_sample.append(line)
                else:
                    test_sample[k] = line
```

The algorithm should be streaming quite fast on the over `500,000` rows of the data matrix. In fact, we really did no preprocessing during the streaming in order to keep it the fastest possible. We consequently now need to transform the data into a NumPy array and standardize the features:

```
In: import numpy as np
from sklearn.preprocessing import StandardScaler
for n,line in enumerate(sample):
        sample[n] = map(float,line.strip().split(','))
y = np.array(sample)[:,-1]
scaling = StandardScaler()
X = scaling.fit_transform(np.array(sample)[:,:-1])
```

Once done with the training data *X, y*, we have to process the test data in the same way; particularly, we will have to standardize the features using standardization parameters (means and standard deviations) as in the training sample:

```
In: for n,line in enumerate(test_sample):
        test_sample[n] = map(float,line.strip().split(','))
yt = np.array(test_sample)[:,-1]
Xt = scaling.transform(np.array(test_sample)[:,:-1])
```

When both train and test sets are ready, we can fit the SVC model and predict the results:

```
In: from sklearn.svm import SVC
h = SVC(kernel='rbf', C=250.0, gamma=0.0025, random_state=101)
h.fit(X,y)
prediction = h.predict(Xt)
from sklearn.metrics import accuracy_score
print accuracy_score(yt, prediction)

Out: 0.75205
```

Achieving SVM at scale with SGD

Given the limitations of subsampling (first of all, the underfitting with respect to models trained on larger datasets), the only available option when using Scikit-learn for linear SVMs applied to large-scale streams remains the `SGDClassifier` and `SGDRegressor` methods, both available in the `linear_model` module. Let's see how to use them at their best and improve our results on the example datasets.

We are going to leverage the previous examples seen in the chapter for linear and logistic regression and transform them into an efficient SVM. As for classification, it is required that you set the loss type using the `loss` hyperparameter. The possible values for the parameter are `'hinge'`, `'squared_hinge'`, and `'modified_huber'`. All such loss functions were previously introduced and discussed in this same chapter when dealing with the SVM formulation.

All of them imply applying a soft-margin linear SVM (no kernels), thus resulting in an SVM resistant to misclassifications and noisy data. However, you may also try to use the loss `'perceptron'`, a type of loss that results in a hinge loss without margin, a solution suitable when it is necessary to resort to a model with more bias than the other possible loss choices.

Two aspects have to be taken into account to gain the best results when using such a range of hinge loss functions:

- When using any loss function, the stochastic gradient descent turns lazy, updating the vector of coefficients only when an example violates the previously defined margins. This is quite contrary to the loss function in the log or squared error, when actually every example is considered for the update of the coefficients' vector. In case there are many features involved in the learning, such a lazy approach leads to a resulting sparser vector of coefficients, thus reducing the overfitting. (A denser vector implies more overfitting because some coefficients are likely to catch more noise than signals from the data.)

- Only the `'modified_huber'` loss allows probability estimation, making it a viable alternative to the log loss (as found in the stochastic logistic regression). A modified Huber is also a better performer when dealing with multiclass **one-vs-all (OVA)** predictions as the probability outputs of the multiple models are better than the standard decision functions characteristic of hinge loss (probabilities work better than the raw output of the decision functions as they are on the same scale, bounded from 0 to 1). This loss function works by deriving a probability estimate directly from the decision function: `(clip(decision_function(X), -1, 1) + 1) / 2`.

As for regression problems, SGDRegressor offers two SVM loss options:

`'epsilon_insensitive'`

`'squared_epsilon_insensitive'`

Both activate a linear support vector regression, where errors (residual from the prediction) within the epsilon value are ignored. Past the epsilon value, the `epsilon_insensitive` loss considers the error as it is. The `squared_epsilon_insensitive` loss operates in a similar way though the error here is more penalizing as it is squared, with larger errors influencing the model building more.

In both cases, setting the correct epsilon hyperparameter is critical. As a default value, Scikit-learn suggests epsilon=0.1, but the best value for your problem has to be found by means of grid-search supported by cross-validation, as we will see in the next paragraphs.

Note that among regression losses, there is also a `'huber'` loss available that does not activate an SVM kind of optimization but just modifies the usual `'squared_loss'` to be insensible to outliers by switching from squared to linear loss past a distance of the value of the epsilon parameter.

As for our examples, we will be repeating the streaming process a certain number of times in order to demonstrate how to set different hyperparameters and transform features; we will use some convenient functions in order to reduce the number of repeated lines of code. Moreover, in order to speed up the execution of the examples, we will put a limit to the number of cases or tolerance values that the algorithm refers to. In such a way, both the training and validation times are kept at a minimum and no example will require you to wait more minutes than the time for a cup of tea or coffee.

As for the convenient wrapper functions, the first one will have the purpose to initially stream part or all the data once (we set a limit using the `max_rows` parameter). After completing the streaming, the function will be able to figure out all the categorical features' levels and record the different ranges of the numeric features. As a reminder, recording ranges is an important aspect to take care of. Both SGD and SVM are algorithms sensible to different range scales and they perform worse when working with a number outside the [-1,1] range.

As an output, our function will return two trained Scikit-learn objects: `DictVectorizer` (able to transform feature ranges present in a dictionary into a feature vector) and `MinMaxScaler` to rescale numeric variables in the [0,1] range (useful to keep values sparse in the dataset, thus keeping memory usage low and achieving fast computations when most values are zero). As a unique constraint, it is necessary for you to know the feature names of the numeric and categorical variables that you want to use for your predictive model. Features not enclosed in the lists' feed to the `binary_features` or `numeric_features` parameters actually will be ignored. When the stream has no features' names, it is necessary for you to name them using the `fieldnames` parameter:

```
In: import csv, time, os
```

```python
import numpy as np
from sklearn.linear_model import SGDRegressor
from sklearn.feature_extraction import DictVectorizer
from sklearn.preprocessing import MinMaxScaler
from scipy.sparse import csr_matrix

def explore(target_file, separator=',', fieldnames= None, binary_
features=list(), numeric_features=list(), max_rows=20000):
    """
    Generate from an online style stream a DictVectorizer and a
MinMaxScaler.

    Parameters
    ----------
    target file = the file to stream from
    separator = the field separator character
    fieldnames = the fields' labels (can be omitted and read from
file)
    binary_features = the list of qualitative features to consider
    numeric_features = the list of numeric futures to consider
    max_rows = the number of rows to be read from the stream (can be
None)
    """
    features = dict()
    min_max  = dict()
    vectorizer = DictVectorizer(sparse=False)
    scaler = MinMaxScaler()
    with open(target_file, 'rb') as R:
        iterator = csv.DictReader(R, fieldnames, delimiter=separator)
        for n, row in enumerate(iterator):
            # DATA EXPLORATION
            for k,v in row.iteritems():
                if k in binary_features:
                    if k+'_'+v not in features:
                        features[k+'_'+v]=0
                elif k in numeric_features:
                    v = float(v)
                    if k not in features:
                        features[k]=0
                        min_max[k] = [v,v]
                    else:
                        if v < min_max[k][0]:
                            min_max[k][0]= v
                        elif v > min_max[k][1]:
                            min_max[k][1]= v
```

```
            else:
                    pass # ignore the feature
             if max_rows and n > max_rows:
                    break
     vectorizer.fit([features])
     A = vectorizer.transform([{f:0 if f not in min_max else min_max[f]
[0] for f in vectorizer.feature_names_},
{f:1 if f not in min_max else min_max[f][1] for f in vectorizer.
feature_names_}])
     scaler.fit(A)
     return vectorizer, scaler
```

 This code snippet can be reused easily for your own machine learning applications for large-scale data. In case your stream is an online one (a continuous streaming) or a too long one, you can apply a different limit on the number of observed examples by setting the `max_rows` parameter.

The second function will instead just pull out the data from the stream and transform it into a feature vector, normalizing the numeric features if a suitable `MinMaxScaler` object is provided instead of a `None` setting:

```
In: def pull_examples(target_file, vectorizer, binary_features,
numeric_features, target, min_max=None, separator=',',
fieldnames=None, sparse=True):
    """
    Reads a online style stream and returns a generator of normalized
feature vectors

    Parameters
    ----------
    target file = the file to stream from
    vectorizer = a DictVectorizer object
    binary_features = the list of qualitative features to consider
    numeric_features = the list of numeric features to consider
    target = the label of the response variable
    min_max = a MinMaxScaler object, can be omitted leaving None
    separator = the field separator character
    fieldnames = the fields' labels (can be omitted and read from
file)
    sparse = if a sparse vector is to be returned from the generator
    """
    with open(target_file, 'rb') as R:
        iterator = csv.DictReader(R, fieldnames, delimiter=separator)
        for n, row in enumerate(iterator):
```

```
# DATA PROCESSING
stream_row = {}
response = np.array([float(row[target])])
for k,v in row.iteritems():
    if k in binary_features:
        stream_row[k+'_'+v]=1.0
    else:
        if k in numeric_features:
            stream_row[k]=float(v)
if min_max:
    features = min_max.transform(vectorizer.
transform([stream_row]))
else:
    features = vectorizer.transform([stream_row])
if sparse:
    yield(csr_matrix(features), response, n)
else:
    yield(features, response, n)
```

Given these two functions, now let's try again to model the first regression problem seen in the previous chapter, the bike-sharing dataset, but using a hinge loss this time instead of the mean squared errors that we used before.

As the first step, we provide the name of the file to stream and a list of qualitative and numeric variables (as derived from the header of the file and initial exploration of the file). The code of our wrapper function will return some information on the hot-coded variables and value ranges. In this case, most of the variables will be binary ones, a perfect situation for a sparse representation, as most values in our dataset are plain zero:

```
In: source = '\\bikesharing\\hour.csv'
local_path = os.getcwd()
b_vars = ['holiday','hr','mnth', 'season','weathersit','weekday','wor
kingday','yr']
n_vars = ['hum', 'temp', 'atemp', 'windspeed']
std_row, min_max = explore(target_file=local_path+'\\'+source, binary_
features=b_vars, numeric_features=n_vars)
print 'Features: '
for f,mv,mx in zip(std_row.feature_names_, min_max.data_min_, min_max.
data_max_):
    print '%s:[%0.2f,%0.2f] ' % (f,mv,mx)

Out:
Features:
atemp:[0.00,1.00]
```

```
holiday_0:[0.00,1.00]
holiday_1:[0.00,1.00]
...
workingday_1:[0.00,1.00]
yr_0:[0.00,1.00]
yr_1:[0.00,1.00]
```

As you can notice from the output, qualitative variables have been encoded using their variable name and adding, after an underscore character, their value and transformed into binary features (which has the value of one when the feature is present, otherwise it is set to zero). Note that we are always using our SGD models with the `average=True` parameter in order to assure a faster convergence (this corresponds to using the **Averaged Stochastic Gradient Descent (ASGD)** model as discussed in the previous chapter.):

```
In:from sklearn.linear_model import SGDRegressor
SGD = SGDRegressor(loss='epsilon_insensitive', epsilon=0.001,
penalty=None, random_state=1, average=True)
val_rmse = 0
val_rmsle = 0
predictions_start = 16000

def apply_log(x): return np.log(x + 1.0)
def apply_exp(x): return np.exp(x) - 1.0

for x,y,n in pull_examples(target_file=local_path+'\\'+source,
                           vectorizer=std_row, min_max=min_max,
                           binary_features=b_vars, numeric_features=n_
vars, target='cnt'):
    y_log = apply_log(y)
# MACHINE LEARNING
    if (n+1) >= predictions_start:
        # HOLDOUT AFTER N PHASE
        predicted = SGD.predict(x)
        val_rmse += (apply_exp(predicted) - y)**2
        val_rmsle += (predicted - y_log)**2
        if (n-predictions_start+1) % 250 == 0 and (n+1) > predictions_
start:
            print n,
            print '%s holdout RMSE: %0.3f' % (time.strftime('%X'),
(val_rmse / float(n-predictions_start+1))**0.5),
            print 'holdout RMSLE: %0.3f' % ((val_rmsle / float(n-
predictions_start+1))**0.5)
    else:
        # LEARNING PHASE
```

```
        SGD.partial_fit(x, y_log)
print '%s FINAL holdout RMSE: %0.3f' % (time.strftime('%X'), (val_rmse
/ float(n-predictions_start+1))**0.5)
print '%s FINAL holdout RMSLE: %0.3f' % (time.strftime('%X'), (val_
rmsle / float(n-predictions_start+1))**0.5)


Out:
16249 07:49:09 holdout RMSE: 276.768 holdout RMSLE: 1.801
16499 07:49:09 holdout RMSE: 250.549 holdout RMSLE: 1.709
16749 07:49:09 holdout RMSE: 250.720 holdout RMSLE: 1.696
16999 07:49:09 holdout RMSE: 249.661 holdout RMSLE: 1.705
17249 07:49:09 holdout RMSE: 234.958 holdout RMSLE: 1.642
07:49:09 FINAL holdout RMSE: 224.513
07:49:09 FINAL holdout RMSLE: 1.596
```

We are now going to try the classification problem of forest covertype:

```
In: source = 'shuffled_covtype.data'
local_path = os.getcwd()
n_vars = ['var_'+'0'*int(j<10)+str(j) for j in range(54)]
std_row, min_max = explore(target_file=local_path+'\\'+source, binary_
features=list(),
                fieldnames= n_vars+['covertype'], numeric_
features=n_vars, max_rows=50000)
print 'Features: '
for f,mv,mx in zip(std_row.feature_names_, min_max.data_min_, min_max.
data_max_):
    print '%s:[%0.2f,%0.2f] ' % (f,mv,mx)


Out:
Features:
var_00:[1871.00,3853.00]
var_01:[0.00,360.00]
var_02:[0.00,61.00]
var_03:[0.00,1397.00]
var_04:[-164.00,588.00]
var_05:[0.00,7116.00]
var_06:[58.00,254.00]
var_07:[0.00,254.00]
var_08:[0.00,254.00]
var_09:[0.00,7168.00]

...
```

After having sampled from the stream and fitted our DictVectorizer and
MinMaxScaler objects, we can start our learning process using a progressive
validation this time (the error measure is given by testing the model on the cases
before they are used for the training), given the large number of examples available.
Every certain number of examples as set by the sample variable in the code, the
script reports the situation with average accuracy from the most recent examples:

```
In: from sklearn.linear_model import SGDClassifier
SGD = SGDClassifier(loss='hinge', penalty=None, random_state=1,
average=True)
accuracy = 0
accuracy_record = list()
predictions_start = 50
sample = 5000
early_stop = 50000
for x,y,n in pull_examples(target_file=local_path+'\\'+source,
                           vectorizer=std_row,
                           min_max=min_max,
                           binary_features=list(), numeric_features=n_
vars,
                           fieldnames= n_vars+['covertype'],
target='covertype'):
    # LEARNING PHASE
    if n > predictions_start:
        accuracy += int(int(SGD.predict(x))==y[0])
        if n % sample == 0:
            accuracy_record.append(accuracy / float(sample))
            print '%s Progressive accuracy at example %i: %0.3f' %
(time.strftime('%X'), n, np.mean(accuracy_record[-sample:]))
            accuracy = 0
    if early_stop and n >= early_stop:
            break
    SGD.partial_fit(x, y, classes=range(1,8))

Out: ...
19:23:49 Progressive accuracy at example 50000: 0.699
```

> Having to process over 575,000 examples, we set an early stop to the
> learning process after 50,000. You are free to modify such parameters
> according to the power of your computer and time availability. Be warned
> that the code may take some time. We experienced about 30 minutes of
> computing on an Intel Core i3 processor clocking at 2.20 GHz.

Feature selection by regularization

In a batch context, it is common to operate feature selection by the following:

- A preliminary filtering based on completeness (incidence of missing values), variance, and high multicollinearity between variables in order to have a cleaner dataset of relevant and operable features.

- Another initial filtering based on the univariate association (chi-squared test, F-value, and simple linear regression) between the features and response variable in order to immediately remove the features that are of no use for the predictive task because they are little or not related to the response.

- During modeling, a recursive approach inserting and/or excluding features on the basis of their capability to improve the predictive power of the algorithm, as tested on a holdout sample. Using a smaller subset of just relevant features allows the machine learning algorithm to be less affected by overfitting because of noisy variables and the parameters in excess due to the high dimensionality of the features.

Applying such approaches in an online setting is certainly still possible, but quite expensive in terms of the required time because of the quantity of data to stream to complete a single model. Recursive approaches based on a large number of iterations and tests require a nimble dataset that can fit in memory. As just previously quoted, in such a case, subsampling would be a good option in order to figure out features and models later to be applied to a larger scale.

Keeping on our out-of-core approach, regularization is the ideal solution as a way to select variables while streaming and filter out noisy or redundant features. Regularization works fine with online algorithms as it operates as the online machine learning algorithm is working and fitting its coefficients from the examples, without any need to run other streams for the purpose of selection. Regularization is, in fact, just a penalty value, which is added to the optimization of the learning process. It is dependent on the features' coefficient and a parameter named `alpha` setting the impact of regularization. The regularization balancing intervenes when coefficients' weights are updated by the model. At that time, regularization acts by reducing the resulting weights if the value of the update is not large enough. The trick of excluding or attenuating redundant variables is achieved because of the regularization `alpha` parameter, which has to be empirically set at the correct magnitude for the best result with respect to each specific data to be learned.

SGD implements the same regularization strategies to be found in batch algorithms:

- L1 penalty pushing to zero redundant and not so important variables
- L2 reducing the weight of less important features
- Elastic Net mixing the effects of L1 and L2 regularization

L1 regularization is the perfect strategy when there are unusual and redundant variables as it will push the coefficients of such features to zero, making them irrelevant when calculating the prediction.

L2 is suitable when there are many correlations between the variables as its strategy is just to reduce the weights of the features whose variation is less important for the loss function minimization. With L2, all the variables keep on contributing to the prediction, though some less so.

Elastic Net mixes L1 and L2 using a weighted sum. This solution is interesting as sometimes L1 regularization is unstable when dealing with highly correlated variables, choosing one or the other with respect to the seen examples. Using `ElasticNet`, many unusual features will still be pushed to zero as in L1 regularization, but correlated ones will be attenuated as in L2.

Both `SGDClassifier` and `SGDRegressor` can implement L1, L2, and Elastic Net regularization using the `penalty`, `alpha`, and `l1_ratio` parameters.

> The alpha parameter is the most critical parameter after deciding what kind of penalty or about the mix of the two. Ideally, you can test suitable values in the range from 0.1 to 10^-7, using the list of values produced by `10.0**-np.arange(1,7)`.

If `penalty` determinates what kind of regularization is chosen, `alpha`, as mentioned, will determinate its strength. As `alpha` is a constant that multiplies the penalization term; low alpha values will bring little influence on the final coefficient, whereas high values will significantly affect it. Finally, `l1_ratio` represents, when `penalty='elasticnet'`, how much percentage is the L1 penalization with respect to L2.

Setting regularization with SGD is very easy. For instance, you may try changing the previous code example inserting a penalty L2 into `SGDClassifier`:

```
SGD = SGDClassifier(loss='hinge', penalty='l2', alpha= 0.0001, random_
state=1, average=True)
```

If you prefer to test an Elastic-Net mixing the effects of the two regularization approaches, all you have to do is explicit the ratio between L1 and L2 by setting `l1_ratio`:

```
SGD = SGDClassifier(loss=''hinge'', penalty=''elasticnet'', \
    alpha= 0.001, l1_ratio=0.5, random_state=1, average=True)
```

As the success of regularization depends on plugging the right kind of penalty and best alpha, regularization will be seen in action in our examples when dealing with the problem of hyperparameter optimization.

Including non-linearity in SGD

The fastest way to insert non-linearity into a linear SGD learner (and basically a no-brainer) is to transform the vector of the example received from the stream into a new vector including both power transformations and a combination of the features upto a certain degree.

Combinations can represent interactions between the features (explicating when two features concur to have a special impact on the response), thus helping the SVM linear model to include a certain amount of non-linearity. For instance, a two-way interaction is made by the multiplication of two features. A three-way is made by multiplying three features and so on, creating even more complex interactions for higher-degree expansions.

In Scikit-learn, the preprocessing module contains the `PolynomialFeatures` class, which can automatically transform the vector of features by polynomial expansion of the desired degree:

```
In: from sklearn.linear_model import SGDRegressor
from  sklearn.preprocessing import PolynomialFeatures

source = '\\bikesharing\\hour.csv'
local_path = os.getcwd()
b_vars = ['holiday','hr','mnth', 'season','weathersit','weekday','wor
kingday','yr']
n_vars = ['hum', 'temp', 'atemp', 'windspeed']
std_row, min_max = explore(target_file=local_path+'\\'+source, binary_
features=b_vars, numeric_features=n_vars)

poly = PolynomialFeatures(degree=2, interaction_only=False, include_
bias=False)
```

```
SGD = SGDRegressor(loss='epsilon_insensitive', epsilon=0.001,
penalty=None, random_state=1, average=True)

val_rmse = 0
val_rmsle = 0
predictions_start = 16000

def apply_log(x): return np.log(x + 1.0)
def apply_exp(x): return np.exp(x) - 1.0

for x,y,n in pull_examples(target_file=local_path+'\\'\
+source,vectorizer=std_row, min_max=min_max, \
sparse = False, binary_features=b_vars,\
numeric_features=n_vars, target='cnt'):
    y_log = apply_log(y)
# Extract only quantitative features and expand them
    num_index = [j for j, i in enumerate(std_row.feature_names_) if i
in n_vars]
    x_poly = poly.fit_transform(x[:,num_index])[:,len(num_index):]
    new_x = np.concatenate((x, x_poly), axis=1)

    # MACHINE LEARNING
    if (n+1) >= predictions_start:
        # HOLDOUT AFTER N PHASE
        predicted = SGD.predict(new_x)
        val_rmse += (apply_exp(predicted) - y)**2
        val_rmsle += (predicted - y_log)**2
        if (n-predictions_start+1) % 250 == 0 and (n+1) > predictions_
start:
            print n,
            print '%s holdout RMSE: %0.3f' % (time.strftime('%X'),
(val_rmse / float(n-predictions_start+1))**0.5),
            print 'holdout RMSLE: %0.3f' % ((val_rmsle / float(n-
predictions_start+1))**0.5)
    else:
        # LEARNING PHASE
        SGD.partial_fit(new_x, y_log)
print '%s FINAL holdout RMSE: %0.3f' % (time.strftime('%X'), (val_rmse
/ float(n-predictions_start+1))**0.5)
print '%s FINAL holdout RMSLE: %0.3f' % (time.strftime('%X'), (val_
rmsle / float(n-predictions_start+1))**0.5)

Out: ...
21:49:24 FINAL holdout RMSE: 219.191
21:49:24 FINAL holdout RMSLE: 1.480
```

`PolynomialFeatures` expects a dense matrix, not a sparse one as an input. Our `pull_examples` function allows the setting of a sparse parameter, which, normally set to `True`, can instead be set to `False`, thus returning a dense matrix as a result.

Trying explicit high-dimensional mappings

Though polynomial expansions are a quite powerful transformation, they can be computationally expensive when we are trying to expand to higher degrees and quickly contrast the positive effects of catching important non-linearity by overfitting caused by over-parameterization (when you have too many redundant and not useful features). As seen in SVC and SVR, kernel transformations can come to our aid. SVM kernel transformations, being implicit, require the data matrix in-memory in order to work. There is a class of transformations in Scikit-learn, based on random approximations, which, in the context of a linear model, can achieve very similar results as a kernel SVM.

The `sklearn.kernel_approximation` module contains a few such algorithms:

- `RBFSampler`: This approximates a feature map of an RBF kernel
- `Nystroem`: This approximates a kernel map using a subset of the training data
- `AdditiveChi2Sampler`: This approximates feature mapping for an additive chi2 kernel, a kernel used in computer vision
- `SkewedChi2Sampler`: This approximates feature mapping similar to the skewed chi-squared kernel also used in computer vision

Apart from the Nystroem method, none of the preceding classes require to learn from a sample of your data, making them perfect for online learning. They just need to know how an example vector is shaped (how many features there are) and then they will produce many random non-linearities that can, hopefully, fit well to your data problem.

There are no complex optimization algorithms to explain in these approximation algorithms; in fact, optimization itself is replaced by randomization and the results largely depend on the number of output features, pointed out by the `n_components` parameters. The more the output features, the higher the probability that by chance you'll get the right non-linearities working perfectly with your problem.

It is important to notice that, if chance has really such a great role in creating the right features to improve your predictions, then reproducibility of the results turns out to be essential and you should strive to obtain it or you won't be able to consistently retrain and tune your algorithm in the same way. Noticeably, each class is provided with a `random_state` parameter, thus allowing the controlling of random feature generation and being able to recreate it later on the same just as on different computers.

The theoretical fundamentals of such feature creation techniques are explained in the scientific articles, *Random Features for Large-Scale Kernel Machines* by *A. Rahimi and Benjamin Recht* (`http://www.eecs.berkeley.edu/~brecht/papers/07.rah.rec.nips.pdf`) and *Weighted Sums of Random Kitchen Sinks: Replacing minimization with randomization in learning* by *A. Rahimi and Benjamin Recht* (`http://www.eecs.berkeley.edu/~brecht/papers/08.rah.rec.nips.pdf`).

For our purposes, it will suffice to know how to implement the technique and have it contribute to improving our SGD models, both linear and SVM-based:

```
In: source = 'shuffled_covtype.data'
local_path = os.getcwd()
n_vars = ['var_'+str(j) for j in range(54)]
std_row, min_max = explore(target_file=local_path+'\\'+source, binary_
features=list(),
                fieldnames= n_vars+['covertype'], numeric_
features=n_vars, max_rows=50000)

from sklearn.linear_model import SGDClassifier
from sklearn.kernel_approximation import RBFSampler

SGD = SGDClassifier(loss='hinge', penalty=None, random_state=1,
average=True)
rbf_feature = RBFSampler(gamma=0.5, n_components=300, random_state=0)
accuracy = 0
accuracy_record = list()
predictions_start = 50
sample = 5000
early_stop = 50000
for x,y,n in pull_examples(target_file=local_path+'\\'+source,
                    vectorizer=std_row,
                    min_max=min_max,
                    binary_features=list(),
                    numeric_features=n_vars,
```

```
                         fieldnames= n_vars+['covertype'],
    target='covertype', sparse=False):

        rbf_x = rbf_feature.fit_transform(x)
        # LEARNING PHASE
        if n > predictions_start:
            accuracy += int(int(SGD.predict(rbf_x))==y[0])
            if n % sample == 0:
                accuracy_record.append(accuracy / float(sample))
                print '%s Progressive accuracy at example %i: %0.3f' %
    (time.strftime('%X'), n, np.mean(accuracy_record[-sample:]))
                accuracy = 0
        if early_stop and n >= early_stop:
                break
        SGD.partial_fit(rbf_x, y, classes=range(1,8))


Out: ...
07:57:45 Progressive accuracy at example 50000: 0.707
```

Hyperparameter tuning

As in batch learning, there are no shortcuts in out-of-core algorithms when testing the best combinations of hyperparameters; you need to try a certain number of combinations to figure out a possible optimal solution and use an out-of-sample error measurement to evaluate their performance.

As you actually do not know if your prediction problem has a simple smooth convex loss or a more complicated one and you do not know exactly how your hyperparameters interact with each other, it is very easy to get stuck into some sub-optimal local-minimum if not enough combinations are tried. Unfortunately, at the moment there are no specialized optimization procedures offered by Scikit-learn for out-of-core algorithms. Given the necessarily long time to train an SGD on a long stream, tuning the hyperparameters can really become a bottleneck when building a model on your data using such techniques.

Here, we present a few rules of thumb that can help you save time and efforts and achieve the best results.

First, you can tune your parameters on a window or a sample of your data that can fit in-memory. As we have seen with kernel SVMs, using a reservoir sample is quite fast even if your stream is huge. Then you can do your optimization in-memory and use the optimal parameters found on your stream.

As Léon Bottou from Microsoft Research has remarked in his technical paper, *Stochastic Gradient Descent Tricks*:

> *"The mathematics of stochastic gradient descent are amazingly independent of the training set size."*

This is true for all the key parameters but especially for the learning rate; the learning rate that works better with a sample will work the best with the full data. In addition, the ideal number of passes over data can be mostly guessed by trying to converge on a small sampled dataset. As a rule of thumb, we report the indicative number of 10**6 examples examined by the algorithm—as pointed out by the Scikit-learn documentation—a number that we have often found accurate, though the ideal number of iterations may change depending on the regularization parameters.

Though most of the work can be done at a relatively small scale when using SGD, we have to define how to approach the problem of fixing multiple parameters. Traditionally, manual search and grid search have been the most used approaches, grid search solving the problem by systematically testing all the combinations of possible parameters at significant values (using, for instance, the log scale checking at the different power degree of 10 or of 2).

Recently, James Bergstra and Yoshua Bengio in their paper, *Random Search for Hyper-Parameter Optimization*, pointed out a different approach based on the random sampling of the values of the hyperparameters. Such an approach, though based on random choices, is often equivalent in results to grid search (but requiring fewer runs) when the number of hyperparameters is low and can exceed the performance of a systematic search when the parameters are many and not all of them are relevant for the algorithm performance.

We leave it to the reader to discover more reasons why this simple and appealing approach works so well in theory by referring to the previously mentioned paper by Bergstra and Bengio. In practice, having experienced its superiority with respect to other approaches, we propose an approach that works well for streams based on Scikit-learn's ParameterSampler function in the following example code snippet. ParameterSampler is able to randomly sample different sets of hyperparameters (both from distribution functions or lists of discrete values) to be applied to your learning SGD by means of the set_params method afterward:

```
In: from sklearn.linear_model import SGDRegressor
from sklearn.grid_search import ParameterSampler

source = '\\bikesharing\\hour.csv'
local_path = os.getcwd()
b_vars = ['holiday','hr','mnth', 'season','weathersit','weekday','wor
kingday','yr']
```

```
n_vars = ['hum', 'temp', 'atemp', 'windspeed']
std_row, min_max = explore(target_file=local_path+'\\'+source, binary_
features=b_vars, numeric_features=n_vars)


val_rmse = 0
val_rmsle = 0
predictions_start = 16000
tmp_rsmle = 10**6


def apply_log(x): return np.log(x + 1.0)
def apply_exp(x): return np.exp(x) - 1.0


param_grid = {'penalty':['l1', 'l2'], 'alpha': 10.0**-np.arange(2,5)}
random_tests = 3
search_schedule = list(ParameterSampler(param_grid, n_iter=random_
tests, random_state=5))
results = dict()


for search in search_schedule:
    SGD = SGDRegressor(loss='epsilon_insensitive', epsilon=0.001,
penalty=None, random_state=1, average=True)
    params =SGD.get_params()
    new_params = {p:params[p] if p not in search else search[p] for p
in params}
    SGD.set_params(**new_params)
    print str(search)[1:-1]
    for iterations in range(200):
        for x,y,n in pull_examples(target_file=local_path+'\\'+source,
                                   vectorizer=std_row, min_max=min_
max, sparse = False,
                                   binary_features=b_vars, numeric_
features=n_vars, target='cnt'):
            y_log = apply_log(y)


# MACHINE LEARNING
            if (n+1) >= predictions_start:
                # HOLDOUT AFTER N PHASE
                predicted = SGD.predict(x)
                val_rmse += (apply_exp(predicted) - y)**2
                val_rmsle += (predicted - y_log)**2
            else:
                # LEARNING PHASE
                SGD.partial_fit(x, y_log)

        examples = float(n-predictions_start+1) * (iterations+1)
```

```
        print_rmse = (val_rmse / examples)**0.5
        print_rmsle = (val_rmsle / examples)**0.5
        if iterations == 0:
            print 'Iteration %i - RMSE: %0.3f - RMSE: %0.3f' %
(iterations+1, print_rmse, print_rmsle)
        if iterations > 0:
            if tmp_rmsle / print_rmsle <= 1.01:
                print 'Iteration %i - RMSE: %0.3f - RMSE: %0.3f\n' %
(iterations+1, print_rmse, print_rmsle)
                results[str(search)]= {'rmse':float(print_rmse),
'rmsle':float(print_rmsle)}
                break
        tmp_rmsle = print_rmsle


Out:
'penalty': 'l2', 'alpha': 0.001
Iteration 1 - RMSE: 216.170 - RMSE: 1.440
Iteration 20 - RMSE: 152.175 - RMSE: 0.857

'penalty': 'l2', 'alpha': 0.0001
Iteration 1 - RMSE: 714.071 - RMSE: 4.096
Iteration 31 - RMSE: 184.677 - RMSE: 1.053

'penalty': 'l1', 'alpha': 0.01
Iteration 1 - RMSE: 1050.809 - RMSE: 6.044
Iteration 36 - RMSE: 225.036 - RMSE: 1.298
```

The code leverages the fact that the bike-sharing dataset is quite small and doesn't require any sampling. In other contexts, it makes sense to limit the number of treated rows or create a smaller sample before by means of reservoir sampling or other sampling techniques for streams seen so far. If you would like to explore optimization in more depth, you can change the `random_tests` variable, fixing the number of sampled hyperparameters' combinations to be tested. Then, you modify the `if tmp_rmsle / print_rmsle <= 1.01` condition using a number nearer to 1.0 — if not 1.0 itself — thus letting the algorithm fully converge until some possible gain in predictive power is feasible.

Though it is recommended to use distribution functions rather than picking from lists of values, you can still appropriately use the hyperparameters' ranges that we suggested before by simply enlarging the number of values to be possibly picked from the lists. For instance, for alpha in L1 and L2 regularization, you could use NumPy's function, `arrange`, with a small step such as `10.0**-np.arange(1, 7, step=0.1)`, or use NumPy `logspace` with a high number for the num parameter: `1.0/np.logspace(1,7,num=50)`.

Other alternatives for SVM fast learning

Though the Scikit-learn package provides enough tools and algorithms to learn out-of-core, there are other interesting alternatives among free software. Some are based on the same libraries that Scikit-learn itself uses, such as the Liblinear/SBM and others are completely new, such as sofia-ml, LASVM and Vowpal Wabbit. For instance, Liblinear/SBMis based on selective block minimization and implemented as a fork `liblinear-cdblock` of the original library (`https://www.csie.ntu.edu.tw/~cjlin/libsvmtools/#large_linear_classification_when_data_cannot_fit_in_memory`). Liblinear/SBM achieves to fit nonlinear SVMs on large amounts of data that cannot fit in-memory using the trick of training the learner using new samples of data and mixing it with previous samples already used for minimization (hence the *blocked* term in the name of the algorithm).

SofiaML (`https://code.google.com/archive/p/sofia-ml/`) is another alternative. SofiaML is based on an online SVM optimization algorithm called Pegasos SVM. This algorithm is an online SVM approximation, just as another software called LaSVM created by Leon Bottou (`http://leon.bottou.org/projects/lasvm`). All these solutions can work with sparse data, especially textual, and solve regression, classification, and ranking problems. To date, no alternative solution that we tested proved as fast and versatile as Vowpal Wabbit, the software that we are going to present in the next sections and use to demonstrate how to integrate external programs with Python.

Nonlinear and faster with Vowpal Wabbit

Vowpal Wabbit (VW) is an open source project for a fast online learner initially released in 2007 by John Langford, Lihong Li, and Alex Strehl from Yahoo! Research (`http://hunch.net/?p=309`) and then successively sponsored by Microsoft Research, as John Langford became the principal researcher at Microsoft. The project has developed over the years, arriving today at version 8.1.0 (at the time this chapter was written), with almost one hundred contributors working on it. (For a visualization of the development of the contributions over time, there is an interesting video using the software **Gource** at `https://www.youtube.com/watch?v=-aXelGLMMgk`.). To date, VW is still being constantly developed and keeps on increasing its learning capabilities at each development iteration.

The striking characteristic of VW is that it is very fast compared to other solutions available (LIBLINEAR, Sofia-ml, svmsgd, and Scikit-learn). Its secret is simple, yet extremely effective: it can load data and learn from it at the same time. An asynchronous thread does the parsing of the examples flowing in as a number of learning threads work on a disjoint set of features, thus assuring a high computational efficiency even when parsing involves high-dimensional feature creation (such as quadratic or cubic polynomial expansion). In most cases, the real bottleneck of the learning process is the transmission bandwidth of the disk or network transmitting the data to VW.

VW can work out classification (even multiclass and multilabel), regression (OLS and quantile), and active learning problems, offering a vast range of accompanying learning tools (called reductions) such as matrix factorization, **Latent Dirichlet Allocation** (LDA), neural networks, n-grams for language models, and bootstrapping.

Installing VW

VW can be retrieved from the online versioning repository GitHub (`https://github.com/JohnLangford/vowpal_wabbit`), where it can be Git-cloned or just downloaded in the form of a packed zip. Being developed on Linux systems, it is easily compiled on any POSIX environment by a simple sequence of make and make install commands. Detailed instructions for installation are available directly on its installation page and you can download Linux precompiled binaries directly from the author (`https://github.com/JohnLangford/vowpal_wabbit/wiki/Download`).

A VW version working on Windows operating systems, unfortunately, is a bit more difficult to obtain. In order to create one, the first reference is the documentation itself of VW where a compiling procedure is explained in detail (`https://github.com/JohnLangford/vowpal_wabbit/blob/master/README.windows.txt`).

On the accompanying website of the book, we will provide both 32-bit and 64-bit Windows binaries of the 8.1.0 version of VW that we have used for the book.

Understanding the VW data format

VW can work with a particular data format and is invoked from a shell. John Langford uses this sample dataset for his online tutorial (https://github.com/JohnLangford/vowpal_wabbit/wiki/Tutorial), representing three houses whose roofs could be replaced. We find it interesting proposing it to you and commenting on it together:

```
In:
with open('house_dataset','wb') as W:
    W.write("0 | price:.23 sqft:.25 age:.05 2006\n")
    W.write("1 2 'second_house | price:.18 sqft:.15 age:.35 1976\n")
    W.write("0 1 0.5 'third_house | price:.53 sqft:.32 age:.87
1924\n")

with open('house_dataset','rb') as R:
    for line in R:
        print line.strip()

Out:
0 | price:.23 sqft:.25 age:.05 2006
1 2 'second_house | price:.18 sqft:.15 age:.35 1976
0 1 0.5 'third_house | price:.53 sqft:.32 age:.87 1924
```

The first noticeable aspect of the file format is that it doesn't have a header. This is because VW uses the hashing trick to allocate the features into a sparse vector, therefore knowing in advance the features that are not necessary at all. Data blocks are divided by pipes (the character |) into namespaces, to be intended as different clusters of features, each one containing one or more features.

The first namespace is always the one containing the response variable. The response can be a real number (or an integer) pointing out a numeric value to be regressed, a binary class, or a class among multiple ones. The response is always the first number to be found on a line. A binary class can be encoded using 1 for positive and -1 for negative (using 0 as a response is allowed only for regression). Multiple classes should be numbered from 1 onward and having gap numbers is not advisable because VW asks for the last class and considers all the integers between 1 and the last one.

The number immediately after the response value is the weight (telling you if you have to consider an example as a multiple example or as a fraction of one), then the base, which plays the role of the initial prediction (a kind of bias). Finally, preceded by the apostrophe character ('), there is the label, which can be a number or text to be later found in the VW outputs (in a prediction, you have an identifier for every estimation). Weight, base, and labels are not compulsory: if omitted, weight will be imputed as 1 and base and label won't matter.

Following the first namespace, you can add as many namespaces as you want, labeling each one by a number or string. In order to be considered the label of the namespace, it should be stuck to the pipe, for instance, |label.

After the label of the namespace, you can add any feature by its name. The feature name can be anything, but should contain a pipe or colon. You can just put entire texts in the namespaces and every word will be treated as a feature. Every feature will be considered valued as 1. If you want to assign a different number, just stick a colon at the end of the feature name and put its value after it.

For instance, a valid row readable by Vowpal Wabbit is:

```
0 1 0.5 'third_house | price:.53 sqft:.32 age:.87 1924
```

In the first namespace, the response is 0, the example weights 1, the base is 0.5, and its label is third_house. The namespace is nameless and is constituted by four features such as price (value is .53), sqft (value is .32), age (value is .87), and 1924 (value is 1).

If you have a feature in an example but not in another one, the algorithm will pretend that the feature value is zero in the second example. Therefore, a feature such as 1924 in the preceding example can be intended as a binary variable as, when it is present, it is automatically valued 1, when missing 0. This also tells you how VW handles missing values—it automatically considers them as 0 values.

You can easily handle missing values by putting a new feature when a value is missing. If the feature is age, for instance, you can add a new feature, age_missing, which will be a binary variable having value as 1. When estimating the coefficients, this variable will act as a missing value estimator.

On the author's website, you can also find an input validator, verifying that your input is correct for VW and displaying how it is interpreted by the software:

http://hunch.net/~vw/validate.html

Python integration

There are a few packages integrating it with Python (**vowpal_porpoise, Wabbit Wappa**, or **pyvw**) and installing them is easy in Linux systems, but much harder on Windows. No matter whether you are working with Jupyter or IDE, the easiest way to use VW integrated with Python's scripts is to leverage the Popen function from the subprocess package. That makes VW run in parallel with Python. Python just waits for VW to complete its operation by capturing its output and printing it on the screen:

```
In: import subprocess

def execute_vw(parameters):
    execution = subprocess.Popen('vw '+parameters, \
               shell=True, stderr=subprocess.PIPE)
    line = ""
    history = ""
    while True:
        out = execution.stderr.read(1)
        history += out
        if out == '' and execution.poll() != None:
            print '----------- COMPLETED -----------\n'
            break
        if out != '':
            line += out
            if '\n' in line[-2:]:
                print line[:-2]
                line = ''
    return history.split('\r\n')
```

The functions return a list of the outputs of the learning process, making it easy to process it, extracting relevant reusable information (like the error measure). As a precondition for its correct functioning, place the VW executable (the vw.exe file) in the Python working directory or system path where it can be found.

By invoking the function on the previously recorded housing dataset, we can have a look at how it works and what outputs it produces:

```
In:
params = "house_dataset"
results = execute_vw(params)

Out:
Num weight bits = 18
learning rate = 0.5
```

```
initial_t = 0
power_t = 0.5
using no cache
Reading datafile = house_dataset
num sources = 1
average    since           example      example  current  current
current
loss       last            counter      weight   label    predict
features
0.000000 0.000000             1            1.0    0.0000   0.0000
5
0.666667 1.000000             2            3.0    1.0000   0.0000
5


finished run
number of examples per pass = 3
passes used = 1
weighted example sum = 4.000000
weighted label sum = 2.000000
average loss = 0.750000
best constant = 0.500000
best constant's loss = 0.250000
total feature number = 15
----------- COMPLETED -----------
```

The initial rows of the output just recall the used parameters and provide confirmation of which data file is being used. Most interesting is the progressive reported by the number of streamed examples (reported by the power of 2, so example 1, 2, 4, 8, 16, and so on). With respect to the loss function, an average loss measure is reported, progressive for the first iteration, based on the hold-out set afterward, whose loss is signaled by postponing the letter h (if holding out is excluded, it is possible that just the in-sample measure is reported). On the example weight column, the weight of the example is reported and then the example is furthermore described as current label, current predict and displays the number of features found on that line (current features). All such information should help you keep an eye on the stream and learning process.

After the learning is completed, a few reporting measures are reported. The average loss is the most important, in particular when a hold-out is used. Using such loss is most useful for comparative reasons as it can be immediately compared with best constant's loss (the baseline predictive power of a simple constant) and with different runs using different parameter configurations.

Another very useful function to integrate VW and Python is a function that we prepared automatically converting CSV files to VW data files. You can find it in the following code snippet. It will help us replicate the previous bike-sharing and covertype problems using VW this time, but it can be easily reused for your own projects:

```
In: import csv

def vw_convert(origin_file, target_file, binary_features, numeric_
features, target, transform_target=lambda(x):x,
               separator=',', classification=True, multiclass=False,
fieldnames= None, header=True, sparse=True):
    """
    Reads a online style stream and returns a generator of normalized
feature vectors

    Parameters
    ----------
    original_file = the CSV file you are taken the data from
    target file = the file to stream from
    binary_features = the list of qualitative features to consider
    numeric_features = the list of numeric features to consider
    target = the label of the response variable
    transform_target = a function transforming the response
    separator = the field separator character
    classification = a Boolean indicating if it is classification
    multiclass =  a Boolean for multiclass classification
    fieldnames = the fields' labels (can be omitted and read from
file)
    header = a boolean indicating if the original file has an header
    sparse = if a sparse vector is to be returned from the generator
    """
    with open(target_file, 'wb') as W:
        with open(origin_file, 'rb') as R:
iterator = csv.DictReader(R, fieldnames, delimiter=separator)
            for n, row in enumerate(iterator):
                if not header or n>0:
                    # DATA PROCESSING
                    response = transform_target(float(row[target]))
                    if classification and not multiclass:
                        if response == 0:
                            stream_row = '-1 '
                        else:
```

```
                              stream_row = '1 '
                    else:
                        stream_row = str(response)+' '
                    quantitative = list()
                    qualitative  = list()
                    for k,v in row.iteritems():
                        if k in binary_features:
                            qualitative.append(str(k)+\
    '_'+str(v)+':1')

                        else:
                            if k in numeric_features and (float(v)!=0
    or not sparse):
                                quantitative.append(str(k)+':'+str(v))
    if quantitative:
                    stream_row += '|n '+\
    ' '.join(quantitative)
                    if qualitative:
                        stream_row += '|q '+\
    ' '.join(qualitative)
    W.write(stream_row+'\n')
```

A few examples using reductions for SVM and neural nets

VW works on minimizing a general cost function, which is as follows:

$$\lambda_1 \|w\|_1 + \frac{\lambda_2}{2} \|w\|_2^2 + \sum_{i=1}^{n} \text{loss}(x_i, y_i, w)$$

As in other formulations seen before, w is the coefficient vector and the optimization is obtained separately for each *xi* and *yi* according to the chosen loss function (OLS, logistic, or hinge). Lambda1 and lambda2 are the regularization parameters that, by default, are zero but can be set using the `--l1` and `--l2` options in the VW command line.

Given such a basic structure, VW has been made more complex and complete over time using the reduction paradigm. A reduction is just a way to reuse an existing algorithm in order to solve new problems without coding new solving algorithms from scratch. In other words, if you have a complex machine learning problem A, you just reduce it to B. Solving B hints at a solution of A. This is also justified by the growing interest in machine learning and the exploding number of problems that cannot be solved creating hosts of new algorithms. It is an interesting approach leveraging the existing possibilities offered by basic algorithms and the reason why VW has grown its applicability over time though the program has stayed quite compact. If you are interested in this approach, you can have a look at these two tutorials from John Langford: `http://hunch.net/~reductions_tutorial/` and `http://hunch.net/~jl/projects/reductions/reductions.html`.

For other illustration purposes, we will briefly introduce you to a couple of reductions to implement an SVM with an `RBFkernel` and a shallow neural network using VW in a purely out-of-core way. We will be using some toy datasets for the purpose.

Here is the Iris dataset, changed to a binary classification problem to guess the Iris Versicolor from the Setosa and Virginica:

```
In: import numpy as np
from sklearn.datasets import load_iris, load_boston
from random import seed
iris = load_iris()
seed(2)
re_order = np.random.permutation(len(iris.target))
with open('iris_versicolor.vw','wb') as W1:
    for k in re_order:
        y = iris.target[k]
        X = iris.values()[1][k,:]
        features = ' |f '+' '.join([a+':'+str(b) for a,b in
zip(map(lambda(a): a[:-5].replace(' ','_'), iris.feature_names),X)])
        target = '1' if y==1 else '-1'
        W1.write(target+features+'\n')
```

Then for a regression problem, we will be using the Boston house pricing dataset:

```
In: boston = load_boston()
seed(2)
re_order = np.random.permutation(len(boston.target))
with open('boston.vw','wb') as W1:
    for k in re_order:
        y = boston.target[k]
        X = boston.data[k,:]
```

```
        features = ' |f '+' '.join([a+':'+str(b) for a,b in
zip(map(lambda(a): a[:-5].replace(' ','_'), iris.feature_names),X)])
        W1.write(str(y)+features+'\n')
```

First, we will be trying SVM. `kvsm` is a reduction based on the LaSVM algorithm (*Fast Kernel Classifiers with Online and Active Learning*—`http://www.jmlr.org/papers/volume6/bordes05a/bordes05a.pdf`) without a bias term. The VW version typically works in just one pass and with a 1-2 reprocessing of a randomly picked support vector (though some problems may need multiple passes and reprocessing). In our case, we are just using a single pass and a couple of reprocessings in order to fit an RBF kernel on our binary problem (KSVM works only for classification problems). Implemented kernels are linear, radial basis function, and polynomial. In order to have it work, use the `--ksvm` option, set a number for reprocessing (default is 1) by `--reprocess`, choose the kernel with `--kernel` (options are `linear`, `poly`, and `rbf`). Then, if the kernel is polynomial, set an integer number for `--degree`, or a float (default is 1.0) for `--bandwidth` if you are using RBF. You also have to compulsorily specify l2 regularization; otherwise, the reduction won't work properly. In our example, we make an `RBFkernel` with bandwidth 0.1:

```
In: params = '--ksvm --l2 0.000001 --reprocess 2 -b 18 --kernel rbf
--bandwidth=0.1 -p iris_bin.test -d iris_versicolor.vw'
results = execute_vw(params)

accuracy = 0
with open('iris_bin.test', 'rb') as R:
    with open('iris_versicolor.vw', 'rb') as TRAIN:
        holdouts = 0.0
        for n,(line, example) in enumerate(zip(R,TRAIN)):
            if (n+1) % 10==0:
                predicted = float(line.strip())
                y = float(example.split('|')[0])
                accuracy += np.sign(predicted)==np.sign(y)
                holdouts += 1
print 'holdout accuracy: %0.3f' % ((accuracy / holdouts)**0.5)

Out: holdout accuracy: 0.966
```

Neural networks are another cool addition to VW; thanks to the work of Paul Mineiro (http://www.machinedlearnings.com/2012/11/unpimp-your-sigmoid. html), VW can implement a single-layer neural network with hyperbolic tangent (*tanh*) activation and, optionally, dropout (using the --dropout option). Though it is only possible to decide the number of neurons, the neural reduction works fine with both regression and classification problems and can smoothly take on other transformations by VW as inputs (such as quadratic variables and n-grams), making it a very well-integrated, versatile (neural networks can solve quite a lot of problems), and fast solution. In our example, we apply it to the Boston dataset using five neurons and dropout:

```
In: params = 'boston.vw -f boston.model --loss_function squared -k
--cache_file cache_train.vw --passes=20 --nn 5 --dropout'
results = execute_vw(params)
params = '-t boston.vw -i boston.model -k --cache_file cache_test.vw
-p boston.test'
results = execute_vw(params)
val_rmse = 0
with open('boston.test', 'rb') as R:
    with open('boston.vw', 'rb') as TRAIN:
        holdouts = 0.0
        for n,(line, example) in enumerate(zip(R,TRAIN)):
            if (n+1) % 10==0:
                predicted = float(line.strip())
                y = float(example.split('|')[0])
                val_rmse += (predicted - y)**2
                holdouts += 1
print 'holdout RMSE: %0.3f' % ((val_rmse / holdouts)**0.5)

Out: holdout RMSE: 7.010
```

Faster bike-sharing

Let's try VW on the previously created bike-sharing example file in order to explain the output components. As the first step, you have to transform the CSV file into a VW file and the previous vw_convert function will come in handy doing this. As before, we will apply a logarithmic transformation on the numeric response, using the apply_log function passed by the transform_target parameter of the vw_convert function:

```
In: import os
import numpy as np

def apply_log(x):
```

```
        return np.log(x + 1.0)

def apply_exp(x):
        return np.exp(x) - 1.0


local_path = os.getcwd()
b_vars = ['holiday','hr','mnth', 'season','weathersit','weekday','wor
kingday','yr']
n_vars = ['hum', 'temp', 'atemp', 'windspeed']
source = '\\bikesharing\\hour.csv'
origin = target_file=local_path+'\\'+source
target = target_file=local_path+'\\'+'bike.vw'
vw_convert(origin, target, binary_features=b_vars, numeric_features=n_
vars, target = 'cnt', transform_target=apply_log,
              separator=',', classification=False, multiclass=False,
fieldnames= None, header=True)
```

After a few seconds, the new file should be ready. We can immediately run our
solution, which is a simple linear regression (the default option in VW). The learning
is expected to run for 100 passes, controlled by the out-of-sample validation that VW
automatically implements (drawing systematically and in a repeatable way, a single
observation out of every 10 as validation). In this case, we decide to set a holdout
sample after 16,000 examples (using the `--holdout_after` option). When the
validation error on the validation increases (instead of decreasing), VW stops after a
few iterations (three by default, but the number can be changed using the `--early_
terminate` option), avoiding overfitting the data:

```
In: params = 'bike.vw -f regression.model -k --cache_file cache_train.
vw --passes=100 --hash strings --holdout_after 16000'
results = execute_vw(params)

Out: …
finished run
number of examples per pass = 15999
passes used = 6
weighted example sum = 95994.000000
weighted label sum = 439183.191893
average loss = 0.427485 h
best constant = 4.575111
total feature number = 1235898
----------- COMPLETED -----------
```

The final report indicates that six passes (out of 100 possible ones) have been
completed and the out-of-sample average loss is 0.428. As we are interested in RMSE
and RMSLE, we have to calculate them ourselves.

We then predict the results in a file (`pred.test`) in order to be able to read them and calculate our error measure using the same holdout strategy as in the training set. The results are indeed much better (in a fraction of the time) than what we previously obtained with Scikit-learn's SGD:

```
In: params = '-t bike.vw -i regression.model -k --cache_file cache_
test.vw -p pred.test'
results = execute_vw(params)
val_rmse = 0
val_rmsle = 0
with open('pred.test', 'rb') as R:
    with open('bike.vw', 'rb') as TRAIN:
        holdouts = 0.0
        for n,(line, example) in enumerate(zip(R,TRAIN)):
            if n > 16000:
                predicted = float(line.strip())
                y_log = float(example.split('|')[0])
                y = apply_exp(y_log)
                val_rmse += (apply_exp(predicted) - y)**2
                val_rmsle += (predicted - y_log)**2
                holdouts += 1

print 'holdout RMSE: %0.3f' % ((val_rmse / holdouts)**0.5)
print 'holdout RMSLE: %0.3f' % ((val_rmsle / holdouts)**0.5)

Out:
holdout RMSE: 135.306
holdout RMSLE: 0.845
```

The covertype dataset crunched by VW

The covertype problem can also be solved better and more easily by VW than we managed before. This time, we will have to set some parameters and decide on the **error correcting tournament** (ECT, invoked by the `--ect` parameter on VW), where each class competes in an elimination tournament to be the label for an example. In many examples, ECT can outperform **one-against-all (OAA)**, but this is not a general rule, and ECT is one of the approaches to be tested when dealing with multiclass problems. (The other possible option is `--log_multi`, using online decision trees to split the sample in smaller sets where we apply single predictive models.) We also set the learning rate to 1.0 and create a third-degree polynomial expansion using the `--cubic` parameter, pointing out which namespaces have to be multiplied by each other (In this case, the namespace f for three times is expressed by the nnn string followed by `--cubic`.):

```
In: import os
local_path = os.getcwd()
```

```
n_vars = ['var_'+'0'*int(j<10)+str(j) for j in range(54)]
source = 'shuffled_covtype.data'
origin = target_file=local_path+'\\'+source
target = target_file=local_path+'\\'+'covtype.vw'
vw_convert(origin, target, binary_features=list(), fieldnames= n_
vars+['covertype'], numeric_features=n_vars,
    target = 'covertype', separator=',', classification=True,
multiclass=True, header=False, sparse=False)
params = 'covtype.vw --ect 7 -f multiclass.model -k --cache_file
cache_train.vw --passes=2 -l 1.0 --cubic nnn'
results = execute_vw(params)
```

```
Out:
finished run
number of examples per pass = 522911
passes used = 2
weighted example sum = 1045822.000000
weighted label sum = 0.000000
average loss = 0.235538 h
total feature number = 384838154
------------ COMPLETED ------------
```

 In order for the example to be speedy, we limit the number of passes to just two. If you have time, raise the number to 100 and witness how the obtained accuracy can be improved furthermore.

Here, we wouldn't need to inspect the error measure further as the reported average loss is the complement to 1.0 of the accuracy measure; we just calculate it for completeness, confirming that our holdout accuracy is exactly 0.769:

```
In: params = '-t covtype.vw -i multiclass.model -k --cache_file cache_
test.vw -p covertype.test'
results = execute_vw(params)
accuracy = 0
with open('covertype.test', 'rb') as R:
    with open('covtype.vw', 'rb') as TRAIN:
        holdouts = 0.0
        for n,(line, example) in enumerate(zip(R,TRAIN)):
            if (n+1) % 10==0:
                predicted = float(line.strip())
                y = float(example.split('|')[0])
                accuracy += predicted ==y
                holdouts += 1
print 'holdout accuracy: %0.3f' % (accuracy / holdouts)
```

```
Out: holdout accuracy: 0.769
```

Summary

In this chapter, we expanded on the initial discussion of out-of-core algorithms by adding SVMs to simple regression-based linear models. Most of the time, we focused on Scikit-learn implementations—mostly SGD—and concluded with an overview of external tools that can be integrated with Python scripts, such as Vowpal Wabbit by John Langford. Along the way, we completed our overview on model improvement and validation technicalities when working out-of-core by discussing reservoir sampling, regularization, explicit and implicit nonlinear transformations, and hyperparameter optimization.

In the next chapter, we will get involved with even more complex and powerful learning approaches while presenting deep learning and neural networks in large scale problems. If your projects revolve around the analysis of images and sounds, what we have seen so far may not yet be the magic solution you were looking for. The next chapter will provide all the desired solutions.

4
Neural Networks and Deep Learning

In this chapter, we will cover one of the most exciting fields in artificial intelligence and machine learning: Deep Learning. This chapter will walk through the most important concepts necessary to apply deep learning effectively. The topics that we will cover in this chapter are as follows:

- Essential neural network theory
- Running neural networks on the GPU or CPU
- Parameter tuning for neural networks
- Large scale deep learning on H2O
- Deep learning with autoencoders (pretraining)

Deep learning emerged from the subfield of artificial intelligence that developed neural networks. Strictly speaking, any large neural network can be considered *deep-learning*. However, recent developments in deep architectures require more than setting up large neural networks. The difference between deep architectures and normal multilayer networks is that a deep architecture consists of multiple preprocessing and unsupervised steps that detect latent dimension in the data to be later fed into further stages of the network. The most important thing to know about deep learning is that new features are learned and transformed through these deep architectures in order to improve the overall learning accuracy. So, an important distinction between the current generation of deep learning methods and other machine learning approaches is that, with deep learning, the task of feature engineering is in part automated. Don't worry too much if these concepts sound abstract, they will be made clear later in this chapter along with practical examples. These deep learning methods introduce new complexities, which make applying them effectively quite challenging.

The biggest challenges are their difficulty in training, computation time, and parameter tuning. Solutions for these difficulties will be dealt with in this chapter.

In the last decade, interesting applications of deep learning can be found in computer vision, natural language processing, and audio processing, applications such as Facebook's deep face project created by a research group at Facebook partly led by the well-known deep learning scholar, Yann LeCun. Deep face aims to extract and identify human faces from digital images. Google has its own project, **DeepMind**, led by Geoffrey Hinton. Google recently introduced **TensorFlow**, an open source library providing deep learning applications, which will be covered in detail in the next chapter.

Before we start unleashing autonomous intelligent agents passing Turing tests and math competitions, let's step back a bit and run through the basics.

The neural network architecture

Let's now focus on how neural networks are organized, starting from their architecture and a few definitions.

A network where the flow of learning is passed forward all the way to the outputs in one pass is referred to as a **feedforward neural network**.

A basic feedforward neural network can easily be depicted by a network diagram, as shown here:

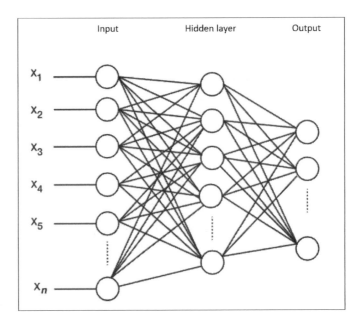

In the network diagram, you can see that this architecture consists of an input layer, hidden layer, and output layer. The input layer contains the feature vectors (where each observation has n features), and the output layer consists of separate units for each class of the output vector in the case of classification and a single numerical vector in the case of regression.

The strength of the connections between the units is expressed through weights later to be passed to an activation function. The goal of an activation function is to transform its input to an output that makes binary decisions more separable.

These activation functions are preferably differentiable so they can be used to learn.

The widely-used activation functions are **sigmoid** and **tanh**, and even more recently the **rectified linear unit (ReLU)** has gained traction. Let's compare the most important activation functions so that we understand their advantages and drawbacks. Note that we mention the output range and active range of the function. The output range is simply the actual output of the function itself. The active range, however, is a little more complicated; it is the range where the gradient has the most variance in the final weight updates. This means that outside of this range, the gradient is near zero and does not add to the parameter updates during learning. This problem of a close-to-zero gradient is also referred to as the **vanishing gradient problem** and is solved by the ReLU activation function, which at this time is the most popular activation for larger neural networks:

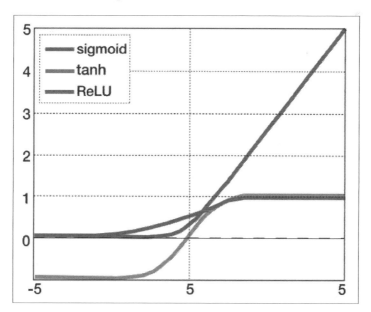

It is important to note that features need to be scaled to the *active range* of the chosen activation function. Most up-to-date packages will have this as a standard preprocessing procedure so you don't need to do this yourself:

sigmoid	$$\dfrac{1}{(1 + e^{-t})}$$	Active range: [sqrt(3), sqrt(3)] Output range: (0, 1)

Sigmoid functions are often used for mathematical convenience because their derivatives are very easy to calculate, which we will use to calculate the weight updates in training algorithms:

tanh function	$$\dfrac{e^t - e^{-t}}{e^t + e^{-t}}$$	Active range: [-2,2] Output range: (-1,+1)

Interestingly the tanh and logistic sigmoid functions are related linearly and tanh can be seen as a rescaled version of the sigmoid function so that its range is between -1 and 1.

rectified linear unit (ReLU)	$f(x) = \max(0, x)$	Active range: [0, inf]

This function is the best choice for deeper architectures. It can be seen as a ramp function whose range lies above 0 to infinity. You can see that it is much easier to calculate than the sigmoid function. The biggest benefit of this function is that it bypasses the vanishing gradient problem. If ReLU is an option during a deep learning project, use it.

Softmax for classification

So far, we have seen that activation functions transform the values within a certain range after they are multiplied with the weight vectors. We also need to transform the outputs of the last hidden layer before providing balanced classes or probability outputs (log-likelihood values).

This will convert the output of the previous layer to probability values so that a final class prediction can be made. The exponentiation in this case will return a near-zero value whenever the output is significantly less than the maximum of all the values; this way the differences are amplified:

$$softmax\left(k, x_1, \ldots, x_n\right) = \frac{e^{xk}}{\sum_{i=1}^{n} e^{xi}}$$

Forward propagation

Now that we understand activation functions and the final outputs of a network, let's see how the input features are fed through the network to provide a final prediction. Computations with huge chunks of units and connections might look like a complex task, but fortunately the feedforward process of a neural network comes down to a sequence of vector computations:

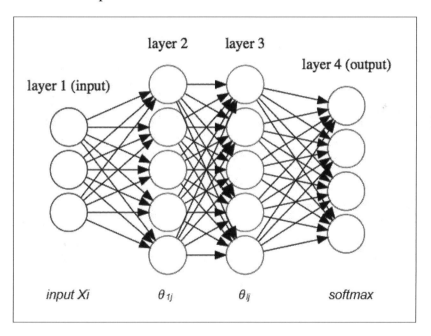

We arrive at a final prediction by performing the following steps:

1. Performing a dot-product on the inputs with the weights between the first and second layer and transforming the result with the activation function.

2. Performing a dot-product on the outputs of the first hidden layer with the weights between the second and third layer. These results are then transformed with the activation function on each unit of the second hidden layer.

3. Finally, we arrive at our prediction by multiplying the vector with the activation function (softmax for classification).

We can treat each layer in the network as a vector and apply simple vector multiplications. More formally, this will look like the following:

θ = the weight vector of layer x

$b1$ and $b2$ are the bias units

f = the activation function

$$z_{(2)} = \theta_{(1)}x + b_{(1)}$$

$$a_{(2)} = f(z_{(2)}) \qquad \text{transformation after layer 1}$$

$$z_{(3)} = \theta_{(2)}a_{(2)} + b_{(2)}$$

$$h_{w,b}(x) = a_{(3)} = f_{(softmax)}(z_{(3)}) \qquad \text{final output with softmax transformation}$$

 Note that this example is based on a single hidden layer network architecture.

Let's perform a simple feedforward pass on a neural network with two hidden layers with basic NumPy. We apply a `softmax` function to the final output:

```
import numpy as np
import math
b1=0 #bias unit 1
b2=0 #bias unit 2

def sigmoid(x):       # sigmoid function
    return 1 /(1+(math.e**-x))

def softmax(x):       #softmax function
```

```
    l_exp = np.exp(x)
    sm = l_exp/np.sum(l_exp, axis=0)
    return sm


# input dataset with 3 features
X = np.array([  [.35,.21,.33],
    [.2,.4,.3],
    [.4,.34,.5],
    [.18,.21,16] ])
len_X = len(X) # training set size
input_dim = 3 # input layer dimensionality
output_dim = 1 # output layer dimensionality
hidden_units=4


np.random.seed(22)
# create random weight vectors
theta0 = 2*np.random.random((input_dim, hidden_units))
theta1 = 2*np.random.random((hidden_units, output_dim))


# forward propagation pass
d1 = X.dot(theta0)+b1
l1=sigmoid(d1)
l2 = l1.dot(theta1)+b2
#let's apply softmax to the output of the final layer
output=softmax(l2)
```

 Note that the bias unit enables the function to move up and down and will help fit the target values more closely. Each hidden layer consists of one bias unit.

Backpropagation

With our simple feedforward example, we have taken our first steps in training the model. Neural networks are trained quite similarly to gradient descent methods that we have seen with other machine learning algorithms. Namely, we upgrade the parameters of a model in order to find the global minimum of the error function. An important difference with neural networks is that we now have to deal with multiple units across the network that we need to train independently. We do this using the partial derivative of the cost function and calculating how much the error curve drops when we change the particular parameter vector by a certain amount (the learning rate). We start with the layer closest to the output and calculate the gradient with respect to the derivative of our loss function. If there are hidden layers, we move to the second hidden layer and update the weights until the first layer in the feedforward network is reached.

The core idea of backpropagation is quite similar to other machine learning algorithms, with the important complication that we are dealing with multiple layers and units. We have seen that each layer in the network is represented by a weight vector θij. So, how do we solve this issue? It might seem intimidating that we have to train a large number of weights independently. However, quite conveniently, we can use vectorized operations. Just like we did with the forward pass, we calculate the gradients and update the weights applied to the weight vectors (θij).

We can summarize the following steps in the backpropagation algorithm:

1. Feedforward pass: We randomly initialize the weight vectors and multiply the input with the subsequent weight vectors toward a final output.

2. Calculate the error: We calculate the error/loss of the output of the feedforward step.

   Randomly initialize the weight vectors.

3. Backpropagation to the last hidden layer (with respect to the output).

   We calculate the gradient of this error and change weights toward the direction of the gradient. We do this by multiplying the weight vector θj with the gradients performed.

4. Update the weights till the stopping criterion is reached (minimum error or number of training rounds):

$$\theta ij := \theta ij - \eta * \Delta_\theta J(\theta ij)$$

We have now covered a feedforward pass of an arbitrary two-layer neural network; let's apply backpropagation with SGD in NumPy to the same input that we used in the previous example. Take special note of how we upgrade the weight parameters:

```
import numpy as np
import math
def sigmoid(x):        # sigmoid function
    return 1 /(1+(math.e**-x))

def deriv_sigmoid(y): #the derivative of the sigmoid function
    return y * (1.0 - y)

alpha=.1    #this is the learning rate
X = np.array([   [.35,.21,.33],
    [.2,.4,.3],
    [.4,.34,.5],
```

```
     [.18,.21,16] ])
y = np.array([[0],
        [1],
        [1],
        [0]])
np.random.seed(1)
#We randomly initialize the layers
theta0 = 2*np.random.random((3,4)) - 1
theta1 = 2*np.random.random((4,1)) - 1


for iter in range(205000): #here we specify the amount of training
rounds.
    # Feedforward the input like we did in the previous exercise
    input_layer = X
    l1 = sigmoid(np.dot(input_layer,theta0))
    l2 = sigmoid(np.dot(l1,theta1))

    # Calculate error
    l2_error = y - l2

    if (iter% 1000) == 0:
        print "Neuralnet accuracy:" + str(np.mean(1-(np.abs(l2_
error))))

    # Calculate the gradients in vectorized form
    # Softmax and bias units are left out for instructional simplicity
    l2_delta = alpha*(l2_error*deriv_sigmoid(l2))
    l1_error = l2_delta.dot(theta1.T)
    l1_delta = alpha*(l1_error * deriv_sigmoid(l1))

    theta1 += l1.T.dot(l2_delta)
    theta0 += input_layer.T.dot(l1_delta)
```

Now look how the accuracy increases with each pass over the network:

```
Neuralnet accuracy:0.983345051044
Neuralnet accuracy:0.983404936523
Neuralnet accuracy:0.983464255273
Neuralnet accuracy:0.983523015841
Neuralnet accuracy:0.983581226603
Neuralnet accuracy:0.983638895759
Neuralnet accuracy:0.983696031345
Neuralnet accuracy:0.983752641234
Neuralnet accuracy:0.983808733139
Neuralnet accuracy:0.98386431462
```

```
Neuralnet accuracy:0.983919393086
Neuralnet accuracy:0.983973975799
Neuralnet accuracy:0.984028069878
Neuralnet accuracy:0.984081682304
Neuralnet accuracy:0.984134819919
```

Common problems with backpropagation

One familiar problem with neural networks is that, during optimization with backpropagation, the gradient can get stuck in local minima. This occurs when the error minimization is tricked into seeing a minimum (the point **S** in the image) where it is really just a local bump to pass the peak **S**:

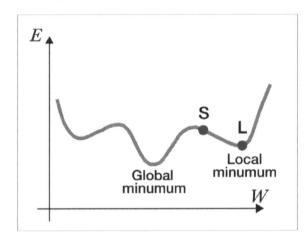

Another common problem is when the gradient descent misses the global minimum, which can sometimes result in surprisingly poor performing models. This problem is referred to as **overshooting**.

It is possible to solve both these problems by choosing a lower learning rate when the model is overshooting or choose a higher learning rate when getting stuck in local minima. Sometimes this adjustment still doesn't lead to a satisfying and quick convergence. Recently, a range of solutions has been found to mitigate these problems. Learning algorithms with tweaks to the vanilla SGDalgorithms that we just covered have been developed. It is important to understand them so that you can choose the right one for any given task. Let's cover these learning algorithms in more detail.

Backpropagation with mini batch

Batch gradient descent computes the gradient using the whole dataset but backpropagation SGD can also work with so-called **mini batches**, where a sample of the dataset with size k (batches) is used to update the learning parameter. The amount of error irregularity between each update can be smoothened out with mini batch, which might avoid getting stuck in and overshooting local minima. In most neural network packages, we can change the batch size of the algorithm (we will look at this later). Depending on the amount of training examples, a batch size anywhere between 10 and 300 can be helpful.

Momentum training

Momentum is a method that adds a fraction of the previous weight update to the current one:

$$v_{t+1} = \mu v_t - \eta \nabla \mathcal{L}(\theta_t)$$
$$\theta_{t+1} = \theta_t + v_{t+1}$$

Here, a fraction of the previous weight update is added to the current one. A high momentum parameter can help increase the speed of convergence reaching the global minimum faster. Looking at the formulation, you can see a v parameter. This is the equivalent of the velocity of the gradient updates with a learning rate η. A simple way to understand this is to see that when the gradient keeps pointing in the same direction over multiple instances, the speed of convergence increases with each step toward the minimum. This also removes irregularities between the gradients by a certain margin. Most packages will have this momentum parameter available (as we will see in a later example). When we set this parameter too high, we have to keep in mind that there is a risk of overshooting the global minimum. On the other hand, when we set the momentum parameter too low, the coefficient might get stuck in local minima and can also slow down learning. Ideal settings for the momentum coefficient are normally in the .5 and .99 range.

Nesterov momentum

Nesterov momentum is a newer and improved version of classical momentum. In addition to classical momentum training, it will *look ahead* in the direction of the gradient. In other words, Nesterov momentum takes a simple step going from x to y, and moves a little bit further in that direction so that x to y becomes x to {y (v1 +1)} in the direction given by the previous point. I will spare you the technical details, but remember that it consistently outperforms normal momentum training in terms of convergence. If there is an option for Nesterov momentum, use it.

Adaptive gradient (ADAGRAD)

ADAGRAD provides a feature-specific learning rate that utilizes information from the previous upgrades:

$$g_{t+1} = g_t + \nabla \mathcal{L}(\theta_t)^2$$

$$\theta_{t+1} = \theta_t - \frac{\eta \nabla \mathcal{L}(\theta_t)}{\sqrt{g_{t+1}} + \epsilon}$$

ADAGRAD updates the learning rate for each parameter according to information from previously iterated gradients for that parameter. This is done by dividing each term by the square root of the sum of squares of its previous gradient. This allows the learning rate to decrease over time because the sum of squares will continue to increase with each iteration. A decreasing learning rate has the advantage of decreasing the risk of overshooting the global minimum quite substantially.

Resilient backpropagation (RPROP)

RPROP is an adaptive method that does not look at historical information, but merely looks at the sign of the partial derivative over a training instance and updates the weights accordingly.

$$\Delta_{ij}^{(t)} = \begin{cases} n^+ * \Delta_{ij}^{(t-1)}, if \, \dfrac{\partial E^{(t-1)}}{\partial w_{ij}} * \dfrac{\partial E^{(t)}}{\partial w_{ij}} > 0 \\[2em] n^- * \Delta_{ij}^{(t-1)}, if \, \dfrac{\partial E^{(t-1)}}{\partial w_{ij}} * \dfrac{\partial E^{(t)}}{\partial w_{ij}} < 0 \\[2em] \Delta_{ij}^{(t-1)}, else \end{cases}$$

$$where \, 0 < \eta^- < 1 < \eta^+$$

A direct adaptive method for faster backpropagation learning: The RPROP Algorithm. Martin Riedmiller 1993

RPROP is an adaptive method that does not look at historical information, but merely looks at the sign of the partial derivative over a training instance and updates the weights accordingly. Inspecting the preceding image closely, we can see that once the partial derivative of the error changes its sign (> 0 or < 0), the gradient starts moving in the opposite direction, leading toward the global minimum correcting for the overshooting. However, if the sign doesn't change at all, larger steps are taken toward the global minimum. Lots of articles have proven the superiority of RPROP over ADAGRAD but in practice, this is not confirmed consistently. Another important thing to keep in mind is that RPROP does not work properly with mini batches.

RMSProp

RMSProp is an adaptive learning method without shrinking the learning rate:

$$\theta_{t+1} = \theta t - \frac{\eta}{\sqrt{E[g2]t+e}} g_t$$

RMSProp is also an adaptive learning method that utilizes ideas from momentum learning and ADAGRAD, with the important addition that it avoids the shrinkage of the learning rate over time. With this technique, the shrinkage is controlled with an exponential decay function over the average of the gradients.

The following is the list of gradient descent optimization algorithms:

	Applications	Common problems	Practical tips
Regular SGD	Widely applicable	Overshooting, stuck in local minima	Use with momentum and mini-batch
ADAGRAD	Smaller datasets <10k	Slow convergence	Use a learning rate between .01 and .1. Widely applicable. Works with sparse data
RPROP	Larger datasets >10k	Not effective with mini-batches	Use RMSProp when possible
RMSProp	Larger datasets >10k	Not effective with wide and shallow nets	Particularly useful for wide sparse data

What and how neural networks learn

Now that we have a basic understanding of backpropagation in all its forms, it is time to address the most difficult task in neural network projects: How do we chose the right architecture? One crucial capability of neural networks is that the weights within an architecture can transform the input into a nonlinear feature space and thereby solve nonlinear classification (decision boundaries) and regression problems. Let's do a simple yet insightful exercise to demonstrate this idea in the neurolab package. We will only use neurolab for a short exercise; for scalable learning problems, we will propose other methods.

First, install the neurolab package with pip.

Install neurolab from the terminal:

```
> $pip install neurolab
```

With this example, we will generate a simple nonlinear cosine function with numpy and train a neural network to predict the cosine function from a variable. We will set up several neural network architectures to see how well each architecture is able to predict the cosine target variable:

```
import neurolab as nl
import numpy as np
from sklearn import preprocessing
import matplotlib.pyplot as plt
plt.style.use('ggplot')
# Create train samples
x = np.linspace(-10,10, 60)
y = np.cos(x) * 0.9
size = len(x)
x_train = x.reshape(size,1)
y_train = y.reshape(size,1)


# Create network with 4 layers and random initialized
# just experiment with the amount of layers

d=[[1,1],[45,1],[45,45,1],[45,45,45,1]]
for i in range(4):
    net = nl.net.newff([[-10, 10]],d[i])
    train_net=nl.train.train_gd(net, x_train, y_train, epochs=1000,
show=100)
    outp=net.sim(x_train)
# Plot results (dual plot with error curve and predicted values)
    import matplotlib.pyplot
    plt.subplot(2, 1, 1)
```

```
plt.plot(train_net)
plt.xlabel('Epochs')
plt.ylabel('squared error')
x2 = np.linspace(-10.0,10.0,150)
y2 = net.sim(x2.reshape(x2.size,1)).reshape(x2.size)
y3 = outp.reshape(size)
plt.subplot(2, 1, 2)

plt.suptitle([i ,'hidden layers'])
plt.plot(x2, y2, '-',x , y, '.', x, y3, 'p')
plt.legend(['y predicted', 'y_target'])
plt.show()
```

Now look closely at how the error curve behaves and how the predicted values start to approximate the target values as we add more layers to the neural network.

With zero hidden layers, the neural network projects a straight line through the target values. The error curve falls to a minimum quickly with a bad fit:

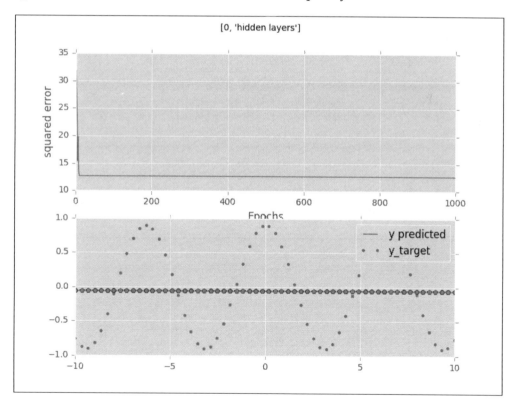

With one hidden layer, the network starts to approximate the target output. Watch how irregular the error curve is:

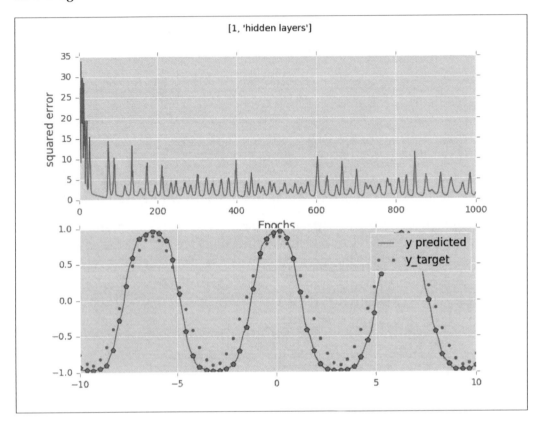

With two hidden layers, the neural network approximates the target value even more closely. The error curve drops faster and behaves less irregularly:

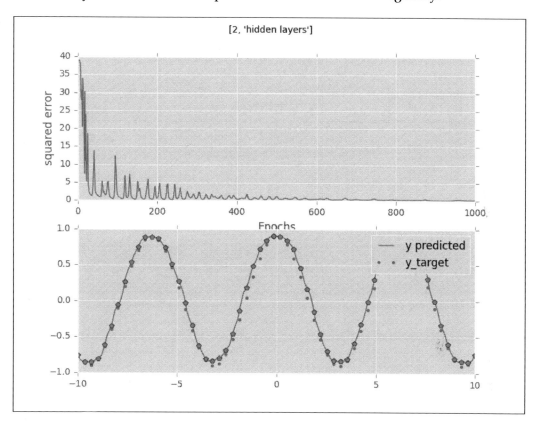

An almost perfect fit with three hidden layers. The error curve drops much faster (around **220** iterations).

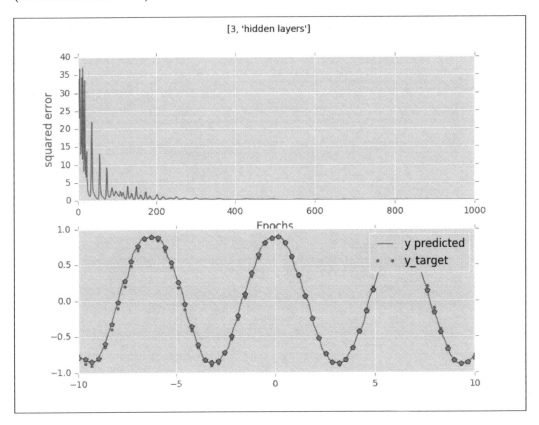

The orange line in the upper plot is a visualization of how the error drops with each epoch (a full pass through the training set). It shows us that we need a certain number of passes through the training set to arrive at a global minimum. If you inspect this error curve more closely, you will see that the error curve behaves differently with each architecture. The lower plot (the dotted line) shows how the predicted values start to approximate the target values. With no hidden layer, the neural network is incapable of detecting nonlinear functions, but once we add hidden layers, the network starts to learn nonlinear functions and increasingly complex functions. In fact, neural networks can learn *any* possible function. This capability of learning every possible function is called the **universal approximation theorem**. We can modify this approximation by adding hidden neurons (units and layers) to the neural network. We do need to be cautious, however, that we don't overfit; adding a high amount of layers and units will lead to memorization of the training data instead of fitting a generalizable function. Quite often, too many layers in a network can be detrimental to predictive accuracy.

Choosing the right architecture

As we have seen, the combinatorial space of possible neural network architectures is almost infinite. So how can we know in advance which architecture will be suitable for our project? We need some sort of heuristic or rule of thumb in order to design an architecture for a specific task. In the last section, we used a simple example with only one output and one feature. However, the recent wave of neural network architectures that we refer to as *deep learning* is very complex and it is crucial to be able to construct the right neural network architectures for any given task. As we have mentioned before, a typical neural network consists of the input layer, one or more hidden layers, and an output layer. Let's look at each layer of the architecture in detail so that we can have a sense of setting up the right architecture for any given task.

The input layer

When we mention the input layer, we are basically talking about the features that will be used as the input of the neural network. The preprocessing steps that are required are highly dependent on the shape and content of the data. If we have features that are measured on different scales, we need to rescale and normalize the data. In cases where we have a high amount of features, a dimension reduction technique such as PCA or SVD will become recommendable.

The following preprocessing techniques can be applied to inputs before learning:

- Normalization, scaling, & outlier detection
- Dimensionality reduction (SVD and factor analysis)
- Pretraining (autoencoders and Boltzmann machines)

We will cover each of these methods in the upcoming examples.

The hidden layer

How do we choose the amount of units in hidden layers? How many hidden layers do we add to the network? We have seen in the the previous example that a neural network without a hidden layer is incapable of learning a nonlinear function (both in curve fitting for regression and in decision boundaries with classification). So if there is a nonlinear pattern or decision boundary to project, we will need hidden layers. When it comes to selecting the amount of units in the hidden layer, we generally want fewer units in the hidden layer than the amount of units in the input layer and more units than the amount of output units:

- Preferably fewer hidden units than the amount of input features
- More units than the amount of output units (classes for classification)

Sometimes, when the target function is very complex in shape, there is an exception. In a case where we add more units than input dimensions, we add an **expansion** of the feature space. Networks with such layers are commonly referred to as **wide networks**.

Complex networks can learn more complex functions, but this does not mean that we can simply keep on stacking layers. It is advisory to keep the amount of layers in check because too many layers will cause problems with overfitting, higher CPU load, and even underfitting. Usually between one and four hidden layers will be sufficient.

> Use preferably between one and four layers as a starting point.

The output layer

Each neural network has one output layer and, just like the input layer, is highly dependent on the structure of the data in question. For classification, we will generally use the `softmax` function. In this case, we should use the same amount of units as the amount of classes we predict.

Neural networks in action

Let's get some hands-on experience with training neural nets for classification. We will use sknn, the Scikit-learn wrapper for lasagne and Pylearn2. You can find out more about the package at `https://github.com/aigamedev/scikit-neuralnetwork/`.

We will use this tool because of its practical and Pythonic interface. It is a great introduction to more sophisticated frameworks like Keras.

The sknn library can run both on CPU or GPU, whichever you might prefer. Note that if you choose to utilize the GPU, sknn will operate on Theano:

```
For CPU (most stable) :
# Use the GPU in 32-bit mode,  from sknn.platform import gpu32

from sknn.platform import cpu32, threading
# Use the CPU in 64-bit mode. from sknn.platform import cpu64

from sknn.platform import cpu64, threading

GPU:
```

```
# Use the GPU in 32-bit mode,
from sknn.platform import gpu32
# Use the CPU in 64-bit mode.
from sknn.platform import cpu64
```

Parallelization for sknn

We can utilize parallel processing in the following way, but this comes with a warning. It is not the most stable method:

```
from sknn.platform import cpu64, threading
```

We can specify Scikit-learn to utilize a specific amount of threads:

```
from sknn.platform import cpu64, threads2 #any desired amount of
threads
```

When you have specified the appropriate number of threads, you can parallelize your code by implementing n_jobs=nthreads in the cross-validation.

Now that we have covered the most important concepts and prepared our environment, let's implement a neural network.

For this example, we will use the convenient yet rather boring Iris dataset.

After this, we will apply preprocessing in the form of normalization and scaling and start building our model:

```
import numpy as np
from sklearn.datasets import load_iris
from sknn.mlp import Classifier, Layer
from sklearn import preprocessing
from sklearn.cross_validation import train_test_split
from sklearn import cross_validation
from sklearn import datasets


# import the familiar Iris data-set
iris = datasets.load_iris()
X_train, X_test, y_train, y_test = train_test_split(iris.data,
iris.target, test_size=0.2, random_state=0)
```

Here we apply preprocessing, normalization, and scaling to our inputs:

```
X_trainn = preprocessing.normalize(X_train, norm='l2')
X_testn = preprocessing.normalize(X_test, norm='l2')

X_trainn = preprocessing.scale(X_trainn)
X_testn = preprocessing.scale(X_testn)
```

Let's set up our neural network architecture and parameters. Let's start with a neural network with two layers. In the Layer part, we specify the settings of each layer independently. (We will see this method again in Tensorflow and Keras.) The Iris dataset consists of four features, but because in this particular case a *wide* neural network works quite well, we will use 13 units in each hidden layer. Note that sknn applies SGD by default:

```
clf = Classifier(
    layers=[
    Layer("Rectifier", units=13),
    Layer("Rectifier", units=13),
    Layer("Softmax")],    learning_rate=0.001,
    n_iter=200)

model1=clf.fit(X_trainn, y_train)
y_hat=clf.predict(X_testn)
scores = cross_validation.cross_val_score(clf, X_trainn, y_train,
cv=5)
print 'train mean accuracy %s' % np.mean(scores)
print 'vanilla sgd test %s' % accuracy_score(y_hat,y_test)


OUTPUT:]
train sgd mean accuracy 0.949909090909
sgd test 0.933333333333
```

A decent result on the training set, but we might be able to do better.

We talked about how Nesterov momentum can shorten the length toward the global minimum; let's run this algorithm with nesterov to see if we can increase accuracy and improve convergence:

```
clf = Classifier(
    layers=[
    Layer("Rectifier", units=13),
    Layer("Rectifier", units=13),
    Layer("Softmax")],         learning_rate=0.001,learning_
rule='nesterov',random_state=101,
```

```
    n_iter=1000)

model1=clf.fit(X_trainn, y_train)
y_hat=clf.predict(X_testn)
scores = cross_validation.cross_val_score(clf, X_trainn, y_train,
cv=5)
print 'Nesterov train mean accuracy %s' % np.mean(scores)
print 'Nesterov  test %s' % accuracy_score(y_hat,y_test)


OUTPUT]
Nesterov train mean accuracy 0.966575757576
Nesterov  test 0.966666666667
```

Our model is improved with Nesterov momentum in this case.

Neural networks and regularization

Even though we didn't overtrain our model in our last example, it is necessary
to think about regularization strategies for neural networks. Three of the most
widely-used ways in which we can apply regularization to a neural network
are as follows:

- **L1** and **L2** regularization with weight decay as a parameter for the
  regularization strength

- **Dropout** means that deactivating units within the neural network at random
  can force other units in the network to take over

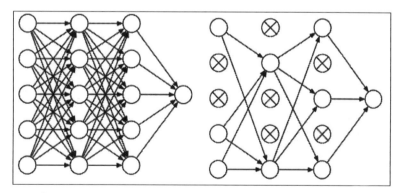

On the left hand, we see an architecture with dropout applied, randomly deactivating units in
the network. On the right hand, we see an ordinary neural network (marked with X).

- **Averaging** or ensembling multiple neural networks (each with different
  settings)

Let's try dropout for this model and see if works:

```
clf = Classifier(
    layers=[
    Layer("Rectifier", units=13),
    Layer("Rectifier", units=13),
    Layer("Softmax")],
    learning_rate=0.01,
    n_iter=2000,
    learning_rule='nesterov',
    regularize='dropout', #here we specify dropout
    dropout_rate=.1,#dropout fraction of neural units in entire
network
    random_state=0)
model1=clf.fit(X_trainn, y_train)

scores = cross_validation.cross_val_score(clf, X_trainn, y_train,
cv=5)
print np.mean(scores)
y_hat=clf.predict(X_testn)
print accuracy_score(y_hat,y_test)


OUTPUT]
dropout train score 0.933151515152
dropout test score 0.866666666667
```

In this case, dropout didn't lead to satisfactory results so we should leave it out altogether. Feel free to experiment with other methods as well. Just change the `learning_rule` parameter and see what it does to the overall accuracy. The models that you can try are `sgd`, `momentum`, `nesterov`, `adagrad`, and `rmsprop`. From this example, you have learned that Nesterov momentum can increase the overall accuracy. In this case, `dropout` was not the best regularization method and was detrimental to model performance. Considering that this large number of parameters all interact and produce unpredictable results, we really need a tuning method. This is exactly what we are going to do in the next section.

Neural networks and hyperparameter optimization

As the parameter space of neural networks and deep learning models is so wide, optimization is a hard task and computationally very expensive. A wrong neural network architecture can be a recipe for failure. These models can only be accurate if we apply the right parameters and choose the right architecture for our problem. Unfortunately, there are only a few applications that provide tuning methods. We found that the best parameter tuning method at the moment is **randomized search**, an algorithm that iterates over the parameter space at random sparing computational resources. The sknn library is really the only library that has this option. Let's walk through the parameter tuning methods with the following example based on the wine-quality dataset.

In this example, we first load the wine dataset. Than we apply transformation to the data, from where we tune our model based on chosen parameters. Note that this dataset has 13 features; we specify the units within each layer to be between 4 and 20. We don't use mini-batch in this case; the dataset is simply too small:

```python
import numpy as np
import scipy as sp
import pandas as pd
from sklearn.grid_search import RandomizedSearchCV
from sklearn.grid_search import GridSearchCV, RandomizedSearchCV
from scipy import stats
from sklearn.cross_validation import train_test_split
from sknn.mlp import  Layer, Regressor, Classifier as skClassifier


# Load data
df = pd.read_csv('http://archive.ics.uci.edu/ml/machine-learning-
databases/wine-quality/winequality-red.csv ' , sep = ';')
X = df.drop('quality' , 1).values # drop target variable


y1 = df['quality'].values # original target variable
y = y1 <= 5 # new target variable: is the rating <= 5?

# Split the data into a test set and a training set
```

```
X_train, X_test, y_train, y_test = train_test_split(X, y, test_
size=0.2, random_state=42)

print X_train.shape


max_net = skClassifier(layers= [Layer("Rectifier",units=10),
                                Layer("Rectifier",units=10),
                                Layer("Rectifier",units=10),
                                Layer("Softmax")])
params={'learning_rate': sp.stats.uniform(0.001, 0.05,.1),
'hidden0__units': sp.stats.randint(4, 20),
'hidden0__type': ["Rectifier"],
'hidden1__units': sp.stats.randint(4, 20),
'hidden1__type': ["Rectifier"],
'hidden2__units': sp.stats.randint(4, 20),
'hidden2__type': ["Rectifier"],
'batch_size':sp.stats.randint(10,1000),
'learning_rule':["adagrad","rmsprop","sgd"]}
max_net2 = RandomizedSearchCV(max_net,param_distributions=params,n_ite
r=25,cv=3,scoring='accuracy',verbose=100,n_jobs=1,\
                              pre_dispatch=None)
model_tuning=max_net2.fit(X_train,y_train)



print "best score %s" % model_tuning.best_score_
print "best parameters %s" % model_tuning.best_params_


OUTPUT:]
[CV]  hidden0__units=11, learning_rate=0.100932183167, hidden2__
units=4, hidden2__type=Rectifier, batch_size=30, hidden1__
units=11, learning_rule=adagrad, hidden1__type=Rectifier, hidden0__
type=Rectifier, score=0.655914 -   3.0s
[Parallel(n_jobs=1)]: Done  74 tasks       | elapsed:  3.0min
[CV] hidden0__units=11, learning_rate=0.100932183167, hidden2__
units=4, hidden2__type=Rectifier, batch_size=30, hidden1__
units=11, learning_rule=adagrad, hidden1__type=Rectifier, hidden0__
type=Rectifier
[CV]  hidden0__units=11, learning_rate=0.100932183167, hidden2__
units=4, hidden2__type=Rectifier, batch_size=30, hidden1__
units=11, learning_rule=adagrad, hidden1__type=Rectifier, hidden0__
type=Rectifier, score=0.750000 -   3.3s
```

```
[Parallel(n_jobs=1)]: Done   75 tasks       | elapsed:   3.0min
[Parallel(n_jobs=1)]: Done   75 out of   75 | elapsed:   3.0min finished
best score 0.721366278222

best parameters {'hidden0__units': 14, 'learning_rate':
0.03202394348494512, 'hidden2__units': 19, 'hidden2__type':
'Rectifier', 'batch_size': 30, 'hidden1__units': 17, 'learning_rule':
'adagrad', 'hidden1__type': 'Rectifier', 'hidden0__type': 'Rectifier'}
```

 Warning: As the parameter space is searched at random, the results can be inconsistent.

We can see that the best parameters for our model are, most importantly, the first layer with 14 units, the second layer contains 17 units, and the third layer contains 19 units. This is quite a complex architecture that we might never have been able to deduce ourselves, which demonstrates the importance of hyperparameter optimization.

Neural networks and decision boundaries

We have covered in the previous section that, by adding hidden units to a neural network, we can approximate the target function more closely. However, we haven't applied it to a classification problem. To do this, we will generate data with a nonlinear target value and look at how the decision surface changes once we add hidden units to our architecture. Let's see the universal approximation theorem at work! First, let's generate some non-linearly separable data with two features, set up our neural network architectures, and see how our decision boundaries change with each architecture:

```
%matplotlib inline
from sknn.mlp import Classifier, Layer
from sklearn import preprocessing
import numpy as np
import matplotlib.pyplot as plt
from sklearn import datasets
from itertools import product


X,y= datasets.make_moons(n_samples=500, noise=.2, random_state=222)
from sklearn.datasets import make_blobs

net1 = Classifier(
    layers=[
```

```
        Layer("Softmax")],random_state=222,
    learning_rate=0.01,
    n_iter=100)
net2 = Classifier(
    layers=[
        Layer("Rectifier", units=4),
        Layer("Softmax")],random_state=12,
    learning_rate=0.01,
    n_iter=100)
net3 =Classifier(
    layers=[
        Layer("Rectifier", units=4),
        Layer("Rectifier", units=4),
        Layer("Softmax")],random_state=22,
    learning_rate=0.01,
    n_iter=100)
net4 =Classifier(
    layers=[
        Layer("Rectifier", units=4),
        Layer("Rectifier", units=4),
        Layer("Rectifier", units=4),
        Layer("Rectifier", units=4),
        Layer("Rectifier", units=4),
        Layer("Rectifier", units=4),
        Layer("Softmax")],random_state=62,
    learning_rate=0.01,
    n_iter=100)


net1.fit(X, y)
net2.fit(X, y)
net3.fit(X, y)
net4.fit(X, y)



# Plotting decision regions
x_min, x_max = X[:, 0].min() - 1, X[:, 0].max() + 1
y_min, y_max = X[:, 1].min() - 1, X[:, 1].max() + 1
xx, yy = np.meshgrid(np.arange(x_min, x_max, 0.1),
                     np.arange(y_min, y_max, 0.1))

f, arxxx = plt.subplots(2, 2, sharey='row',sharex='col', figsize=(8,
8))
plt.suptitle('Neural Network - Decision Boundary')
for idx, clf, ti in zip(product([0, 1], [0, 1]),
```

```
                [net1, net2, net3,net4],
                ['0 hidden layer', '1 hidden layer',
                 '2 hidden layers','6 hidden layers']):

    Z = clf.predict(np.c_[xx.ravel(), yy.ravel()])
    Z = Z.reshape(xx.shape)

    arxxx[idx[0], idx[1]].contourf(xx, yy, Z, alpha=0.5)
    arxxx[idx[0], idx[1]].scatter(X[:, 0], X[:, 1], c=y, alpha=0.5)
    arxxx[idx[0], idx[1]].set_title(ti)

plt.show()
```

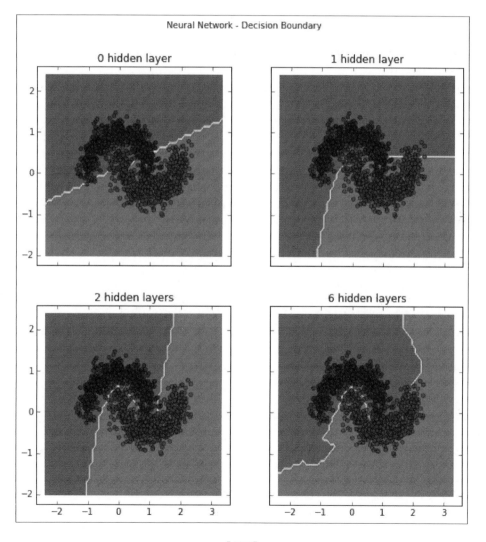

In this screenshot, we can see that, as we add hidden layers to the neural network, we can learn increasingly complex decision boundaries. An interesting side note is that the network with two layers produced the most accurate predictions.

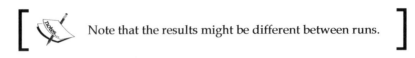 Note that the results might be different between runs.

Deep learning at scale with H2O

In previous sections, we covered neural networks and deep architectures running on a local computer and we found that neural networks are already highly vectorized but still computationally expensive. There is not much that we can do if we want to make the algorithm more scalable on a desktop computer other than utilizing Theano and GPU computing. So if we want to scale deep learning algorithms more drastically, we will need to find a tool that can run algorithms out-of-core instead of on a local CPU/GPU. H2O is, at this moment, the only open source out-of-core platform that can run deep learning algorithms quickly. It is also cross-platform; besides Python, there are APIs for R, Scala, and Java.

H2O is compiled on a Java-based platform developed for a wide range of data science-related tasks such as datahandling and machine learning. H2O runs on distributed and parallel CPUs in-memory so that data will be stored in the H2O cluster. The H2O platform—as of yet—has applications for **General Linear Models (GLM)**, Random Forests, **Gradient Boosting Machines (GBM)**, K Means, Naive Bayes, Principal Components Analysis, Principal Components Regression, and, of course our main focus for this chapter, Deep Learning.

Great, now we are ready to perform our first H2O out-of-core analysis.

Let's start the H2O instance and load a file in H2O's distributed memory system:

```
import sys
sys.prefix = "/usr/local"
import h2o

h2o.init(start_h2o=True)

Type this to get interesting information about the specifications of
your cluster.
Look at the memory that is allowed and the number of cores.

h2o.cluster_info()
```

This will look more or less like the following (slight differences might occur between trials and systems):

```
OUTPUT:]


Java Version: java version "1.8.0_60"
Java(TM) SE Runtime Environment (build 1.8.0_60-b27)
Java HotSpot(TM) 64-Bit Server VM (build 25.60-b23, mixed mode)



Starting H2O JVM and connecting: ................. Connection
successful!
---------------------------  ------------------------------------
--
H2O cluster uptime:            2 seconds 346 milliseconds
H2O cluster version:           3.8.2.3
H2O cluster name:              H2O_started_from_
                               python**********nzb520
H2O cluster total nodes:       1
H2O cluster total free memory: 3.56 GB
H2O cluster total cores:       8
H2O cluster allowed cores:     8
H2O cluster healthy:           True
H2O Connection ip:             1**.***.***.***
H2O Connection port:           54321
H2O Connection proxy:
Python Version:                2.7.10
---------------------------  ------------------------------------
--
---------------------------  ------------------------------------
--
H2O cluster uptime:            2 seconds 484 milliseconds
H2O cluster version:           3.8.2.3
H2O cluster name:              H2O_started_from_python_quandbee_
nzb520
H2O cluster total nodes:       1
H2O cluster total free memory: 3.56 GB
H2O cluster total cores:       8
H2O cluster allowed cores:     8
H2O cluster healthy:           True
H2O Connection ip:             1**.***.***.***
H2O Connection port:           54321
H2O Connection proxy:
```

```
Python Version:                2.7.10
------------------------------- -------------------------------------
--
Sucessfully closed the H2O Session.
Successfully stopped H2O JVM started by the h2o python module.
```

Large scale deep learning with H2O

In H2O deep learning, the dataset that we will use to train is the famous MNIST dataset. It consists of pixel intensities of 28 x 28 images of handwritten digits. The training set has 70,000 training items with 784 features together with a label for each record containing the target label *digits*.

Now that we are more comfortable with managing data in H2O, let's perform a deep learning example.

In H2O, we don't have to transform or normalize the input data; it is standardized internally and automatically. Each feature is transformed into the N(0,1) space.

Let's import the famous handwritten digits image dataset MNIST from the Amazon server to the H2O cluster:

```
import h2o
h2o.init(start_h2o=True)
train_url ="https://h2o-public-test-data.s3.amazonaws.com/bigdata/
laptop/mnist/train.csv.gz"
test_url="https://h2o-public-test-data.s3.amazonaws.com/bigdata/
laptop/mnist/test.csv.gz"


train=h2o.import_file(train_url)
test=h2o.import_file(test_url)

train.describe()
test.describe()


y='C785'
x=train.names[0:784]
train[y]=train[y].asfactor()
test[y]=test[y].asfactor()

from h2o.estimators.deeplearning import H2ODeepLearningEstimator

model_cv=H2ODeepLearningEstimator(distribution='multinomial'
```

```
                                    ,activation='RectifierWithDropout',hi
dden=[32,32,32],

                                    input_dropout_ratio=.2,
                                    sparse=True,
                                    l1=.0005,
                                        epochs=5)
```

The output of this print model will provide a lot of detailed information. The first table that you will see is the following one. This provides all the specifics about the architecture of the neural network. You can see that we have used a neural network with an input dimension of 717 with three hidden layers (consisting of 32 units each) with softmax activation applied to the output layer and ReLU between the hidden layers:

```
model_cv.train(x=x,y=y,training_frame=train,nfolds=3)
print model_cv
```

OUTPUT]

```
Model Details
==============
H2ODeepLearningEstimator :  Deep Learning
Model Key:  DeepLearning_model_python_1463889677812_3

Status of Neuron Layers: predicting C785, 10-class classification, multinomial distribution, CrossEntropy loss, 25,418
weights/biases, 371.3 KB, 300,525 training samples, mini-batch size 1
```

layer	units	type	dropout	l1	l2	mean_rate	rate_RMS	momentum	mean_weight	weight_RMS	mean_bias	bias_RMS
1	717	Input	20.0									
2	32	RectifierDropout	50.0	0.0005	0.0	0.0370441	0.1916480	0.0	-0.0061157	0.0612413	0.4243763	0.0918573
3	32	RectifierDropout	50.0	0.0005	0.0	0.0004112	0.0002142	0.0	-0.0279839	0.1946866	0.7527754	0.2369041
4	32	RectifierDropout	50.0	0.0005	0.0	0.0006548	0.0002914	0.0	-0.0397208	0.2000279	0.6407341	0.3597416
5	10	Softmax		0.0005	0.0	0.0025825	0.0024549	0.0	-0.2988227	0.8903637	-1.0314634	0.8309324

```
ModelMetricsMultinomial: deeplearning
** Reported on train data. **

MSE: 0.142497867237
R^2: 0.982924289006
LogLoss: 0.455262748035
```

If you want a short overview of model performance, this is a very practical method.

In the following table, the most interesting metrics are the training classification error and validation classification error over each fold. You can easily compare these in case you want to validate your model:

```
print model_cv.scoring_history()
```

```
              timestamp    duration  training_speed      epochs   iterations  \
0   2016-05-22 06:09:35   0.000 sec  training_speed    0.000000            0
1   2016-05-22 06:09:36   3.161 sec  30039 rows/sec    0.500650            1
2   2016-05-22 06:09:41   8.279 sec  40768 rows/sec    4.008217            8
3   2016-05-22 06:09:43  10.002 sec  40360 rows/sec    5.008750           10

     samples  training_MSE  training_r2  training_logloss  \
0          0           NaN          NaN               NaN
1      30039      0.434316     0.947955          1.154869
2     240493      0.163368     0.980423          0.507394
3     300525      0.142498     0.982924          0.455263

     training_classification_error
0                              NaN
1                         0.327284
2                         0.114081
3                         0.096430
```

Our training classification error of **.096430** and accuracy in the .907 range on the MNIST dataset is pretty good; it's almost as good as Yann LeCun's convolutional neural network submission.

H2O provides a convenient method to acquire validation metrics as well. We can do this by passing the validation dataframe to the cross-validation function:

```
model_cv.train(x=x,y=y,training_frame=train,validation_
frame=test,nfolds=3)
print model_cv
```

Scoring History:

training_r2	training_logloss	training_classification_error	validation_MSE	validation_r2	validation_logloss	validation_classification_error
nan	nan	nan	nan	nan	nan	nan
0.9412354	1.2943441	0.3213827	0.4909360	0.9414521	1.2906389	0.3221
0.9857803	0.4101554	0.0889877	0.1234896	0.9852729	0.4234574	0.0954

In this case, we can easily compare **training_classification_error** (.089) with our **validation_classification_error** (.0954).

Maybe we can improve our score; let's use a hyperparameter optimization model.

Gridsearch on H2O

Considering that our previous model performed quite well, we will focus our tuning efforts on the architecture of our network. H2O's gridsearch function is quite similar to Scikit-learn's randomized search; namely, instead of searching the full parameter space, it iterates over a random list of parameters. First, we will set up a parameter list that we will pass to the gridsearch function. H2O will provide us with an output of each model and the corresponding score in the parameters' search:

```
hidden_opt = [[18,18],[32,32],[32,32,32],[100,100,100]]
# l1_opt = [s/1e6 for s in range(1,1001)]

# hyper_parameters = {"hidden":hidden_opt, "l1":l1_opt}
hyper_parameters = {"hidden":hidden_opt}

#important: here we specify the search parameters
#be careful with these, training time can explode (see max_models)
search_c = {"strategy":"RandomDiscrete",

"max_models":10, "max_runtime_secs":100,

"seed":222}


from h2o.grid.grid_search import H2OGridSearch

model_grid = H2OGridSearch(H2ODeepLearningEstimator, hyper_
params=hyper_parameters)

#We have added a validation set to the gridsearch method in order to
have a better #estimate of the model performance.


model_grid.train(x=x, y=y, distribution="multinomial", epochs=1000,
training_frame=train, validation_frame=test,
    score_interval=2, stopping_rounds=3, stopping_
tolerance=0.05,search_criteria=search_c)
```

```
print model_grid


# Grid Search Results for H2ODeepLearningEstimator:


OUTPUT]

deeplearning Grid Build Progress: [##################################
###############] 100%
     hidden   \
0     [100, 100, 100]
1         [32, 32, 32]
2             [32, 32]
3             [18, 18]


     model_ids     logloss
0  Grid_DeepLearning_py_1_model_python_1464790287811_3_model_3
0.148162   ←------
1  Grid_DeepLearning_py_1_model_python_1464790287811_3_model_2
0.173675
2  Grid_DeepLearning_py_1_model_python_1464790287811_3_model_1
0.212246
3  Grid_DeepLearning_py_1_model_python_1464790287811_3_model_0
0.227706
```

We can see that our best architecture would be one with three layers with 100 units each. We can also clearly see that gridsearch increases training time substantially even on a powerful computing cluster like the one that H2O operates on. So, even on H2O, we should use gridsearch with caution and be conservative with the parameters that are parsed in the model.

Now let's shutdown the H2O instance before we proceed:

```
h2o.shutdown(prompt=False)
```

Deep learning and unsupervised pretraining

In this section, we will introduce the most important concept in deep learning: how to improve learning by unsupervised pretraining. With unsupervised pretraining, we use neural networks to find latent features and factors in the data to later pass to a neural network. This method has the powerful capability of training networks to learn tasks that other machine learning methods can't, without handcrafting features. We will get into the specifics and introduce a new powerful library.

Deep learning with theanets

Scikit-learn's neural network application is especially interesting for parameter tuning purposes. Unfortunately, its capabilities for unsupervised neural network applications are limited. For the next subject, where we dive into more sophisticated deep learning methods, we need another library. In this chapter, we will focus on theanets. We love theanets because of its ease of use and stability; it's a very smooth and well-maintained package developed by Lief Johnson at the University of Texas. Setting up a neural network architecture works quite similarly to sklearn; namely, we instantiate a learning objective (classification or regression), specify the layers, and train it. For more information, you can visit `http://theanets.readthedocs.org/en/stable/`.

All you have to do is install theanets with `pip`:

```
$ pip install theanets
```

As theanets is built on top of Theano, you also need to have the Theano properly installed. Let's run a basic neural network model to see how theanets works. The resemblance with Scikit-learn will be obvious. Note that we use momentum for this example, and softmax is used by default in theanets so we don't have to specify it:

```
import climate # This package provides the reporting of iterations
from sklearn.metrics import confusion_matrix
import numpy as np
from sklearn import datasets
from sklearn.cross_validation import train_test_split
from sklearn.metrics import mean_squared_error
import theanets
import theano
import numpy as np
import matplotlib.pyplot as plt
import climate
```

```
from sklearn.cross_validation import train_test_split
import theanets
from sklearn.metrics import confusion_matrix
from sklearn import preprocessing
from sklearn.metrics import accuracy_score
from sklearn import datasets
climate.enable_default_logging()


digits = datasets.load_digits()
digits = datasets.load_digits()
X = np.asarray(digits.data, 'float32')


Y = digits.target


Y=np.array(Y, dtype=np.int32)
#X = (X - np.min(X, 0)) / (np.max(X, 0) + 0.0001)  # 0-1 scaling


X_train, X_test, y_train, y_test = train_test_split(X, Y,
                                            test_size=0.2,
                                            random_state=0)



# Build a classifier model with 64 inputs, 1 hidden layer with 100
units   and 10 outputs.
net = theanets.Classifier([64,100,10])


# Train the model using Resilient backpropagation and momentum.
net.train([X_train,y_train], algo='sgd', learning_rate=.001,
momentum=0.9,patience=0,
validate_every=N,
min_improvement=0.8)


# Show confusion matrices on the training/validation splits.
print(confusion_matrix(y_test, net.predict(X_test)))
print (accuracy_score(y_test, net.predict(X_test)))


OUTPUT ]


[[27  0  0  0  0  0  0  0  0  0]
 [ 0 32  0  0  0  1  0  0  0  2]
 [ 0  1 34  0  0  0  0  1  0  0]
```

```
[ 0   0   0  29   0   0   0   0   0   0]
[ 0   0   0   0  29   0   0   1   0   0]
[ 0   0   0   0   0  38   0   0   0   2]
[ 0   1   0   0   0   0  43   0   0   0]
[ 0   0   0   0   1   0   0  38   0   0]
[ 0   2   1   0   0   0   0   0  36   0]
[ 0   0   0   0   0   1   0   0   0  40]]
0.961111111111
```

Autoencoders and unsupervised learning

Up until now, we discussed neural networks with multiple layers and a wide variety of parameters to optimize. The current generation of neural networks that we often refer to as deep learning is capable of more; it is capable of learning new features automatically so that very little feature engineering and domain expertise is required. These features are created by unsupervised methods on unlabeled data later to be fed into a subsequent layer in a neural network. This method is referred to as (unsupervised) **pretraining**. This approach has been proven to be highly successful in image recognition, language learning, and even vanilla machine learning projects. The most important and dominant technique in recent years is called **denoising autoencoders** and algorithms based on Boltzmann techniques. **Boltzmann machines**, which were the building blocks for **Deep Belief Networks (DBN)**, have lately fallen out of favor in the deep learning community because they turned out to be hard to train and optimize. For this reason, we will focus only on autoencoders. Let's cover this important topic in small manageable steps.

Autoencoders

We try to find a function (F) that has an output as its input with the least possible error $F(x) \approx {}'x$. This function is commonly referred to as the **identity function**, which we try to optimize so that x is as close as possible to ${}'x$. The difference between x and ${}'x$ is referred to as **reconstruction error**.

Let's look at a simple single-layer architecture to get an intuition of what's going on. We will see that these architectures are very flexible and need careful tuning:

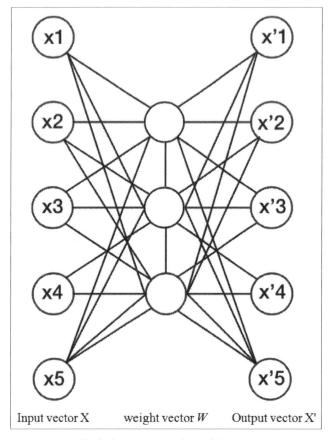

Single-layer autoencoder architecture

It is important to understand that when we have fewer units in the hidden layer than the input space, we force the weights to compress the input data.

In this case, we have a dataset containing five features. In the middle is a hidden layer containing three units (*Wij*). These units have the same property as the weight vector that we have seen in neural networks; namely, they are made up of weights that can be trained with backpropagation. With the output of the hidden layer, we get the feature representations as output by the same feedforward vector operations as we have seen with neural networks.

The process of calculating the vector $'x$ is quite similar to what we have seen with forward propagation by calculating the dot products of the weight vectors of each layer:

W=the weights

$$h_i=\text{sigmoid}((W_1.x*x)+b_1(i,1))$$

$$'x=\text{sigmoid}(W_2.x*h_i)+b_2(i,1)$$

The reconstruction error can be measured with the squared error or in cross-entropy form, which we have seen in so many other methods. In this case, $\hat{y}$ represents the reconstructed output and y the true input:

Cross entropy $\qquad L(x,y)=-\frac{1}{m}\sum_{i=l}^{m}[y_n\text{log}\hat{y}_n+(1-y_n)\text{log}(1-\hat{y}_n)]$

An important notion is that, with only one hidden layer, the dimensions in the data captured by the autoencoder model approximate the results of **Principal Component Analysis (PCA)**. However, an autoencoder behaves much differently if there is non-linearity involved. The autoencoder will detect different latent factors that PCA will never be able to detect. Now that we know more about the architecture of the autoencoder and how we can calculate the error from its identity approximation, let's look at these **sparsity parameters** with which we compress the input.

You might ask: why do we even need this scarcity parameter? Can't we just run the algorithm to find the identity function and move on?

Unfortunately, it is not quite that simple. There are cases where the identity function projects the input almost perfectly but still fails to extract the latent dimensions of the input features. In that case, the function simply memorizes the input data instead of extracting meaningful features. We can do two things. First, we deliberately add noise to the signal (**denoising autoencoders**) and second, we introduce a sparsity parameter, forcing the deactivation of weakly-activated units. Let's first look at how sparsity works.

We discussed the activation threshold of a biological neuron; we can think of a neuron as being *active* if its potential is close to 1 or being *inactive* if its output value is close to 0. We can constraint the neurons to be inactive most of the time by increasing the activation threshold. We do this by decreasing the average activation probability of each neuron/unit. Looking at the following formula, we can see how we can minimize the activation threshold:

$$\hat{p}_j = \frac{1}{m} \sum_{i=1}^{m} \left[a_j^{(2)} \left(x^{(i)} \right) \right]$$

$\hat{p}_j$: The average activation threshold of each neuron in the hidden layer.

ρ: The desired activation threshold of the network, which we specify upfront. In most cases, this value is set at .05.

a: The weight vector of the hidden layers.

Here, we see an opportunity for optimization by penalizing a training round on the error rate between $\hat{p}_j$ and ρ.

In this chapter, we will not worry too much about the technical details of this optimization objective. In most packages, we can use a very simple instruction to do this (as we will see in the next example). The most important thing to understand is that with autoencoders, we have two main learning objectives: minimizing the error between the input vector x and output vector 'x by optimizing the identity function, and minimizing the difference between the desired activation threshold and average activation of each neuron in the network.

The second way in which we can force the autoencoder to detect latent features is by introducing noise in the model; this is where the name **denoising autoencoders** comes from. The idea is that by *corrupting* the input, we force the autoencoder to learn a more robust representation of the data. In the upcoming example, we will simply introduce Gaussian noise to the auto-encoder model.

Really deep learning with stacked denoising autoencoders – pretraining for classification

With this exercise, you will set yourself apart from the many people who talk about deep learning and the few who actually do it! Now we will apply an autoencoder to the mini version of the famous MNIST dataset, which can conveniently be loaded from within Scikit-learn. The dataset consists of pixel intensities of 28 x 28 images of handwritten digits. The training set has 1,797 training items with 64 features with a label for each record containing the target label *digits* from 0 to 9. So we have 64 features with a target variable consisting of 10 classes (digits from 0-9) to predict.

First, we train the stacked denoising autoencoder model with a sparsity of .9 and inspect the reconstruction error. We will use the results from deep learning research papers as a guideline for the settings. You can read this paper for more information (http://arxiv.org/pdf/1312.5663.pdf). However, we have some limitations because of the enormous computational load for these types of models. So, for this autoencoder, we use five layers with ReLU activation and compress the data from 64 features to 45 features:

```
model = theanets.Autoencoder([64,(45,'relu'),(45,'relu'),(45,'relu'),(
45,'relu'),(45,'relu'),64])
dAE_model=model.train([X_train],algo='rmsprop',input_noise=0.1,hidden_
l1=.001,sparsity=0.9,num_updates=1000)
X_dAE=model.encode(X_train)
X_dAE=np.asarray(X_dAE, 'float32')
:OUTPUT:
I 2016-04-20 05:13:37 downhill.base:232 RMSProp 2639 loss=0.660185
err=0.645118
I 2016-04-20 05:13:37 downhill.base:232 RMSProp 2640 loss=0.660031
err=0.644968
I 2016-04-20 05:13:37 downhill.base:232 validation 264 loss=0.660188
err=0.645123
I 2016-04-20 05:13:37 downhill.base:414 patience elapsed!
I 2016-04-20 05:13:37 theanets.graph:447 building computation graph
I 2016-04-20 05:13:37 theanets.losses:67 using loss: 1.0 *
MeanSquaredError (output out:out)
I 2016-04-20 05:13:37 theanets.graph:551 compiling feed_forward
function
```

Now we have the output from our autoencoder that we created from a new set of compressed features. Let's look closer at this new dataset:

```
X_dAE.shape
Output: (1437, 45)
```

Here, we can actually see that we have compressed the data from 64 to 45 features. The new dataset is less sparse (meaning fewer zeroes) and numerically more continuous. Now that we have our pretrained data from the autoencoder, we can apply a deep neural network to it for supervised learning:

```
#By default, hidden layers use the relu transfer function so we don't
need to specify #them. Relu is the best option for auto-encoders.
# Theanets classifier also uses softmax by default so we don't need to
specify them.
net = theanets.Classifier(layers=(45,45,45,10))
autoe=net.train([X_dAE, y_train], algo='rmsprop',learning_
rate=.0001,batch_size=110,min_improvement=.0001,momentum=.9,
nesterov=True,num_updates=1000)
## Enjoy the rare pleasure of 100% accuracy on the training set.
OUTPUT:
I 2016-04-19 10:33:07 downhill.base:232 RMSProp 14074 loss=0.000000
err=0.000000 acc=1.000000
I 2016-04-19 10:33:07 downhill.base:232 RMSProp 14075 loss=0.000000
err=0.000000 acc=1.000000
I 2016-04-19 10:33:07 downhill.base:232 RMSProp 14076 loss=0.000000
err=0.000000 acc=1.000000
```

Before we predict this neural network on the test set, it is important that we apply the autoencoder model that we have trained to the test set:

```
dAE_model=model.train([X_test],algo='rmsprop',input_noise=0.1,hidden_
l1=.001,sparsity=0.9,num_updates=100)
X_dAE2=model.encode(X_test)
X_dAE2=np.asarray(X_dAE2, 'float32')
```

Now let's check the performance on the test set:

```
final=net.predict(X_dAE2)
from sklearn.metrics import accuracy_score
print accuracy_score(final,y_test)
OUTPUT: 0.972222222222
```

We can see that the final accuracy of the model with auto-encoded features (.9722) outperforms the model without it (.9611).

Summary

In this chapter, we looked at the most important concepts behind deep learning together with scalable solutions.

We took away some of the black-boxiness by learning how to construct the right architecture for any given task and worked through the mechanics of forward propagation and backpropagation. Updating the weights of a neural network is a hard task, regular stochastic gradient descent can result in getting stuck in global minima or overshooting. More sophisticated algorithms like momentum, ADAGRAD, RPROP and RMSProp can provide solutions. Even though neural networks are harder to train than other machine learning methods, they have the power of transforming feature representations and can learn any given function (universal approximation theorem). We also dived into large scale deep learning with H2O, and even utilized the very hot topic of parameter optimization for deep learning.

Unsupervised pre-training with auto-encoders can increase accuracy of any given deep network and we walked through a practical example within the theanets framework to get there.

In this chapter, we primarily worked with packages built on top of the Theano framework. In the next chapter, we will cover deep learning techniques with packages built on top of the new open source framework Tensorflow.

5
Deep Learning with TensorFlow

In this chapter, we will focus on TensorFlow and cover the following topics:

- Basic TensorFlow operations
- Machine learning from scratch with TensorFlow — regression, SGD classifier, and neural network
- Deep learning with SkFlow
- Incremental deep learning with large files
- Convolutional Neural Networks with Keras

The TensorFlow framework was introduced at the time of writing this book and already has proven to be a great addition to the machine learning landscape.

TensorFlow was started by the Google Brain Team consisting of most of the researchers that worked on important developments in deep learning in the recent decade (Geoffrey Hinton, Samy Bengio, and others). It is basically a next-generation development of an earlier generation of frameworks called DistBelief, a platform for distributed deep neural networks. Contrary to TensorFlow, **DistBelief** is not open source. Interesting examples of successful DistBelief projects are the reversed image search engine, Google deep dream, and speech recognition in Google apps. DistBelief enabled Google developers to utilize thousands of cores (both CPU and GPU) for distributed training.

TensorFlow is an improvement over DistBelief in that it is now completely open source and its programming language is less abstract. TensorFlow claims to be more flexible and has a wider range of applications. At the time of writing (late 2015), the TensorFlow framework is in its infancy and interesting lightweight packages built on top of TensorFlow have already emerged, as we will see later in this chapter.

Similarly to Theano, TensorFlow operates with symbolic computations on tensors; this means that most of its computations are based on vector-and matrix multiplications.

Regular programming languages define **variables** that contain values or characters to which operations can be applied to.

In symbolic programming languages such as Theano or TensorFlow, operations are structured around graphs instead of variables. This has computational advantages because they can be distributed and parallelized across computational units (GPU and CPU):

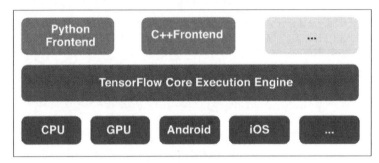

TensorFlow's architecture as introduced in November 2015

Tensorflow has the following features and applications:

- TensorFlow can be parallelized (horizontally) with multiple GPUs
- A development framework is also available for mobile deployment
- **TensorBoard** is a dashboard for visualizations (at a premature stage)
- It's a frontend for several programming languages (Python Go, Java, Lua, JavaScript, R, C++, and soon Julia)
- It provides integration for large scale solutions such as Spark and Google Cloud Platform (https://cloud.google.com/ml/)

The idea that tensor operations in a graph-like structure provide new ways of parallelized computations (so Google claims) can become quite clear with the following image:

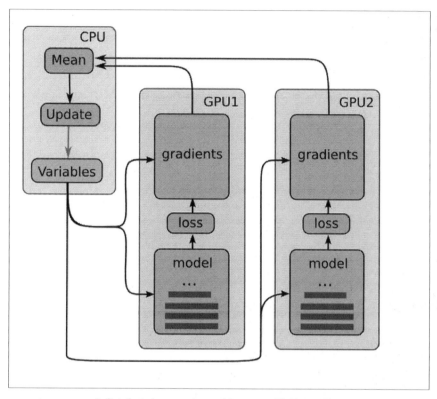

A distributed processing architecture with TensorFlow

We can see from this image that each model can be assigned to separate GPUs. After which the average of the predictions is calculated from each model. Among other methods, this approach has been the central idea to train very large distributed neural networks on GPU clusters.

TensorFlow installation

The version of TensorFlow that we will use in this chapter is 0.8 so make sure that you install this version. As TensorFlow is in heavy development, small changes are due. We can install TensorFlow quite easily with `pip install`, independent of which operating system you use:

```
pip install tensorflow
```

If you already have previous versions installed, you can upgrade according to your operating system:

```
# Ubuntu/Linux 64-bit, CPU only:
$ sudo pip install --upgrade https://storage.googleapis.com/
tensorflow/linux/cpu/tensorflow-0.8.1-cp27-none-linux_x86_64.whl

# Ubuntu/Linux 64-bit, GPU enabled:
$ sudo pip install --upgrade https://storage.googleapis.com/
tensorflow/linux/gpu/tensorflow-0.8.1-cp27-none-linux_x86_64.whl

# Mac OS X, CPU only:
$ sudo easy_install --upgrade six
$ sudo pip install --upgrade https://storage.googleapis.com/
tensorflow/mac/tensorflow-0.8.1-cp27-none-any.whl
```

Now that TensorFlow is installed, you can test it in the terminal:

```
$python
import tensorflow as tf
hello = tf.constant('Hello, TensorFlow!')
sess = tf.Session()
print(sess.run(hello))
Output Hello, TensorFlow!
```

TensorFlow operations

Let's walk through some simple examples to get a feel for how it works.

An important distinction is that with TensorFlow, we first need to initialize the variables before we can apply operations to them. TensorFlow operates on a C++ backend to perform computations so, in order to connect to this backend, we need to instantiate a session first:

```
x = tf.constant([22,21,32], name='x')
d=tf.constant([12,23,43],name='x')
y = tf.Variable(x * d, name='y')
print(y)
```

Instead of providing the output vector of *x*d*, you will see something like this:

```
OUTPUT ]
<tensorflow.python.ops.variables.Variable object at 0x114a95710>
```

To actually produce the provided results of a computation from the C++ backend, we instantiate the session in the following way:

```
x = tf.constant([22,21,32], name='x')
d=tf.constant([12,23,43],name='d')
y = tf.Variable(x * d, name='y')

model = tf.initialize_all_variables()

with tf.Session() as session:
    session.run(model)
    print(session.run(y))
```

```
Output [ 264   483 1376]
```

Up until now, we have used variables directly, but to be more flexible with tensor operations, it can be convenient if we can assign data to a prespecified container. This way, we can perform operations on the computation graph without loading the data in-memory beforehand. In TensorFlow terminology, we then feed data into the graph through what are called *placeholders*. This is exactly where the resemblance with the Theano language becomes clear (see the *Appendix, Introduction to GPUs and Theano*).

These TensorFlow placeholders are simply containers of objects with certain prespecified settings and classes. So in order to perform operations on an object, we first create a placeholder for that object, together with its corresponding class (an integer in this case):

```
a = tf.placeholder(tf.int8)
b = tf.placeholder(tf.int8)
sess = tf.Session()
sess.run(a+b, feed_dict={a: 111, b: 222})
```

```
Output   77
```

Matrix multiplications will work like this:

```
matrix1 = tf.constant([[1, 2,32], [3, 4,2],[3,2,11]])

matrix2 = tf.constant([[21,3,12], [3, 56,2],[35,21,61]])

product = tf.matmul(matrix1, matrix2)

with tf.Session() as sess:
```

```
    result = sess.run(product)
    print result
```

OUTPUT

```
[[1147  787 1968]
 [ 145  275  166]
 [ 454  352  711]]
```

It is interesting to note that the output of the object `result` is a NumPy `ndarray` object that we can apply operations to outside of TensorFlow.

GPU computing

If we want to perform TensorFlow operations on a GPU, we only need to specify a device. Be warned; this only works with a properly installed, CUDA-compatible, NVIDIA GPU unit:

```
with tf.device('/gpu:0'):
    product = tf.matmul(matrix1, matrix2)
with tf.Session() as sess:
    result = sess.run(product)
    print result
```

If we want to utilize multiple GPUs, we need to assign a GPU device to a specific task:

```
matrix3 = tf.constant([[13, 21,53], [4, 3,6],[3,1,61]])
matrix4 = tf.constant([[13,23,32], [23, 16,2],[35,51,31]])

with tf.device('/gpu:0'):
    product = tf.matmul(matrix1, matrix2)
with tf.Session() as sess:
    result = sess.run(product)
    print result




with tf.device('/gpu:1'):
    product = tf.matmul(matrix3, matrix4)
with tf.Session() as sess:
    result = sess.run(product)
    print result
```

Linear regression with SGD

Now that we have covered the basics, we can start writing our first machine learning algorithm from scratch within the TensorFlow framework. Later, we will use more practical lightweight applications in higher abstractions on top of TensorFlow.

We will perform a very simple linear regression with stochastic gradient descent in order to get a sense of how training and evaluation works in TensorFlow. First, we will create some variables to work with in order to parse them in placeholders to contain those variables. We then feed x and y to a `cost` function and train the model with gradient descent:

```
import tensorflow as tf
import numpy as np


X = tf.placeholder("float") # create symbolic variables
Y = tf.placeholder("float")
X_train = np.asarray([1,2.2,3.3,4.1,5.2])
Y_train =  np.asarray([2,3,3.3,4.1,3.9,1.6])

def model(X, w):
    return tf.mul(X, w)


w = tf.Variable(0.0, name="weights")
y_model = model(X, w) # our predicted values

cost = (tf.pow(Y-y_model, 2)) # squared error cost

train_op = tf.train.GradientDescentOptimizer(0.01).minimize(cost) #sgd
optimization
sess = tf.Session()
init = tf.initialize_all_variables()
sess.run(init)

for trials in range(50):   #
    for (x, y) in zip(X_train, Y_train):
        sess.run(train_op, feed_dict={X: x, Y: y})

print(sess.run(w))

OUTPUT ]
0.844732
```

To summarize, we perform linear regression with SGD in the following way: first, we initialize the regression weights (coefficients), then in the second step, we set up the cost function to later train and optimize the function with gradient descent. In the end, we need to write a `for` loop in order to specify the amount of training rounds we want and calculate the final predictions. The same basic structure will become apparent in neural networks.

A neural network from scratch in TensorFlow

Now let's perform a neural network in the TensorFlow language and dissect the process.

We will also use the Iris dataset and some Scikit-learn applications to preprocess in this case:

```
import tensorflow as tf
import numpy as np
from sklearn import cross_validation
from sklearn.cross_validation import train_test_split
from sklearn.preprocessing import OneHotEncoder
from sklearn.utils import shuffle
from sklearn import preprocessing
import os
import pandas as pd
from datetime import datetime as dt
import logging

iris = datasets.load_iris()
X = np.asarray(iris.data, 'float32')

Y = iris.target

from sklearn import preprocessing
X= preprocessing.scale(X)
min_max_scaler = preprocessing.MinMaxScaler()
X = min_max_scaler.fit_transform(X)

lb = preprocessing.LabelBinarizer()
Y=lb.fit_transform(iris.target)
```

This is an important step. Neural networks in TensorFlow cannot work with target labels within a singular vector. Target labels need to be transformed into binarized features (some will know this as dummy variables) so that the neural network will work with a one versus all output:

```
X_train, x_test, y_train, y_test = train_test_split(X,Y,test_
size=0.3,random_state=22)
```

```
def init_weights(shape):
    return tf.Variable(tf.random_normal(shape, stddev=0.01))
```

Here, we can see the feedforward pass:

```
def model(X, w_h, w_o):
    h = tf.nn.sigmoid(tf.matmul(X, w_h))
    return tf.matmul(h, w_o)
```

```
X = tf.placeholder("float", [None, 4])
Y = tf.placeholder("float", [None, 3])
```

Here, we set up our layer architecture with one hidden layer:

```
w_h = init_weights([4, 4])
w_o = init_weights([4, 3])
py_x = model(X, w_h, w_o)
```

```
cost = tf.reduce_mean(tf.nn.softmax_cross_entropy_with_logits(py_x,
Y)) # compute costs
train_op = tf.train.GradientDescentOptimizer(learning_rate=0.01).
minimize(cost) # construct an optimizer

predict_op = tf.argmax(py_x, 1)

sess = tf.Session()
init = tf.initialize_all_variables()
sess.run(init)
```

```
for i in range(500):
    for start, end in zip(range(0, len(X_train),1 ), range(1, len(X_
train),1)):
```

```
        sess.run(train_op, feed_dict={X: X_train[start:end], Y: y_
train[start:end]})
    if i % 100 == 0:
        print i, np.mean(np.argmax(y_test, axis=1) ==
                    sess.run(predict_op, feed_dict={X: x_test, Y: y_
test}))
```

```
OUTPUT:]
0 0.288888888889
100 0.666666666667
200 0.933333333333
300 0.977777777778
400 0.977777777778
```

The accuracy of this neural network is around .977% but can yield slightly different results across runs. It is more or less the benchmark for a neural network with a single hidden layer and vanilla SGD.

Like we saw in the previous examples, it is quite intuitive to implement an optimization method and set up the tensors. It is a lot more intuitive than when we do the same in NumPy. (See *Chapter 4, Neural Networks and Deep Learning.*) The downside at this moment is that evaluation and prediction requires a sometimes tedious for loop, whereas packages such as Scikit-learn can provide these methods with a simple line of script. Luckily, there are higher-level packages developed on top of TensorFlow that make training and evaluation a lot easier. One of those packages is SkFlow; as the name implies, it is a wrapper based on a scripting style that works just like Scikit-learn.

Machine learning on TensorFlow with SkFlow

Now that we have seen the basic operations of TensorFlow, let's dive into the higher-level applications built on top of TensorFlow to make machine learning a little more practical. SkFlow is the first application that we will cover. In SkFlow, we don't have to specify types and placeholders. We can load and manage data in the same way that we would do with Scikit-learn and NumPy. Let's install the package with pip.

The safest way is to install the package from GitHub directly:

```
$ pip install git+git://github.com/tensorflow/skflow.git
```

SkFlow has three main classes of learning algorithms: linear classifiers, linear regression, and neural networks. A linear classifier is basically a simple SGD (multi) classifier, and neural networks is where SkFlow excels. It provides relatively easy-to-use wrappers for very deep neural networks, recurrent networks, and Convolutional Neural Networks. Unfortunately, other algorithms such as Random Forest, gradient boosting, SVM, and Naïve Bayes are not yet implemented. However, there were discussions on GitHub about implementing a Random Forest algorithm in SkFlow that will probably be named tf_forest, which is an exciting development.

Let's apply our first multiclass classification algorithm in SkFlow. For this example, we will use the wine dataset—a dataset originally from the UCI machine learning repository. It consists of 13 features of continuous chemical metrics such as Magnesium, Alcohol, Malic acid, and so on. It's a light dataset with only 178 instances and a target feature with three classes. The target variable consists of three different cultivars. Wines are classified according to their respective cultivar (type of grapes used for the wine) using the chemical analysis of the thirteen chemical metrics. You can see that we load the data from a URL in the same way that we would do it when we work in a Scikit-learn environment:

```
import numpy as np
from sklearn.metrics import accuracy_score
import skflow
import urllib2
url = 'https://www.csie.ntu.edu.tw/~cjlin/libsvmtools/datasets/
multiclass/wine.scale'
set1 = urllib2.Request(url)
wine = urllib2.urlopen(set1)


from sklearn.datasets import load_svmlight_file
X_train, y_train = load_svmlight_file(wine)
X_train=X_train.toarray()

from sklearn.cross_validation import train_test_split
X_train, X_test, y_train, y_test = train_test_split(X_train,
y_train, test_size=0.30, random_state=4)


classifier = skflow.TensorFlowLinearClassifier(n_classes=4,learning_
rate=0.01, optimizer='SGD',continue_training=True, steps=1000)
classifier.fit(X_train, y_train)
score = accuracy_score(y_train, classifier.predict(X_train))
d=classifier.predict(X_test)
```

```
print("Accuracy: %f" % score)

c=accuracy_score(d,y_test)
print('validation/test accuracy: %f' % c)
```

```
OUTPUT:
Step #1, avg. loss: 1.58672
Step #101, epoch #25, avg. loss: 1.45840
Step #201, epoch #50, avg. loss: 1.09080
Step #301, epoch #75, avg. loss: 0.84564
Step #401, epoch #100, avg. loss: 0.68503
Step #501, epoch #125, avg. loss: 0.57680
Step #601, epoch #150, avg. loss: 0.50120
Step #701, epoch #175, avg. loss: 0.44486
Step #801, epoch #200, avg. loss: 0.40151
Step #901, epoch #225, avg. loss: 0.36760
Accuracy: 0.967742
validation/test accuracy: 0.981481
```

By now, this method will be quite familiar; it is basically the same way a classifier in Scikit-learn would work. However, there are two important things to notice. With SkFlow, we can use NumPy and TensorFlow objects interchangeably so that we don't have to merge and convert objects in and out of tensor frames. This makes working with TensorFlow through a higher-level method like SkFlow much more flexible. The second thing to notice is that we applied the `toarray` method to the main data object. This is because the dataset is quite sparse (lots of zero entries), and TensorFlow is not able to process sparse data well.

Neural networks is where TensorFlow excels and in SkFlow, it is quite easy to train a neural network with multiple layers. Let's perform a neural network on the diabetes dataset. This dataset contains diabetes metrics (binary target) diagnostic features of pregnant females of over 21 years of age and of Pima heritage. The Pima Indians of Arizona have the highest reported prevalence of diabetes of any population in the world and therefore this ethnic group has been a voluntary subject of diabetes research. The dataset consists of the following features:

- Number of times pregnant
- Plasma glucose concentration at two hours in an oral glucose tolerance test
- Diastolic blood pressure (mm Hg)
- Triceps skin fold thickness (mm)
- 2-hour serum insulin (mu U/ml)

- Body mass index (weight in kg/(height in m)^2)
- Diabetes pedigree function
- Age (years)
- Class variable (0 or 1)

In this example, we first load and scale the data:

```
import tensorflow
import tensorflow as tf
import numpy as np
import urllib
import skflow
from sklearn.preprocessing import Normalizer
from sklearn import datasets, metrics, cross_validation
from sklearn.cross_validation import train_test_split
# Pima Indians Diabetes dataset (UCI Machine Learning Repository)
url = "http://archive.ics.uci.edu/ml/machine-learning-databases/pima-
indians-diabetes/pima-indians-diabetes.data"
# download the file
raw_data = urllib.urlopen(url)
dataset = np.loadtxt(raw_data, delimiter=",")
print(dataset.shape)
X = dataset[:,0:7]
y = dataset[:,8]
X_train, X_test, y_train, y_test = train_test_split(X, y,
                                                    test_size=0.2,
                                                    random_state=0)


from sklearn import preprocessing
X= preprocessing.scale(X)
min_max_scaler = preprocessing.MinMaxScaler()
X = min_max_scaler.fit_transform(X)
```

This step is very interesting; for neural networks to converge better, we can use more flexible decay rates. While training multilayer neural networks, it is usually helpful to decrease the learning rate over time. Generally speaking, when we have a too high learning rate, we might overshoot the optimum. On the other hand, when the learning rate is too low, we will waste computational resources and get stuck in local minima. Exponential decay is a method to dampen the learning rate over time so that it becomes more sensitive when it starts to approach a minimum. There are three common ways of implementing the learning rate decay; namely, step decay, 1/t decay, and exponential decay:

Exponential decay: $a = a_0 e^{-kt}$

In this case, *a* is the learning rate, *k* is the hyperparameter, and *t* is the iteration.

In this example, we will use exponential decay because it seemed to have worked very well for this dataset. This is how we implement an exponential decay function (with TensorFlow's built-in `tf.train.exponential_decay` function):

```
def exp_decay(global_step):
    return tf.train.exponential_decay(
        learning_rate=0.01, global_step=global_step,
        decay_steps=steps, decay_rate=0.01)
```

We can now pass the decay function in the TensorFlow neural network model. For this neural network, we will provide a two-layer network, with the first layer consisting of five units and the second layer of four units. By default, SkFlow implements the ReLU activation function as we prefer it over the other ones (tanh, sigmoid, and so on) and so we stick with it.

Following this example, we can also implement optimization algorithms other than stochastic gradient descent. Let's implement an adaptive algorithm called Adam based on an article by Diederik Kingma and Jimmy Ba (http://arxiv.org/abs/1412.6980).

Adam, developed in the University of Amsterdam, stands for adaptive moment estimation. In the previous chapter, we saw how ADAGRAD works—by lowering the gradients over time as they move toward the (hopefully) global minimum. Adam also uses adaptive methods, but in combination with the idea of momentum training where previous gradient updates are taken into account:

```
steps = 5000
classifier = skflow.TensorFlowDNNClassifier(
    hidden_units=[5,4],
    n_classes=2,
    batch_size=300,
    steps=steps,
    optimizer='Adam',#SGD   #RMSProp
    learning_rate=exp_decay #here is the decay function
    )
classifier.fit(X_train,y_train)
score1a = metrics.accuracy_score(y_train, classifier.predict(X_train))
print("Accuracy: %f" % score1a)
score1b = metrics.accuracy_score(y_test, classifier.predict(X_test))
print("Validation Accuracy: %f" % score1b)

OUTPUT
(768, 9)
```

```
Step #1, avg. loss: 12.83679
Step #501, epoch #167, avg. loss: 0.69306
Step #1001, epoch #333, avg. loss: 0.56356
Step #1501, epoch #500, avg. loss: 0.54453
Step #2001, epoch #667, avg. loss: 0.54554
Step #2501, epoch #833, avg. loss: 0.53300
Step #3001, epoch #1000, avg. loss: 0.53266
Step #3501, epoch #1167, avg. loss: 0.52815
Step #4001, epoch #1333, avg. loss: 0.52639
Step #4501, epoch #1500, avg. loss: 0.52721
Accuracy: 0.754072
Validation Accuracy: 0.740260
```

The accuracy is not so convincing; we might improve the accuracy by applying **Principal Component Analysis (PCA)** to the input. In this article by Stavros J Perantonis and Vassilis Virvilis from 1999 (http://rexa.info/paper/dc4f2babc5ca4534b435280aec32f5816ddb53b0), it has been proposed that this diabetes dataset benefits well from a PCA dimension reduction before passing in the neural network. We will use the Scikit-learn pipeline method for this dataset:

```
from sklearn.decomposition import PCA
from sklearn import linear_model, decomposition, datasets
from sklearn.pipeline import Pipeline
from sklearn.metrics import accuracy_score

pca = PCA(n_components=4,whiten=True)

lr = pca.fit(X)
classifier = skflow.TensorFlowDNNClassifier(
    hidden_units=[5,4],
    n_classes=2,
    batch_size=300,
    steps=steps,
    optimizer='Adam',#SGD  #RMSProp
    learning_rate=exp_decay
    )


pipe = Pipeline(steps=[('pca', pca), ('NNET', classifier)])

X_train, X_test, Y_train, Y_test = train_test_split(X, y,
                                        test_size=0.2,
```

```
                                                    random_state=0)
pipe.fit(X_train, Y_train)


score2 = metrics.accuracy_score(Y_test, pipe.predict(X_test))
print("Accuracy Validation, with pca: %f" % score2)


OUTPUT:
Step #1, avg. loss: 1.07512
Step #501, epoch #167, avg. loss: 0.54236
Step #1001, epoch #333, avg. loss: 0.50186
Step #1501, epoch #500, avg. loss: 0.49243
Step #2001, epoch #667, avg. loss: 0.48541
Step #2501, epoch #833, avg. loss: 0.46982
Step #3001, epoch #1000, avg. loss: 0.47928
Step #3501, epoch #1167, avg. loss: 0.47598
Step #4001, epoch #1333, avg. loss: 0.47464
Step #4501, epoch #1500, avg. loss: 0.47712
Accuracy Validation, with pca: 0.805195
```

We have been able to improve the performance of the neural network quite a bit with that simple PCA preprocessing step. We went from seven features to a reduction of four dimensions, thus four features. PCA generally smoothens the signal by zero-centering the features, reducing the feature space using only the vectors containing the highest *eigenvalue*. **Whitening** makes sure that the features are transformed into zero-correlated ones. This results in a smoother signal and smaller feature set enabling the neural network to converge faster. See the *Chapter 7, Unsupervised Learning at Scale* for a more detailed explanation of PCA.

Deep learning with large files – incremental learning

Until now, we have dealt with some TensorFlow operations and machine learning techniques on SkFlow on relatively small datasets. However, this book is about large scale and scalable machine learning; what has the TensorFlow framework to offer us in that regard?

Until recently, parallel computation was in its infancy and not stable enough to be covered in this book. Multi-GPU computing is not accessible to readers without CUDA-compatible NVIDIA cards. Large scale cloud services (`https://cloud.google.com/products/machine-learning/`) or Amazon EC2 come with a considerable fee. This leaves only one way we can scale our project—by incremental learning.

Generally speaking, any file size exceeding about 25% of the available RAM of a computer will cause memory overload problems. So if you have a 2 GB computer and want to apply machine learning solutions to a 500 MB file, it is time to start thinking about ways to bypass memory consumption.

In order to prevent memory overload, we advise an out-of-core learning method that breaks the data down into smaller chunks to incrementally train and update models. The partial fit methods in Scikit-learn that we covered in *Chapter 2, Scalable Learning in Scikit-learn*, are examples of this.

SkFlow also provides a great incremental learning method for all its machine learning models just like the partial fit method in Scikit-learn. In this section, we are going to use a deep learning classifier incrementally because we think it is the most exciting one.

In this section, we will use two strategies for our scalable and out-of-core deep learning project; namely, incremental learning and random subsampling.

First, we generate some data, then we build a subsample function where we can draw random subsamples from that dataset and incrementally train a deep learning model on these subsets:

```
import numpy as np
import pandas as pd
import skflow
from sklearn.datasets import make_classification
import random
from sklearn.cross_validation import train_test_split
import gc
import tensorflow as tf
from sklearn.metrics import accuracy_score
```

First, we are going to generate some example data and write it to disk:

```
X, y = make_classification(n_samples=5000000,n_features=10, n_
classes=4,n_informative=6,random_state=222,n_clusters_per_class=1)
X_train, X_test, y_train, y_test = train_test_split(X,y, test_
size=0.2, random_state=22)

Big_trainm=pd.DataFrame(X_train,y_train)
Big_testm = pd.DataFrame(X_test,y_test)


Big_trainm.to_csv('lsml-Bigtrainm', sep=',')
Big_testm.to_csv('lsml-Bigtestm', sep=',')
```

Let's free up memory by deleting all the objects that we created.

With `gc.collect` we force Python's garbage collector to empty memory:

```
del(X,y,X_train,y_train,X_test)
gc.collect
```

Here, we create a function that draws random subsamples from disk. Note that we use a sample fraction of ⅓. We could use smaller fractions but we also need to adjust two important things if we do so. First, we need to match the batch size of the deep learning model so that the batch size never exceeds the sample size. Second, we need to adjust our amount of epochs in our `for` loop in such a way that we make sure that the largest portion of the training data is used to train the model:

```
import pandas as pd
import random
def sample_file():
    global skip_idx
    global train_data
    global X_train
    global y_train
    big_train='lsml-Bigtrainm'
```

Count the number of rows in the entire set:

```
num_lines = sum(1 for i in open(big_train))
```

We use one-third fraction of the training set:

```
size = int(num_lines / 3)
```

Skip indexes and keep indices:

```
skip_idx = random.sample(range(1, num_lines), num_lines - size)
train_data = pd.read_csv(big_train, skiprows=skip_idx)
X_train=train_data.drop(train_data.columns[[0]], axis=1)
y_train = train_data.ix[:,0]
```

We saw weight decay in a previous section; we will use it again here:

```
def exp_decay(global_step):
    return tf.train.exponential_decay(
        learning_rate=0.01, global_step=global_step,
        decay_steps=steps, decay_rate=0.01)
```

Here, we set up our neural network DNN classifier with three hidden layers with 5, 4, and 4 units respectively. Note that we set the batch size to 300, which means that we use 300 training cases in each epoch. This also helps prevent memory from overloading:

```
steps = 5000
clf = skflow.TensorFlowDNNClassifier(
    hidden_units=[5,4,4],
    n_classes=4,
    batch_size=300,
    steps=steps,
    optimizer='Adam',
    learning_rate=exp_decay
     )
```

Here, we set our amount of subsamples to three (epochs=3). This means that we incrementally train our deep learning model on three consecutive subsamples:

```
epochs=3
for i in range(epochs):
    sample_file()
    clf.partial_fit(X_train,y_train)


test_data = pd.read_csv('lsml-Bigtestm',sep=',')
X_test=test_data.drop(test_data.columns[[0]], axis=1)
y_test = test_data.ix[:,0]
score = accuracy_score(y_test, clf.predict(X_test))
print score

OUTPUT

Step #501, avg. loss: 0.55220
```

```
Step #1001, avg. loss: 0.31165
Step #1501, avg. loss: 0.27033
Step #2001, avg. loss: 0.25250
Step #2501, avg. loss: 0.24156
Step #3001, avg. loss: 0.23438
Step #3501, avg. loss: 0.23113
Step #4001, avg. loss: 0.23335
Step #4501, epoch #1, avg. loss: 0.23303
Step #1, avg. loss: 2.57968
Step #501, avg. loss: 0.57755
Step #1001, avg. loss: 0.33215
Step #1501, avg. loss: 0.27509
Step #2001, avg. loss: 0.26172
Step #2501, avg. loss: 0.24883
Step #3001, avg. loss: 0.24343
Step #3501, avg. loss: 0.24265
Step #4001, avg. loss: 0.23686
Step #4501, epoch #1, avg. loss: 0.23681
0.929022
```

We managed to get an accuracy of .929 on the test set within a very manageable training time and without overloading our memory, considerably faster than if we would have trained the same model on the entire dataset at once.

Keras and TensorFlow installation

Previously, we have seen practical examples of the SkFlow wrapper for TensorFlow applications. For a more sophisticated approach to neural networks and deep learning where we have more control over parameters, we propose Keras (http://keras.io/). This package was originally developed within the Theano framework, but recently is also adapted to TensorFlow. This way, we can use Keras as a higher abstract package on top of TensorFlow. Keep in mind though that Keras is slightly less straightforward than SkFlow in its methods. Keras can run on both GPU and CPU, which makes this package really flexible when porting it to different environments.

Let's first install Keras and make sure that it utilizes the TensorFlow backend.

Installation works simply using pip in the command line:

```
$pip install Keras
```

Keras is originally built on top of Theano, so we need to specify Keras to utilize TensorFlow instead. In order to do this, we first need to run Keras once on its default platform, Theano.

First, we need to run some Keras code to make sure that all the library items are properly installed. Let's train a basic neural network and get introduced to some key concepts.

Out of convenience, we will make use of generated data with Scikit-learn consisting of four features and a target variable consisting of three classes. These dimensions are very important because we need them to specify the architecture of the neural network:

```
import numpy as np
import keras
from sklearn.datasets import make_classification
from sklearn.cross_validation import train_test_split
from sklearn.preprocessing import OneHotEncoder
from keras.utils import np_utils, generic_utils
from keras.models import Sequential
from keras.layers import Dense, Dropout, Activation
from keras.optimizers import SGD

nb_classes=3
X, y = make_classification(n_samples=1000, n_features=4, n_classes=nb_
classes,n_informative=3, n_redundant=0, random_state=101)
```

Now that we have specified the variables, it is important to convert the target variable to a one-hot encoding array (just like we did in TensorFlow). Otherwise, Keras won't be able to compute the one versus all target outputs. For Keras, we want to use np_utils instead of sklearn's one-hot encoder. This is how we will use it:

```
y=np_utils.to_categorical(y,nb_classes)
print y
```

Our array of y will look like this:

```
OUTPUT]
array([[ 1.,    0.,    0.],
       [ 0.,    0.,    1.],
       [ 0.,    0.,    1.],
       ...,
```

Now let's split the data into test and train:

```
x_train, x_test, y_train, y_test = train_test_split(X, y,test_
size=0.30, random_state=222)
```

This is where we start to give form to the neural network architecture that we have in mind. Let's start a two-hidden layer neural network with `relu` activation and three units in each hidden layer. Our first layer has four inputs because we have four features in this case. After that, we add the hidden layers with three units, hence (`model.add(dense(3)`).

Like we have seen before, we will use a `softmax` function to pass the network to the output layer:

```
model = Sequential()
model.add(Dense(4, input_shape=(4,)))
model.add(Activation('relu'))
model.add(Dense(3))
model.add(Activation('relu'))
model.add(Dense(3))
model.add(Activation('softmax'))
```

First, we specify our SGD function, where we implement the most important parameters that are familiar to us by now, namely:

- **lr**: The learning rate.
- **decay**: The decay function to decay the learning rate. Do not confuse this with weight decay, which is a regularization parameter.
- **momentum**: We use this to prevent from getting stuck in local minima.
- **nesterov**: This is a Boolean that specifies whether we want to use nesterov momentum and is only applicable if we have specified an integer for the momentum parameter. (Refer to *Chapter 4, Neural Networks and Deep Learning*, for a more detailed explanation.)
- **optimizer**: Here, we will specify our optimization algorithm of choice (consisting of SGD, RMSProp, ADAGRAD, Adadelta, and Adam).

Let us see the following code snippet:

```
#We use this for reproducibility
seed = 22
np.random.seed(seed)

model = Sequential()
model.add(Dense(4, input_shape=(4,)))
model.add(Activation('relu'))
model.add(Dense(3))
model.add(Activation('relu'))
model.add(Dense(3))
```

```
model.add(Activation('softmax'))

sgd = SGD(lr=0.01, decay=1e-6, momentum=0.9, nesterov=True)
model.compile(loss='categorical_crossentropy', optimizer=sgd)
model.fit(x_train, y_train, verbose=1, batch_size=100, nb_
epoch=50,show_accuracy=True,validation_data=(x_test, y_test))
time.sleep(0.1)
```

In this case, we have used `batch_size` of `100`, which means that we have used minibatch gradient descent with 100 training examples in each epoch. In this model, we have used `50` training epochs. This will give you the following output:

```
OUTPUT:

acc: 0.8129 - val_loss: 0.5391 - val_acc: 0.8000
Train on 700 samples, validate on 300 samples
```

In the last model where we used SGD with nesterov, we couldn't improve our score no matter how many epochs we used for its training.

In order to increase accuracy. it is advisable to try out other optimization algorithms. We have already used the Adam optimization method successfully before, so let's use it again here and see if we can increase the accuracy. As adaptive learning rates such as Adam, lower the learning rate over time, it requires more epochs to arrive at an optimum solution. Therefore, in this example, we will set the amount of epochs to 200:

```
adam=keras.optimizers.Adam(lr=0.01)
model.compile(loss='categorical_crossentropy', optimizer=adam)
model.fit(x_train, y_train, verbose=1, batch_size=100, nb_
epoch=200,show_accuracy=True,validation_data=(x_test, y_test))
time.sleep(0.1)
```

```
OUTPUT:
Epoch 200/200
700/700 [==============================] - 0s - loss: 0.3755 - acc:
0.8657 - val_loss: 0.4725 - val_acc: 0.8200
```

We now have managed to achieve a convincing improvement from 0.8 to 0.82 with the Adam optimization algorithm.

For now, we have covered the most important elements of neural networks in Keras. Let's now proceed setting up Keras so that it will utilize the TensorFlow framework. By default, Keras will use the Theano backend. In order to instruct Keras to work on TensorFlow, we need to first locate the Keras folder in the packages folder:

```
import os
print keras.__file__
```

Your path might look different:

```
Output: /Library/Python/2.7/site-packages/keras/__init__.pyc
```

Now that we have located the package folder of Keras, we need to look for the `~/.keras/keras.json` file.

There is a piece of script in this file that looks like this:

```
{"epsilon": 1e-07, "floatx": "float32", "backend": "theano"}
```

You simply need to change `"backend":"theano"` to `"backend":"tensorflow"`, resulting in the following:

```
{"epsilon": 1e-07, "floatx": "float32", "backend": "tensorflow"}
```

If, for some reason, the `.json` file is not present in the Keras folder, that is, `/Library/Python/2.7/site-packages/keras/`, you can just copy paste this to a text editor:

```
{"epsilon": 1e-07, "floatx": "float32", "backend": "tensorflow"}
```

Save it as a `.json` file and put it in the `keras` folder.

To test if the TensorFlow environment is properly utilized from within TensorFlow, we can type the following:

```
from keras import backend as K
input = K.placeholder(shape=(4, 4, 5))
# also works:
input = K.placeholder(shape=(None, 2, 5))
# also works:
input = K.placeholder(ndim=2)

OUTPUT:

Using Theano backend.
```

Some users might get no output at all, which is fine. Your TensorFlow backend should be ready to use.

Convolutional Neural Networks in TensorFlow through Keras

Between this and the previous chapter, we have come quite a long way covering the most important topics in deep learning. We now understand how to construct architectures by stacking multiple layers in a neural network and how to discern and utilize backpropagation methods. We also covered the concept of unsupervised pretraining with stacked and denoising autoencoders. The next and really exciting step in deep learning is the rapidly evolving field of **Convolutional Neural Networks (CNN)**, a method of building multilayered, locally connected networks. CNNs, commonly referred to as **ConvNets**, are so rapidly evolving at the time of writing this book that we literally had to rewrite and update this chapter within a month's timeframe. In this chapter, we will cover the most fundamental and important concepts behind CNNs so that we will be able to run some basic examples without becoming overwhelmed by the sometimes enormous complexity. However, we won't be able to do justice fully to the enormous theoretical and computational background so this paragraph provides a practical starting point.

The best way to understand CNNs conceptually is to go back in history, start with a little bit of cognitive neuroscience, and look at Huber and Wiesel's research on the visual cortex of cats. Huber and Wiesel recorded neuro-activations of the visual cortex in cats while measuring neural activity by inserting microelectrodes in the visual cortex of the brain. (Poor cats!) They did this while the cats were watching primitive images of shapes projected on a screen. Interestingly, they found that certain neurons responded only to contours of specific orientation or shape. This led to the theory that the visual cortex is composed of local and orientation-specific neurons. This means that specific neurons respond only to images of specific orientation and shape (triangles, circles, or squares). Considering that cats and other mammals can perceive complex and evolving shapes into a coherent whole, we can assume that perception is an aggregate of all these locally and hierarchically organized neurons. By that time, the first multilayer perceptrons were already fully developed so it didn't take too long before this idea of locality and specific sensitivity in neurons was modeled in perceptron architectures. From a computational neuroscience perspective, this idea was developed into maps of local receptive regions in the brain with the addition of selectively connected layers. This was adopted by the already ongoing field of neural networks and artificial intelligence. The first *reported* scientist who applied this notion of local specific computationally to a multilayer perceptron was Fukushima with his so-called neocognitron (1982).

Yann LeCun developed the idea of the neocognitron into his version called LeNet. It added the gradient descent backpropagation algorithm. This LeNet architecture is still the foundation for many more evolved CNN architectures introduced recently. A basic CNN like LeNet learns to detect edges from raw pixels in the first layer, then use these edges to detect simple shapes in the second layer, and later in the process uses these shapes to detect higher-level features, such as objects in an environment in higher layers. The layer further down the neural sequence is then a final classifier that uses these higher-level features. We can see the feedforward pass in a CNN like this: we move from a matrix input to pixels, we detect edges from pixels, then shapes from edges, and detect increasingly distinctive and more abstract and complex features from shapes.

Each convolution or layer in the network is receptive for a specific feature (such as shape, angle, or color).

Deeper layers will combine these features into a more complex aggregate. This way, it can process complete images without burdening the network with the full input space of the image at step.

Up until now, we have only worked with fully connected neural networks where each layer is connected to each neighboring layer. These networks have proven to be quite effective, but have the downside of dramatically increasing the number of parameters that we have to train. On a side note, we might imagine that when we train a small image (28 x 28) in size, we can get away with a fully connected network. However, training a fully connected network on larger images that span across the entire image would be tremendously computationally expansive.

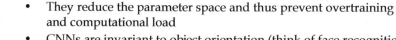

To summarize, we can state that CNNs have the following benefits over fully connected neural networks:

- They reduce the parameter space and thus prevent overtraining and computational load
- CNNs are invariant to object orientation (think of face recognition classifying faces with different locations)
- CNNs capable of learning and generalizing complex multidimensional features
- CNNs can be usefull in speech recogntion, image classification, and lately complex recommendation engines

CNNs utilize so-called receptive fields to connect the input to a feature map. The best way to understand CNNs is to dive deeper into the architecture, and of course get hands-on experience. So let's run through the types of layers that make up CNNs. The architecture of a CNN consists of three types of layers; namely, convolutional layer, pooling layer, and a fully-connected layer, where each layer accepts an input 3D volume (h, w, d) and transforms it into a 3D output through a differentiable function.

The convolution layer

We can understand the concept of convolution by imagining a spotlight of a certain size sliding over the input (pixel-values and RGB color dimensions), conveniently after which we compute a dot product between the filtered values (also referred to as patches) and the true input. This does two important things: first, it compresses the input, and more importantly, second, the network learns filters that only activate when they see some specific type of feature spatial position in the input.

Look at the following image to see how this works:

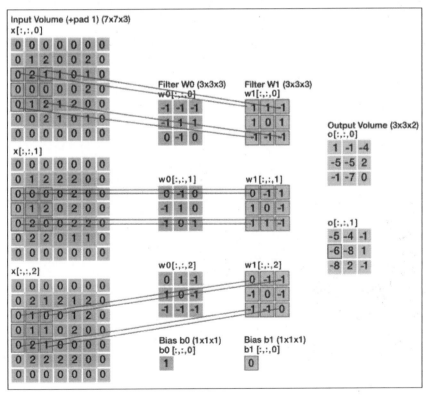

Two convolutional layers processing image input
[7x7x3] input volume: an image of width 7, height 7, and with three color channels R,G,B

We can see from this image that we have two levels of filters (W0 and W1) and three dimensions (in the form of arrays) of inputs, all resulting in the dot product of the sliding spotlight/window over the input matrix. We refer to the size of this spotlight as *stride*, which means that the larger the stride, the smaller the output.

As you can see, when we apply a 3 x 3 filter, the full scope of the filter is processed at the center of the matrix, but once we move close to or past the edges, we start to lose out on the edges of the input. In this case, we apply what is called *zero-padding*. All elements that fall outside of the input dimensions are set to zero in this case. Zero-padding became more or less a default setting for most CNN applications recently.

The pooling layer

The next type of layer that is often placed in between the filter layers is called a pooling layer or *subsampling* layer. What this does is it performs a downsampling operation along the spatial dimensions (width, height), which in turn helps with overfitting and reducing computational load. There are several ways to perform this downsampling, but recently Max Pooling turned out to be the most effective method.

Max-pooling is a simple method that compresses features by taking the maximum value of a patch of the neighboring feature. The following image will clarify this idea; each color box within the matrix represents a subsample of stride size 2:

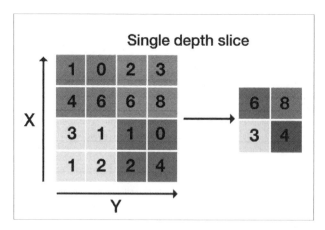

A max-pooling layer with a stride of 2

The pooling layers are used mainly for the following reasons:

- Reduce the amount of parameters and thus computational load
- Regularization

Interestingly, the latest research findings suggest to leave out the pooling layer altogether, which will result in better accuracy (although at the expense of more strain on the CPU or GPU).

The fully connected layer

There is not much to explain about this type of layer. The final output where the classifications are computed (mostly with softmax) is a fully connected layer. However, in between convolutional layers, there (although rarely) are fully connected layers as well.

Before we apply a CNN ourselves, let's take what you have learned so far and inspect a CNN architecture to check our understanding. When we look at the ConvNet architecture in the following image, we can already get a sense of what a ConvNet will do to the input. The example is an effective convolutional neural network called AlexNet aimed at classifying 1.2 million images into 1,000 classes. It was used for the ImageNet contest in 2012. ImageNet is the most important image classification and localization competition in the world, which is held each year. AlexNet refers to Alex Krizhevsky (together with Vinod Nair and Geoffrey Hinton).

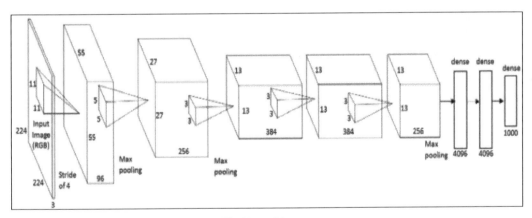

AlexNet architecture

When we look at the architecture, we can immediately see the input dimension 224 by 224 with three-dimensional depth. The stride size of four in the input, where max pooling layers are stacked, reduces the dimensionality of the input. In turn, this is followed by the convolutional layer. The two dense layers of size 4,096 are the fully connected layers leading to the final output that we mentioned before.

On a side note, we mentioned in a previous paragraph that TensorFlow's graph computation allows parallelization across GPUs. AlexNet did the same thing; look at the following image to see how they parallelized the architecture across GPUs:

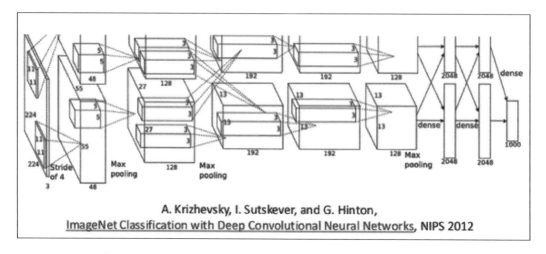

A. Krizhevsky, I. Sutskever, and G. Hinton,
ImageNet Classification with Deep Convolutional Neural Networks, NIPS 2012

The preceding image is taken from http://www.cs.toronto.edu/~fritz/absps/imagenet.pdf.

AlexNet let different models utilize GPUs by splitting up the architecture vertically to later be merged into the final classification output. That CNNs are more suitable for distributed processing is one of the biggest advantages of locally connected networks over fully connected ones. This model trained a set of 1.2 million images and took five days to complete on two NVIDIA GTX 580 3GB GPUs. Two multiple GPU units (a total of six GPUs) were used for this project.

CNN's with an incremental approach

Now that we have a decent understanding of the architectures of CNNs, let's get our hands dirty in Keras and apply a CNN.

For this example, we will use the famous CIFAR-10 face image dataset, which is conveniently available within the Keras domain. The dataset consists of 60,000, 32 x 32 color images with 10 target classes consisting of an airplane, automobile, bird, cat, deer, dog, frog, horse, ship, and truck. This is a smaller dataset than the one that was used for the AlexNet example. For more information, you can refer to https://www.cs.toronto.edu/~kriz/cifar.html.

In this CNN, we will use the following architecture to classify the image according to the 10 classes that we specified:

```
input->convolution 1 (32,3,3)->convolution 2(32,3,3)->pooling-
>dropout -> Output (Fully connected layer and softmax)
```

GPU Computing

If you have a CUDA compatible graphics card installed, you can utilize your GPU for this CNN example by placing the following piece of code on top of your IDE:

```
import os
os.environ['THEANO_FLAGS'] = 'device=gpu0, assert_no_cpu_op=raise, on_
unused_input=ignore, floatX=float32'
```

We do recommend however to first try this example on your regular CPU.

Let's first import and prepare the data.

We use a 32 x 32 input size considering this is the actual size of the image:

```
from keras.datasets import cifar10
from keras.preprocessing.image import ImageDataGenerator
from keras.models import Sequential
from keras.layers.core import Dense, Dropout, Activation, Flatten
from keras.layers.convolutional import Convolution2D, MaxPooling2D
from keras.optimizers import SGD
from keras.utils import np_utils

batch_size = 32
nb_classes = 10
nb_epoch = 5 #these are the number of epochs, watch out because it
might set your #cpu/gpu on fire.


# input image dimensions
img_rows, img_cols = 32, 32
# the CIFAR10 images are RGB
img_channels = 3

# the data, shuffled and split between train and test sets
(X_train, y_train), (X_test, y_test) = cifar10.load_data()
print('X_train shape:', X_train.shape)
print(X_train.shape[0], 'train samples')
```

```
print(X_test.shape[0], 'test samples')

#remember we need to encode the target variable
Y_train = np_utils.to_categorical(y_train, nb_classes)
Y_test = np_utils.to_categorical(y_test, nb_classes)
```

Now let's setup our CNN architecture and construct the model according to the architecture we have in mind.

For this example, we will train our CNN model with vanilla SGD and Nesterov momentum:

```
model = Sequential()

#this is the first convolutional layer, we set the filter size
model.add(Convolution2D(32, 3, 3, border_mode='same',
                        input_shape=(img_channels, img_rows, img_
cols)))
model.add(Activation('relu'))
#the second convolutional layer
model.add(Convolution2D(32, 3, 3))
model.add(Activation('relu'))
#here we specify the pooling layer
model.add(MaxPooling2D(pool_size=(2, 2)))
model.add(Dropout(0.25))


#first we flatten the input towards the fully connected layer into the
softmax function
model.add(Flatten())
model.add(Dense(512))
model.add(Activation('relu'))
model.add(Dropout(0.2))
model.add(Dense(nb_classes))
model.add(Activation('softmax'))

# let's train the model using SGD + momentum like we have done before.
sgd = SGD(lr=0.01, decay=1e-6, momentum=0.9, nesterov=True)
model.compile(loss='categorical_crossentropy', optimizer=sgd)

X_train = X_train.astype('float32')
X_test = X_test.astype('float32')

#Here we apply scaling to the features
X_train /= 255
X_test /= 255
```

This step is very important because here we specify the CNN to train incrementally. We saw in previous chapters (refer to *Chapter 2, Scalable Learning in Scikit-learn*), and in a previous paragraph, the computational efficiency of online and incremental learning. We can mimic some of its properties and apply it to CNNs by using a very small epoch size with a smaller batch_size (fraction of the training set in each epoch), and train them incrementally in a for loop. This way, we can given the same amount of epochs and train our CNN in a much shorter time with also a lower burden on main memory. We can implement this very powerful idea with a simple for loop as follows:

```
for epoch in xrange(nb_epoch):
    model.fit(X_train, Y_train, batch_size=batch_size, nb_
epoch=1,show_accuracy=True
            ,validation_data=(X_test, Y_test), shuffle=True)


OUTPUT:]


X_train shape: (50000, 3, 32, 32)
50000 train samples
10000 test samples
Train on 50000 samples, validate on 10000 samples
Epoch 1/1
50000/50000 [==============================] - 1480s - loss: 1.4464 -
acc: 0.4803 - val_loss: 1.1774 - val_acc: 0.5785
Train on 50000 samples, validate on 10000 samples
Epoch 1/1
50000/50000 [==============================] - 1475s - loss: 1.0701 -
acc: 0.6212 - val_loss: 0.9959 - val_acc: 0.6525
Train on 50000 samples, validate on 10000 samples
Epoch 1/1
50000/50000 [==============================] - 1502s - loss: 0.8841 -
acc: 0.6883 - val_loss: 0.9395 - val_acc: 0.6750
Train on 50000 samples, validate on 10000 samples
Epoch 1/1
50000/50000 [==============================] - 1555s - loss: 0.7308 -
acc: 0.7447 - val_loss: 0.9138 - val_acc: 0.6920
Train on 50000 samples, validate on 10000 samples
Epoch 1/1
50000/50000 [==============================] - 1587s - loss: 0.5972 -
acc: 0.7925 - val_loss: 0.9351 - val_acc: 0.6820
```

We can see our CNN train to finally arrive at a validation accuracy approaching 0.7. Considering we have trained a complex model on a high-dimensional dataset with 50,000 training examples and 10 target classes, this is already satisfying. The maximum possible score that can be achieved with a CNN on this dataset requires at least 200 epochs. The method proposed in this example is by no means final. This is quite a basic implementation to get you started with CNNs. Feel free to experiment by adding or removing layers, adjusting the batch size, and so on. Play with the parameters to get a feel of how this works.

If you want to learn more about the latest developments in convolutional layers, take a look at **residual network (ResNet)**, which is one of the latest improvements on CNN architectures.

Kaiming He and others were the winners of ImageNet 2015 (ILSVRC). It features an interesting architecture that uses a method called batch normalization, a method that normalizes the feature transformation between layers. There is a batch normalization function in Keras that you might want to experiment with (`http://keras.io/layers/normalization/`).

To give you an overview of the latest generation of ConvNets, you might want to familiarize yourself with the following parameter settings for CNNs that have been found to be more effective:

- Small stride
- Weight decay (regularization instead of dropout)
- No dropout
- Batch normalization between mid-level layers
- Less to no pre-training (Autoencoders and Boltzman machines slowly fall out of fashion for image classification)

Another interesting notion is that recently convolutional networks are used for applications besides image detection. They are used for language and text classification, sentence completion, and even recommendation systems. An interesting example is Spotify's music recommendation engine, which is based on Convolutional Neural Networks. You can take a look here for further information:

- `http://benanne.github.io/2014/08/05/spotify-cnns.html`
- `http://machinelearning.wustl.edu/mlpapers/paper_files/NIPS2013_5004.pdf`

Currently, convolutional networks are used for the following actions:

- Face detection (Facebook)
- Film classification (YouTube)
- Speech and text
- Generative art (Google DeepDream, for instance)
- Recommendation engines (music recommendation — Spotify)

Summary

In this chapter, we have come quite a long way covering the TensorFlow landscape and its corresponding methods. We got acquainted with how to set up basic regressors, classifiers, and single-hidden layer neural networks. Even though the programming TensorFlow operations are relatively straightforward, for off-the-shelf machine learning tasks, TensorFlow might be a little bit too tedious. This is exactly where SkFlow comes in, a higher-level library with an interface quite similar to Scikit-learn. For incremental or even out-of-core solutions, SkFlow provides a partial fit method, which can easily be set up. Other large scale solutions are either restricted to GPU applications or are at a premature stage. So for now, we have to settle for incremental learning strategies when it comes to scalable solutions.

We also provided an introduction to Convolutional Neural Networks and saw how they can be set up in Keras.

6
Classification and Regression Trees at Scale

In this chapter, we will focus on scalable methods for classification and regression trees. The following topics will be covered:

- Tips and tricks for fast random forest applications in Scikit-learn
- Additive random forest models and subsampling
- GBM gradient boosting
- XGBoost together with streaming methods
- Very fast GBM and random forest in H2O

The aim of a decision tree is to learn a series of decision rules to infer the target labels based on the training data. Using a recursive algorithm, the process starts at the tree root and splits the data on the feature that results in the lowest impurity. Currently, the most widely applicable scalable tree-based applications are based on CART. Introduced by Breiman, Friedman Stone, and Ohlson in 1984, **CART** is an abbreviation of **Classification and Regression Trees**. CART is different from other decision tree models (such as ID3, C4.5/C5.0, CHAID, and MARS) in two ways. First, CART is applicable to both classification and regression problems. Second, it builds binary trees (at each split, resulting in a binary split). This enables CART trees to operate recursively on given features and optimize in a greedy fashion on an error metric in the form of impurity. These binary trees together with scalable solutions are the focus of this chapter.

Let's look closely at how these trees are constructed. We can see a decision tree as a graph with nodes, passing information down from top to bottom. Each decision within the tree is made by binary splits for either classes (Boolean) or continuous variables (a threshold value) resulting in a final prediction.

Trees are constructed and learned by the following procedure:

- Recursively finding the variable that best splits the target label from root to terminal node. This is measured by the impurity of each feature that we minimize based on the target outcome. In this chapter, the relevant impurity measures are Gini impurity and cross entropy.

Gini impurity

$$Gini\left(S\right) = 1 - \sum_{i=1}^{k} p_i^2$$

Gini impurity is a metric that measures the divergence between the probability pi of the target classes (k) so that an equal spread of probability values over the target classes result in a high Gini impurity.

Cross entropy

$$D = -\sum_{k=1}^{k} \hat{p}_{mk} \, log \, \hat{p}_{mk}.$$

With cross entropy, we look at the log probability of misclassification. Both metrics are proven to yield quite similar results. However, Gini impurity is computationally more efficient because it does not require calculating the logs.

We do this until a stopping criterion is met. This criteria can roughly mean two things: one, adding new variables no longer improves the target outcome, and second, a maximum tree depth or tree complexity threshold is reached. Note that very deep and complex trees with many nodes can easily lead to overfitting. In order to prevent this, we generally prune the tree by limiting the tree depth.

To get an intuition for how this process works, let's build a decision tree with Scikit-learn and visualize it with graphviz. First, create a toy dataset to see if we can predict who is a smoker and who is not based on IQ (numeric), age (numeric), annual income (numeric), business owner (Boolean), and university degree (Boolean). You need to download the software from `http://www.graphviz.org` in order to load a visualization of the `tree.dot` file that we are going to create with Scikit-learn:

```
import numpy as np
from sklearn import tree
iq=[90,110,100,140,110,100]
age=[42,20,50,40,70,50]
anincome=[40,20,46,28,100,20]
businessowner=[0,1,0,1,0,0]
univdegree=[0,1,0,1,0,0]
smoking=[1,0,0,1,1,0]
ids=np.column_stack((iq, age, anincome,businessowner,univdegree))
names=['iq','age','income','univdegree']
dt = tree.DecisionTreeClassifier(random_state=99)
dt.fit(ids,smoking)
dt.predict(ids)
tree.export_graphviz(dt,out_file='tree2.dot',feature_
names=names,label=all,max_depth=5,class_names=True)
```

You can now find the `tree.dot` file in your working directory. Once you find this file, you can open it with the graphviz software:

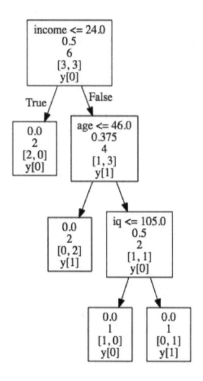

- Root node (Income): This is the starting node that represents the feature with the highest information gain and lowest impurity (Gini=.5)

- Internal nodes (Age and IQ):This is each node between the root node and terminal. Parent nodes pass down decision rules to the receiving end — child nodes (left and right)

- Terminal nodes (leaf nodes): The target labels partitioned by the tree structure

Tree-depth is the number of edges from the root node to the terminal nodes. In this case, we have a tree depth of 3.

We can now see all the binary splits resulting from the generated tree. At the top in the root node, we can see that a person with an income lower than 24k is not a smoker (income < 24). We can also see the corresponding Gini impurity (.5) for that split at each node. There are no left child nodes because the decision is final. The path simply ends there because it fully divides the target class. However, in the right child node (age) of income, the tree branches out. Here, if age is less than or equal to 46, then that person is not a smoker, but with an age older than 46 and an IQ lower than 105, that person is a smoker. Just as important are the few features we created that are not part of the tree—degree and business owner. This is because the variables in the tree are able to classify the target labels without them. These omitted features simply don't contribute to decreasing the impurity level of the tree.

Single trees have their drawbacks because they easily overtrain and therefore don't generalize well to unseen data. The current generation of these techniques are trained with ensemble methods where single trees are aggregated into much more powerful models. These CART ensemble techniques are one of the most used methods for machine learning because of their accuracy, ease of use, and capability to handle heterogeneous data. These techniques have been successfully applied in recent datascience competitions such as Kaggle and KDD-cup. As ensemble methods for classification and regression trees are currently the norm in the world of AI and data science, scalable solutions for CART-ensemble methods will be the main topic for this chapter.

Generally, we can discern two classes of ensemble methods that we use with CART models, namely bagging and boosting. Let's work through these concepts to form a better understanding of how the process of ensemble formation works.

Bootstrap aggregation

Bagging is an abbreviation of **bootstrap aggregation**. The bootstrapping technique originated in a context where analysts had to deal with a scarcity of data. With this statistical approach, subsamples were used to estimate population parameters when a statistical distribution couldn't be figured out a priori. The goal of bootstrapping is to provide a more robust estimate for population parameters where more variability is introduced to a smaller dataset by random subsampling with replacement. Generally, bootstrapping follows the following basic steps:

1. Randomly sample a batch of size x with replacement from a given dataset.

2. Calculate a metric or parameter from each sample to estimate the population parameters.

3. Aggregate the results.

In recent years, bootstrap methods have been used for parameters of machine learning models as well. An ensemble is most effective when its classifiers provide highly diverse decision boundaries. This diversity in ensembles can be achieved in the diversity of its underlying models and data these models are trained on. Trees are very well-suited for such diversity among classifiers because the structure of trees can be highly variable. However, the most popular method to ensemble is to use different training datasets to train individual classifiers. Often, such datasets are obtained through subsampling-sampling techniques, such as bootstrapping and bagging. Everything started from the idea that by leveraging more data, we can reduce the variance of the estimates. If it is not possible to have more data at hand, resampling can provide a significant improvement because it allows retraining the algorithm over many versions of the training sample. This is where the idea of bagging comes in; using bagging, we take the original bootstrap idea a bit further by aggregation (averaging, for instance) of the results of many resamples in order to arrive at a final prediction where the errors due to in-sample overfitting are reciprocally smoothed out.

When we apply an ensemble technique such as bagging to tree models, we build multiple trees on each separate bootstrapped sample (or subsampled using sampling without replacement) of the original dataset and then aggregate the results (usually by arithmetic, geometric averaging, or voting).

In such a fashion, a standard bagging algorithm will look as follows:

1. Draw an n amount of random samples with size K with replacement from the full dataset ($S1, S2, \ldots Sn$).

2. Train distinct trees on ($S1, S2, \ldots Sn$).

3. Calculate predictions on samples ($S1, S2, \ldots Sn$) on new data and aggregate their results.

CART models benefit very well from bagging methods because of the stochasticity and diversity it introduces.

Random forest and extremely randomized forest

Apart from bagging, based on training examples, we can also draw random subsamples based on features. Such a method is referred to as Random Subspaces. Random subspaces are particularly useful for high-dimensional data (data with lots of features) and it is the foundation of the method that we refer to as random forest. At the time of writing this, random forest is the most popular machine learning algorithm because of its ease of use, robustness to messy data, and parallelizability. It found its way into all sorts of applications such as location apps, games, and screening methods for healthcare applications. For instance, the Xbox Kinect uses a random forest model for motion detection purposes. Considering that the random forest algorithm is based on bagging methods, the algorithm is relatively straightforward:

1. Bootstrap m samples of size N from the available sample.
2. Trees are constructed independently on each subset ($S1, S2, \ldots Sn$) using a different fraction of the feature set G (without replacement) at every node split.
3. Minimize the error of the node splits (based on the Gini index or entropy measure).
4. Have each tree make a prediction and aggregate the results, using voting for classification and averaging for regression.

As bagging relies on multiple subsamples, it's an excellent candidate for parallelization where each CPU unit is dedicated to calculating separate models. In this way, we can speed up the learning using the widespread availability of multiple cores. As a limit in such a scaling strategy, we have to be aware that Python is single-threaded and we will have to replicate many Python instances, each replicating the memory space with the in-sample examples we have to employ. Consequently, we will need to have a lot of RAM memory available in order to fit the training matrix and the number of processes. If the available RAM does not suffice, setting the number of parallel tree computations running at once on our computer will not help scaling the algorithm. In this case, CPU usage and RAM memory are important bottlenecks.

Random forests models are quite easy to employ for machine learning because they don't require a lot of hyperparameter tuning to perform well. The most important parameters of interest are the *amount of trees* and depth of the trees (tree depth) that have the most influence on the performance of the model. When operating on these two hyperparameters, it results in an accuracy/performance trade-off where more trees and more depth lead to higher computational load. Our experience as practitioners suggests not to set the value of the *amount of trees* too high because eventually, the model will reach a plateau in performance and won't improve anymore when adding more trees but will just result in taxing the CPU cores. Under such considerations, although a random forest model with default parameters performs well just out of the box, we can still increase its performance by tuning the number of trees. See the following table for an overview of the hyperparameters for random forests.

The most important parameters for bagging with a random forest:

- `n_estimators`: The number of trees in the model
- `max_features`: The number of features used for tree construction
- `min_sample_leaf`: Node split is removed if a terminal node contains less samples than the minimum
- `max_depth`: The number of nodes that we pass top-down from the root to the terminal node
- `criterion`: The method used to calculate the best split (Gini or entropy)
- `min_samples_split`: The minimum number of samples required to split an internal node

Scikit-learn provides a wide range of powerful CART ensemble applications, some of which are quite computationally efficient. When it comes to random forests, there is an often-overlooked algorithm called extra-trees, better known as **Extremely Randomized Forest**. When it comes to CPU efficiency, extra-trees can deliver a considerable speedup from regular random forests—sometimes even in tenfolds.

In the following table, you can see the computation speed for each method. Extra-trees is considerably faster with a more pronounced difference once we increase the sample size:

samplesize	extratrees	randomforest
100000	25.9 s	164 s
50000	9.95 s	35.1 s
10000	2.11 s	6.3 s

Models were trained with 50 features and 100 estimators for both extra trees and random forest. We used a quad-core MacBook Pro with 16GB RAM for this example. We measured the training time in seconds.

In this paragraph, we will use extreme forests instead of the vanilla random forest method in Scikit-learn. So you might ask: how are they different? The difference is not strikingly complex. In random forests, the node split decision rules are based on a best score resulting from the randomly selected features at each iteration. In extremely randomized forests, a random split is generated on each feature in the random subset (so there are no computations spent on looking for the best split for each feature) and then the best scoring threshold is selected. Such an approach brings about some advantageous properties because the method leads to achieving models with lower variance even if each individual tree is grown until having the greatest possible accuracy in terminal nodes. As more randomness is added to branch splits, the tree learner makes errors, which are consequently less correlated among the trees in the ensemble. This will lead to much more uncorrelated estimations in the ensemble and, depending on the learning problem (there is no free lunch, after all), to a lower generalization error than a standard random forest ensemble. In practice, however, a regular random forest model can provide a slightly higher accuracy.

Given such interesting learning properties, with a more efficient node split calculation and the same parallelism that can be leveraged for random forests, we consider extremely randomized trees as an excellent candidate in the range of ensemble tree algorithms, if we want to speed up in-core learning.

To read a detailed description of the extremely randomized forest algorithm, you can read the following article that started everything:

P. Geurts, D. Ernst, and L. Wehenkel, *Extremely randomized trees*, Machine Learning, 63(1), 3-42, 2006. This article can be freely accessed at https://www.semanticscholar.org/paper/Extremely-randomized-trees-Geurts-Ernst/336a165c17c9c56160d332b9f4a2b403fccbdbfb/pdf.

As an example of how to scale in-core tree ensembles, we will run an example where we apply an efficient random forest method to credit data. This dataset is used to predict credit card clients' default rates. The data consists of 18 features and 30,000 training examples. As we need to import a file in XLS format, you will need to install the xlrd package, and we can achieve this by typing the following in the command-line terminal:

```
$ pip install xlrd
import pandas as pd
import numpy as np
import os
```

```
import xlrd
import urllib
#set your path here
os.chdir('/your-path-here')

url = 'http://archive.ics.uci.edu/ml/machine-learning-databases/00350/
default%20of%20credit%20card%20clients.xls'
filename='creditdefault.xls'
urllib.urlretrieve(url, filename)

target = 'default payment next month'
data = pd.read_excel('creditdefault.xls', skiprows=1)

target = 'default payment next month'
y = np.asarray(data[target])
features = data.columns.drop(['ID', target])
X = np.asarray(data[features])

from sklearn.ensemble import ExtraTreesClassifier
from sklearn.cross_validation import cross_val_score
from sklearn.datasets import make_classification
from sklearn.cross_validation import train_test_split

X_train, X_test, y_train, y_test = train_test_split(X, y,test_size=0.30,
random_state=101)

clf = ExtraTreesClassifier(n_estimators=500, random_state=101)
clf.fit(X_train,y_train)
scores = cross_val_score(clf, X_train, y_train, cv=3,scoring='accuracy',
n_jobs=-1)
print "ExtraTreesClassifier -> cross validation accuracy: mean = %0.3f
std = %0.3f" % (np.mean(scores), np.std(scores))

Output]

ExtraTreesClassifier -> cross validation accuracy: mean = 0.812 std =
0.003
```

Now that we have some base estimation of the accuracy on the training set, let's see how well it performs on the test set. In this case, we want to monitor the false positives and false negatives and also check for class imbalances on the target variable:

```
y_pred=clf.predict(X_test)
from sklearn.metrics import confusion_matrix
confusionMatrix = confusion_matrix(y_test, y_pred)
print confusionMatrix
from sklearn.metrics import accuracy_score
accuracy_score(y_test, y_pred)

OUTPUT:
[[6610  448]
 [1238  704]]

Our overall test accuracy:
0.81266666666666665
```

Interestingly, the test set accuracy is equal to our training results. As our baseline model is just using the default setting, we can try to improve performance by tuning the hyperparameters, a task that can be computationally expensive. Recently, more computationally efficient methods have been developed for hyperparameter optimization, which we will cover in the next section.

Fast parameter optimization with randomized search

You might already be familiar with Scikit-learn's gridsearch functionalities. It is a great tool but when it comes to large files, it can ramp up training time enormously depending on the parameter space. For extreme random forests, we can speed up the computation time for parameter tuning using an alternative parameter search method named **randomized search**. Where common gridsearch taxes both CPU and memory by systematically testing all possible combinations of the hyperparameter settings, randomized search selects combinations of hyperparameters at random. This method can lead to a considerable computational speedup when the gridsearch is testing more than 30 combinations (for smaller search spaces, gridsearch is still competitive). The gain achievable is in the same order as we have seen when we switched from random forests to extremely randomized forests (think between a two to tenfold gain, depending on hardware specifications, hyperparameter space, and the size of the dataset).

We can specify the number of hyperparameter settings that are evaluated randomly by the `n_iter` parameter:

```
from sklearn.grid_search import GridSearchCV, RandomizedSearchCV


param_dist = {"max_depth": [1,3, 7,8,12,None],
    "max_features": [8,9,10,11,16,22],
    "min_samples_split": [8,10,11,14,16,19],
    "min_samples_leaf": [1,2,3,4,5,6,7],
    "bootstrap": [True, False]}

#here we specify the search settings, we use only 25 random parameter
#valuations but we manage to keep training times in check.
rsearch = RandomizedSearchCV(clf, param_distributions=param_dist,
    n_iter=25)

rsearch.fit(X_train,y_train)
rsearch.grid_scores_

bestclf=rsearch.best_estimator_
print bestclf
```

Here, we can see the list of optimal parameter settings for our model.

We can now use this model to make predictions on our test set:

```
OUTPUT:
ExtraTreesClassifier(bootstrap=False, class_weight=None,
criterion='gini',
    max_depth=12, max_features=11, max_leaf_nodes=None,
    min_samples_leaf=4, min_samples_split=10,
    min_weight_fraction_leaf=0.0, n_estimators=500, n_jobs=1,
    oob_score=False, random_state=101, verbose=0, warm_start=False)

y_pred=bestclf.predict(X_test)
confusionMatrix = confusion_matrix(y_test, y_pred)
print confusionMatrix
accuracy=accuracy_score(y_test, y_pred)
print accuracy

OUT
[[6733  325]
```

```
[1244   698]]

Out[152]:
0.8256666666666666
```

We managed to increase the performance of our model within a manageable range of training time and increase accuracy at the same time.

Extremely randomized trees and large datasets

So far, we have looked at solutions to scale up leveraging multicore CPUs and randomization thanks to the specific characteristics of random forest and its more efficient alternative, extremely randomized forest. However, if you have to deal with a large dataset that won't fit in memory or is too CPU-demanding, you may want to try an out-of-core solution. The best solution for an out-of-core approach with ensembles is the one provided by H2O, which will be covered in detail later in this chapter. However, we can exert another practical trick in order to have random forest or extra-trees running smoothly on a large-scale dataset. A second-best solution would be to train models on subsamples of the data and then ensemble the results from each model built on different subsamples of the data (after all, we just have to average or group the results). In *Chapter 3*, *Fast-Learning SVMs*, we already introduced the concept of reservoir sampling, dealing with sampling on data streams. In this chapter, we will use sampling again, resorting to a larger choice of sampling algorithms. First, let's install a really handy tool called subsample developed by Paul Butler (https://github.com/paulgb/subsample), a command-line tool to sample data from a large, newline-separated dataset (typically, a CSV-like file). This tool provides quick and easy sampling methods such as reservoir sampling.

As seen in *Chapter 3*, *Fast-Learning SVMs*, reservoir sampling is a sampling algorithm that helps sampling fixed-size samples from a stream. Conceptually simple (we have seen the formulation in Chapter 3), it just needs a simple pass over the data to produce a sample that will be stored in a new file on disk. (Our script in Chapter 3 stored it in memory, instead.)

In the next example, we will use this subsample tool together with a method to ensemble the models trained on these subsamples.

To recap, in this section, we are going to perform the following actions:

1. Create our dataset and split it into test and training data.
2. Draw subsamples of the training data and save them as separate files on our harddrive.
3. Load these subsamples and train extremely randomized forest models on them.
4. Aggregate the models.
5. Check the results.

Let's install this subsample tool with `pip`:

```
$pip install subsample
```

In the command line, set the working directory containing the file that you want to sample:

```
$ cd /yourpath-here
```

At this point, using the `cd` command, you can specify your working directory where you will need to store the file that we will create in the next step.

We do this in the following way:

```
from sklearn.datasets import fetch_covtype
import numpy as np
from sklearn.cross_validation import train_test_split
dataset = fetch_covtype(random_state=111, shuffle=True)
dataset = fetch_covtype()
X, y = dataset.data, dataset.target
X_train, X_test, y_train, y_test = train_test_split(X,y, test_
size=0.3, random_state=0)
del(X,y)
covtrain=np.c_[X_train,y_train]
covtest=np.c_[X_test,y_test]
np.savetxt('covtrain.csv', covtrain, delimiter=",")
np.savetxt('covtest.csv', covtest, delimiter=",")
```

Now that we have split the dataset into test and training sets, let's subsample the training set in order to obtain chunks of data that we can manage to upload in-memory. Considering that the size of the full training dataset is 30,000 examples, we will subsample three smaller datasets, each one made of 10,000 items. If you have a computer equipped with less than 2GB of RAM memory, you may find it more manageable to split the initial training set into smaller files, though the modeling results that you will obtain will likely differ from our example based on three subsamples. As a rule, the fewer the examples in the subsamples, the greater will be the bias of your model. When subsampling, we are actually trading the advantage of working on a more manageable amount of data against an increased bias of the estimates:

```
$ subsample --reservoir -n 10000 covtrain.csv > cov1.csv

$ subsample --reservoir -n 10000 covtrain.csv > cov2.csv

$ subsample --reservoir -n 10000 covtrain.csv>cov3.csv
```

You can now find these subsets in the folder that you specified in the command line.

Now make sure that you set the same path in your IDE or notebook.

Let's load the samples one by one and train a random forest model on them.

To combine them later for a final prediction, note that we keep a single line-by-line approach so that you can follow the consecutive steps closely.

In order for these examples to be successful, make sure that you are working on the same path set in your IDE or Jupyter Notebook:

```
import os
os.chdir('/your-path-here')
```

At this point, we are ready to start learning from the data and we can load the samples in-memory one by one and train an ensemble of trees on them:

```
import numpy as np
from sklearn.ensemble import ExtraTreesClassifier
from sklearn.cross_validation import cross_val_score
from sklearn.cross_validation import train_test_split
import pandas as pd
import os
```

After reporting a validation score, the code will proceed training our model on all the data chunks, one at a time. As we are learning separately from different data partitions, data chunk after data chunk, we initialize the ensemble learner (in this case, `ExtraTreeClassifier`) using the `warm_start=True` parameter and `set_params` method that incrementally adds trees from the previous training sessions as the fit method is called multiple times:

```
#here we load sample 1
df = pd.read_csv('/yourpath/cov1.csv')
y=df[df.columns[54]]
X=df[df.columns[0:54]]
```

```
clf1=ExtraTreesClassifier(n_estimators=100, random_state=101,warm_
start=True)
clf1.fit(X,y)
scores = cross_val_score(clf1, X, y, cv=3,scoring='accuracy', n_jobs=-
1)
print "ExtraTreesClassifier -> cross validation accuracy: mean = %0.3f
std = %0.3f" % (np.mean(scores), np.std(scores))
print scores
print 'amount of trees in the model: %s' % len(clf1.estimators_)


#sample 2
df = pd.read_csv('/yourpath/cov2.csv')
y=df[df.columns[54]]
X=df[df.columns[0:54]]


clf1.set_params(n_estimators=150, random_state=101,warm_start=True)
clf1.fit(X,y)
scores = cross_val_score(clf1, X, y, cv=3,scoring='accuracy', n_jobs=-
1)
print "ExtraTreesClassifier after params -> cross validation accuracy:
mean = %0.3f std = %0.3f" % (np.mean(scores), np.std(scores))
print scores
print 'amount of trees in the model: %s' % len(clf1.estimators_)


#sample 3
df = pd.read_csv('/yourpath/cov3.csv')
y=df[df.columns[54]]
X=df[df.columns[0:54]]
clf1.set_params(n_estimators=200, random_state=101,warm_start=True)
clf1.fit(X,y)
```

```
scores = cross_val_score(clf1, X, y, cv=3,scoring='accuracy', n_jobs=-
1)
print "ExtraTreesClassifier after params -> cross validation accuracy:
mean = %0.3f std = %0.3f" % (np.mean(scores), np.std(scores))
print scores
print 'amount of trees in the model: %s' % len(clf1.estimators_)


# Now let's predict our combined model on the test set and check our
score.

df = pd.read_csv('/yourpath/covtest.csv')
X=df[df.columns[0:54]]
y=df[df.columns[54]]
pred2=clf1.predict(X)
scores = cross_val_score(clf1, X, y, cv=3,scoring='accuracy', n_jobs=-
1)
print "final test score %r" % np.mean(scores)


OUTPUT:]
ExtraTreesClassifier -> cross validation accuracy: mean = 0.803 std =
0.003
[ 0.805997    0.79964007  0.8021021 ]
amount of trees in the model: 100
ExtraTreesClassifier after params -> cross validation accuracy: mean =
0.798 std = 0.003
[ 0.80155875  0.79651861  0.79465626]
amount of trees in the model: 150
ExtraTreesClassifier after params -> cross validation accuracy: mean =
0.798 std = 0.006
[ 0.8005997   0.78974205  0.8033033 ]
amount of trees in the model: 200
final test score 0.92185447181058278
```

 Warning: This method looks un-Pythonic but is quite effective.

We have improved the score on the final prediction now; we went from an accuracy of around .8 to an accuracy of .922 on the test set. This is because we have a final combined model containing all the tree information combined of the previous three random forest models. In the code's output, you can also notice the number of trees that are added to the initial model.

From here, you might want to try such an approach on even larger datasets leveraging more subsamples, or apply randomized search to one of the subsamples for better tuning.

CART and boosting

We started this chapter with bagging; now we will complete our overview with boosting, a different ensemble method. Just like bagging, boosting can be used for both regression and classification and has recently overshadowed random forest for higher accuracy.

As an optimization process, boosting is based on the stochastic gradient descent principle that we have seen in other methods, namely optimizing models by minimizing error according to gradients. The most familiar boosting methods to date are **AdaBoost** and Gradient Boosting (GBM and recently XGBoost). The AdaBoost algorithm comes down to minimizing the error of those cases where the prediction is slightly wrong so that cases that are harder to classify get more attention. Recently, AdaBoost fell out of favor as other boosting methods were found to be generally more accurate.

In this chapter, we will cover the two most effective boosting algorithms available to date to Python users: **Gradient Boosting Machine** (**GBM**) found in the Scikit-learn package and **extreme gradient boosting** (**XGBoost**). As GBM is sequential in nature, the algorithm is hard to parallelize and thus harder to scale than random forest, but some tricks will do the job. Some tips and tricks to speed up the algorithm will be covered with a nice out-of-memory solution for H2O.

Gradient Boosting Machines

As we have seen in the previous sections, random forests and extreme trees are efficient algorithms and both work quite well with minimum effort. Though recognized as a more accurate method, GBM is not very easy to use and it is always necessary to tune its many hyperparameters in order to achieve the best results. Random forest, on the other hand, can perform quite well with only a few parameters to consider (mostly tree depth and number of trees). Another thing to pay attention to is overtraining. Random forests are less sensitive to overtraining than GBM. So, with GBM, we also need to think about regularization strategies. Above all, random forests are much easier to perform parallel operations where as GBM is sequential and thus slower to compute.

In this chapter, we will apply GBM in Scikit-learn, look at the next generation of tree boosting algorithms named XGBoost, and implement boosting on a larger scale on H2O.

The GBM algorithm that we use in Scikit-learn and H2O is based on two important concepts: **additive expansion** and gradient optimization by the **steepest descent** algorithm. The general idea of the former is to generate a sequence of relatively simple trees (weak learners), where each successive tree is added along a gradient. Let's assume that we have M trees that aggregate the final predictions in the ensemble. The tree in each iteration fk is now part of a much broader space of all the possible trees in the model (ϕ) (in Scikit-learn, this parameter is better known as `n_estimators`):

$$\hat{y} = \sum_{m=1}^{M} f_k(x_i), f_k \in \phi$$

The additive expansion will add new trees to previous trees in a stage-wise manner:

$\hat{y}_i^{(0)} = 0$

$\hat{y}_i^{(1)} = f_1(x_i) = \hat{y}_i^{(0)} + f_1(x_i)$ *(this is our first tree)*

$\hat{y}_i^{(2)} = f_1(x_i) + f_2(x_i) = \hat{y}_i^{(1)} + f_2(x_i)$ *(our second tree added to the previous)*

And so on... till stopping criteria is reached

The prediction of our gradient boosting ensemble is simply the sum of the predictions of all the previous trees and the newly added tree $(\hat{y}_i^{(t-1)}) + f_1(x_i)$, more formally leading to the following:

$$\hat{y}_i^{(t)} = \sum_{m=1}^{M} f_k(x_i) = \hat{y}_i^{(t-1)} + f_i(x_i)$$

The second important and yet quite tricky part of the GBM algorithm is gradient optimization by **steepest descent**. This means that we add increasingly more powerful trees to the additive model. This is achieved by applying gradient optimization to the new trees. How do we perform gradient updates with trees as there are no parameters like we have seen with traditional learning algorithms? First, we parameterize the trees; we do this by recursively upgrading the node split values along a gradient where the nodes are represented by a vector. This way, the steepest descent direction is the negative gradient of the loss function and the node splits will be upgraded and learned, leading to:

- λ : A shrinkage parameter (also referred to as learning rate in this context) that will cause the ensemble to learn slowly with the addition of more trees

- γ_{mi} : The gradient upgrade parameter also referred to as the step length

The prediction score for each leaf is thus the final score for the new tree that then simply is the sum over each leaf:

$$\hat{y}_i^{(t)} = \sum_{m=1}^{M} f_k\left(x_i\right) = \hat{y}_i^{(t-1)} + \lambda \gamma_{mi} f_i\left(x_i\right)$$

So to summarize, GBM works by incrementally adding more accurate trees learned along the gradient.

Now that we understand the core concepts, let's run a GBM example and look at the most important parameters. For GBM, these parameters are extra important because when we set this number of trees too high, we are bound to strain our computational resources exponentially. So be careful with these parameters. Most parameters in Scikit-learn's GBM application are the same as in random forest, which we have covered in the previous paragraph. There are three parameters that we need to take into account that need special attention.

max_depth

Contrary to random forests, which perform better when they build their tree structures to their maximum extension (thus building and ensembling predictors with high variance), GBM tends to work better with smaller trees (thus leveraging predictors with a higher bias, that is, weak learners). Working with smaller decision trees or just with stumps (decision trees with only one single branch) can alleviate the training time, trading off the speediness of execution against a larger bias (because a smaller tree can hardly intercept more complex relationships in data).

learning_rate

Also known as shrinkage λ, this is a parameter related to the gradient descent optimization and how each tree will contribute to the ensemble. Smaller values of this parameter can improve the optimization in the training process, though it will require more estimators to converge and thus more computational time. As it affects the weight of each tree in the ensemble, smaller values imply that each tree will contribute a small part to the optimization process and you will need more trees before reaching a good solution. Consequently, when optimizing this parameter for performance, we should avoid too large values that may lead to sub-optimal models; we also have to avoid using too low values because this will affect the computation time heavily (more trees will be needed for the ensemble to converge to a solution). In our experience, a good starting point is to use a learning rate in the range <0.1 and >.001.

Subsample

Let's recall the principles of bagging and pasting, where we take random samples and construct trees on those samples. If we apply subsampling to GBM, we randomize the tree constructions and prevent overfitting, reduce memory load, and even sometimes increase accuracy. We can apply this procedure to GBM as well, making it more stochastic and thus leveraging the advantages of bagging. We can randomize the tree construction in GBM by setting the subsample parameter to .5.

Faster GBM with warm_start

This parameter allows storing new tree information after each iteration is added to the previous one without generating new trees. This way, we can save memory and speed up computation time extensively.

Using the GBM available in Scikit-learn, there are two actions that we can take in order to increase memory and CPU efficiency:

- Warm start for (semi) incremental learning
- We can use parallel processing during cross-validation

Let's run through a GBM classification example where we use the spam dataset from the UCI machine learning library. We will first load the data, preprocess it, and look at the variable importance of each feature:

```
import pandas
import urllib2
import urllib2
from sklearn import ensemble
```

```
columnNames1_url = 'https://archive.ics.uci.edu/ml/machine-learning-
databases/spambase/spambase.names'
columnNames1 = [
    line.strip().split(':')[0]
    for line in urllib2.urlopen(columnNames1_url).readlines()[33:]]

columnNames1
n = 0
for i in columnNames1:
    columnNames1[n] = i.replace('word_freq_','')
    n += 1
print columnNames1

spamdata = pandas.read_csv(
    'https://archive.ics.uci.edu/ml/machine-learning-databases/
spambase/spambase.data',
    header=None, names=(columnNames1 + ['spam'])
)

X = spamdata.values[:,:57]
y=spamdata['spam']

spamdata.head()

import numpy as np
from sklearn import cross_validation
from sklearn.metrics import classification_report
from sklearn.cross_validation import cross_val_score
from sklearn.cross_validation import cross_val_predict
from sklearn.cross_validation import train_test_split
from sklearn.metrics  import recall_score, f1_score
from sklearn.cross_validation import cross_val_predict
import matplotlib.pyplot as plt
from sklearn.metrics import confusion_matrix
from sklearn.metrics import accuracy_score
from sklearn.ensemble import GradientBoostingClassifier

X_train, X_test, y_train, y_test = train_test_split(X,y, test_
size=0.3, random_state=22)

clf = ensemble.GradientBoostingClassifier(n_estimators=300,random_
state=222,max_depth=16,learning_rate=.1,subsample=.5)
scores=clf.fit(X_train,y_train)
```

```
scores2 = cross_val_score(clf, X_train, y_train, cv=3,
scoring='accuracy',n_jobs=-1)
print scores2.mean()

y_pred = cross_val_predict(clf, X_test, y_test, cv=10)
print 'validation accuracy %s' % accuracy_score(y_test, y_pred)

OUTPUT:]
validation accuracy 0.928312816799

confusionMatrix = confusion_matrix(y_test, y_pred)
print confusionMatrix

from sklearn.metrics import accuracy_score
accuracy_score(y_test, y_pred)

clf.feature_importances_

def featureImp_order(clf, X, k=5):
    return X[:,clf.feature_importances_.argsort()[::-1][:k]]
newX = featureImp_order(clf,X,2)
print newX

# let's order the features in amount of importance

print sorted(zip(map(lambda x: round(x, 4), clf.feature_importances_),
columnNames1),
    reverse=True)
OUTPUT]
```

```
0.945030177548
    precision    recall  f1-score    support

    0         0.93      0.96      0.94        835
    1         0.93      0.88      0.91        546

avg / total      0.93      0.93      0.93       1381

[[799  36]
 [ 63 483]]


Feature importance:

[(0.2262, 'char_freq_;'),
```

```
(0.0945, 'report'),
(0.0637, 'capital_run_length_average'),
(0.0467, 'you'),
(0.0461, 'capital_run_length_total')
(0.0403, 'business')
(0.0397, 'char_freq_!')
(0.0333, 'will')
(0.0295, 'capital_run_length_longest')
(0.0275, 'your')
(0.0259, '000')
(0.0257, 'char_freq_(')
(0.0235, 'char_freq_$')
(0.0207, 'internet')
```

We can see that the character ; is the most discriminative in classifying spam.

 Variable importance shows us how much splitting each feature reduces the relative impurity across all the splits in the tree.

Speeding up GBM with warm_start

Unfortunately, there is no parallel processing for GBM in Scikit-learn. Only cross-validation and gridsearch can be parallelized. So what can we do to make it faster? We saw that GBM works with the principle of additive expansion where trees are added incrementally. We can utilize this idea in Scikit-learn with the warm-start parameter. We can model this with Scikit-learn's GBM functionalities by building tree models incrementally with a handy for loop. So let's do this with the same dataset and inspect the computational advantage that it provides:

```
gbc = GradientBoostingClassifier(warm_start=True, learning_rate=.05,
max_depth=20,random_state=0)
for n_estimators in range(1, 1500, 100):
    gbc.set_params(n_estimators=n_estimators)
    gbc.fit(X_train, y_train)
y_pred = gbc.predict(X_test)
print(classification_report(y_test, y_pred))
print(gbc.set_params)
OUTPUT:
 precision    recall  f1-score   support

      0       0.93      0.95      0.94       835
```

1	0.92	0.89	0.91	546
avg / total	0.93	0.93	0.93	1381

```
<bound method GradientBoostingClassifier.set_params of GradientBoostin
gClassifier(init=None, learning_rate=0.05, loss='deviance',
    max_depth=20, max_features=None, max_leaf_nodes=None,
    min_samples_leaf=1, min_samples_split=2,
    min_weight_fraction_leaf=0.0, n_estimators=1401,
    presort='auto', random_state=0, subsample=1.0, verbose=0,
    warm_start=True)>
```

It's adviable to pay special attention to the output of the settings of the tree (n_estimators=1401). You can see that the size of the tree we used is 1401. This little trick helped us reduce the training time a lot (think half or even less) when we compare it to a similar GBM model, which we would have trained with 1401 trees at once. Note that we can use this method for random forest and extreme random forest as well. Nevertheless, we found this useful specifically for GBM.

Let's look at the figure that shows the training time for a regular GBM and our warm_start method. The computation speedup is considerable with the accuracy remaining relatively the same:

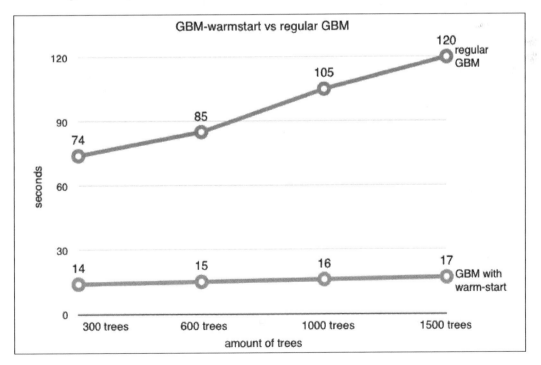

Training and storing GBM models

Ever thought of training a model on three computers at the same time? Or training a GBM model on an EC2 instance? There might be a case where you train a model and want to store it to use it again later on. When you have to wait for two days for a full training round to complete, we don't want to have to go through that process again. A case where you have trained a model in the cloud on an Amazon EC2 instance, you can store that model and reuse it later on another computer using Scikit-learn's `joblib`. So let's walk through this process as Scikit-learn has provided us with a handy tool to manage it.

Let's import the right libraries and set our directories for our file locations:

```
import errno
import os
#set your path here
path='/yourpath/clfs'
clfm=os.makedirs(path)
os.chdir(path)
```

Now let's export the model to the specified location on our harddrive:

```
from sklearn.externals import joblib
joblib.dump( gbc,'clf_gbc.pkl')
```

Now we can load the model and reuse it for other purposes:

```
model_clone = joblib.load('clf_gbc.pkl')
zpred=model_clone.predict(X_test)
print zpred
```

XGBoost

We have just discussed that there are no options for parallel processing when using GBM from Scikit-learn, and this is exactly where XGBoost comes in. Expanding on GBM, XGBoost introduces more scalable methods leveraging multithreading on a single machine and parallel processing on clusters of multiple servers (using sharding). The most important improvement of XGBoost over GBM lies in the capability of the latter to manage sparse data. XGBoost automatically accepts sparse data as input without storing zero values in memory. A second benefit of XGBoost lies in the way in which the best node split values are calculated while branching the tree, a method named quantile sketch. This method transforms the data by a weighting algorithm so that candidate splits are sorted based on a certain accuracy level. For more information read the article at http://arxiv.org/pdf/1603.02754v3.pdf.

XGBoost stands for Extreme Gradient Boosting, an open source gradient boosting algorithm that has gained a lot of popularity in data science competitions such as Kaggle (`https://www.kaggle.com/`) and KDD-cup 2015. (The code is available on GitHub at `https://github.com/dmlc/XGBoost`, as we described in *Chapter 1, First Steps to Scalability*.) As the authors (Tianqui Chen, Tong He, and Carlos Guestrin) report on papers that they wrote on their algorithm, XGBoost, among 29 challenges held on Kaggle during 2015, 17 winning solutions used XGBoost as a standalone or part of some kind of ensemble of multiple models. In their paper *XGBoost: A Scalable Tree Boosting System* (which can be found at `http://learningsys.org/papers/LearningSys_2015_paper_32.pdf`), the authors report that, in the recent KDD-cup 2015, XGBoost was used by every team that ended in the top ten of the competition. Apart from successful performances in both accuracy and computational efficiency, our principal concern in this book is scalability, and XGBoost is indeed a scalable solution from different points of view. XGBoost is a new generation of GBM algorithms with important tweaks to the initial tree boost GBM algorithm. XGBoost provides parallel processing; the scalability offered by the algorithm is due to quite a few new tweaks and additions developed by its authors:

- An algorithm that accepts sparse data, which can leverage sparse matrices, saving both memory (no need for dense matrices) and computation time (zero values are handled in a special way)

- An approximate tree learning (weighted quantile sketch), which bears similar results but in much less time than the classical complete explorations of possible branch cuts

- Parallel computing on a single machine (using multithreading in the phase of the search for the best split) and similarly distributed computations on multiple ones

- Out-of-core computations on a single machine leveraging a data storage solution called Column Block, which arranges data on disk by columns, thus saving time by pulling data from disk as the optimization algorithm (which works on column vectors) expects it

From a practical point of view, XGBoost features mostly the same parameters as GBM. XGBoost is also quite capable of dealing with missing data. Other tree ensembles, based on standard decisions trees, require missing data first to be imputed using an off-scale value (such as a large negative number) in order to develop an appropriate branching of the tree to deal with missing values. XGBoost, instead, first fits all the non-missing values and, after having created the branching for the variable, it decides which branch is better for the missing values to take in order to minimize the prediction error. Such an approach leads to trees that are more compact and an effective imputation strategy leading to more predictive power.

The most important XGBoost parameters are as follows:

- `eta` (default=0.3): This is the equivalent of the learning rate in Scikit-learn's GBM
- `min_child_weight` (default=1): Higher values prevent overfitting and tree complexity
- `max_depth` (default=6): This is the number of interactions in the trees
- `subsample` (default=1): This is a fraction of samples of the training data that we take in each iteration
- `colsample_bytree` (default=1): This is the fraction of features in each iteration
- `lambda` (default=1): This is the L2 regularization (Boolean)
- `seed` (default=0): This is the equivalent of Scikit-learn's `random_state` parameter, allowing reproducibility of learning processes across multiple tests and different machines

Now that we know XGBoost's most important parameters, let's run an XGBoost example on the same dataset that we used for GBM with the same parameter settings (as much as possible). XGBoost is a little less straightforward to use than the Scikit-learn package. So we will provide some basic examples that you can use as a starting point for more complex models. Before we dive deeper into XGBoost applications, let's compare it to the GBM method in `sklearn` on the spam dataset; we have already loaded the data in-memory:

```
import xgboost as xgb
import numpy as np
from sklearn.metrics import classification_report
from sklearn import cross_validation

clf = xgb.XGBClassifier(n_estimators=100,max_depth=8,
    learning_rate=.1,subsample=.5)

clf1 = GradientBoostingClassifier(n_estimators=100,max_depth=8,
    learning_rate=.1,subsample=.5)

%timeit xgm=clf.fit(X_train,y_train)
%timeit gbmf=clf1.fit(X_train,y_train)

y_pred = xgm.predict(X_test)
y_pred2 = gbmf.predict(X_test)

print 'XGBoost results %r' % (classification_report(y_test, y_pred))
```

```
print 'gbm results %r' % (classification_report(y_test, y_pred2))

OUTPUT:
1 loop, best of 3: 1.71 s per loop
1 loop, best of 3: 2.91 s per loop
XGBoost results '                precision    recall  f1-score   support\
n\n          0        0.95      0.97      0.96       835\n          1
0.95        0.93      0.94       546\n\navg / total      0.95      0.95
0.95       1381\n'
gbm results '              precision    recall  f1-score   support\n\n
0        0.95      0.97      0.96       835\n          1        0.95
0.92        0.93       546\n\navg / total      0.95      0.95      0.95
1381\n
```

We can clearly see that XGBoost is quite faster than GBM (1.71s versus 2.91s) even though we didn't use parallelization for XGBoost. Later, we can even arrive at a greater speedup when we use parallelization and out-of-core methods for XGBoost when we apply out-of-memory streaming. In some cases, the XGBoost model results in a higher accuracy than GBM, but (almost) never the other way around.

XGBoost regression

Boosting methods are often used for classification but can be very powerful for regression tasks as well. As regression is often overlooked, let's run a regression example and walk through the key issues. Let's fit a boosting model on the California housing set with gridsearch. The California house dataset has recently been added to Scikit-learn, which saves us some preprocessing steps:

```
import numpy as np
import scipy.sparse
import xgboost as xgb
import os
import pandas as pd
from sklearn.cross_validation import train_test_split
import numpy as np
from sklearn.datasets import fetch_california_housing
from sklearn.metrics import mean_squared_error
pd=fetch_california_housing()

#because the y  variable is highly skewed we apply the log
transformation
y=np.log(pd.target)
X_train, X_test, y_train, y_test = train_test_split(pd.data,
    y,
    test_size=0.15,
```

```
        random_state=111)
names = pd.feature_names
print names

import xgboost as xgb
from xgboost.sklearn import XGBClassifier
from sklearn.grid_search import GridSearchCV

clf=xgb.XGBRegressor(gamma=0,objective= "reg:linear",nthread=-1)



clf.fit(X_train,y_train)
y_pred = clf.predict(X_test)
print 'score before gridsearch %r' % mean_squared_error(y_test, y_
pred)

params = {
 'max_depth':[4,6,8],
 'n_estimators':[1000],
'min_child_weight':range(1,3),
'learning_rate':[.1,.01,.001],
'colsample_bytree':[.8,.9,1]
,'gamma':[0,1]}

#with the parameter nthread we specify XGBoost for parallelisation
cvx = xgb.XGBRegressor(objective= "reg:linear",nthread=-1)
clf=GridSearchCV(estimator=cvx,param_grid=params,n_jobs=-
1,scoring='mean_absolute_error',verbose=True)

clf.fit(X_train,y_train)
print clf.best_params_
y_pred = clf.predict(X_test)
print 'score after gridsearch %r' %mean_squared_error(y_test, y_pred)



#Your output might look a little different based on your hardware.

OUTPUT
['MedInc', 'HouseAge', 'AveRooms', 'AveBedrms', 'Population',
'AveOccup', 'Latitude', 'Longitude']
score before gridsearch 0.07110580252173157
Fitting 3 folds for each of 108 candidates, totalling 324 fits
[Parallel(n_jobs=-1)]: Done  34 tasks      | elapsed:  1.9min
```

```
[Parallel(n_jobs=-1)]: Done 184 tasks       | elapsed: 11.3min
[Parallel(n_jobs=-1)]: Done 324 out of 324  | elapsed: 22.3min finished
{'colsample_bytree': 0.8, 'learning_rate': 0.1, 'min_child_weight': 1,
'n_estimators': 1000, 'max_depth': 8, 'gamma': 0}
score after gridsearch 0.049878294113796254
```

We have been able to improve our score quite a bit with gridsearch; you can see the optimal parameters of our gridsearch. You can see its resemblance with regular boosting methods in sklearn. However, XGBoost by default parallelizes the algorithm over all available cores. You can improve the performance of the model by increasing the `n_estimators` parameter to around 2,500 or 3,000. However, we found that the training time would be a little too long for readers with less powerful computers.

XGBoost and variable importance

XGBoost has some very practical built-in functionalities to plot the variable importance. First, there's an handy tool for feature selection relative to the model at hand. As you probably know, variable importance is based on the relative influence of each feature at the tree construction. It provides practical methods for feature selection and insight into the nature of the predictive model. So let's see how we can plot importance with XGBoost:

```
import numpy as np
import os
from matplotlib import pylab as plt
# %matplotlib inline    <- this only works in jupyter notebook

#our best parameter set
# {'colsample_bytree': 1, 'learning_rate': 0.1, 'min_child_weight': 1,
'n_estimators': 500, #'max_depth': 8, 'gamma': 0}

params={'objective': "reg:linear",
        'eval_metric': 'rmse',
        'eta': 0.1,
        'max_depth':8,
        'min_samples_leaf':4,
        'subsample':.5,
        'gamma':0
        }

dm = xgb.DMatrix(X_train, label=y_train,
                feature_names=names)
regbgb = xgb.train(params, dm, num_boost_round=100)
np.random.seed(1)
```

```
regbgb.get_fscore()
```

```
regbgb.feature_names
regbgb.get_fscore()
xgb.plot_importance(regbgb,color='magenta',title='california-
housing|variable importance')
```

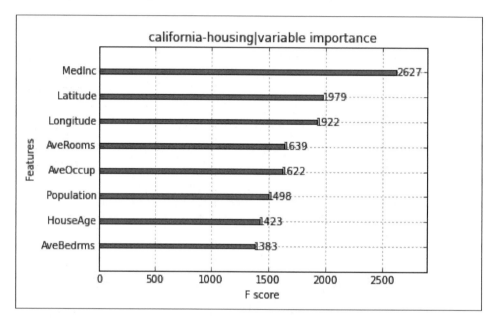

Feature importance should be used with some caution (for GBM and random forest as well). The feature importance metrics are purely based on the tree structure built on the specific model trained with the parameters of that model. This means that if we change the parameters of the model, the importance metrics, and some of the rankings, will change as well. Therefore, it's important to note that for any importance metric, they should not be taken as a generic variable conclusion that generalizes across models.

XGBoost streaming large datasets

In terms of accuracy/performance trade-off, this is simply the best desktop solution. We saw that, with the previous random forest example, we needed to perform subsampling in order to prevent overloading our main memory.

An often-overlooked capability of XGBoost is the method of streaming data through memory. This method parses data through the main memory in a stage-wise fashion to subsequently be parsed into XGBoost model training. This method is a prerequisite to train models on large datasets that are impossible to fit in the main memory. Streaming with XGBoost only works with LIBSVM files, which means that we first have to parse our dataset to the LIBSVM format and import it in the memory cache preserved for XGBoost. Another thing to note is that we use different methods to instantiate XGBoost models. The Scikit-learn-like interface for XGBoost only works on regular NumPy objects. So let's look at how this works.

First, we need to load our dataset in the LIBSVM format and split it into train and test sets before we proceed with preprocessing and training. Parameter tuning with gridsearch is unfortunately not possible with this XGBoost method. If you want to tune parameters, we need to transform the LIBSVM file into a Numpy object, which will dump the data from the memory cache to the main memory. This is unfortunately not scalable, so if you want to perform tuning on large datasets, I would suggest using the reservoir sampling tools we previously introduced and apply tuning to subsamples:

```
import urllib
from sklearn.datasets import dump_svmlight_file
from sklearn.datasets import load_svmlight_file
trainfile = urllib.URLopener()
trainfile.retrieve("http://www.csie.ntu.edu.tw/~cjlin/libsvmtools/
datasets/multiclass/poker.bz2", "pokertrain.bz2")
X,y = load_svmlight_file('pokertrain.bz2')
dump_svmlight_file(X, y,'pokertrain', zero_based=True,query_id=None,
multilabel=False)
testfile = urllib.URLopener()
testfile.retrieve("http://www.csie.ntu.edu.tw/~cjlin/libsvmtools/
datasets/multiclass/poker.t.bz2", "pokertest.bz2")
X,y = load_svmlight_file('pokertest.bz2')
dump_svmlight_file(X, y,'pokertest', zero_based=True,query_id=None,
multilabel=False)
del(X,y)
from sklearn.metrics import classification_report
import numpy as np
import xgboost as xgb
dtrain = xgb.DMatrix('/yourpath/pokertrain#dtrain.cache')
dtest = xgb.DMatrix('/yourpath/pokertest#dtestin.cache')

# For parallelisation it is better to instruct "nthread" to match the
exact amount of cpu cores you want #to use.
```

```
param = {'max_depth':8,'objective':'multi:softmax','nthread':2,'num_
class':10,'verbose':True}
num_round=100
watchlist = [(dtest,'eval'), (dtrain,'train')]
bst = xgb.train(param, dtrain, num_round,watchlist)
print bst
OUTPUT:
[89]    eval-merror:0.228659    train-merror:0.016913
[90]    eval-merror:0.228599    train-merror:0.015954
[91]    eval-merror:0.227671    train-merror:0.015354
[92]    eval-merror:0.227777    train-merror:0.014914
[93]    eval-merror:0.226247    train-merror:0.013355
[94]    eval-merror:0.225397    train-merror:0.012155
[95]    eval-merror:0.224070    train-merror:0.011875
[96]    eval-merror:0.222421    train-merror:0.010676
[97]    eval-merror:0.221881    train-merror:0.010116
[98]    eval-merror:0.221922    train-merror:0.009676
[99]    eval-merror:0.221733    train-merror:0.009316
```

We can really experience a great speedup from in-memory XGBoost. We would need a lot more training time if we had used the internal memory version. In this example, we already included the test set as a validation round in the *watchlist*. However, if we want to predict values on unseen data, we can simply use the same prediction procedure as with any other model in Scikit-learn and XGBoost:

```
bst.predict(dtest)
OUTPUT:
array([ 0.,  0.,  1., ...,  0.,  0.,  1.], dtype=float32)
```

XGBoost model persistence

In the previous chapter, we covered how to store a GBMmodel to disk to later import and use it for predictions. XGBoost provides the same functionalities. So let's see how we can store and import the model:

```
import pickle
bst.save_model('xgb.model')
```

Now you can import the saved model from the directory that you previously specified:

```
imported_model = xgb.Booster(model_file='xgb.model')
```

Great, now you can use this model for predictions:

```
imported_model.predict(dtest)
OUTPUT array([ 9.,  9.,  9., ...,  1.,  1.,  1.], dtype=float32)
```

Out-of-core CART with H2O

Up until now, we have only dealt with desktop solutions for CART models. In *Chapter 4, Neural Networks and Deep Learning*, we introduced H2O for deep learning out of memory that provided a powerful scalable method. Luckily, H2O also provides tree ensemble methods utilizing its powerful parallel Hadoop ecosystem. As we covered GBM and random forest extensively in previous sections, let's get to it right away. For this exercise, we will use the spam dataset that we used before.

Random forest and gridsearch on H2O

Let's implement a random forest with gridsearch hyperparameter optimization. In this section, we first load the spam dataset from the URL source:

```
import pandas as pd
import numpy as np
import os
import xlrd
import urllib
import h2o

#set your path here
os.chdir('/yourpath/')

url = 'https://archive.ics.uci.edu/ml/machine-learning-databases/
spambase/spambase.data'
filename='spamdata.data'
urllib.urlretrieve(url, filename)
```

Now that we have loaded the data, we can initialize the H2O session:

```
h2o.init(max_mem_size_GB = 2)
```

OUTPUT:

H2O cluster uptime:	1 days 1 hours 33 minutes 47 seconds 112 milliseconds
H2O cluster version:	●●●●
H2O cluster name:	H2O_started_from_python
H2O cluster total nodes:	1
H2O cluster total memory:	1.78 GB
H2O cluster total cores:	4
H2O cluster allowed cores:	4
H2O cluster healthy:	True
H2O Connection ip:	▓▓▓▓
H2O Connection port:	54321

Here, we preprocess the data where we split the data into train, validation, and test sets. We do this with an H2O function (.split_frame). Also note the important step where we convert the target vector C58 to a factor variable:

```
spamdata = h2o.import_file(os.path.realpath("/yourpath/"))
spamdata['C58']=spamdata['C58'].asfactor()
train, valid, test= spamdata.split_frame([0.6,.2], seed=1234)
spam_X = spamdata.col_names[:-1]
spam_Y = spamdata.col_names[-1]
```

In this part, we will set up the parameters that we will optimize with gridsearch. First of all, we set the number of trees in the model to a single value of 300. The parameters that are iterated with gridsearch are as follows:

- max_depth: The maximum depth of the tree
- balance_classes: Each iteration uses balanced classes for the target outcome
- sample_rate: This is the fraction of the rows that are sampled for each iteration

Now let's pass these parameters into a Python list to be used in our H2O gridsearch model:

```
hyper_parameters={'ntrees':[300], 'max_depth':[3,6,10,12,50],'balance_
classes':['True','False'],'sample_rate':[.5,.6,.8,.9]}
grid_search = H2OGridSearch(H2ORandomForestEstimator, hyper_
params=hyper_parameters)
grid_search.train(x=spam_X, y=spam_Y,training_frame=train)
print 'this is the optimum solution for hyper parameters search %s' %
grid_search.show()
OUTPUT:
```

```
drf Grid Build Progress: [##############################################] 100%
```

Grid Search Results for H2ORandomForestEstimator:

Model Id	Hyperparameters: [ntrees, sample_rate, max_depth, balance_classes]	mse
Grid_DRF_py_87_model_python_1466382079157_49_model_19	[300, 0.9, 50, True]	0.0249340
Grid_DRF_py_87_model_python_1466382079157_49_model_18	[300, 0.8, 50, True]	0.0258412
Grid_DRF_py_87_model_python_1466382079157_49_model_17	[300, 0.6, 50, True]	0.0289790
Grid_DRF_py_87_model_python_1466382079157_49_model_16	[300, 0.5, 50, True]	0.0314358
Grid_DRF_py_87_model_python_1466382079157_49_model_38	[300, 0.8, 50, False]	0.0417964
---	---	---
Grid_DRF_py_87_model_python_1466382079157_49_model_23	[300, 0.9, 3, False]	0.0914980
Grid_DRF_py_87_model_python_1466382079157_49_model_1	[300, 0.6, 3, True]	0.1040888
Grid_DRF_py_87_model_python_1466382079157_49_model_0	[300, 0.5, 3, True]	0.1042337
Grid_DRF_py_87_model_python_1466382079157_49_model_2	[300, 0.8, 3, True]	0.1042843
Grid_DRF_py_87_model_python_1466382079157_49_model_3	[300, 0.9, 3, True]	0.1060737

Of all the possible combinations, the model with a row sample rate of .9, a tree depth of 50, and balanced classes yields the highest accuracy. Now let's train a new random forest model with optimal parameters resulting from our gridsearch and predict the outcome on the test set:

```
final = H2ORandomForestEstimator(ntrees=300, max_depth=50,balance_
classes=True,sample_rate=.9)
final.train(x=spam_X, y=spam_Y,training_frame=train)
print final.predict(test)
```

The final output of the predictions in H2O results in an array with the first column containing the actual predicted classes and columns containing the class probabilities of each target label:

OUTPUT:

predict	p0	p1
1	0.531042	0.468958
1	0.510856	0.489144
1	0.51637	0.48363
1	0.542997	0.457003
1	0.544576	0.455424
1	0.560277	0.439723
1	0.544576	0.455424
1	0.5408	0.4592
1	0.535741	0.464259
1	0.498822	0.501178

Stochastic gradient boosting and gridsearch on H2O

We have seen in previous examples that most of the time, a well-tuned GBM model outperforms random forest. So now let's perform a GBM with gridsearch in H2O and see if we can improve our score. For this session, we introduce the same random subsampling method that we used for the random forest model in H2O (`sample_rate`). Based on Jerome Friedman's article (`https://statweb.stanford.edu/~jhf/ftp/stobst.pdf`) from 1999, a method named **stochastic gradient boosting** was introduced. This stochasticity added to the model utilizes random subsampling without replacement from the data at each tree iteration that is considered to prevent overfitting and increase overall accuracy. In this example, we take this idea of stochasticity further by introducing random subsampling based on the features at each iteration.

This method of randomly subsampling features is also referred to as the **random subspace method**, which we have already seen in the *Random forest and extremely randomized forest* section of this chapter. We achieve this with the `col_sample_rate` parameter. So to summarize, in this GBM model, we are going to perform gridsearch optimization on the following parameters:

- `max_depth`: Maximum tree depth
- `sample_rate`: Fraction of the rows used at each iteration
- `col_sample_rate`: Fraction of the features used at each iteration

We use exactly the same spam dataset as the previous section so we can get right down to it:

```
hyper_parameters={'ntrees':[300],'max_depth':[12,30,50],'sample_
rate':[.5,.7,1],'col_sample_rate':[.9,1],
'learn_rate':[.01,.1,.3],}
grid_search = H2OGridSearch(H2OGradientBoostingEstimator, hyper_
params=hyper_parameters)
grid_search.train(x=spam_X, y=spam_Y, training_frame=train)
print 'this is the optimum solution for hyper parameters search %s' %
grid_search.show()
```

```
gbm Grid Build Progress: [#############################################] 100%

Grid Search Results for H2OGradientBoostingEstimator:
```

Model Id	Hyperparameters: [learn_rate, col_sample_rate, ntrees, sample_rate, max_depth]	mse
Grid_GBM_py_87_model_python_1466382079157_52_model_23	[0.3, 0.9, 300, 1.0, 30]	0.0001859
Grid_GBM_py_87_model_python_1466382079157_52_model_20	[0.3, 0.9, 300, 1.0, 12]	0.0001859
Grid_GBM_py_87_model_python_1466382079157_52_model_47	[0.3, 1.0, 300, 1.0, 12]	0.0001859
Grid_GBM_py_87_model_python_1466382079157_52_model_26	[0.3, 0.9, 300, 1.0, 50]	0.0001859
Grid_GBM_py_87_model_python_1466382079157_52_model_53	[0.3, 1.0, 300, 1.0, 50]	0.0001859
~~	~~~	~~~
Grid_GBM_py_87_model_python_1466382079157_52_model_33	[0.01, 1.0, 300, 0.5, 50]	0.0196867
Grid_GBM_py_87_model_python_1466382079157_52_model_6	[0.01, 0.9, 300, 0.5, 50]	0.0197013

```
gbm Grid Build Progress: [#############################################
#######] 100%
```

The upper part of our gridsearch output shows that we should use an exceptionally high learning rate of .3, a column sample rate of .9, and a maximum tree depth of 30. Random subsampling based on rows didn't increase performance, but subsampling based on features with a fraction of .9 was quite effective in this case. Now let's train a new GBM model with the optimal parameters resulting from our gridsearch optimization and predict the outcome on the test set:

```
spam_gbm2 = H2OGradientBoostingEstimator(
    ntrees=300,
    learn_rate=0.3,
    max_depth=30,
    sample_rate=1,
    col_sample_rate=0.9,
    score_each_iteration=True,
    seed=2000000
)
spam_gbm2.train(spam_X, spam_Y, training_frame=train, validation_
frame=valid)

confusion_matrix = spam_gbm2.confusion_matrix(metrics="accuracy")
print confusion_matrix
OUTPUT:
```

```
gbm Model Build Progress: [#############################################] 100%

Confusion Matrix (Act/Pred) for max accuracy @ threshold = 0.99983413575:
```

	0	1	Error	Rate
0	1639.0	0.0	0.0	(0.0/1639.0)
1	1.0	1050.0	0.001	(1.0/1051.0)
Total	1640.0	1050.0	0.0004	(1.0/2690.0)

This delivers interesting diagnostics of the model's performance such as `accuracy`, `rmse`, `logloss`, and AUC. However, its output is too large to include here. Look at the output of your IPython notebook for the complete output.

You can utilize this with the following:

```
print spam_gbm2.score_history()
```

Of course, the final predictions can be achieved as follows:

```
print spam_gbm2.predict(test)
```

Great, we have been able to improve the accuracy of our model close to 100%. As you can see, in H2O, you might be less flexible in terms of modeling and munging your data, but the speed of processing and accuracy that can be achieved is unrivaled. To round off this session, you can do the following:

```
h2o.shutdown(prompt=False)
```

Summary

We saw that CART methods trained with ensemble routines are powerful when it comes to predictive accuracy. However, they can be computationally expensive and we have covered some techniques in speeding them up in sklearn's applications. We noticed that using extreme randomized forests tuned with randomized search could speed up by tenfold when used properly. For GBM, however, there is no parallelization implemented in sklearn, and this is exactly where XGBoost comes in.

XGBoost comes with an effective parallelized boosting algorithm speeding up the algorithm nicely. When we use larger files (>100k training examples), there is an out-of-core method that makes sure we don't overload our main memory while training models.

The biggest gains in speed and memory can be found with H2O; we saw powerful tuning capabilities together with an impressive training speed.

7
Unsupervised Learning at Scale

In the previous chapters, the focus of the problem was on predicting a variable, which could have been a number, class, or category. In this chapter, we will change the approach and try to create new features and variables at scale, hopefully better for our prediction purposes than the ones already included in the observation matrix. We will first introduce the unsupervised methods and illustrate three of them, which are able to scale to big data:

- **Principal Component Analysis (PCA)**, an effective way to reduce the number of features
- **K-means**, a scalable algorithm for clustering
- **Latent Dirichlet Allocation (LDA)**, a very effective algorithm able to extract topics from a series of text documents

Unsupervised methods

Unsupervised learning is a branch of machine learning whose algorithms reveal inferences from data without an explicit label (unlabeled data). The goal of such techniques is to extract hidden patterns and group similar data.

In these algorithms, the unknown parameters of interests of each observation (the group membership and topic composition, for instance) are often modeled as latent variables (or a series of hidden variables), hidden in the system of observed variables that cannot be observed directly, but only deduced from the past and present outputs of the system. Typically, the output of the system contains noise, which makes this operation harder.

In common problems, unsupervised methods are used in two main situations:

- With labeled datasets to extract additional features to be processed by the classifier/regressor down to the processing chain. Enhanced by additional features, they may perform better.

- With labeled or unlabeled datasets to extract some information about the structure of the data. This class of algorithms is commonly used during the **Exploratory Data Analysis (EDA)** phase of the modeling.

First of all, before starting with our illustration, let's import the modules that will be necessary along the chapter in our notebook:

```
In : import matplotlib
import numpy as np
import pandas as pd
import matplotlib.pyplot as plt
from matplotlib import pylab
%matplotlib inline
import matplotlib.cm as cm
import copy
import tempfile
import os
```

Feature decomposition – PCA

PCA is an algorithm commonly used to decompose the dimensions of an input signal and keep just the *principal* ones. From a mathematical perspective, PCA performs an orthogonal transformation of the observation matrix, outputting a set of linear uncorrelated variables, named principal components. The output variables form a basis set, where each component is orthonormal to the others. Also, it's possible to rank the output components (in order to use just the principal ones) as the first component is the one containing the largest possible variance of the input dataset, the second is orthogonal to the first (by definition) and contains the largest possible variance of the residual signal, and the third is orthogonal to the first two and it's built on the residual variance, and so on.

A generic transformation with PCA can be expressed as a projection to a space. If just the principal components are taken from the transformation basis, the output space will have a smaller dimensionality than the input one. Mathematically, it can be expressed as follows:

$$\hat{X} = X \cdot T$$

Here, *X* is a generic point of the training set of dimension *N*, *T* is the transformation matrix coming from PCA, and $\hat{X}$ is the output vector. Note that the symbol indicates a dot product in this matrix equation. From a practical perspective, also note that all the features of *X* must be zero-centered before doing this operation.

Let's now start with a practical example; later, we will explain math PCA in depth. In this example, we will create a dummy dataset composed of two blobs of points—one cantered in (-5, 0) and the other one in (5, 5).Let's use PCA to transform the dataset and plot the output compared to the input. In this simple example, we will use all the features, that is, we will not perform feature reduction:

```
In:from sklearn.datasets.samples_generator import make_blobs
from sklearn.decomposition import PCA

X, y = make_blobs(n_samples=1000, random_state=101, \
centers=[[-5, 0], [5, 5]])
pca = PCA(n_components=2)
X_pca = pca.fit_transform(X)
pca_comp = pca.components_.T

test_point = np.matrix([5, -2])
test_point_pca = pca.transform(test_point)

plt.subplot(1, 2, 1)
plt.scatter(X[:, 0], X[:, 1], c=y, edgecolors='none')
plt.quiver(0, 0, pca_comp[:,0], pca_comp[:,1], width=0.02, \
          scale=5, color='orange')
plt.plot(test_point[0, 0], test_point[0, 1], 'o')
plt.title('Input dataset')

plt.subplot(1, 2, 2)
plt.scatter(X_pca[:, 0], X_pca[:, 1], c=y, edgecolors='none')
```

```
plt.plot(test_point_pca[0, 0], test_point_pca[0, 1], 'o')
plt.title('After "lossless" PCA')

plt.show()
```

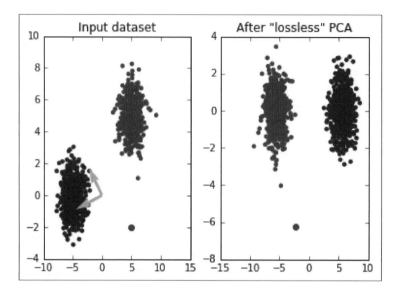

As you can see, the output is more organized than the original features' space and, if the next task is a classification, it would require just one feature of the dataset, saving almost 50% of the space and computation needed. In the image, you can clearly see the core of PCA: it's just a projection of the input dataset to the transformation basis drawn in the image on the left in orange. Are you unsure about this? Let's test it:

```
In:print "The blue point is in", test_point[0, :]
print "After the transformation is in", test_point_pca[0, :]
print "Since (X-MEAN) * PCA_MATRIX = ", np.dot(test_point - \
pca.mean_, pca_comp)

Out:The blue point is in [[ 5 -2]]
After the transformation is in [-2.34969911 -6.2575445 ]
Since (X-MEAN) * PCA_MATRIX =  [[-2.34969911 -6.2575445 ]
```

Now, let's dig into the core problem: how is it possible to generate T from the training set? It should contain orthonormal vectors, and the vectors should be ranked according to the quantity of variance (that is, the energy or information carried by the observation matrix) that they can explain. Many solutions have been implemented, but the most common implementation is based on **Singular Value Decomposition (SVD)**.

SVD is a technique that decomposes any matrix M into three matrixes (U, Σ, W) with special properties and whose multiplication gives back M again:

$$M = U \cdot \Sigma \cdot W^T$$

Specifically, given M, a matrix of m rows and n columns, the resulting elements of the equivalence are as follows:

- U is a matrix $m \times m$ (square matrix), it's unitary, and its columns form an orthonormal basis. Also, they're named left singular vectors, or input singular vectors, and they're the eigenvectors of the matrix product $M \cdot M^T$.

- Σ is a matrix $m \times n$, which has only non-zero elements on its diagonal. These values are named singular values, are all non-negative, and are the eigenvalues of both $M \cdot M^T$ and $M^T \cdot M$.

- W is a unitary matrix $n \times n$ (square matrix), its columns form an orthonormal basis, and they're named right (or output) singular vectors. Also, they are the eigenvectors of the matrix product $M^T \cdot M$.

Why is this needed? The solution is pretty easy: the goal of PCA is to try and estimate the directions where the variance of the input dataset is larger. For this, we first need to remove the mean from each feature and then operate on the covariance matrix $X^T \cdot X$.

Given that, by decomposing the matrix X with SVD, we have the columns of the matrix W that are the principal components of the covariance (that is, the matrix T we are looking for), the diagonal of Σ that contains the variance explained by the principal components, and the columns of U the principal components. Here's why PCA is always done with SVD.

Let's see it now on a real example. Let's test it on the Iris dataset, extracting the first two principal components (that is, passing from a dataset composed by four features to one composed by two):

```
In:from sklearn import datasets

iris = datasets.load_iris()
X = iris.data
y = iris.target

print "Iris dataset contains", X.shape[1], "features"

pca = PCA(n_components=2)
```

```
X_pca = pca.fit_transform(X)

print "After PCA, it contains", X_pca.shape[1], "features"
print "The variance is [% of original]:", \
        sum(pca.explained_variance_ratio_)


plt.scatter(X_pca[:, 0], X_pca[:, 1], c=y, edgecolors='none')
plt.title('First 2 principal components of Iris dataset')

plt.show()

Out:Iris dataset contains 4 features
After PCA, it contains 2 features
The variance is [% of original]: 0.977631775025
```

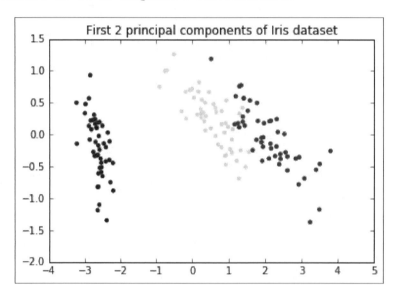

This is the analysis of the outputs of the process:

- The explained variance is almost 98% of the original variance from the input. The number of features has been halved, but only 2% of the information is not in the output, hopefully just noise.

- From a visual inspection, it seems that the different classes, composing the Iris dataset, are separated from each other. This means that a classifier working on such a reduced set will have comparable performance in terms of accuracy, but will be faster to train and run prediction.

As a proof of the second point, let's now try to train and test two classifiers, one using the original dataset and another using the reduced set, and print their accuracy:

```
In:from sklearn.linear_model import SGDClassifier
from sklearn.cross_validation import train_test_split
from sklearn.metrics import accuracy_score

def test_classification_accuracy(X_in, y_in):
    X_train, X_test, y_train, y_test = \
        train_test_split(X_in, y_in, random_state=101, \
        train_size=0.50)

    clf = SGDClassifier('log', random_state=101)
clf.fit(X_train, y_train)

    return accuracy_score(y_test, clf.predict(X_test))

print "SGDClassifier accuracy on Iris set:", \
        test_classification_accuracy(X, y)
print "SGDClassifier accuracy on Iris set after PCA
    (2 components):", \
        test_classification_accuracy(X_pca, y)

Out:SGDClassifier accuracy on Iris set: 0.586666666667
SGDClassifier accuracy on Iris set after PCA (2 components): 0.72
```

As you can see, this technique not only reduces the complexity and space of the learner down in the chain, but also helps achieve generalization (exactly as a Ridge or Lasso regularization).

Now, if you are unsure how many components should be in the output, typically as a rule of thumb, choose the minimum number that is able to explain at least 90% (or 95%) of the input variance. Empirically, such a choice usually ensures that only the noise is cut off.

So far, everything seems perfect: we found a great solution to reduce the number of features, building some with very high predictive power, and we also have a rule of thumb to guess the right number of them. Let's now check how scalable this solution is: we're investigating how it scales when the number of observations and features increases. The first thing to note is that the SVD algorithm, the *core* piece of PCA, is not stochastic; therefore, it needs the whole matrix in order to be able to extract its principal components. Now, let's see how scalable PCA is in practice on some synthetic datasets with an increasing number of features and observations. We will perform a full (lossless) decomposition (the argument while instantiating the object PCA is None), as asking for a lower number of features doesn't impact the performance (it's just a matter of slicing the output matrixes of SVD).

In the following code, we first create matrixes with 10,000 points and 20, 50, 100, 250, 1,000, and 2,500 features to be processed by PCA. Then, we create matrixes with 100 features and 1, 5, 10, 25, 50, and 100 thousand observations to be processed with PCA:

```
In:import time

def check_scalability(test_pca):
    pylab.rcParams['figure.figsize'] = (10, 4)

    # FEATURES
    n_points = 10000
    n_features = [20, 50, 100, 250, 500, 1000, 2500]
    time_results = []

    for n_feature in n_features:
        X, _ = make_blobs(n_points, n_features=n_feature, \
random_state=101)

        pca = copy.deepcopy(test_pca)
        tik = time.time()
        pca.fit(X)
        time_results.append(time.time()-tik)

    plt.subplot(1, 2, 1)
    plt.plot(n_features, time_results, 'o--')
    plt.title('Feature scalability')
    plt.xlabel('Num. of features')
    plt.ylabel('Training time [s]')

    # OBSERVATIONS
```

```
n_features = 100
n_observations = [1000, 5000, 10000, 25000, 50000, 100000]
time_results = []

for n_points in n_observations:
    X, _ = make_blobs(n_points, n_features=n_features, \
random_state=101)
    pca = copy.deepcopy(test_pca)
    tik = time.time()
    pca.fit(X)
    time_results.append(time.time()-tik)

plt.subplot(1, 2, 2)
plt.plot(n_observations, time_results, 'o--')
plt.title('Observations scalability')
plt.xlabel('Num. of training observations')
plt.ylabel('Training time [s]')



plt.show()

check_scalability(PCA(None))
```

Out:

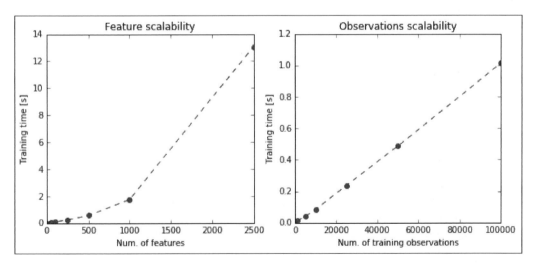

As you can clearly see, PCA based on SVD is not scalable: if the number of features increases linearly, the time needed to train the algorithm increases exponentially. Also, the time needed to process a matrix with a few hundred observations becomes too high and (not shown in the image) the memory consumption makes the problem unfeasible for a domestic computer (with 16 or fewer GB of RAM). It seems clear that a PCA based on SVD is not the solution for big data; fortunately, in recent years, many workarounds have been introduced. In the following sections, you'll find a short introduction for each of them.

Randomized PCA

The correct name of this technique should be *PCA based on randomized SVD*, but it has become popular with the name **Randomized PCA**. The core idea behind the randomization is the redundancy of all the principal components; in fact, if the goal of the method is dimension reduction, one should expect that only a few vectors are needed in the output (the K principal ones). By focusing on the problem of finding the best K principal vectors, the algorithm scales more. Note that in this algorithm, K — the number of principal components to be outputted — is a key parameter: set it too large and the performance won't be better than PCA; set it too low and the variance explained with the resulting vectors will be too low.

As in PCA, we want to find an approximation of the matrix containing observations X, such that $X \approx Q \cdot Q^T \cdot X$; we also want the matrix Q with K orthonormal columns (they will be called principal components). With SVD, we can now compute the decomposition of the *small* matrix $Q^T \cdot X = U \cdot \Sigma \cdot W^T$. As we proved, it won't take a long time. As $X \approx Q \cdot Q^T \cdot X = Q \cdot U \cdot \Sigma \cdot W^T$, by taking $Q \cdot U = S$, we now have a truncated approximation of X based on a low rank SVD, $X \approx S \cdot \Sigma \cdot W^T$.

Mathematically, it seems perfect, but there are still two missing points: what role does the randomization have? How to get the matrix Q? Both questions are answered here: a Gaussian random matrix is extracted, Ω , and it's computed Y as $Y = X \cdot \Omega$. Then, Y is QR-decomposed, creating $Y = Q \cdot R$, and here is Q, the matrix of K orthonormal columns that we are looking for.

The math underneath this decomposition is pretty heavy, and fortunately everything has been implemented in Scikit-learn, so you don't need to figure out how to deal with Gaussian random variables and so on. Let's initially see how bad it performs when a full (lossless) decomposition is computed with randomized PCA:

```
In:from sklearn.decomposition import RandomizedPCA
check_scalability(RandomizedPCA(None))
```

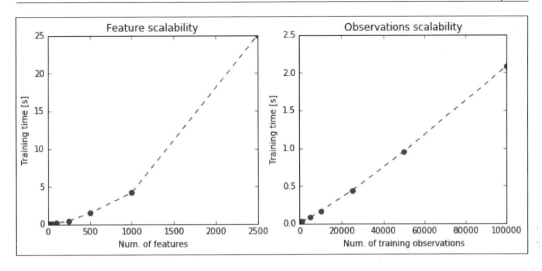

Performances are worse than the classic PCA; in fact, this transformation works very well when a reduced set of components is asked. Let's now see the performance when *K=20*:

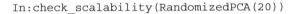

```
In:check_scalability(RandomizedPCA(20))
```

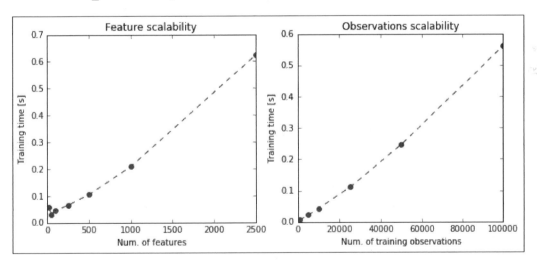

As expected, the computations are very quick; in less than a second, the algorithm is able to perform the most complex factorizations.

Checking the results and the algorithm, we still notice something odd: the training dataset, *X*, must all fit in-memory in order to be decomposed, even in the case of the randomized PCA. Does an online version of PCA exist that is able to incrementally fit the principal vectors without having the whole dataset in-memory? Yes, there is — incremental PCA.

Incremental PCA

Incremental PCA, or mini-batch PCA, is the online version of Principal Component Analysis. The core of the algorithm is very simple: the batch of data is initially split into mini-batches with the same number of observations. (The only limitation is that the number of observations per mini-batch should be greater than the number of features.) Then, the first mini-batch is centered (the mean is removed) and its SVD decomposition is performed, storing the principal components. Then, when the next mini-batch enters the process, it's first centered and then stacked with the principal components extracted from the previous mini-batch (they're inserted as additional observations). Now, another SVD is performed and the principal components are overwritten with the new ones. The process goes till the last mini-batch: for each of them, first there is the centering, then the stacking, and finally the SVD. Doing so, instead of a *big* SVD, we're performing as many *small* SVD as the number of mini-batches.

As you can understand, this technique doesn't outperform randomized PCA, but its goal is to offer a solution (or the only solution) when PCA is needed on a dataset that doesn't fit in-memory. Incremental PCA doesn't run to win a speed challenge, but to limit memory consumption; the memory usage is constant throughout the training and can be tuned by setting the mini-batch size. As a rule of thumb, the memory footprint is approximately the same order of magnitude as the square of the size of the mini-batch.

As a code example, let's now check how incremental PCA is able to cope with a large dataset, which is, in our exemplification, composed of 10 million observations and 100 features. None of the previous algorithms are able to do so, unless you want to crash your computer (or witness an enormous amount of swap between memory and the storage disk). With incremental PCA, such a task turns into a piece of cake and, all things considered, the process is not all that slow (Note that we're doing a complete lossless decomposition with a stable amount of memory consumed):

```
In:from sklearn.decomposition import IncrementalPCA

X, _ = make_blobs(100000, n_features=100, random_state=101)
pca = IncrementalPCA(None, batch_size=1000)

tik = time.time()
```

```
for i in range(100):
    pca.partial_fit(X)
print "PCA on 10M points run with constant memory usage in ", \
    time.time() - tik, "seconds"

Out:PCA on 10M points run with constant memory usage in  155.642718077
seconds
```

Sparse PCA

Sparse PCA operates in a different way than the previous algorithms; instead of operating a feature reduction using an SVD applied on the covariance matrix (after being centered), it operates a feature selection-like operation of that matrix, finding the set of sparse components that best reconstruct the data. As in Lasso regularization, the amount of sparseness is controllable by a penalty (or constraint) on the coefficients.

With respect to PCA, sparse PCA doesn't guarantee that the resulting components will be orthogonal, but the result is more interpretable as principal vectors are actually a portion of the input dataset. Moreover, it's scalable in terms of the number of features: if PCA and its scalable versions are stuck when the number of features is getting larger (let's say, more than 1,000), sparse PCA is still an optimal solution in terms of speed thanks to the internal method to solve the Lasso problem, typically based on Lars or Coordinate Descent. (Remember that Lasso tries to minimize the L1 norm of the coefficients.) Moreover, it's great when the number of features is greater than the number of observations as, for example, some image datasets.

Let's now see how it works on a 25,000 observations dataset with 10,000 features. For this example, we're using the mini-batch version of the SparsePCA algorithm that ensures constant memory usage and is able to cope with massive datasets, eventually larger than the available memory (note that the batch version is named SparsePCA but doesn't support the online training):

```
In:from sklearn.decomposition import MiniBatchSparsePCA

X, _ = make_blobs(25000, n_features=10000, random_state=101)

tik = time.time()
pca = MiniBatchSparsePCA(20, method='cd', random_state=101, \
                n_iter=1000)
pca.fit(X)
```

```
print "SparsePCA on matrix", X.shape, "done in ", time.time() - \
       tik, "seconds"
```

```
Out:
SparsePCA on matrix (25000, 10000) done in  41.7692570686 seconds
```

In about 40 seconds, `SparsePCA` is able to produce a solution using a constant amount of memory.

PCA with H2O

We can also use the PCA implementation provided by H2O. (We've already seen H2O in the previous chapter and mentioned it along the book.)

With H2O, we first need to turn on the server with the `init` method. Then, we dump the dataset on a file (precisely, a CSV file) and finally run the PCA analysis. As the last step, we shut down the server.

We're trying this implementation on some of the biggest datasets seen so far—the one with 100K observations and 100 features and the one with 10K observations and 2,500 features:

```
In: import h2o
from h2o.transforms.decomposition import H2OPCA
h2o.init(max_mem_size_GB=4)

def testH2O_pca(nrows, ncols, k=20):
    temp_file = tempfile.NamedTemporaryFile().name
    X, _ = make_blobs(nrows, n_features=ncols, random_state=101)
np.savetxt(temp_file, np.c_[X], delimiter=",")
    del X

pca = H2OPCA(k=k, transform="NONE", pca_method="Power")
    tik = time.time()
    pca.train(x=range(100), \
training_frame=h2o.import_file(temp_file))

    print "H2OPCA on matrix ", (nrows, ncols), \
" done in ", time.time() - tik, "seconds"
os.remove(temp_file)

testH2O_pca(100000, 100)
```

```
testH2O_pca(10000, 2500)
h2o.shutdown(prompt=False)


Out:[...]
H2OPCA on matrix  (100000, 100) done in  12.9560530186 seconds
[...]
H2OPCA on matrix  (10000, 2500) done in  10.1429388523 seconds
```

As you can see, in both cases, H2O indeed performs very fast and is well-comparable (if not outperforming) to Scikit-learn.

Clustering – K-means

K-means is an unsupervised algorithm that creates K disjoint clusters of points with equal variance, minimizing the distortion (also named inertia).

Given only one parameter K, representing the number of clusters to be created, the K-means algorithm creates K sets of points $S_1, S_2, ..., S_K$, each of them represented by its centroid: $C_1, C_2, ..., C_K$. The generic centroid, C_i, is simply the mean of the samples of the points associated to the cluster Si in order to minimize the intra-cluster distance. The outputs of the system are as follows:

1. The composition of the clusters $S_1, S_2, ..., S_K$, that is, the set of points composing the training set that are associated to the cluster number 1, 2, ..., K.

2. The centroids of each cluster, $C_1, C_2, ..., C_K$. Centroids can be used for future associations.

3. The distortion introduced by the clustering, computed as follows:

$$D = \sum_{i=i}^{K} \sum_{x \in S_i} ||x - Ci||^2$$

This equation denotes the optimization intrinsically done in the K-means algorithm: the centroids are chosen to minimize the intra-cluster distortion, that is, the sum of Euclidean norms of the distances between each input point and the centroid of the cluster to which the point is associated to. In other words, the algorithm tries to fit the best vectorial quantization.

The training phase of the K-means algorithm is also called Lloyd's algorithm, named after Stuart Lloyd, who first proposed the algorithm. It's an iterative algorithm composed of two phases iterated over and over till convergence (the distortion reaches a minimum). It's a variant of the generalized **expectation-maximization (EM)** algorithm as the first step creates a function for the **expectation (E)** of a score, and the **maximization (M)** step computes the parameters that maximize the score. (Note that in this formulation, we try to achieve the opposite, that is, the minimization of the distortion.) Here's its formulation:

- The expectation step: In this step, the points in the training set are assigned to the closest centroid:

$$S_i^{(t)} = \{\ x : \|x - Ci\|^2 = \min_j \|x - Cj\|^2\ \}$$

This step is also named assignment or vectorial quantization.

- The maximization step: The centroid of each cluster is moved to the middle of the cluster by averaging the points composing it:

$$C_i^{(t+1)} = \frac{1}{|S_i^{(t)}|} \cdot \sum_{x \in S_i^{(t)}} x \ for \ i = 1, ..., K$$

This step is also named update step.

These two steps are performed till convergence (points are stable in their cluster), or till the algorithm reaches a preset number of iterations. Note that, per composition, the distortion cannot increase throughout the training phase (unlike Stochastic Gradient Descent-based methods); therefore, in this algorithm, the more iterations, the better the result.

Let's now see how it looks like on a dummy two-dimensional dataset. We first create a set of 1,000 points concentrated in four locations symmetric with respect to the origin. Each cluster, per construction, has the same variance:

```
In:import matplotlib
import numpy as np
import pandas as pd
import matplotlib.pyplot as plt
```

```
%matplotlib inline

In:from sklearn.datasets.samples_generator import make_blobs


centers = [[1, 1], [1, -1], [-1, -1], [-1, 1]]
X, y = make_blobs(n_samples=1000, centers=centers,
                  cluster_std=0.5, random_state=101)
```

Let's now plot the dataset. To make things easier, we will color the clusters with different colors:

```
In:plt.scatter(X[:,0], X[:,1], c=y, edgecolors='none', alpha=0.9)
plt.show()
```

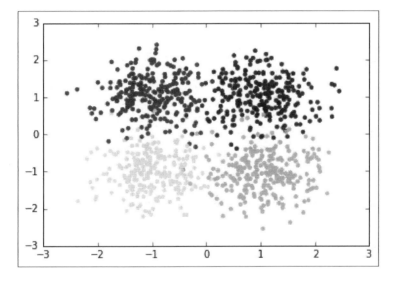

Let's now run K-means and inspect what's going on at each iteration. For this, we stop the iteration to 1, 2, 3, and 4 iterations and plot the points with their associated cluster (color-coded) as well as the centroid, distortion (in the title), and decision boundaries (also named Voronoi cells). The initial choice of the centroids is at random, that is, four training points are elected centroids in the first iteration during the expectation phase of the training:

```
In:pylab.rcParams['figure.figsize'] = (10.0, 8.0)

from sklearn.cluster import KMeans

for n_iter in range(1, 5):

    cls = KMeans(n_clusters=4, max_iter=n_iter, n_init=1,
                init='random', random_state=101)
    cls.fit(X)


    # Plot the voronoi cells

    plt.subplot(2, 2, n_iter)
    h=0.02
    xx, yy = np.meshgrid(np.arange(-3, 3, h), np.arange(-3, 3, h))
    Z = cls.predict(np.c_[xx.ravel(), \
        yy.ravel()]).reshape(xx.shape)
    plt.imshow(Z, interpolation='nearest', cmap=plt.cm.Accent, \
               extent=(xx.min(), xx.max(), yy.min(), yy.max()), \
               aspect='auto', origin='lower')


    plt.scatter(X[:,0], X[:,1], c=cls.labels_, \
edgecolors='none', alpha=0.7)
    plt.scatter(cls.cluster_centers_[:,0], \
                cls.cluster_centers_[:,1], \
                marker='x', color='r', s=100, linewidths=4)
    plt.title("iter=%s, distortion=%s" %(n_iter, \
                int(cls.inertia_)))

plt.show()
```

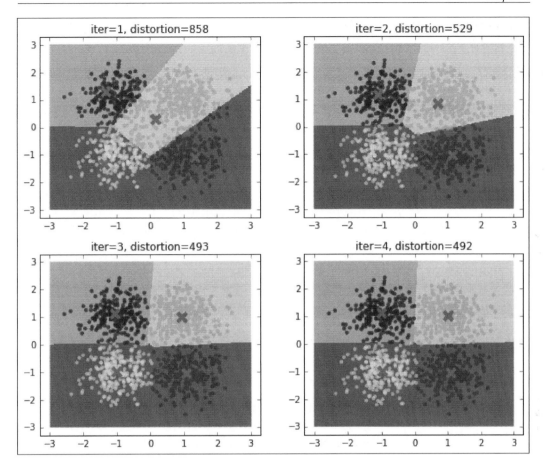

As you can see, the distortion is getting lower and lower as the number of iterations increases. For this dummy dataset, it seems that using a few iterations (five iterations), we've reached the convergence.

Initialization methods

Finding the global minimum of the distortion in K-means is a NP-hard problem; moreover, exactly as with Stochastic Gradient Descent, this method is prone to converge to local minima especially if the number of dimensions is high. In order to avoid such behavior and limit the maximum number of iterations, you can use the following countermeasures:

- Run the algorithm multiple times using different initial conditions. In Scikit-learn, the KMeans class has the n_init parameter that controls how many times the K-means algorithm will be run with different centroid seeds. At the end, the model that ensures the lower distortion is selected. If multiple cores are available, this process can be run in parallel by setting the n_jobs parameter to the number of desired jobs to spin off. Note that the memory consumption is linearly dependent on the number of parallel jobs.

- Prefer the k-means++ initialization (the KMeans class is the default) to the random choice of training points. K-means++ initialization selects points that are *far* among each other; this should ensure that the centroids are able to form clusters in uniform subspaces of the space. It's also proved that this fact ensures that *it's more likely* to find the best solution.

K-means assumptions

K-means relies on the assumptions that each cluster has a (hyper-) spherical shape, that is, it doesn't have an elongated shape (like an arrow), all the clusters have the same variance internally, and their size is comparable (or they are very far away).

All of these hypotheses can be guaranteed with a strong feature preprocessing step; PCA, KernelPCA, feature normalization, and sampling can be a good start.

Let's now see what happens when the assumptions behind K-means are not met:

```
In:pylab.rcParams['figure.figsize'] = (5.0, 10.0)
from sklearn.datasets import make_moons

# Oblong/elongated sets
X, _ = make_moons(n_samples=1000, noise=0.1, random_state=101)
cls = KMeans(n_clusters=2, random_state=101)
y_pred = cls.fit_predict(X)

plt.subplot(3, 1, 1)
plt.scatter(X[:, 0], X[:, 1], c=y_pred, edgecolors='none')
plt.scatter(cls.cluster_centers_[:,0], cls.cluster_centers_[:,1],
            marker='x', color='r', s=100, linewidths=4)
plt.title("Elongated clusters")

# Different variance between clusters
centers = [[-1, -1], [0, 0], [1, 1]]
X, _ = make_blobs(n_samples=1000, cluster_std=[0.1, 0.4, 0.1],
                  centers=centers, random_state=101)
cls = KMeans(n_clusters=3, random_state=101)
y_pred = cls.fit_predict(X)

plt.subplot(3, 1, 2)
plt.scatter(X[:, 0], X[:, 1], c=y_pred, edgecolors='none')
plt.scatter(cls.cluster_centers_[:,0], cls.cluster_centers_[:,1],
            marker='x', color='r', s=100, linewidths=4)
plt.title("Unequal Variance between clusters")

# Unevenly sized blobs
centers = [[-1, -1], [1, 1]]
centers.extend([[0,0]]*20)
X, _ = make_blobs(n_samples=1000, centers=centers,
                  cluster_std=0.28, random_state=101)
cls = KMeans(n_clusters=3, random_state=101)
y_pred = cls.fit_predict(X)

plt.subplot(3, 1, 3)
plt.scatter(X[:, 0], X[:, 1], c=y_pred, edgecolors='none')
```

```
plt.scatter(cls.cluster_centers_[:,0], cls.cluster_centers_[:,1],
            marker='x', color='r', s=100, linewidths=4)
plt.title("Unevenly Sized Blobs")

plt.show()
```

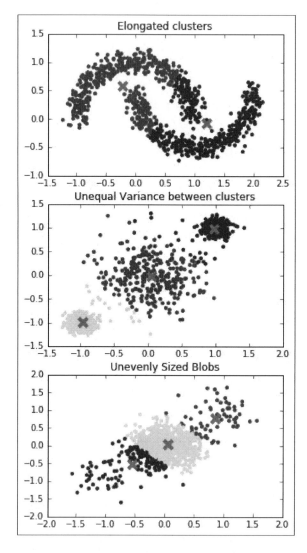

In all the preceding examples, the clustering operation is not perfect, outputting a wrong and unstable result.

So far, we've assumed to know exactly which is the exact K, the number of clusters that we're expecting to use in the clustering operation. Actually, in real-world problems, this is not always true. We often use an unsupervised learning method to discover the underlying structure of the data, including the number of clusters composing the dataset. Let's see what happens when we try to run K-means with a wrong K on a simple dummy dataset; we will try both a lower K and a higher one:

```
In:pylab.rcParams['figure.figsize'] = (10.0, 4.0)
X, _ = make_blobs(n_samples=1000, centers=3, random_state=101)

for K in [2, 3, 4]:
    cls = KMeans(n_clusters=K, random_state=101)
    y_pred = cls.fit_predict(X)

    plt.subplot(1, 3, K-1)
    plt.title("K-means, K=%s" % K)
    plt.scatter(X[:, 0], X[:, 1], c=y_pred, edgecolors='none')
    plt.scatter(cls.cluster_centers_[:,0], cls.cluster_centers_[:,1],
                marker='x', color='r', s=100, linewidths=4)

plt.show()
```

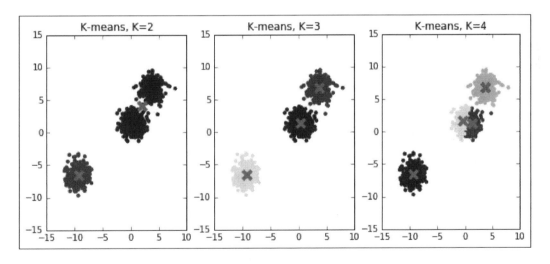

As you can see, the results are massively wrong in case the right K is not guessed, even for this simple dummy dataset. In the next section, we will explain some tricks to best select the K.

Selection of the best K

There are several methods to detect the best K if the assumptions behind K-means are met. Some of them are based on cross-validation and metrics on the output; they can be used on all clustering methods, but only when a ground truth is available (they're named supervised metrics). Some others are based on intrinsic parameters of the clustering algorithm and can be used independently by the presence or absence of the ground truth (also named unsupervised metrics). Unfortunately, none of them ensures 100% accuracy to find the correct result.

Supervised metrics require a ground truth (containing the true associations in sets) and they're usually combined with a gridsearch analysis to understand the best K. Some of these metrics are derived from equivalent classification ones, but they allow having a different number of unordered sets as predicted labels. The first one that we're going to see is named **homogeneity**; as you can expect, it gives a measure of how many of the predicted clusters contain just points of one class. It's a measure based on entropy, and it's the cluster equivalent of the precision in classification. It's a measure bound between 0 (worst) and 1 (best); its mathematical formulation is as follows:

$$h = 1 - \frac{H(C|K)}{H(C)}$$

Here, $H(C|K)$ is the conditional entropy of the class distribution given the proposed clustering assignment, and $H(C)$ is the entropy of the classes. $H(C|K)$ is maximal and equals $H(C)$ when the clustering provides no new information; it is zero when each cluster contains only a member of a single class.

Connected to it, as in precision and recall for classification, there is the **completeness** score: it gives a measure about how much all members of a class are assigned to the same cluster. Even this one is bound between 0 (worst) and 1 (best), and its mathematical formulation is deeply based on entropy:

$$c = 1 - \frac{H(K|C)}{H(K)}$$

Here, *H(K | C)* is the conditional entropy of the proposed cluster distribution given the class, and *H(K)* is the entropy of the clusters.

Finally, equivalent to the f1 score for the classification task, the V-measure is the harmonic mean of homogeneity and completeness:

$$v = 2 \cdot \frac{h \cdot c}{h + c}$$

Let's get back to the first dataset (four symmetric noisy clusters), and try to see how these scores operate and whether they are able to highlight the best K to use:

```
In:pylab.rcParams['figure.figsize'] = (6.0, 4.0)
from sklearn.metrics import homogeneity_completeness_v_measure


centers = [[1, 1], [1, -1], [-1, -1], [-1, 1]]
X, y = make_blobs(n_samples=1000, centers=centers,
                  cluster_std=0.5, random_state=101)

Ks = range(2, 10)
HCVs = []
for K in Ks:
    y_pred = KMeans(n_clusters=K, random_state=101).fit_predict(X)
    HCVs.append(homogeneity_completeness_v_measure(y, y_pred))

plt.plot(Ks, [el[0] for el in HCVs], 'r', label='Homogeneity')
plt.plot(Ks, [el[1] for el in HCVs], 'g', label='Completeness')
plt.plot(Ks, [el[2] for el in HCVs], 'b', label='V measure')
plt.ylim([0, 1])
plt.legend(loc=4)
plt.show()
```

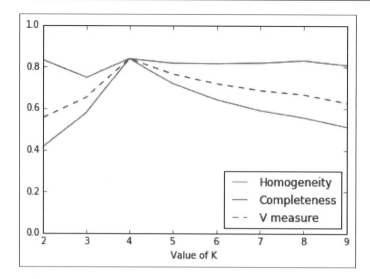

In the plot, initially (*K<4*) completeness is high, but homogeneity is low; for *K>4*, it is the opposite: homogeneity is high, but completeness is low. In both cases, the V-measure is low. For *K=4*, instead, all the measure reaches their maximum, indicating that's the best value for *K*, the number of clusters.

Beyond these metrics that are supervised, there are others named unsupervised that don't require a ground truth, but are just based on the learner itself.

The first that we're going to see in this section is the **Elbow method**, applied to the distortion. It's very easy and doesn't require any math: you just need to plot the distortion of many K-means models with different Ks, then select the one in which increasing K doesn't introduce *much lower* distortion in the solution. In Python, this is very simple to achieve:

```
In:Ks = range(2, 10)
Ds = []
for K in Ks:
    cls = KMeans(n_clusters=K, random_state=101)
    cls.fit(X)
    Ds.append(cls.inertia_)

plt.plot(Ks, Ds, 'o-')
plt.xlabel("Value of K")
plt.ylabel("Distortion")
plt.show()
```

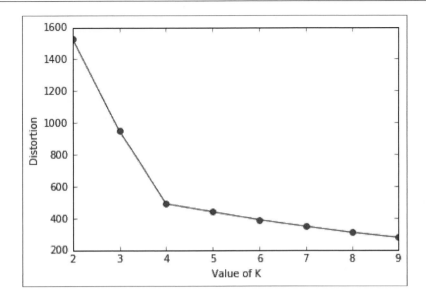

As you can expect, the distortion drops till *K=4*, then it decreases slowly. Here, the best-obtained K is 4.

Another unsupervised metric that we're going to see is the **Silhouette**. It's more complex, but also more powerful than the previous heuristics. At a very high level, it measures how close (similar) an observation is to the assigned cluster and how loosely (dissimilarly) it is matched to the data of nearby clusters. A Silhouette score of 1 indicates that all the data is in the best cluster, and -1 indicates a completely wrong cluster result. To obtain such a measure using Python code is very easy, thanks to the Scikit-learn implementation:

```
In:from sklearn.metrics import silhouette_score

Ks = range(2, 10)
Ds = []
for K in Ks:
    cls = KMeans(n_clusters=K, random_state=101)
    Ds.append(silhouette_score(X, cls.fit_predict(X)))

plt.plot(Ks, Ds, 'o-')
plt.xlabel("Value of K")
plt.ylabel("Silhouette score")
plt.show()
```

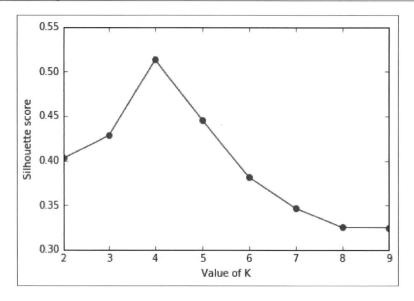

Even in this case, we've arrived at the same conclusion: the best value for K is 4 as the silhouette score is much lower with a lower and higher K.

Scaling K-means – mini-batch

Let's now test the scalability of K-means. From the website of UCI, we've selected an appropriate dataset for this task: the US Census 1990 Data. This dataset contains almost 2.5 million observations and 68 categorical (but already number-encoded) attributes. There is no missing data and the file is in the CSV format. Each observation contains the ID of the individual (to be removed before the clustering) and other information about gender, income, marital status, work, and so on.

 Further information about the dataset can be found at
http://archive.ics.uci.edu/ml/datasets/
US+Census+Data+%281990%29 or in the paper published in The Journal of Machine Learning Research by Meek, Thiesson, and Heckerman (2001) entitled *The Learning Curve Method Applied to Clustering.*

As the first thing to be done, you have to download the file containing the dataset and store it in a temporary directory. Note that it's 345MB in size, therefore its download might require a long time on slow connections:

```
In:import urllib
import os.path

url = "http://archive.ics.uci.edu/ml/machine-learning-databases/
census1990-mld/USCensus1990.data.txt"
census_csv_file = "/tmp/USCensus1990.data.txt"

import os.path
if not os.path.exists(census_csv_file):
    testfile = urllib.URLopener()
    testfile.retrieve(url, census_csv_file)
```

Now, let's run some tests clocking the times needed to train a K-means learner with K equal to 4, 8, and 12, and with a dataset containing 20K, 200K, and 0.5M observations. As we don't want to saturate the memory of the machine, consequently we will just read the first 500K lines and drop the column containing the identifier of the user. Finally, let's plot the training times for a complete performance evaluation:

```
In:piece_of_dataset = pd.read_csv(census_csv_file, iterator=True).get_
chunk(500000).drop('caseid', axis=1).as_matrix()

time_results = {4: [], 8:[], 12:[]}
dataset_sizes = [20000, 200000, 500000]


for dataset_size in dataset_sizes:
    print "Dataset size:", dataset_size
    X = piece_of_dataset[:dataset_size,:]

    for K in [4, 8, 12]:
        print "K:", K
        cls = KMeans(K, random_state=101)
        timeit = %timeit -o -n1 -r1 cls.fit(X)

        time_results[K].append(timeit.best)

plt.plot(dataset_sizes, time_results[4], 'r', label='K=4')
plt.plot(dataset_sizes, time_results[8], 'g', label='K=8')
plt.plot(dataset_sizes, time_results[12], 'b', label='K=12')

plt.xlabel("Training set size")
```

```
plt.ylabel("Training time")
plt.legend(loc=0)
plt.show()

Out:Dataset size: 20000
K: 4
1 loops, best of 1: 478 ms per loop
K: 8
1 loops, best of 1: 1.22 s per loop
K: 12
1 loops, best of 1: 1.76 s per loop
Dataset size: 200000
K: 4
1 loops, best of 1: 6.35 s per loop
K: 8
1 loops, best of 1: 10.5 s per loop
K: 12
1 loops, best of 1: 17.7 s per loop
Dataset size: 500000
K: 4
1 loops, best of 1: 13.4 s per loop
K: 8
1 loops, best of 1: 48.6 s per loop
K: 12
1 loops, best of 1: 1min 5s per loop
```

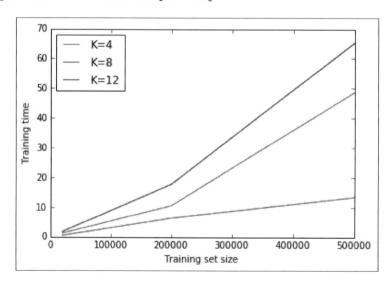

It seems clear that, given the plot and actual timings, the training time increases linearly with K and the training set size, but for large Ks and training sizes, such a relation becomes nonlinear. Doing an exhaustive search with the whole training set for many Ks does not seem scalable.

Fortunately, there's an online version of K-means based on mini-batches, already implemented in Scikit-learn and named MiniBatchKMeans. Let's try it on the slowest case of the previous cell, that is, with *K=12*. With the classic K-means, the training on 500,000 samples (circa 20% of the full dataset) took more than a minute; let's see the performance of the online mini-batch version, setting the batch size to 1,000 and importing chunks of 50,000 observations from the dataset. As an output, we plot the training time versus the number of chunks already passed thought the training phase:

```
In:from sklearn.cluster import MiniBatchKMeans
import time

cls = MiniBatchKMeans(12, batch_size=1000, random_state=101)
ts = []

tik = time.time()
for chunk in pd.read_csv(census_csv_file, chunksize=50000):
    cls.partial_fit(chunk.drop('caseid', axis=1))
    ts.append(time.time()-tik)

plt.plot(range(len(ts)), ts)
plt.xlabel('Training batches')
plt.ylabel('time [s]')

plt.show()
```

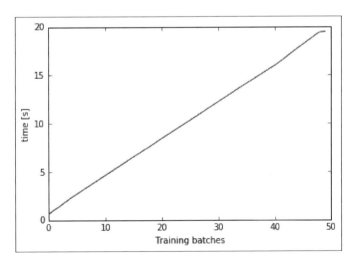

Training time is linear for each chunk, performing the clustering on the full 2.5 million observations dataset in nearly 20 seconds. With this implementation, we can run a full search to select the best K using the elbow method on the distortion. Let's do a gridsearch, with K spanning from 4 to 12, and plot the distortion:

```
In:Ks = list(range(4, 13))
ds = []

for K in Ks:
    cls = MiniBatchKMeans(K, batch_size=1000, random_state=101)

    for chunk in pd.read_csv(census_csv_file, chunksize=50000):
        cls.partial_fit(chunk.drop('caseid', axis=1))
    ds.append(cls.inertia_)

plt.plot(Ks, ds)
plt.xlabel('Value of K')
plt.ylabel('Distortion')

plt.show()

Out:
```

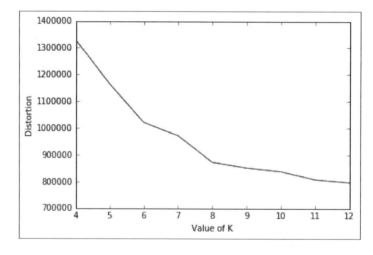

From the plot, the elbow seems in correspondence of K=8. Beyond the value, we would like to point out that in less than a couple of minutes, we've been able to perform this massive operation on a large dataset, thanks to the batch implementation; therefore remember never to use the plain vanilla K-means if the dataset is getting big.

K-means with H2O

Here, we're comparing the K-means implementation of H2O with Scikit-learn. More specifically, we will run the mini-batch experiment using `H2OKMeansEstimator`, the object for K-means available in H2O. The setup is similar to the one shown in the *PCA with H2O* section, and the experiment is the same as seen in the preceding section:

```
In:import h2o
from h2o.estimators.kmeans import H2OKMeansEstimator
h2o.init(max_mem_size_GB=4)

def testH2O_kmeans(X, k):

    temp_file = tempfile.NamedTemporaryFile().name
    np.savetxt(temp_file, np.c_[X], delimiter=",")

    cls = H2OKMeansEstimator(k=k, standardize=True)
    blobdata = h2o.import_file(temp_file)

    tik = time.time()
    cls.train(x=range(blobdata.ncol), training_frame=blobdata)
    fit_time = time.time() - tik

    os.remove(temp_file)

    return fit_time

piece_of_dataset = pd.read_csv(census_csv_file, iterator=True).get_
chunk(500000).drop('caseid', axis=1).as_matrix()
time_results = {4: [], 8:[], 12:[]}
dataset_sizes = [20000, 200000, 500000]

for dataset_size in dataset_sizes:
    print "Dataset size:", dataset_size
    X = piece_of_dataset[:dataset_size,:]

    for K in [4, 8, 12]:
        print "K:", K
        fit_time = testH2O_kmeans(X, K)
        time_results[K].append(fit_time)

plt.plot(dataset_sizes, time_results[4], 'r', label='K=4')
plt.plot(dataset_sizes, time_results[8], 'g', label='K=8')
```

```
plt.plot(dataset_sizes, time_results[12], 'b', label='K=12')

plt.xlabel("Training set size")
plt.ylabel("Training time")
plt.legend(loc=0)
plt.show()

testH2O_kmeans(100000, 100)

h2o.shutdown(prompt=False)
```

Out:

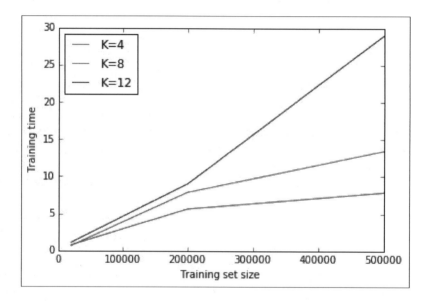

Thanks to the H2O architecture, its implementation of K-means is very fast and scalable and able to perform the clustering of the 500K point datasets in less than 30 seconds for all the selected Ks.

LDA

LDA stands for **Latent Dirichlet Allocation**, and it's one of the widely-used techniques to analyze collections of textual documents.

 LDA is an acronym also used by another technique, Linear Discriminant Analysis, which is a supervised method for classification. Pay attention to how LDA is used as there's no connection between these two algorithms.

A full mathematical explanation of LDA would require the knowledge of probabilistic modeling, which is beyond the scope of this practical book. Here, instead, we will give you the most important intuitions behind the model and how to practically apply this model on a massive dataset.

First at all, LDA is used in a branch of data science named text mining, where the focus is on building learners to understand the natural language, for instance, based on textual examples. Specifically, LDA belongs to the category of topic-modeling algorithms as it tries to model the topics included in a document. Ideally, LDA is able to understand whether a document is about finance, politics, or religion, for example. However, differently from a classifier, it is also able to quantify the presence of topics in a document. For example, let's think about a Harry Potter novel, by Rowling. A classifier would be able to assess its category (fantasy novel); LDA, instead, is able to understand how much comedy, drama, mystery, romance, and adventure is in there. Moreover, LDA doesn't require any label; it's an unsupervised method and internally builds the output categories or topic and its composition (that is, given by the set of words composing a topic).

During the processing, LDA builds both a topics-per-document model and a words-per-topic model, modeled as Dirichlet distributions. Although the complexity is high, the processing time needed to output stable results is not all that long, thanks to an iterative Monte Carlo-like core function.

The LDA model is easy to understand: each document is modeled as a distribution of topics, and each topic is modeled as a distribution of words. Distributions assume to have a Dirichlet prior (with different parameters as the number of words per topic are usually different than the number of topics per document). Thanks to Gibbs sampling, distributions shouldn't be directly sampled, but an accurate approximate of it is obtained iteratively. Similar results can be obtained using the variational Bayes technique, where the approximation is generated with an Expectation-Maximization approach.

The resulting LDA model is generative (as happens with Hidden Markov Models, Naïve Bayes, and Restricted Boltzmann Machines), therefore each variable can be simulated and observed.

Let's now see how it works on a real-world dataset—the 20 Newsgroup dataset. It's composed of a collection of e-mails exchanged in 20 newsgroups. Let's initially load it, removing the e-mail headers, footers, and quotes from replied e-mails:

```
In:from sklearn.datasets import fetch_20newsgroups
documents = fetch_20newsgroups(remove=('headers', 'footers', \
            'quotes'), random_state=101).data
```

Check the size of the dataset (that is, how many documents), and print one of them to see what one document is actually composed of:

```
In:len(documents)

Out:11314

In:document_num = 9960
print documents[document_num]

Out:Help!!!

I have an ADB graphicsd tablet which I want to connect to my
Quadra 950. Unfortunately, the 950 has only one ADB port and
it seems I would have to give up my mouse.

Please, can someone help me? I want to use the tablet as well as
the mouse (and the keyboard of course!!!).

Thanks in advance.
```

As in the example, one guy is looking for help for his video socket on his tablet.

Now, we import the Python packages needed to run LDA. The Gensim package is one of the best ones and, as you'll see at the end of the section, it is also very scalable:

```
In:import gensim
from gensim.utils import simple_preprocess
from gensim.parsing.preprocessing import STOPWORDS
from nltk.stem import WordNetLemmatizer, SnowballStemmer

np.random.seed(101)
```

As the first step, we should clean the text. A few steps are necessary, which is typical of any NLP text processing:

1. Tokenization is where the text is split into sentences and sentences are split into words. Finally, words are lowercased. At this point, punctuation (and accents) is removed.

2. Words composed of fewer than three characters are removed. (This step removes most of the acronyms, emoticons, and conjunctions.)

3. Words appearing in the list of English *stopwords* are removed. Words in this list are very common and have no predictive power (such as the, an, so, then, have, and so on).

4. Tokens are then lemmatized; words in third-person are changed to first-person, and verbs in past and future tenses are changed into present (for example, goes, went, and gone all become go).

5. Finally, stemming removes the inflection, reducing the word to its root (for example, shoes becomes shoe).

In the following piece of code, we will do exactly this: try to clean the text as much as possible and list the words composing each of them. At the end of the cell, we see how this operation changes the document seen previously:

```
In:lm = WordNetLemmatizer()
stemmer = SnowballStemmer("english")

def lem_stem(text):
    return stemmer.stem(lm.lemmatize(text, pos='v'))

def tokenize_lemmatize(text):
    return [lem_stem(token)
            for token in gensim.utils.simple_preprocess(text)
            if token not in gensim.parsing.preprocessing.STOPWORDS and
len(token) > 3]

print tokenize_lemmatize(documents[document_num])

Out:[u'help', u'graphicsd', u'tablet', u'want', u'connect', u'quadra',
u'unfortun', u'port', u'mous', u'help', u'want', u'tablet', u'mous',
u'keyboard', u'cours', u'thank', u'advanc']
```

Now, as the next step, let's operate the cleaning steps on all the documents. After this, we have to build a dictionary containing how many times a word appears in the training set. Thanks to the Gensim package, this operation is straightforward:

```
In:processed_docs = [tokenize(doc) for doc in documents]
   word_count_dict = gensim.corpora.Dictionary(processed_docs)
```

Now, as we want to build a generic and fast solution, let's remove all the very rare and very common words. For example, we can filter out all the words appearing less than 20 times (in total) and in no more than 20% of the documents:

```
In:word_count_dict.filter_extremes(no_below=20, no_above=0.2)
```

As the next step, with such a reduced set of words, we now build the bag-of-words model for each document; that is, for each document, we create a dictionary reporting how many words and how many times the words appear:

```
In:bag_of_words_corpus = [word_count_dict.doc2bow(pdoc) \
   for pdoc in processed_docs]
```

As an example, let's have a peek at the bag-of-words model of the preceding document:

```
In:bow_doc1 = bag_of_words_corpus[document_num]

for i in range(len(bow_doc1)):
    print "Word {} (\"{}\") appears {} time[s]" \
.format(bow_doc1[i][0], \
word_count_dict[bow_doc1[i][0]], bow_doc1[i][1])


Out:Word 178 ("want") appears 2 time[s]
Word 250 ("keyboard") appears 1 time[s]
Word 833 ("unfortun") appears 1 time[s]
Word 1037 ("port") appears 1 time[s]
Word 1142 ("help") appears 2 time[s]
Word 1543 ("quadra") appears 1 time[s]
Word 2006 ("advanc") appears 1 time[s]
Word 2124 ("cours") appears 1 time[s]
Word 2391 ("thank") appears 1 time[s]
Word 2898 ("mous") appears 2 time[s]
Word 3313 ("connect") appears 1 time[s]
```

Now, we have arrived at the core part of the algorithm: running LDA. As for our decision, let's ask for 12 topics (there are 20 different newsletters, but some are similar):

```
In:lda_model = gensim.models.LdaMulticore(bag_of_words_corpus, num_
topics=10, id2word=word_count_dict, passes=50)
```

 If you get an error with such a code, try to mono-process the version with the gensim.models.LdaModel class instead of gensim.models.LdaMulticore.

Let's now print the topic composition, that is, the words appearing in each topic and their relative weight:

```
In:for idx, topic in lda_model.print_topics(-1):
    print "Topic:{} Word composition:{}".format(idx, topic)
    print


Out:
Topic:0 Word composition:0.015*imag + 0.014*version + 0.013*avail
+ 0.013*includ + 0.013*softwar + 0.012*file + 0.011*graphic +
0.010*program + 0.010*data + 0.009*format

Topic:1 Word composition:0.040*window + 0.030*file + 0.018*program
+ 0.014*problem + 0.011*widget + 0.011*applic + 0.010*server +
0.010*entri + 0.009*display + 0.009*error

Topic:2 Word composition:0.011*peopl + 0.010*mean + 0.010*question
+ 0.009*believ + 0.009*exist + 0.008*encrypt + 0.008*point +
0.008*reason + 0.008*post + 0.007*thing

Topic:3 Word composition:0.010*caus + 0.009*good + 0.009*test +
0.009*bike + 0.008*problem + 0.008*effect + 0.008*differ + 0.008*engin
+ 0.007*time + 0.006*high

Topic:4 Word composition:0.018*state + 0.017*govern + 0.015*right +
0.010*weapon + 0.010*crime + 0.009*peopl + 0.009*protect + 0.008*legal
+ 0.008*control + 0.008*drug

Topic:5 Word composition:0.017*christian + 0.016*armenian +
0.013*jesus + 0.012*peopl + 0.008*say + 0.008*church + 0.007*bibl +
0.007*come + 0.006*live + 0.006*book
```

```
Topic:6 Word composition:0.018*go + 0.015*time + 0.013*say +
0.012*peopl + 0.012*come + 0.012*thing + 0.011*want + 0.010*good +
0.009*look + 0.009*tell

Topic:7 Word composition:0.012*presid + 0.009*state + 0.008*peopl +
0.008*work + 0.008*govern + 0.007*year + 0.007*israel + 0.007*say +
0.006*american + 0.006*isra

Topic:8 Word composition:0.022*thank + 0.020*card + 0.015*work +
0.013*need + 0.013*price + 0.012*driver + 0.010*sell + 0.010*help +
0.010*mail + 0.010*look

Topic:9 Word composition:0.019*space + 0.011*inform + 0.011*univers +
0.010*mail + 0.009*launch + 0.008*list + 0.008*post + 0.008*anonym +
0.008*research + 0.008*send

Topic:10 Word composition:0.044*game + 0.031*team + 0.027*play +
0.022*year + 0.020*player + 0.016*season + 0.015*hockey + 0.014*leagu
+ 0.011*score + 0.010*goal

Topic:11 Word composition:0.075*drive + 0.030*disk + 0.028*control
+ 0.028*scsi + 0.020*power + 0.020*hard + 0.018*wire + 0.015*cabl +
0.013*instal + 0.012*connect
```

Unfortunately, LDA doesn't provide a name for each topic; we should do it manuall yourselves, based on our interpretation of the results of the algorithm. After having carefully examined the composition, we can name the discovered topics as follows:

Topic	Name
0	Software
1	Applications
2	Reasoning
3	Transports
4	Government
5	Religion
6	People actions
7	Middle-East
8	PC Devices
9	Space
10	Games
11	Drives

Let's now try to understand what topics are represented in the preceding document and their weights:

```
In:
for index, score in sorted( \
lda_model[bag_of_words_corpus[document_num]], \
key=lambda tup: -1*tup[1]):
    print "Score: {}\t Topic: {}".format(score, lda_model.print_
topic(index, 10))
Out:Score: 0.938887758964      Topic: 0.022*thank + 0.020*card +
0.015*work + 0.013*need + 0.013*price + 0.012*driver + 0.010*sell +
0.010*help + 0.010*mail + 0.010*look
```

The highest score is associated with the topic *PC Devices*. Based on our previous knowledge of the collections of documents, it seems that the topic extraction has performed quite well.

Now, let's evaluate the model as a whole. The perplexity (or its logarithm) provides us with a metric to understand how well LDA has performed on the training dataset:

```
In:print "Log perplexity of the model is", lda_model.log_
perplexity(bag_of_words_corpus)

Out:Log perplexity of the model is -7.2985188569
```

In this case, the perplexity is 2-7.298, and it's connected to the (log) likelihood that the LDA model is able to generate the documents in the test set, given the distribution of topics for those documents. The lower the perplexity, the better the model, because it basically means that the model can regenerate the text quite well.

Now, let's try to use the model on an unseen document. For simplicity, the document contains only the sentences, *Golf or tennis? Which is the best sport to play?*:

```
In:unseen_document = "Golf or tennis? Which is the best sport to
play?"

bow_vector = word_count_dict.doc2bow(\
tokenize_lemmatize(unseen_document))
for index, score in sorted(lda_model[bow_vector], \
key=lambda tup: -1*tup[1]):
    print "Score: {}\t Topic: {}".format(score, \
                lda_model.print_topic(index, 5))

Out:Score: 0.610691655136      Topic: 0.044*game + 0.031*team +
0.027*play + 0.022*year + 0.020*player

Score: 0.222640440339      Topic: 0.018*state + 0.017*govern +
0.015*right + 0.010*weapon + 0.010*crime
```

As expected, the topic with a higher score is the one about "Games", followed by others with a relatively smaller score.

How does LDA scale with the size of the corpus? Fortunately, very well; the algorithm is iterative and allows online learning, similar to the mini-batch one. The key for the online process is the `.update()` method offered by `LdaModel` (or `LdaMulticore`).

We will do this test on a subset of the original corpus composed of the first 1,000 documents, and we will update our LDA model with batches of 50, 100, 200, and 500 documents. For each mini-batch updating the model, we will record the time and plot them on a graph:

```
In:small_corpus = bag_of_words_corpus[:1000]
batch_times = {}

for batch_size in [50, 100, 200, 500]:
    print "batch_size =", batch_size
    tik0 = time.time()
    lda_model = gensim.models.LdaModel(num_topics=12, \
                id2word=word_count_dict)
    batch_times[batch_size] = []

    for i in range(0, len(small_corpus), batch_size):
        lda_model.update(small_corpus[i:i+batch_size], \
update_every=25, \
passes=1+500/batch_size)
        batch_times[batch_size].append(time.time() - tik0)

Out:batch_size = 50
batch_size = 100
batch_size = 200
batch_size = 500
```

Note that we've set the `update_every` and `passes` parameters in the model update. This is necessary to make the model converge at each iteration and not return a non-converging model. Note that 500 has been chosen heuristically; if you set it lower, you'll have many warnings from Gensim about the non-convergence of the model.

Let's now plot the results:

```
In:plt.plot(range(50, 1001, 50), batch_times[50], 'g', \
label='size 50')
plt.plot(range(100, 1001, 100), batch_times[100], 'b', \
label='size 100')
```

```
plt.plot(range(200, 1001, 200), batch_times[200], 'k', \
label='size 200')
plt.plot(range(500, 1001, 500), batch_times[500], 'r', \
label='size 500')

plt.xlabel("Training set size")
plt.ylabel("Training time")
plt.xlim([0, 1000])
plt.legend(loc=0)
plt.show()
```

Out:

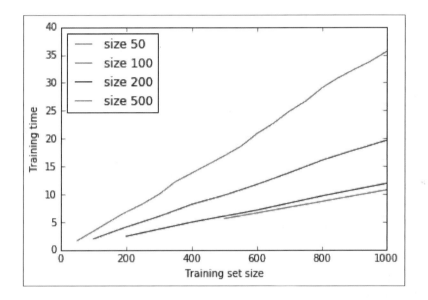

The bigger the batch, the faster the training. (Remember that big batches need fewer passes while updating the model.) On the other hand, the bigger the batch, the greater the amount of memory you need in order to store and process the corpora. Thanks to the mini-batches update method, LDA is able to scale to process a corpora of million documents. In fact, the implementation provided by the Gensim package is able to scale and process the whole of Wikipedia in a couple of hours on a domestic computer. If you're brave enough to try it yourself, here are the complete instructions to accomplish the task, provided by the author of the package:

```
https://radimrehurek.com/gensim/wiki.html
```

Scaling LDA – memory, CPUs, and machines

Gensim is very flexible and built to crunch big textual corpora; in fact, this library is able to scale without any modification or additional download:

1. With the number of CPUs, allowing parallel processes on a single node (with the classes, as seen in the first example).

2. With the number of observations, allowing online learning based on mini-batches. This can be achieved with the `update` method available in `LdaModel` and `LdaMulticore` (as shown in the previous example).

3. Running it on a cluster, distributing the workload across the nodes in the cluster, thanks to the Python library Pyro4 and the `models.lda_dispatcher` (as a scheduler) and `models.lda_worker` (as a worker process) objects, both provided by Gensim.

Beyond the classical LDA algorithm, Gensim also provides its hierarchical version, named **Hierarchical Dirichlet Processing (HDP)**. Using this algorithm, topics follow a multilevel structure, enabling the user to understand complex corpora better (that is, where some documents are generic and some specific on a topic). This module is fairly new and, as of the end of 2015, not as scalable as the classic LDA.

Summary

In this chapter, we've introduced three popular unsupervised learners able to scale to cope with big data. The first, PCA, is able to reduce the number of features by creating ones containing the majority of variance (that is, the principal ones). K-means is a clustering algorithm able to group similar points together and associate them with a centroid. LDA is a powerful method to do topic modeling on textual data, that is, model the topics per document and the words appearing in a topic jointly.

In the next chapter, we will introduce some advanced and very recent methods of machine learning, still not part of the mainstream, naturally great for small datasets, but also suitable to process large scale machine learning.

8
Distributed Environments – Hadoop and Spark

In this chapter, we will introduce a new way to process data, scaling horizontally. So far, we've focused our attention primarily on processing big data on a standalone machine; here, we will introduce some methods that run on a cluster of machines.

Specifically, we will first illustrate the motivations and circumstances when we need a cluster to process big data. Then, we will introduce the Hadoop framework and all its components with a few examples (HDFS, MapReduce, and YARN), and finally, we will introduce the Spark framework and its Python interface—pySpark.

From a standalone machine to a bunch of nodes

The amount of data stored in the world is increasing exponentially. Nowadays, for a data scientist, having to process a few Terabytes of data a day is not an unusual request. To make things more complex, usually data comes from many different heterogeneous systems and the expectation of business is to produce a model within a short time.

Handling big data, therefore, is not just a matter of size, it's actually a three-dimensional phenomenon. In fact, according to the 3V model, systems operating on big data can be classified using three (orthogonal) criteria:

1. The first criterion is the velocity that the system archives to process the data. Although a few years ago, speed was indicating how quickly a system was able to process a batch; nowadays, velocity indicates whether a system can provide real-time outputs on streaming data.

2. The second criterion is volume, that is, how much information is available to be processed. It can be expressed in number of rows, features, or just a bare count of the bytes. To stream data, volume indicates the throughput of data arriving in the system.

3. The last criterion is variety, that is, the type of data sources. A few years ago, variety was limited by structured datasets; nowadays, data can be structured (tables, images, and so on), semi-structured (JSON, XML, and so on), and unstructured (webpages, social data, and so on). Usually, big data systems try to process as many relevant sources as possible, mixing all kinds of sources.

Beyond these criteria, many other Vs have appeared in the last years, trying to explain other features of big data. Some of these are as follows:

- Veracity (providing an indication of abnormality, bias, and noise contained in the data; ultimately, its accuracy)

- Volatility (indicating for how long the data can be used to extract meaningful information)

- Validity (the correctness of the data)

- Value (indicating the return over investment of the data)

In the recent years, all of the Vs have increased dramatically; now many companies have found that the data they retain has a huge value that can be monetized and they want to extract information out of it. The technical challenge has moved to have enough storage and processing power in order to be able to extract meaningful insights quickly, at scale, and using different input data streams.

Current computers, even the newest and most expensive ones, have a limited amount of disk, memory, and CPU. It looks very hard to process terabytes (or petabytes) of information per day, producing a quick model. Moreover, a standalone server containing both data and processing software needs to be replicated; otherwise, it could become the single point of failure of the system.

The world of big data has therefore moved to clusters: they're composed by a variable number of *not very expensive* nodes and sit on a high-speed Internet connection. Usually, some clusters are dedicated to storing data (a big hard disk, little CPU, and low amount of memory), and others are devoted to processing the data (a powerful CPU, medium-to-big amount of memory, and small hard disk). Moreover, if a cluster is properly set, it can ensure reliability (no single point of failure) and high availability.

Pay attention that, when we store data in a distributed environment (like a cluster), we should also consider the limitation of the CAP theorem; in the system, we can just ensure two out of the following three properties:

- Consistency: All the nodes are able to deliver the same data at the same time to a client

- Availability: A client requesting data is guaranteed to always receive a response, for both succeeded and failed requests

- Partition tolerance: If the network experiences failures and all the nodes cannot be in contact, the system is able to keep working

Specifically, the following are the consequences of the CAP theorem:

- If you give up on consistency, you'll create an environment where data is distributed across the nodes, and even though the network experiences some problems, the system is still able to provide a response to each request, although it is not guaranteed that the response to the same question is the same (it can be inconsistent). Typical examples of this configuration are DynamoDB, CouchDB, and Cassandra.

- If you give up on availability, you'll create a distributed system that can fail to respond to a query. Examples of this class are distributed-cache databases such as Redis, MongoDb, and MemcacheDb.

- Lastly, if you vice up on partition tolerance, you fall in the rigid schema of relational databases that don't allow the network to be split. This category includes MySQL, Oracle, and SQL Server.

Why do we need a distributed framework?

The easiest way to build a cluster is to use some nodes as storage nodes and others as processing ones. This configuration seems very easy as we don't need a complex framework to handle this situation. In fact, many small clusters are exactly built in this way: a couple of servers handle the data (plus their replica) and another bunch process the data.

Although this may appear as a great solution, it's not often used for many reasons:

- It just works for embarrassingly parallel algorithms. If an algorithm requires a common area of memory shared among the processing servers, this approach cannot be used.

- If one or many storage nodes die, the data is not guaranteed to be consistent. (Think about a situation where a node and its replica dies at the same time or where a node dies just after a write operation which has not yet been replicated.

- If a processing node dies, we are not able to keep track of the process that it was executing, making it hard to resume the processing on another node.

- If the network experiences failures, it's very hard to predict the situation after it's back to normality.

Let's now compute what the probability of a node failure is. Is it so rare that we can discard it? Is it something more concrete that we shall always take into consideration? The solution is easy: let's take into consideration a 100-node cluster, where each node has a probability of 1% of failure (cumulative of hardware and software crash) in the first year. What's the probability that all of the 100 will survive the first year? Under the hypothesis that every server is independent (that is, each node can crash independently of all the others), it's simply a multiplication:

$$P(cluster = ok) = P(note_1 = ok, node_2 = ok, ..., node_{100} = ok)$$
$$= \left(1 - P(fail)\right)^{100}$$
$$= 37\%$$

The result is very surprising at the beginning, but it explains why the big data community has put a lot of emphasis on the problem and developed many solutions for the cluster management in the past decade. From the formula's results, it seems that a crash event (or even more than one) is quite likely, a fact requiring that such an occurrence must be thought of in advance and handled properly to ensure the continuity of operations on the data. Furthermore, using cheap hardware or a bigger cluster, it looks almost certain that at least a node will fail.

The learning point here is that, once you go enterprise with big data, you must adopt enough countermeasures for node failures; it's the norm rather than the exception and should be handled properly to ensure the continuity of operations.

So far, the vast majority of cluster frameworks use the approach named *divide et impera* (split and conquer):

- There are modules *specialized* for the data nodes and some others *specialized* for data processing nodes (also named worker).

- Data is replicated across the data nodes, and one node is the master, ensuring that both the write and read operations succeed.

- The processing steps are split across the worker nodes. They don't share any state (unless stored in the data nodes) and their master ensures that all the tasks are performed positively and in the right order.

Later on, we will introduce the Apache Hadoop framework in this chapter; although it is now a mature cluster management system, it still relies on solid foundations. Before that, let's set up the right working environment on our machines.

Setting up the VM

Setting up a cluster is a long and difficult operation; senior big data engineers earn their (high) salaries not just downloading and executing a binary application, but skillfully and carefully adapting the cluster manager to the desired working environment. It's a tough and complex operation; it may take a long time and if results are below the expectations, the whole business (including data scientists and software developers) won't be able to be productive. Data engineers must know every small detail of the nodes, data, operations that will be carried out, and network before starting to build the cluster. The output is usually a balanced, adaptive, fast, and reliable cluster, which can be used for years by all the technical people in the company.

Is a cluster with a low number of very powerful nodes better than a cluster with many less powerful servers? The answer should be evaluated case-by-case, and it's highly dependent on the data, processing algorithms, number of people accessing it, speed at which we want the results, overall price, robustness of the scalability, network speed, and many other factors. Simply stated, it's not easy at all to decide for the best!

As setting up an environment is very difficult, we authors prefer to provide readers with a virtual machine image containing everything that you need in order to try some operations on a cluster. In the following sections, you'll learn how to set up a guest operating system on your machine, containing one node of a cluster with all the software you'd find on a real cluster.

Why only one node? As the framework that we've used is not lightweight, we decided to go for the atomic piece of a cluster ensuring that the environment you'll find in the node is exactly the same you'll find in a real-world situation. In order to run the virtual machine on your computer, you need two software: Virtualbox and Vagrant. Both of them are free of charge and open source.

VirtualBox

VirtualBox is an open source software used to virtualize one-to-many guest operative systems on Windows, macOS, and Linux host machines. From the user's point of view, a virtualized machine looks like another computer running in a window, with all its functionalities.

VirtualBox has become very popular because of its high performance, simplicity, and clean **graphical user interface** (**GUI**). Starting, stopping, importing, and terminating a virtual machine with VirtualBox is just a matter of a click.

Technically, VirtualBox is a hypervisor, which supports the creation and management of multiple **virtual machines** (**VM**) including many versions of Windows, Linux, and BSD-like distributions. The machine where VirtualBox runs is named *host*, while the virtualized machines are named *guests*. Note that there are no restrictions between the host and guests; for example, a Windows host can run Windows (the same version, a previous, or the most recent one) as well as any Linux and BSD distribution that is VirtualBox-compatible.

Virtualbox is often used to run software Operative-System specific; some software runs only on Windows or just a specific version of Windows, some is available only in Linux, and so on. Another application is to simulate new features on a cloned production environment; before trying the modifications in the live (production) environment, software developers usually test it on a clone, like one running on VirtualBox. Thanks to the guest isolation from the host, if something goes wrong in the guest (even formatting the hard disk), this doesn't impact the host. To have it back, just clone your machine before doing anything dangerous; you'll always be in time to recover it.

For those who want to start from scratch, VirtualBox supports virtual hard drives (including hard disks, CDs, DVDs, and floppy disks); this makes the installation of a new OS very simple. For example, if you want to install a plain vanilla version of Linux Ubuntu 14.04, you first download the `.iso` file. Instead of burning it on a CD/DVD, you can simply add it as a virtual drive to VirtualBox. Then, thanks to the simple step-by-step interface, you can select the hard drive size and the features of the guest machine (RAM, number of CPUs, video memory, and network connectivity). When operating with real bios, you can select the boot order: selecting the CD/DVD as a higher priority, you can start the process of the installation of Ubuntu as soon as you turn on the guest.

Now, let's download VirtualBox; remember to select the right version for your operating system.

To install it on your computer, follow the instructions at
`https://www.virtualbox.org/wiki/Downloads`.

At the time of writing this, the latest version is 5.1. Once installed, the graphical
interface looks like the one in the following screenshot:

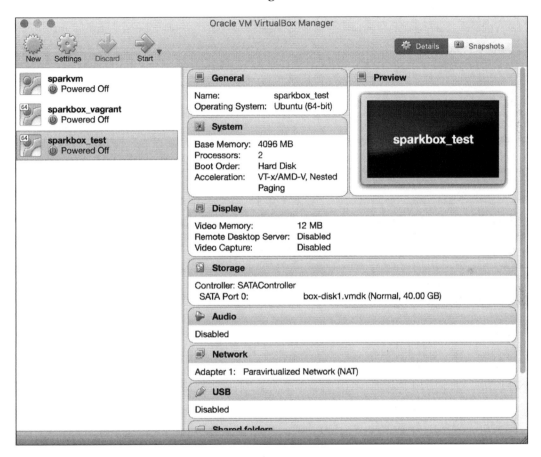

We strongly advise you to take a look at how to set up a guest machine on your
machine. Each guest machine will appear on the left-hand side of the window.
(In the image, you can see that, on our computer, we have three stopped guests.)
By clicking on each of them, on the right side will appear the detailed description
of the virtualized hardware. In the example image, if the virtual machine named
`sparkbox_test` (the one highlighted on the left) is turned on, it will be run on a
virtual computer whose hardware is composed by a 4GB RAM, two processors,
40GB hard drive, and a video card with 12MB of RAM attached to the network
with NAT.

Vagrant

Vagrant is a software that configures virtual environments at a high level. The core piece of Vagrant is the scripting capability, often used to create programmatically and automatically specific virtual environments. Vagrant uses VirtualBox (but also other virtualizers) to build and configure the virtual machines.

 To install it, follow the instructions at `https://www.vagrantup.com/downloads.html`.

Using the VM

With Vagrant and VirtualBox installed, you're now ready to run the node of a cluster environment. Create an empty directory and insert the following Vagrant commands into a new file named `Vagrantfile`:

```
Vagrant.configure("2") do |config|
    config.vm.box = "sparkpy/sparkbox_test_1"
    config.vm.hostname = "sparkbox"
    config.ssh.insert_key = false

    # Hadoop ResourceManager
    config.vm.network :forwarded_port, guest: 8088, host: 8088, auto_
correct: true

    # Hadoop NameNode
    config.vm.network :forwarded_port, guest: 50070, host: 50070,
auto_correct: true

    # Hadoop DataNode
    config.vm.network :forwarded_port, guest: 50075, host: 50075,
auto_correct: true

    # Ipython notebooks (yarn and standalone)
    config.vm.network :forwarded_port, guest: 8888, host: 8888, auto_
correct: true

    # Spark UI (standalone)
    config.vm.network :forwarded_port, guest: 4040, host: 4040, auto_
correct: true


    config.vm.provider "virtualbox" do |v|
```

```
    v.customize ["modifyvm", :id, "--natdnshostresolver1", "on"]
   v.customize ["modifyvm", :id, "--natdnsproxy1", "on"]
v.customize ["modifyvm", :id, "--nictype1", "virtio"]
   v.name = "sparkbox_test"
   v.memory = "4096"
   v.cpus = "2"
   end

  end
```

From top to bottom, the first lines download the right virtual machine (that we authors created and uploaded on a repository). Then, we set some ports to be forwarded to the guest machine; in this way, you'll be able to access some webservices of the virtualized machine. Finally, we set the hardware of the node.

> The configuration is set for a virtual machine with exclusive use of 4GB RAM and two cores. If your system can't meet these requirements, modify v.memory and v.cpus values to those good for your machine. Note that some of the following code examples may fail if the configuration that you set is not adequate.

Now, open a terminal and navigate to the directory containing the Vagrantfile. Here, launch the virtual machine with the following command:

```
$ vagrant up
```

The first time, this command will take a while as it downloads (it's an almost 2GB download) and builds the correct structure of the virtual machine. The next time, this command takes a smaller amount of time as there is nothing more to download.

After having turned on the virtual machine on your local system, you can access it as follows:

```
$ vagrant ssh
```

This command simulates an SSH access, and you'll be inside the virtualized machine finally.

> On Windows machines, this command may fail with an error due to the missing SSH executable. In such a situation, download and install an SSH client for Windows, such as Putty (http://www.putty.org/), Cygwin openssh (http://www.cygwin.com/), or Openssh for Windows (http://sshwindows.sourceforge.net/). Unix systems should not be affected by this problem.

To turn if off, you first need to exit the machine. From inside the VM, simply use the `exit` command to exit the SSH connection and then shut down the VM:

```
$ vagrant halt
```

 The virtual machine consumes resources. Remember to turn it off when you're done with the work with the `vagranthalt` command from the directory where the VM is located.

The preceding command shuts down the virtual machine, exactly as you would do with a server. To remove it and delete all its content, use the `vagrant destroy` command. Use it carefully: after having destroyed the machine, you won't be able to recover the files in there.

Here are the instructions to use IPython (Jupyter) Notebook inside the virtual machine:

1. Launch `vagrant up` and `vagrant ssh` from the folder containing the `Vagrantfile`. You should now be inside the virtual machine.

2. Now, launch the script:

   ```
   vagrant@sparkbox:~$ ./start_hadoop.sh
   ```

3. At this point, launch the following shell script:

   ```
   vagrant@sparkbox:~$ ./start_jupyter_yarn.sh
   ```

   Open a browser on your local machine and point it to `http://localhost:8888`.

Here is the notebook that's backed by the cluster node. To turn the notebook and virtual machine off, perform the following steps:

1. To terminate the Jupyter console, press *Ctrl + C* (and then type *Y* for Yes).

2. Terminate the Hadoop framework as follows:

   ```
   vagrant@sparkbox:~$ ./stop_hadoop.sh
   ```

3. Exit the virtual machine with the following command:

   ```
   vagrant@sparkbox:~$ exit
   ```

4. Shut down the VirtualBox machine with `vagrant halt`.

The Hadoop ecosystem

Apache Hadoop is a very popular software framework for distributed storage and distributed processing on a cluster. Its strengths are in the price (it's free), flexibility (it's open source, and although being written in Java, it can by used by other programming languages), scalability (it can handle clusters composed by thousands of nodes), and robustness (it was inspired by a published paper from Google and has been around since 2011), making it the de facto standard to handle and process big data. Moreover, lots of other projects from the Apache foundation extend its functionalities.

Architecture

Logically, Hadoop is composed of two pieces: distributed storage (HDFS) and distributed processing (YARN and MapReduce). Although the code is very complex, the overall architecture is fairly easy to understand. A client can access both storage and processing through two dedicated modules; they are then in charge of distributing the job across all the working nodes:

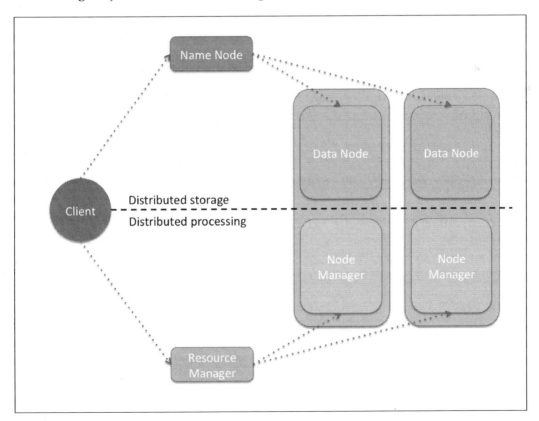

All the Hadoop modules run as services (or instances), that is, a physical or virtual node can run many of them. Typically, for small clusters, all the nodes run both distributed computing and processing services; for big clusters, it may be better to separate the two functionalities specializing the nodes.

We will see the functionalities offered by the two layers in detail.

HDFS

The **Hadoop Distributed File System (HDFS)** is a fault-tolerant distributed filesystem, designed to run on commodity low-cost hardware and able to handle very large datasets (in the order of hundred petabytes to exabytes). Although HDFS requires a fast network connection to transfer data across nodes, the latency can't be as low as in classic filesystems (it may be in the order of seconds); therefore, HDFS has been designed for batch processing and high throughput. Each HDFS node contains a part of the filesystem's data; the same data is also replicated in other instances and this ensures a high throughput access and fault-tolerance.

HDFS's architecture is master-slave. If the master (Name Node) fails, there is a secondary/backup one ready to take control. All the other instances are slaves (Data Nodes); if one of them fails, there's no problem as HDFS has been designed with this in mind.

Data Nodes contain blocks of data: each file saved in HDFS is broken up in chunks (or blocks), typically 64MB each, and then distributed and replicated in a set of Data Nodes.

The Name Node stores just the metadata of the files in the distributed filesystem; it doesn't store any actual data, but just the right indications on how to access the files in the multiple Data Nodes that it manages.

A client asking to read a file shall first contact the Name Node, which will give back a table containing an ordered list of blocks and their locations (as in Data Nodes). At this point, the client should contact the Data Nodes separately, downloading all the blocks and reconstructing the file (by appending the blocks together).

To write a file, instead, a client should first contact the Name Node, which will first decide how to handle the request, updating its records and then replying to the client with an ordered list of Data Nodes of where to write each block of the file. The client will now contact and upload the blocks to the Data Nodes, as reported in the Name Node reply.

Namespace queries (for example, listing a directory content, creating a folder, and so on) are instead completely handled by the Name Node by accessing its metadata information.

Moreover, Name Node is also responsible for handling a Data Node failure properly (it's marked as dead if no Heartbeat packets are received) and its data re-replication to other nodes.

Although these operations are long and hard to be implemented with robustness, they're completely transparent to the user, thanks to many libraries and the HDFS shell. The way you operate on HDFS is pretty similar to what you're currently doing on your filesystem and this is a great benefit of Hadoop: hiding the complexity and letting the user use it with simplicity.

Let's now take a look at the HDFS shell and later, a Python library.

 Use the preceding instructions to turn the VM on and launch the IPython Notebook on your computer.

Now, open a new notebook; this operation will take more time than usual as each notebook is connected to the Hadoop cluster framework. When the notebook is ready to be used, you'll see a flag saying **Kernel starting, please wait ...** on the top right disappear.

The first piece is about the HDFS shell; therefore, all the following commands can be run at a prompt or shell of the virtualized machine. To run them in an IPython Notebook, all of them are anticipated by a question mark !, which is a short way to execute bash code in a notebook.

The common denominator of the following command lines is the executable; we will always run the `hdfs` command. It's the main interface to access and manage the HDFS system and the main command for the HDFS shell.

We start with a report on the state of HDFS. To obtain the details of the **distributed filesystem (dfs)** and its Data Nodes, use the `dfsadmin` subcommand:

```
In:!hdfs dfsadmin -report

Out:Configured Capacity: 42241163264 (39.34 GB)
Present Capacity: 37569168058 (34.99 GB)
DFS Remaining: 37378433024 (34.81 GB)
DFS Used: 190735034 (181.90 MB)
DFS Used%: 0.51%
Under replicated blocks: 0
Blocks with corrupt replicas: 0
```

```
Missing blocks: 0


-------------------------------------------------
Live datanodes (1):

Name: 127.0.0.1:50010 (localhost)
Hostname: sparkbox
Decommission Status : Normal
Configured Capacity: 42241163264 (39.34 GB)
DFS Used: 190735034 (181.90 MB)
Non DFS Used: 4668290330 (4.35 GB)
DFS Remaining: 37380775936 (34.81 GB)
DFS Used%: 0.45%
DFS Remaining%: 88.49%
Configured Cache Capacity: 0 (0 B)
Cache Used: 0 (0 B)
Cache Remaining: 0 (0 B)
Cache Used%: 100.00%
Cache Remaining%: 0.00%
Xceivers: 1
Last contact: Tue Feb 09 19:41:17 UTC 2016
```

The dfs subcommand allows using some well-known Unix commands to access and interact with the distributed filesystem. For example, list the content of the the root directory as follows:

```
In:!hdfs dfs -ls /


Out:Found 2 items
drwxr-xr-x   - vagrant supergroup          0 2016-01-30 16:33 /spark
drwxr-xr-x   - vagrant supergroup          0 2016-01-30 18:12 /user
```

The output is similar to the ls command provided by Linux, listing the permissions, number of links, user and group owning the file, size, timestamp of the last modification, and name for each file or directory.

Similar to the df command, we can invoke the -df argument to display the amount of available disk space in HDFS. The -h option will make the output more readable (using gigabytes and megabytes instead of bytes):

```
In:!hdfs dfs -df -h /


Out:Filesystem              Size    Used  Available  Use%
hdfs://localhost:9000   39.3 G  181.9 M    34.8 G     0%
```

Similar to du, we can use the -du argument to display the size of each folder contained in the root. Again, -h will produce a more human readable output:

```
In:!hdfs dfs -du -h /

Out:178.9 M  /spark
1.4 M    /user
```

So far, we've extracted some information from HDFS. Let's now do some operations on the distributed filesystem, which will modify it. We can start with creating a folder with the -mkdir option followed by the name. Note that this operation may fail if the directory already exists (exactly as in Linux, with the mkdir command):

```
In:!hdfs dfs -mkdir /datasets
```

Let's now transfer some files from the hard disk of the node to the distributed filesystem. In the VM that we've created, there is already a text file in the ../ datasets directory; let's download a text file from the Internet. Let's move both of them to the HDFS directory that we've created with the previous command:

```
In:
!wget -q http://www.gutenberg.org/cache/epub/100/pg100.txt \
    -O ../datasets/shakespeare_all.txt

!hdfs dfs -put ../datasets/shakespeare_all.txt \
/datasets/shakespeare_all.txt

!hdfs dfs -put ../datasets/hadoop_git_readme.txt \
/datasets/hadoop_git_readme.txt
```

Was the importing successful? Yes, we didn't have any errors. However, to remove any doubt, let's list the HDFS directory/datasets to see the two files:

```
In:!hdfs dfs -ls /datasets

Out:Found 2 items
-rw-r--r--  1 vagrant supergroup       1365 2016-01-31 12:41 /
datasets/hadoop_git_readme.txt
-rw-r--r--  1 vagrant supergroup    5589889 2016-01-31 12:41 /
datasets/shakespeare_all.txt
```

To concatenate some files to the standard output, we can use the `-cat` argument. In the following piece of code, we're counting the new lines appearing in a text file. Note that the first command is piped into another command that is operating on the local machine:

```
In:!hdfs dfs -cat /datasets/hadoop_git_readme.txt | wc -l
```

```
Out:30
```

Actually, with the `-cat` argument, we can concatenate multiple files from both the local machine and HDFS. To see it, let's now count how many newlines are present when the file stored on HDFS is concatenated to the same one stored on the local machine. To avoid misinterpretations, we can use the full **Uniform Resource Identifier (URI)**, referring to the files in HDFS with the `hdfs:` scheme and to local files with the `file:` scheme:

```
In:!hdfs dfs -cat \
    hdfs:///datasets/hadoop_git_readme.txt \
    file:///home/vagrant/datasets/hadoop_git_readme.txt | wc -l
```

```
Out:60
```

In order to copy in HDFS, we can use the `-cp` argument:

```
In : !hdfs dfs -cp /datasets/hadoop_git_readme.txt \
/datasets/copy_hadoop_git_readme.txt
```

To delete a file (or directories, with the right option), we can use the `-rm` argument. In this snippet of code, we're removing the file that we've just created with the preceding command. Note that HDFS has the thrash mechanism; consequently, a deleted file is not actually removed from the HDFS but just moved to a special directory:

```
In:!hdfs dfs -rm /datasets/copy_hadoop_git_readme.txt
```

```
Out:16/02/09 21:41:44 INFO fs.TrashPolicyDefault: Namenode trash
configuration: Deletion interval = 0 minutes, Emptier interval = 0
minutes.
```

```
Deleted /datasets/copy_hadoop_git_readme.txt
```

To empty the thrashed data, here's the command:

```
In:!hdfs dfs -expunge

Out:16/02/09 21:41:44 INFO fs.TrashPolicyDefault: Namenode trash
configuration: Deletion interval = 0 minutes, Emptier interval = 0
minutes.
```

To obtain (get) a file from HDFS to the local machine, we can use the `-get` argument:

```
In:!hdfs dfs -get /datasets/hadoop_git_readme.txt \
/tmp/hadoop_git_readme.txt
```

To take a look at a file stored in HDFS, we can use the `-tail` argument. Note that there's no head function in HDFS as it can be done using `cat` and the result then piped in a local head command. As for the tail, the HDFS shell just displays the last kilobyte of data:

```
In:!hdfs dfs -tail /datasets/hadoop_git_readme.txt

Out:ntry, of
encryption software.  BEFORE using any encryption software, please
check your country's laws, regulations and policies concerning the
import, possession, or use, and re-export of encryption software, to
see if this is permitted.  See <http://www.wassenaar.org/> for more
information.
[...]
```

The `hdfs` command is the main entry point for HDFS, but it's slow and invoking system commands from Python and reading back the output is very tedious. For this, there exists a library for Python, Snakebite, which wraps many distributed filesystem operations. Unfortunately, the library is not as complete as the HDFS shell and is bound to a Name Node. To install it on your local machine, simply use `pip install snakebite`.

To instantiate the client object, we should provide the IP (or its alias) and the port of the Name Node. In the VM we provided, it's running on port 9000:

```
In:from snakebite.client import Client
client = Client("localhost", 9000)
```

To print some information about the HDFS, the client object has the `serverdefaults` method:

```
In:client.serverdefaults()

Out:{'blockSize': 134217728L,
 'bytesPerChecksum': 512,
 'checksumType': 2,
 'encryptDataTransfer': False,
 'fileBufferSize': 4096,
 'replication': 1,
 'trashInterval': 0L,
 'writePacketSize': 65536}
```

To list the files and directories in the root, we can use the `ls` method. The result is a list of dictionaries, one for each file, containing information such as permissions, timestamp of the last modification, and so on. In this example, we're just interested in the paths (that is, the names):

```
In:for x in client.ls(['/']):
    print x['path']

Out:/datasets
/spark
/user
```

Exactly as the preceding code, the Snakebite client has the `du` (for disk usage) and `df` (for disk free) methods available. Note that many methods (like `du`) return generators, which means that they need to be consumed (like an iterator or list) to be executed:

```
In:client.df()

Out:{'capacity': 42241163264L,
 'corrupt_blocks': 0L,
 'filesystem': 'hdfs://localhost:9000',
 'missing_blocks': 0L,
 'remaining': 37373218816L,
 'under_replicated': 0L,
 'used': 196237268L}

In:list(client.du(["/"]))

Out:[{'length': 5591254L, 'path': '/datasets'},
 {'length': 187548272L, 'path': '/spark'},
 {'length': 1449302L, 'path': '/user'}]
```

As for the HDFS shell example, we will now try to count the newlines appearing in the same file with Snakebite. Note that the `.cat` method returns a generator:

```
In:
for el in client.cat(['/datasets/hadoop_git_readme.txt']):
    print el.next().count("\n")


Out:30
```

Let's now delete a file from HDFS. Again, pay attention that the `delete` method returns a generator and the execution never fails, even if we're trying to delete a non-existing directory. In fact, Snakebite doesn't raise exceptions, but just signals to the user in the output dictionary that the operation failed:

```
In:client.delete(['/datasets/shakespeare_all.txt']).next()


Out:{'path': '/datasets/shakespeare_all.txt', 'result': True}
```

Now, let's copy a file from HDFS to the local filesystem. Observe that the output is a generator, and you need to check the output dictionary to see if the operation was successful:

```
In:
(client
.copyToLocal(['/datasets/hadoop_git_readme.txt'],
            '/tmp/hadoop_git_readme_2.txt')
.next())


Out:{'error': '',
  'path': '/tmp/hadoop_git_readme_2.txt',
  'result': True,
  'source_path': '/datasets/hadoop_git_readme.txt'}
```

Finally, create a directory and delete all the files matching a string:

```
In:list(client.mkdir(['/datasets_2']))


Out:[{'path': '/datasets_2', 'result': True}]


In:client.delete(['/datasets*'], recurse=True).next()


Out:{'path': '/datasets', 'result': True}
```

Where is the code to put a file in HDFS? Where is the code to copy an HDFS file to another one? Well, these functionalities are not yet implemented in Snakebite. For them, we shall use the HDFS shell through system calls.

MapReduce

MapReduce is the programming model implemented in the earliest versions of Hadoop. It's a very simple model, designed to process large datasets on a distributed cluster in parallel batches. The core of MapReduce is composed of two programmable functions—a mapper that performs filtering and a reducer that performs aggregation—and a shuffler that moves the objects from the mappers to the right reducers.

> Google has published a paper in 2004 on Mapreduce, a few months after having been granted a patent on it.

Specifically, here are the steps of MapReduce for the Hadoop implementation:

1. Data chunker. Data is read from the filesystem and split into chunks. A chunk is a piece of the input dataset, typically either a fixed-size block (for example, a HDFS block read from a Data Node) or another more appropriate split.

   For example, if we want to count the number of characters, words, and lines in a text file, a nice split can be a line of text.

2. Mapper: From each chunk, a series of key-value pairs is generated. Each mapper instance applies the same mapping function on different chunks of data.

   Continuing the preceding example, for each line, three key-value pairs are generated in this step—one containing the number of characters in the line (the key can simply be a *chars* string), one containing the number of words (in this case, the key must be different, let's say *words*), and one containing the number of lines, which is always one (in this case, the key can be *lines*).

3. Shuffler: From the key and number of available reducers, the shuffler distributes all the key-value pairs with the same key to the same reducers. Typically, this operation is the hash of the key, modulo the number of reducers. This should ensure a fair amount of keys for each reducer. This function is not user-programmable, but provided by the MapReduce framework.

4. Reducer: Each reducer receives all the key-value pairs for a specific set of keys and can produce zero or more aggregate results.

   In the example, all the values connected to the *words* key arrive at a reducer; its job is just summing up all the values. The same happens for the other keys, resulting in three final values: the number of characters, number of words, and number of lines. Note that these results may be on different reducers.

5. Output writer: The outputs of the reducers are written on the filesystem (or HDFS). In the default Hadoop configuration, each reducer writes a file (part-r-00000 is the output of the first reducer, part-r-00001 of the second, and so on). To have a full list of results on a file, you should concatenate all of them.

   Visually, this operation can be simply communicated and understood as follows:

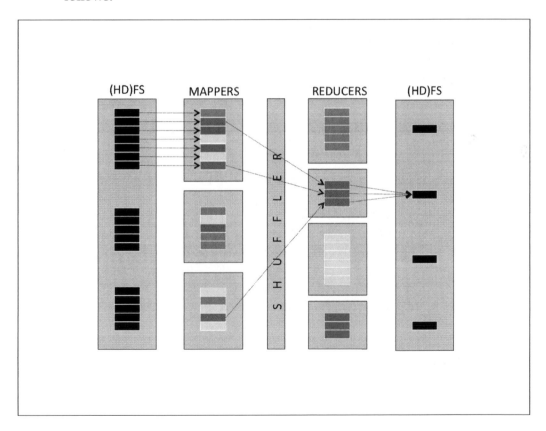

There's also an optional step that can be run by each mapper instance after the mapping step—the combiner. It basically anticipates, if possible, the reducing step on the mapper and is often used to decrease the amount of information to shuffle, speeding up the process. In the preceding example, if a mapper processes more than one line of the input file, during the (optional) combiner step, it can pre-aggregate the results, outputting the smaller number of key-value pairs. For example, if the mapper processes 100 lines of text in each chunk, why output 300 key-value pairs (100 for the number of chars, 100 for words, and 100 for lines) when the information can be aggregated in three? That's actually the goal of the combiner.

In the MapReduce implementation provided by Hadoop, the shuffle operation is distributed, optimizing the communication cost, and it's possible to run more than one mapper and reducer per node, making full use of the hardware resources available on the nodes. Also, the Hadoop infrastructure provides redundancy and fault-tolerance as the same task can be assigned to multiple workers.

Let's now see how it works. Although the Hadoop framework is written in Java, thanks to the Hadoop Streaming utility, mappers and reducers can be any executable, including Python. Hadoop Streaming uses the pipe and standard inputs and outputs to stream the content; therefore, mappers and reducers must implement a reader from stdin and a key-value writer on stdout.

Now, turn on the virtual machine and open a new IPython notebook. Even in this case, we will first introduce the command line way to run MapReduce jobs provided by Hadoop, then introduce a pure Python library. The first example will be exactly what we've described: a counter of the number of characters, words, and lines of a text file.

First, let's insert the datasets into HDFS; we're going to use the Hadoop Git readme (a short text file containing the readme file distributed with Apache Hadoop) and the full text of all the Shakespeare books, provided by Project Gutenberg (although it's just 5MB, it contains almost 125K lines). In the first cell, we'll be cleaning up the folder from the previous experiment, then, we download the file containing the Shakespeare bibliography in the dataset folder, and finally, we put both datasets on HDFS:

```
In:!hdfs dfs -mkdir -p /datasets
!wget -q http://www.gutenberg.org/cache/epub/100/pg100.txt \
    -O ../datasets/shakespeare_all.txt
!hdfs dfs -put -f ../datasets/shakespeare_all.txt /datasets/
shakespeare_all.txt
!hdfs dfs -put -f ../datasets/hadoop_git_readme.txt /datasets/hadoop_
git_readme.txt
!hdfs dfs -ls /datasets
```

Now, let's create the Python executable files containing the mapper and reducer. We will use a very dirty hack here: we're going to write Python files (and make them executable) using a write operation from the Notebook.

Both the mapper and reducer read from the stdin and write to the stdout (with simple print commands). Specifically, the mapper reads lines from the stdin and prints the key-value pairs of the number of characters (except the newline), the number of words (by splitting the line on the whitespace), and the number of lines, always one. The reducer, instead, sums up the values for each key and prints the grand total:

```
In:
with open('mapper_hadoop.py', 'w') as fh:
    fh.write("""#!/usr/bin/env python

import sys

for line in sys.stdin:
    print "chars", len(line.rstrip('\\n'))
    print "words", len(line.split())
    print "lines", 1
    """)

with open('reducer_hadoop.py', 'w') as fh:
    fh.write("""#!/usr/bin/env python

import sys

counts = {"chars": 0, "words":0, "lines":0}

for line in sys.stdin:
    kv = line.rstrip().split()
    counts[kv[0]] += int(kv[1])

for k,v in counts.items():
    print k, v
    """)

In:!chmod a+x *_hadoop.py
```

To see it at work, let's try it locally without using Hadoop. In fact, as mappers and reducers read and write to the standard input and output, we can just pipe all the things together. Note that the shuffler can be replaced by the `sort -k1,1` command, which sorts the input strings using the first field (that is, the key):

```
In:!cat ../datasets/hadoop_git_readme.txt | ./mapper_hadoop.py | sort
-k1,1 | ./reducer_hadoop.py

Out:chars 1335
lines 31
words 179
```

Let's now use the Hadoop MapReduce way to get the same result. First of all, we should create an empty directory in HDFS able to store the results. In this case, we create a directory named `/tmp` and we remove anything inside named in the same way as the job output (Hadoop will fail if the output file already exists). Then, we use the right command to run the MapReduce job. This command includes the following:

- The fact that we want to use the Hadoop Streaming capability (indicating the Hadoop streaming jar file)
- The mappers and reducers that we want to use (the `-mapper` and `-reducer` options)
- The fact that we want to distribute these files to each mapper as they're local files (with the `-files` option)
- The input file (the `-input` option) and the output directory (the `-output` option)

```
In:!hdfs dfs -mkdir -p /tmp
!hdfs dfs -rm -f -r /tmp/mr.out

!hadoop jar /usr/local/hadoop/share/hadoop/tools/lib/hadoop-streaming-
2.6.4.jar \
-files mapper_hadoop.py,reducer_hadoop.py \
-mapper mapper_hadoop.py -reducer reducer_hadoop.py \
-input /datasets/hadoop_git_readme.txt -output /tmp/mr.out

Out:[...]
16/02/04 17:12:22 INFO mapreduce.Job: Running job:
job_1454605686295_0003
16/02/04 17:12:29 INFO mapreduce.Job: Job job_1454605686295_0003
running in uber mode : false
16/02/04 17:12:29 INFO mapreduce.Job:  map 0% reduce 0%
```

```
16/02/04 17:12:35 INFO mapreduce.Job:   map 50% reduce 0%
16/02/04 17:12:41 INFO mapreduce.Job:   map 100% reduce 0%
16/02/04 17:12:47 INFO mapreduce.Job:   map 100% reduce 100%
16/02/04 17:12:47 INFO mapreduce.Job: Job job_1454605686295_0003
completed successfully
[...]
    Shuffle Errors
            BAD_ID=0
            CONNECTION=0
            IO_ERROR=0
            WRONG_LENGTH=0
            WRONG_MAP=0
            WRONG_REDUCE=0
[...]
16/02/04 17:12:47 INFO streaming.StreamJob: Output directory: /tmp/
mr.out
```

The output is very verbose; we just extracted three important sections in it.
The first indicates the progress of the MapReduce job, and it's very useful to
track and estimate the time needed to complete the operation. The second section
highlights the errors, which may have occurred during the job, and the last section
reports the output directory and timestamp of the termination. The whole process
on the small file (of 30 lines) took almost half a minute! The reasons are very simple:
first, Hadoop MapReduce has been designed for robust big data processing and
contains a lot of overhead, and second, the ideal environment is a cluster of powerful
machines, not a virtualized VM with 4GB of RAM. On the other hand, this code can
be run on much bigger datasets and a cluster of a very powerful machine, without
changing anything.

Let's not see the results immediately. First, let's take a peek at the output directory
in HDFS:

```
In:!hdfs dfs -ls /tmp/mr.out

Out:Found 2 items
-rw-r--r--   1 vagrant supergroup          0 2016-02-04 17:12 /tmp/
mr.out/_SUCCESS
-rw-r--r--   1 vagrant supergroup         33 2016-02-04 17:12 /tmp/
mr.out/part-00000
```

There are two files: the first is empty and named _SUCCESS and indicates that the MapReduce job has finished the writing stage in the directory, and the second is named part-00000 and contains the actual results (as we're operating on a node with just one reducer). Reading this file will provide us with the final results:

```
In:!hdfs dfs -cat /tmp/mr.out/part-00000

Out:chars 1335
lines 31
words 179
```

As expected, they're the same as the piped command line shown previously.

Although conceptually simple, Hadoop Streaming is not the best way to run Hadoop jobs with Python code. For this, there are many libraries available on Pypy; the one we're presenting here is one of the most flexible and maintained open source one—**MrJob**. It allows you to run the jobs seamlessly on your local machine, your Hadoop cluster, or the same cloud cluster environments, such as Amazon Elastic MapReduce; it merges all the code in a standalone file even if multiple MapReduce steps are needed (think about iterative algorithms) and interprets Hadoop errors in the code. Also, it's very simple to install; to have the MrJob library on your local machine, simply use `pip install mrjob`.

Although MrJob is a great piece of software, it doesn't work very well with IPython Notebook as it requires a main function. Here, we need to write the MapReduce Python code in a separate file and then run a command line.

We start with the example that we've seen many times so far: counting characters, words, and lines in a file. First, let's write the Python file using the MrJob functionalities; mappers and reducers are *wrapped* in a subclass of MRJob. Inputs are not read from stdin, but passed as a function argument, and outputs are not printed, but yielded (or returned).

Thanks to MrJob, the whole MapReduce program becomes just a few lines of code:

```
In:
with open("MrJob_job1.py", "w") as fh:
    fh.write("""
from mrjob.job import MRJob


class MRWordFrequencyCount(MRJob):

    def mapper(self, _, line):
        yield "chars", len(line)
```

```
        yield "words", len(line.split())
        yield "lines", 1

    def reducer(self, key, values):
        yield key, sum(values)


if __name__ == '__main__':
    MRWordFrequencyCount.run()
    """)
```

Let's now execute it locally (with the local version of the dataset). The MrJob library, beyond executing the mapper and reducer steps (locally, in this case), also prints the result and cleans up the temporary directory:

```
In:!python MrJob_job1.py ../datasets/hadoop_git_readme.txt

Out: [...]
Streaming final output from /tmp/MrJob_job1.
vagrant.20160204.171254.595542/output
"chars"    1335
"lines"    31
"words"    179
removing tmp directory /tmp/MrJob_job1.vagrant.20160204.171254.595542
```

To run the same process on Hadoop, just run the same Python file, this time inserting the -r hadoop option in the command line, and automatically MrJob will execute it using Hadoop MapReduce and HDFS. In this case, remember to point the hdfs path of the input file:

```
In:
!python MrJob_job1.py -r hadoop hdfs:///datasets/hadoop_git_readme.txt

Out:[...]
HADOOP: Running job: job_1454605686295_0004
HADOOP: Job job_1454605686295_0004 running in uber mode : false
HADOOP:  map 0% reduce 0%
HADOOP:  map 50% reduce 0%
HADOOP:  map 100% reduce 0%
HADOOP:  map 100% reduce 100%
HADOOP: Job job_1454605686295_0004 completed successfully
[...]
HADOOP:     Shuffle Errors
HADOOP:         BAD_ID=0
HADOOP:         CONNECTION=0
```

```
HADOOP:             IO_ERROR=0
HADOOP:             WRONG_LENGTH=0
HADOOP:             WRONG_MAP=0
HADOOP:             WRONG_REDUCE=0
[...]
Streaming final output from hdfs:///user/vagrant/tmp/mrjob/MrJob_job1.
vagrant.20160204.171255.073506/output
"chars"     1335
"lines"     31
"words"     179
removing tmp directory /tmp/MrJob_job1.vagrant.20160204.171255.073506
deleting hdfs:///user/vagrant/tmp/mrjob/MrJob_job1.
vagrant.20160204.171255.073506 from HDFS
```

You will see the same output of the Hadoop Streaming command line as seen previously, plus the results. In this case, the HDFS temporary directory, used to store the results, is removed after the termination of the job.

Now, to see the flexibility of MrJob, let's try running a process that requires more than one MapReduce Step. While done from the command line, this is a very difficult task; in fact, you have to run the first iteration of MapReduce, check the errors, read the results, and then launch the second iteration of MapReduce, check the errors again, and finally read the results. This sounds very time-consuming and prone to errors. Thanks to MrJob, this operation is very easy: within the code, it's possible to create a cascade of MapReduce operations, where each output is the input of the next stage.

As an example, let's now find the most common word used by Shakespeare (using, as input, the 125K lines file). This operation cannot be done in a single MapReduce step; it requires at least two of them. We will implement a very simple algorithm based on two iterations of MapReduce:

- Data chunker: Just as for the MrJob default, the input file is split on each line.

- Stage 1 – map: A key-map tuple is yielded for each word; the key is the lowercased word and the value is always 1.

- Stage 1 – reduce: For each key (lowercased word), we sum all the values. The output will tell us how many times the word appears in the text.

- Stage 2 – map: During this step, we flip the key-value tuples and put them as values of a new key pair. To force one reducer to have all the tuples, we assign the same key, *None*, to each output tuple.

- Stage 2 – reduce: We simply discard the only key available and extract the maximum of the values, resulting in extracting the maximum of all the tuples (count, word).

```
In:
with open("MrJob_job2.py", "w") as fh:
    fh.write("""
from mrjob.job import MRJob
from mrjob.step import MRStep
import re

WORD_RE = re.compile(r"[\w']+")


class MRMostUsedWord(MRJob):

    def steps(self):
        return [
            MRStep(mapper=self.mapper_get_words,
                   reducer=self.reducer_count_words),
            MRStep(mapper=self.mapper_word_count_one_key,
                   reducer=self.reducer_find_max_word)
        ]

    def mapper_get_words(self, _, line):
        # yield each word in the line
        for word in WORD_RE.findall(line):
            yield (word.lower(), 1)

    def reducer_count_words(self, word, counts):
        # send all (num_occurrences, word) pairs to the same reducer.
        yield (word, sum(counts))

    def mapper_word_count_one_key(self, word, counts):
        # send all the tuples to same reducer
        yield None, (counts, word)

    def reducer_find_max_word(self, _, count_word_pairs):
        # each item of word_count_pairs is a tuple (count, word),
        yield max(count_word_pairs)


if __name__ == '__main__':
    MRMostUsedWord.run()
""")
```

We can then decide to run it locally or on the Hadoop cluster, obtaining the same result: the most common word used by William Shakespeare is the word *the*, used more than 27K times. In this piece of code, we just want the result outputted; therefore, we launch the job with the `--quiet` option:

```
In:!python MrJob_job2.py --quiet ../datasets/shakespeare_all.txt

Out:27801    "the"

In:!python MrJob_job2.py -r hadoop --quiet hdfs:///datasets/
shakespeare_all.txt

Out:27801    "the"
```

YARN

With Hadoop 2 (the current branch as of 2016),a layer has been introduced on top of HDFS that allows multiple applications to run, for example, MapReduce is one of them (targeting batch processing). The name of this layer is **Yet Another Resource Negotiator (YARN)** and its goal is to manage the resource management in the cluster.

YARN follows the paradigm of master/slave and is composed of two services: Resource Manager and Node Manager.

The Resource Manager is the master and is responsible for two things: scheduling (allocating resources) and application management (handling job submission and tracking their status). Each Node Manager, the slaves of the architecture, is the per-worker framework running the tasks and reporting to the Resource Manager.

The YARN layer introduced with Hadoop 2 ensures the following:

- Multitenancy, that is, having multiple engines to use Hadoop
- Better cluster utilization as the allocation of the tasks is dynamic and schedulable
- Better scalability; YARN does not provide a processing algorithm, it's just a resource manager of the cluster
- Compatibility with MapReduce (the higher layer in Hadoop 1)

Spark

Apache Spark is an evolution of Hadoop and has become very popular in the last few years. Contrarily to Hadoop and its Java and batch-focused design, Spark is able to produce iterative algorithms in a fast and easy way. Furthermore, it has a very rich suite of APIs for multiple programming languages and natively supports many different types of data processing (machine learning, streaming, graph analysis, SQL, and so on).

Apache Spark is a cluster framework designed for quick and general-purpose processing of big data. One of the improvements in speed is given by the fact that data, after every job, is kept in-memory and not stored on the filesystem (unless you want to) as would have happened with Hadoop, MapReduce, and HDFS. This thing makes iterative jobs (such as the clustering K-means algorithm) faster and faster as the latency and bandwidth provided by the memory are more performing than the physical disk. Clusters running Spark, therefore, need a high amount of RAM memory for each node.

Although Spark has been developed in Scala (which runs on the JVM, like Java), it has APIs for multiple programming languages, including Java, Scala, Python, and R. In this book, we will focus on Python.

Spark can operate in two different ways:

- Standalone mode: It runs on your local machine. In this case, the maximum parallelization is the number of cores of the local machine and the amount of memory available is exactly the same as the local one.

- Cluster mode: It runs on a cluster of multiple nodes, using a cluster manager such as YARN. In this case, the maximum parallelization is the number of cores across all the nodes composing the cluster and the amount of memory is the sum of the amount of memory of each node.

pySpark

In order to use the Spark functionalities (or pySpark, containing the Python APIs of Spark), we need to instantiate a special object named SparkContext. It tells Spark how to access the cluster and contains some application-specific parameters. In the IPython Notebook provided in the virtual machine, this variable is already available and named sc (it's the default option when an IPython Notebook is started); let's now see what it contains.

First, open a new IPython Notebook; when it's ready to be used, type the following in the first cell:

```
In:sc._conf.getAll()

Out:[(u'spark.rdd.compress', u'True'),
 (u'spark.master', u'yarn-client'),
 (u'spark.serializer.objectStreamReset', u'100'),
 (u'spark.yarn.isPython', u'true'),
 (u'spark.submit.deployMode', u'client'),
 (u'spark.executor.cores', u'2'),
 (u'spark.app.name', u'PySparkShell')]
```

It contains multiple information: the most important is the `spark.master`, in this case set as a client in YARN, `spark.executor.cores` set to two as the number of CPUs of the virtual machine, and `spark.app.name`, the name of the application. The name of the app is particularly useful when the (YARN) cluster is shared; going to `ht/127.0.0.1:8088`, it is possible to check the state of the application:

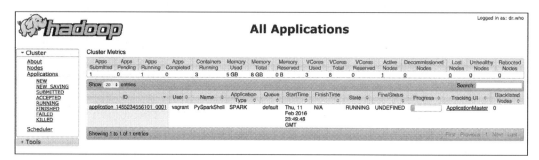

The data model used by Spark is named **Resilient Distributed Dataset (RDD)**, which is a distributed collection of elements that can be processed in parallel. An RDD can be created from an existing collection (a Python list, for example) or from an external dataset, stored as a file on the local machine, HDFS, or other sources.

Let's now create an RDD containing integers from 0 to 9. To do so, we can use the `parallelize` method provided by the `SparkContext` object:

```
In:numbers = range(10)
numbers_rdd = sc.parallelize(numbers)

numbers_rdd

Out:ParallelCollectionRDD[1] at parallelize at PythonRDD.scala:423
```

As you can see, you can't simply print the RDD content as it's split into multiple partitions (and distributed in the cluster). The default number of partitions is twice the number of CPUs (so, it's four in the provided VM), but it can be set manually using the second argument of the parallelize method.

To print out the data contained in the RDD, you should call the collect method. Note that this operation, while run on a cluster, collects all the data on the node; therefore, the node should have enough memory to contain it all:

```
In:numbers_rdd.collect()
```

```
Out:[0, 1, 2, 3, 4, 5, 6, 7, 8, 9]
```

To obtain just a partial peek, use the take method indicating how many elements you'd want to see. Note that as it's a distributed dataset, it's not guaranteed that elements are in the same order as when we inserted it:

```
In:numbers_rdd.take()
```

```
Out:[0, 1, 2, 3]
```

To read a text file, we can use the textFile method provided by the Spark Context. It allows reading both HDFS files and local files, and it splits the text on the newline characters; therefore, the first element of the RDD is the first line of the text file (using the first method). Note that if you're using a local path, all the nodes composing the cluster should access the same file through the same path:

```
In:sc.textFile("hdfs:///datasets/hadoop_git_readme.txt").first()
```

```
Out:u'For the latest information about Hadoop, please visit our
website at:'
```

```
In:sc.textFile("file:///home/vagrant/datasets/hadoop_git_readme.txt").
first()
```

```
Out:u'For the latest information about Hadoop, please visit our
website at:'
```

To save the content of an RDD on disk, you can use the saveAsTextFile method provided by the RDD. Here, you can use multiple destinations; in this example, let's save it in HDFS and then list the content of the output:

```
In:numbers_rdd.saveAsTextFile("hdfs:///tmp/numbers_1_10.txt")
```

```
In:!hdfs dfs -ls /tmp/numbers_1_10.txt
```

```
Out:Found 5 items
```

```
-rw-r--r--    1 vagrant supergroup           0 2016-02-12 14:18 /tmp/
numbers_1_10.txt/_SUCCESS
-rw-r--r--    1 vagrant supergroup           4 2016-02-12 14:18 /tmp/
numbers_1_10.txt/part-00000
-rw-r--r--    1 vagrant supergroup           4 2016-02-12 14:18 /tmp/
numbers_1_10.txt/part-00001
-rw-r--r--    1 vagrant supergroup           4 2016-02-12 14:18 /tmp/
numbers_1_10.txt/part-00002
-rw-r--r--    1 vagrant supergroup           8 2016-02-12 14:18 /tmp/
numbers_1_10.txt/part-00003
```

Spark writes one file for each partition, exactly as MapReduce, writing one file for each reducer. This way speeds up the saving time as each partition is saved independently, but on a 1-node cluster, it makes things harder to read.

Can we take all the partitions to 1 before writing the file or, generically, can we lower the number of partitions in an RDD? The answer is yes, through the `coalesce` method provided by the RDD, passing the number of partitions we'd want to have as an argument. Passing `1` forces the RDD to be in a standalone partition and, when saved, produces just one output file. Note that this happens even when saving on the local filesystem: a file is created for each partition. Mind that doing so on a cluster environment composed by multiple nodes won't ensure that all the nodes see the same output files:

```
In:
numbers_rdd.coalesce(1) \
.saveAsTextFile("hdfs:///tmp/numbers_1_10_one_file.txt")

In : !hdfs dfs -ls /tmp/numbers_1_10_one_file.txt

Out:Found 2 items
-rw-r--r--    1 vagrant supergroup           0 2016-02-12 14:20 /tmp/
numbers_1_10_one_file.txt/_SUCCESS
-rw-r--r--    1 vagrant supergroup          20 2016-02-12 14:20 /tmp/
numbers_1_10_one_file.txt/part-00000

In:!hdfs dfs -cat /tmp/numbers_1_10_one_file.txt/part-00000

Out:0
1
2
3
4
5
6
7
```

```
8
9

In: numbers_rdd.saveAsTextFile("file:///tmp/numbers_1_10.txt")

In: !ls /tmp/numbers_1_10.txt

Out: part-00000  part-00001   part-00002  part-00003   _SUCCESS
```

An RDD supports just two types of operations:

- Transformations transform the dataset into a different one. Inputs and outputs of transformations are both RDDs; therefore, it's possible to chain together multiple transformations, approaching a functional style programming. Moreover, transformations are lazy, that is, they don't compute their results straightaway.

- Actions return values from RDDs, such as the sum of the elements and the count, or just collect all the elements. Actions are the trigger to execute the chain of (lazy) transformations as an output is required.

Typical Spark programs are a chain of transformations with an action at the end. By default, all the transformations on the RDD are executed each time you run an action (that is, the intermediate state after each transformer is not saved). However, you can override this behavior using the persist method (on the RDD) whenever you want to cache the value of the transformed elements. The persist method allows both memory and disk persistency.

In the next example, we will square all the values contained in an RDD and then sum them up; this algorithm can be executed through a mapper (square elements) followed by a reducer (summing up the array). According to Spark, the map method is a transformer as it just transforms the data element by element; reduce is an action as it creates a value out of all the elements together.

Let's approach this problem step by step to see the multiple ways in which we can operate. First, start with the mapping: we first define a function that returns the square of the input argument, then we pass this function to the map method in the RDD, and finally we collect the elements in the RDD:

```
In:
def sq(x):
    return x**2

numbers_rdd.map(sq).collect()

Out: [0, 1, 4, 9, 16, 25, 36, 49, 64, 81]
```

Although the output is correct, the `sq` function is taking a lot of space; we can rewrite the transformation more concisely, thanks to Python's lambda expression, in this way:

```
In:numbers_rdd.map(lambda x: x**2).collect()

Out:[0, 1, 4, 9, 16, 25, 36, 49, 64, 81]
```

Remember: why did we need to call collect to print the values in the transformed RDD? This is because the `map` method will not spring to action, but will be just lazily evaluated. The `reduce` method, on the other hand, is an action; therefore, adding the reduce step to the previous RDD should output a value. As for map, reduce takes as an argument a function that should have two arguments (left value and right value) and should return a value. Even in this case, it can be a verbose function defined with `def` or a `lambda` function:

```
In:numbers_rdd.map(lambda x: x**2).reduce(lambda a,b: a+b)

Out:285
```

To make it even simpler, we can use the sum action instead of the reducer:

```
In:numbers_rdd.map(lambda x: x**2).sum()

Out:285
```

So far, we've shown a very simple example of pySpark. Think about what's going on under the hood: the dataset is first loaded and partitioned across the cluster, then the mapping operation is run on the distributed environment, and then all the partitions are collapsed together to generate the result (sum or reduce), which is finally printed on the IPython Notebook. A huge task, yet made super simple by pySpark.

Let's now advance one step and introduce the key-value pairs; although RDDs can contain any kind of object (we've seen integers and lines of text so far), a few operations can be made when the elements are tuples composed by two elements: key and value.

To show an example, let's now first group the numbers in the RDD in odds and evens and then compute the sum of the two groups separately. As for the MapReduce model, it would be nice to map each number with a key (odd or even) and then, for each key, reduce using a sum operation.

We can start with the map operation: let's first create a function that tags the numbers, outputting even if the argument number is even, odd otherwise. Then, create a key-value mapping that creates a key-value pair for each number, where the key is the tag and the value is the number itself:

```
In:
def tag(x):
    return "even" if x%2==0 else "odd"


numbers_rdd.map(lambda x: (tag(x), x) ).collect()

Out:[('even', 0),
 ('odd', 1),
 ('even', 2),
 ('odd', 3),
 ('even', 4),
 ('odd', 5),
 ('even', 6),
 ('odd', 7),
 ('even', 8),
 ('odd', 9)]
```

To reduce each key separately, we can now use the reduceByKey method (which is not a Spark action). As an argument, we should pass the function that we should apply to all the values of each key; in this case, we will sum up all of them. Finally, we should call the collect method to print the results:

```
In:
numbers_rdd.map(lambda x: (tag(x), x) ) \
.reduceByKey(lambda a,b: a+b).collect()

Out:[('even', 20), ('odd', 25)]
```

Now, let's list some of the most important methods available in Spark; it's not an exhaustive guide, but just includes the most used ones.

We start with transformations; they can be applied to an RDD and they produce an RDD:

- map(function): This returns an RDD formed by passing each element through the function.
- flatMap(function): This returns an RDD formed by flattening the output of the function for each element of the input RDD. It's used when each value at the input can be mapped to 0 or more output elements.

For example, to count the number of times that each word appears in a text, we should map each word to a key-value pair (the word would be the key, 1 the value), producing more than one key-value element for each input line of text in this way:

- `filter(function)`: This returns a dataset composed by all the values where the function returns true.

- `sample(withReplacement, fraction, seed)`: This bootstraps the RDD, allowing you to create a sampled RDD (with or without replacement) whose length is a fraction of the input one.

- `distinct()`: This returns an RDD containing distinct elements of the input RDD.

- `coalesce(numPartitions)`: This decreases the number of partitions in the RDD.

- `repartition(numPartitions)`: This changes the number of partitions in the RDD. This methods always shuffles all the data over the network.

- `groupByKey()`: This creates an RDD where, for each key, the value is a sequence of values that have that key in the input dataset.

- `reduceByKey(function)`: This aggregates the input RDD by key and then applies the reduce function to the values of each group.

- `sortByKey(ascending)`: This sorts the elements in the RDD by key in ascending or descending order.

- `union(otherRDD)`: This merges two RDDs together.

- `intersection(otherRDD)`: This returns an RDD composed by just the values appearing both in the input and argument RDD.

- `join(otherRDD)`: This returns a dataset where the key-value inputs are joined (on the key) to the argument RDD.

  Similar to the join function in SQL, there are available these methods as well: `cartesian`, `leftOuterJoin`, `rightOuterJoin`, and `fullOuterJoin`.

Now, let's overview what are the most popular actions available in pySpark. Note that actions trigger the processing of the RDD through all the transformers in the chain:

- `reduce(function)`: This aggregates the elements of the RDD producing an output value

- `count()`: This returns the count of the elements in the RDD

- `countByKey()`: This returns a Python dictionary, where each key is associated with the number of elements in the RDD with that key

- `collect()`: This returns all the elements in the transformed RDD locally

- `first()`: This returns the first value of the RDD

- `take(N)`: This returns the first *N* values in the RDD

- `takeSample(withReplacement, N, seed)`: This returns a bootstrap of *N* elements in the RDD with or without replacement, eventually using the random seed provided as argument

- `takeOrdered(N, ordering)`: This returns the top *N* element in the RDD after having sorted it by value (ascending or descending)

- `saveAsTextFile(path)`: This saves the RDD as a set of text files in the specified directory

There are also a few methods that are neither transformers nor actions:

- `cache()`: This caches the elements of the RDD; therefore, future computations based on the same RDD can reuse this as a starting point

- `persist(storage)`: This is the same as cache, but you can specify where to store the elements of RDD (memory, disk, or both)

- `unpersist()`: This undoes the persist or cache operation

Let's now try to replicate the examples that we've seen in the section about MapReduce with Hadoop. With Spark, the algorithm should be as follows:

1. The input file is read and parallelized on an RDD. This operation can be done with the `textFile` method provided by the Spark Context.

2. For each line of the input file, three key-value pairs are returned: one containing the number of chars, one the number of words, and the last the number of lines. In Spark, this is a flatMap operation as three outputs are generated for each input line.

3. For each key, we sum up all the values. This can be done with the `reduceByKey` method.

4. Finally, results are collected. In this case, we can use the `collectAsMap` method that collects the key-value pairs in the RDD and returns a Python dictionary. Note that this is an action; therefore, the RDD chain is executed and a result is returned.

```
In:
def emit_feats(line):
    return [("chars", len(line)), \
            ("words", len(line.split())), \
            ("lines", 1)]

print (sc.textFile("/datasets/hadoop_git_readme.txt")
 .flatMap(emit_feats)
 .reduceByKey(lambda a,b: a+b)
 .collectAsMap())

Out:{'chars': 1335, 'lines': 31, 'words': 179}
```

We can immediately note the enormous speed of this method compared to the MapReduce implementation. This is because all of the dataset is stored in-memory and not in HDFS. Secondly, this is a pure Python implementation and we don't need to call external command lines or libraries—pySpark is self-contained.

Let's now work on the example on the larger file, containing the Shakespeare texts, to extract the most popular word. In the Hadoop MapReduce implementation, it takes two map-reduce steps and therefore four write/read on HDFS. In pySpark, we can do all this in an RDD:

1. The input file is read and parallelized on an RDD with the `textFile` method.

2. For each line, all the words are extracted. For this operation, we can use the flatMap method and a regular expression.

3. Each word in the text (that is, each element of the RDD) is now mapped to a key-value pair: the key is the lowercased word and the value is always 1. This is a map operation.

4. With a `reduceByKey` call, we count how many times each word (key) appears in the text (RDD). The output is key-value pairs, where the key is a word and value is the number of times the word appears in the text.

5. We flip keys and values, creating a new RDD. This is a map operation.

6. We sort the RDD in descending order and extract (take) the first element. This is an action and can be done in one operation with the `takeOrdered` method.

```
In:import re
WORD_RE = re.compile(r"[\w']+")

print (sc.textFile("/datasets/shakespeare_all.txt")
  .flatMap(lambda line: WORD_RE.findall(line))
  .map(lambda word: (word.lower(), 1))
  .reduceByKey(lambda a,b: a+b)
  .map(lambda (k,v): (v,k))
  .takeOrdered(1, key = lambda x: -x[0]))

Out:[(27801, u'the')]
```

The results are the same that we had using Hadoop and MapReduce, but in this case, the computation takes far less time. We can actually further improve the solution, collapsing the second and third steps together (flatMap-ing a key-value pair for each word, where the key is the lowercased word and value is the number of occurrences) and the fifth and sixth steps together (taking the first element and ordering the elements in the RDD by their value, that is, the second element of the pair):

```
In:
print (sc.textFile("/datasets/shakespeare_all.txt")
  .flatMap(lambda line: [(word.lower(), 1) for word in WORD_
RE.findall(line)])
  .reduceByKey(lambda a,b: a+b)
  .takeOrdered(1, key = lambda x: -x[1]))

Out:[(u'the', 27801)]
```

To check the state of the processing, you can use the Spark UI: it's a graphical interface that shows the jobs run by Spark step-by-step. To access the UI, you should first figure out what's the name of the pySpark IPython application, searching in the bash shell where you've launched the notebook by its name (typically, it is in the form `application_<number>_<number>`), and then point your browser to the page: `http://localhost:8088/proxy/application_<number>_<number>`

The result is similar to the one in the following image. It contains all the jobs run in Spark (as IPython Notebook cells), and you can also visualize the execution plan as a **directed acyclic graph (DAG)**:

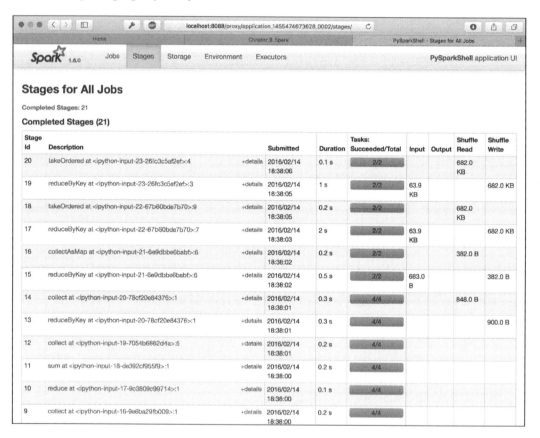

Summary

In this chapter, we've introduced some primitives to be able to run distributed jobs on a cluster composed by multiple nodes. We've seen the Hadoop framework and all its components, features, and limitations, and then we illustrated the Spark framework.

In the next chapter, we will dig deep in to Spark, showing how it's possible to do data science in a distributed environment.

9
Practical Machine Learning with Spark

In the previous chapter, we saw the main functionalities of data processing with Spark. In this chapter, we will focus on data science with Spark on a real data problem. During the chapter, you will learn the following topics:

- How to share variables across a cluster's nodes
- How to create DataFrames from structured (CSV) and semi-structured (JSON) files, save them on disk, and load them
- How to use SQL-like syntax to select, filter, join, group, and aggregate datasets, thus making the preprocessing extremely easy
- How to handle missing data in the dataset
- Which algorithms are available out of the box in Spark for feature engineering and how to use them in a real case scenario
- Which learners are available and how to measure their performance in a distributed environment
- How to run cross-validation for hyperparameter optimization in a cluster

Setting up the VM for this chapter

As machine learning needs a lot of computational power, in order to save some resources (especially memory) we will use the Spark environment not backed by YARN in this chapter. This mode of operation is named standalone and creates a Spark node without cluster functionalities; all the processing will be on the driver machine and won't be shared. Don't worry; the code that we will see in this chapter will work in a cluster environment as well.

In order to operate this way, perform the following steps:

1. Turn on the virtual machine using the `vagrant up` command.

2. Access the virtual machine when it's ready, with `vagrant ssh`.

3. Launch Spark standalone mode with the IPython Notebook from inside the virtual machine with `./start_jupyter.sh`.

4. Open a browser pointing to `http://localhost:8888`.

To turn it off, use the *Ctrl + C* keys to exit the IPython Notebook and `vagrant halt` to turn off the virtual machine.

> Note that, even in this configuration, you can access the Spark UI (when at least an IPython Notebook is running) at the following URL:
> `http://localhost:4040`

Sharing variables across cluster nodes

When we're working on a distributed environment, sometimes it is required to share information across nodes so that all the nodes can operate using consistent variables. Spark handles this case by providing two kinds of variables: read-only and write-only variables. By not ensuring that a shared variable is both readable and writable anymore, it also drops the consistency requirement, letting the hard work of managing this situation fall on the developer's shoulders. Usually, a solution is quickly reached as Spark is really flexible and adaptive.

Broadcast read-only variables

Broadcast variables are variables shared by the driver node, that is, the node running the IPython Notebook in our configuration, with all the nodes in the cluster. It's a read-only variable as the variable is broadcast by one node and never read back if another node changes it.

Let's now see how it works on a simple example: we want to one-hot encode a dataset containing just gender information as a string. Precisely, the dummy dataset contains just a feature that can be male *M*, female *F*, or unknown *U* (if the information is missing). Specifically, we want all the nodes to use a defined one-hot encoding, as listed in the following dictionary:

```
In:one_hot_encoding = {"M": (1, 0, 0),
                       "F": (0, 1, 0),
                       "U": (0, 0, 1)
                      }
```

Let's now try doing it step by step.

The easiest solution (it's not working though) is to parallelize the dummy dataset (or read it from the disk) and then use the map method on the RDD with a lambda function to map a gender to its encoded tuple:

```
In:(sc.parallelize(["M", "F", "U", "F", "M", "U"])
    .map(lambda x: one_hot_encoding[x])
    .collect())
```

```
Out:
[(1, 0, 0), (0, 1, 0), (0, 0, 1), (0, 1, 0), (1, 0, 0), (0, 0, 1)]
```

This solution works locally, but it won't operate on a real distributed environment as all the nodes don't have the one_hot_encoding variable available in their workspace. A quick workaround is to include the Python dictionary in the mapped function (that's distributed) as we manage to do here:

```
In:
def map_ohe(x):
    ohe = {"M": (1, 0, 0),
           "F": (0, 1, 0),
           "U": (0, 0, 1)
          }
    return ohe[x]

sc.parallelize(["M", "F", "U", "F", "M", "U"]).map(map_ohe).collect()
```

```
Out:
[(1, 0, 0), (0, 1, 0), (0, 0, 1), (0, 1, 0), (1, 0, 0), (0, 0, 1)]
here are you I love you hello hi is that email with all leave formal
minutes very worrying A hey
```

Such a solution works both locally and on the server, but it's not very nice: we mixed data and process, making the mapping function not reusable. It would be better if the mapping function refers to a broadcasted variable so that it can be used with whatsoever mapping we need to one-hot encode the dataset.

For this, we first broadcast the Python dictionary (calling the `broadcast` method provided by the Spark context, `sc`) inside the mapped function; using its `.value` property, we can now have access to it. After doing this, we have a generic map function that can work on any one-hot map dictionary:

```
In:bcast_map = sc.broadcast(one_hot_encoding)

def bcast_map_ohe(x, shared_ohe):
    return shared_ohe[x]

(sc.parallelize(["M", "F", "U", "F", "M", "U"])
 .map(lambda x: bcast_map_ohe(x, bcast_map.value))
 .collect())

Out:
[(1, 0, 0), (0, 1, 0), (0, 0, 1), (0, 1, 0), (1, 0, 0), (0, 0, 1)]
```

Think about the broadcasted variable as a file written in HDFS. Then, when a generic node wants to access it, it just needs the HDFS path (which is passed as an argument of the map method) and you're sure that all of them will read the same thing, using the same path. Of course, Spark doesn't use HDFS, but an in-memory variation of it.

> Broadcasted variables are saved in-memory in all the nodes composing a cluster; therefore, they never share a large amount of data that can fill them and make the following processing impossible.

To remove a broadcasted variable, use the `unpersist` method on the broadcasted variable. This operation will free up the memory of that variable on all the nodes:

```
In:bcast_map.unpersist()
```

Accumulators write-only variables

The other variables that can be shared in a Spark cluster are accumulators. Accumulators are write-only variables that can be added together and are used typically to implement sums or counters. Just the driver node, the one that is running the IPython Notebook, can read its value; all the other nodes can't.

Let's see how it works using an example: we want to process a text file and understand how many lines are empty while processing it. Of course, we can do this by scanning the dataset twice (using two Spark jobs): the first one counting the empty lines, and the second time doing the real processing, but this solution is not very effective.

In the first, ineffective solution—extracting the number of empty lines using two standalone Spark jobs—we can read the text file, filter the empty lines, and count them, as shown here:

```
In:print "The number of empty lines is:"

(sc.textFile('file:///home/vagrant/datasets/hadoop_git_readme.txt')
    .filter(lambda line: len(line) == 0)
    .count())

Out:The number of empty lines is:
6
```

The second solution is instead more effective (and more complex). We instantiate an accumulator variable (with the initial value of 0) and we add 1 for each empty line that we find while processing each line of the input file (with a map). At the same time, we can do some processing on each line; in the following piece of code, for example, we simply return 1 for each line, counting all the lines in the file in this way.

At the end of the processing, we will have two pieces of information: the first is the number of lines, from the result of the count() action on the transformed RDD, and the second is the number of empty lines contained in the value property of the accumulator. Remember, both of these are available after having scanned the dataset once:

```
In:accum = sc.accumulator(0)

def split_line(line):
    if len(line) == 0:
        accum.add(1)
    return 1

tot_lines = (
    sc.textFile('file:///home/vagrant/datasets/hadoop_git_readme.txt')
      .map(split_line)
      .count())

empty_lines = accum.value
```

```
print "In the file there are %d lines" % tot_lines
print "And %d lines are empty" % empty_lines

Out:In the file there are 31 lines
And 6 lines are empty
```

Natively, Spark supports accumulators of numeric types, and the default operation is a sum. With a bit more coding, we can turn it into something more complex.

Broadcast and accumulators together – an example

Although broadcast and accumulators are simple and very limited variables (one is read-only, the other one is write-only), they can be actively used to create very complex operations. For example, let's try to apply different machine learning algorithms on the Iris dataset in a distributed environment. We will build a Spark job in the following way:

1. The dataset is read and broadcasted to all the nodes (as it's small enough to fit in-memory).

2. Each node will use a different classifier on the dataset and return the classifier name and its accuracy score on the full dataset. Note that, to keep things easy in this simple example, we won't do any preprocessing, train/test splitting, or hyperparameter optimization.

3. If the classifiers raise any exception, the string representation of the error along with the classifier name should be stored in an accumulator.

4. The final output should contain a list of the classifiers that performed the classification task without errors and their accuracy score.

As the first step, we load the Iris dataset and broadcast it to all the nodes in the cluster:

```
In:from sklearn.datasets import load_iris

bcast_dataset = sc.broadcast(load_iris())
```

Now, let's create a custom accumulator. It will contain a list of tuples to store the classifier name and the exception it experienced as a string. The custom accumulator is derived by the AccumulatorParam class and should contain at least two methods: zero (which is called when it's initialized) and addInPlace (which is called when the add method is called on the accumulator).

The easiest way to do this is shown in the following code, followed by its initialization as an empty list. Mind that the additive operation is a bit tricky: we need to combine two elements, a tuple, and a list, but we don't know which element is the list and which is the tuple; therefore, we first ensure that both elements are lists and then we can proceed to concatenate them in an easy way (with the + operator):

```
In:from pyspark import AccumulatorParam

class ErrorAccumulator(AccumulatorParam):
    def zero(self, initialList):
        return initialList

    def addInPlace(self, v1, v2):
        if not isinstance(v1, list):
            v1 = [v1]
        if not isinstance(v2, list):
            v2 = [v2]
        return v1 + v2


errAccum = sc.accumulator([], ErrorAccumulator())
```

Now, let's define the mapping function: each node should train, test, and evaluate a classifier on the broadcasted Iris dataset. As an argument, the function will receive the classifier object and should return a tuple containing the classifier name and its accuracy score contained in a list.

If any exception is raised by doing so, the classifier name and exception as a string are added to the accumulator, and it's returned as an empty list:

```
In:
def apply_classifier(clf, dataset):

    clf_name = clf.__class__.__name__
    X = dataset.value.data
    y = dataset.value.target

    try:
        from sklearn.metrics import accuracy_score

        clf.fit(X, y)
        y_pred = clf.predict(X)
        acc = accuracy_score(y, y_pred)

        return [(clf_name, acc)]

    except Exception as e:
        errAccum.add((clf_name, str(e)))
        return []
```

Finally, we have arrived at the core of the job. We're now instantiating a few objects from Scikit-learn (some of them are not classifiers, in order to test the accumulator). We will transform them into an RDD and apply the map function that we created in the previous cell. As the returned value is a list, we can use `flatMap` to collect just the outputs of the mappers that didn't get caught in any exception:

```
In:from sklearn.linear_model import SGDClassifier
from sklearn.dummy import DummyClassifier
from sklearn.decomposition import PCA
from sklearn.manifold import MDS

classifiers = [DummyClassifier('most_frequent'),
               SGDClassifier(),
               PCA(),
               MDS()]

(sc.parallelize(classifiers)
    .flatMap(lambda x: apply_classifier(x, bcast_dataset))
    .collect())

Out:[('DummyClassifier', 0.33333333333333331),
  ('SGDClassifier', 0.66666666666666663)]
```

As expected, only the *real* classifiers are contained in the output. Let's now see which classifiers generated an error. Unsurprisingly, here we spot the two missing ones from the preceding output:

```
In:print "The errors are:"
errAccum.value

Out:The errors are:
  [('PCA', "'PCA' object has no attribute 'predict'"),
  ('MDS', "Proximity must be 'precomputed' or 'euclidean'. Got
euclidean instead")]
```

As a final step, let's clean up the broadcasted dataset:

```
In:bcast_dataset.unpersist()
```

Remember that in this example, we've used a small dataset that could be broadcasted. In real-world big data problems, you'll need to load the dataset from HDFS, broadcasting the HDFS path.

Data preprocessing in Spark

So far, we've seen how to load text data from the local filesystem and HDFS. Text files can contain either unstructured data (like a text document) or structured data (like a CSV file). As for semi-structured data, just like files containing JSON objects, Spark has special routines able to transform a file into a DataFrame, similar to the DataFrame in R and Python pandas. DataFrames are very similar to RDBMS tables, where a schema is set.

JSON files and Spark DataFrames

In order to import JSON-compliant files, we should first create a SQL context, creating a `SQLContext` object from the local Spark Context:

```
In:from pyspark.sql import SQLContext
sqlContext = SQLContext(sc)
```

Now, let's see the content of a small JSON file (it's provided in the Vagrant virtual machine). It's a JSON representation of a table with six rows and three columns, where some attributes are missing (such as the `gender` attribute for the user with `user_id=0`):

```
In:!cat /home/vagrant/datasets/users.json

Out:{"user_id":0, "balance": 10.0}
{"user_id":1, "gender":"M", "balance": 1.0}
{"user_id":2, "gender":"F", "balance": -0.5}
{"user_id":3, "gender":"F", "balance": 0.0}
{"user_id":4, "balance": 5.0}
{"user_id":5, "gender":"M", "balance": 3.0}
```

Using the `read.json` method provided by `sqlContext`, we already have the table well formatted and with all the right column names in a variable. The output variable is typed as Spark DataFrame. To show the variable in a nice, formatted table, use its `show` method:

```
In:
df = sqlContext.read \
.json("file:///home/vagrant/datasets/users.json")
df.show()

Out:
+-------+------+-------+
|balance|gender|user_id|
+-------+------+-------+
```

```
|    10.0|  null|       0|
|     1.0|     M|       1|
|    -0.5|     F|       2|
|     0.0|     F|       3|
|     5.0|  null|       4|
|     3.0|     M|       5|
+-------+------+-------+
```

Additionally, we can investigate the schema of the DataFrame using the
printSchema method. We realize that, while reading the JSON file, each column
type has been inferred by the data (in the example, the user_id column contains
long integers, the gender column is composed by strings, and the balance is a double
floating point):

```
In:df.printSchema()
```

```
Out:root
 |-- balance: double (nullable = true)
 |-- gender: string (nullable = true)
 |-- user_id: long (nullable = true)
```

Exactly like a table in an RDBMS, we can slide and dice the data in the DataFrame,
making selections of columns and filtering the data by attributes. In this example,
we want to print the balance, gender, and user_id of the users whose gender is not
missing and have a balance strictly greater than zero. For this, we can use the filter
and select methods:

```
In:(df.filter(df['gender'] != 'null')
.filter(df['balance'] > 0)
    .select(['balance', 'gender', 'user_id'])
    .show())
```

```
Out:
+-------+------+-------+
|balance|gender|user_id|
+-------+------+-------+
|    1.0|     M|       1|
|    3.0|     M|       5|
+-------+------+-------+
```

We can also rewrite each piece of the preceding job in a SQL-like language. In fact, `filter` and `select` methods can accept SQL-formatted strings:

```
In:(df.filter('gender is not null')
   .filter('balance > 0').select("*").show())
```

```
Out:
+-------+------+-------+
|balance|gender|user_id|
+-------+------+-------+
|    1.0|     M|      1|
|    3.0|     M|      5|
+-------+------+-------+
```

We can also use just one call to the `filter` method:

```
In:df.filter('gender is not null and balance > 0').show()
```

```
Out:
+-------+------+-------+
|balance|gender|user_id|
+-------+------+-------+
|    1.0|     M|      1|
|    3.0|     M|      5|
+-------+------+-------+
```

Dealing with missing data

A common problem of data preprocessing is to handle missing data. Spark DataFrames, similar to pandas DataFrames, offer a wide range of operations that you can do on them. For example, the easiest option to have a dataset composed by complete rows only is to discard rows containing missing information. For this, in a Spark DataFrame, we first have to access the `na` attribute of the DataFrame and then call the `drop` method. The resulting table will contain only the complete rows:

```
In:df.na.drop().show()
```

```
Out:
+-------+------+-------+
|balance|gender|user_id|
+-------+------+-------+
|    1.0|     M|      1|
|   -0.5|     F|      2|
|    0.0|     F|      3|
|    3.0|     M|      5|
+-------+------+-------+
```

If such an operation is removing too many rows, we can always decide what columns should be accounted for the removal of the row (as the augmented subset of the drop method):

```
In:df.na.drop(subset=["gender"]).show()
```

```
Out:
+-------+------+-------+
|balance|gender|user_id|
+-------+------+-------+
|    1.0|     M|      1|
|   -0.5|     F|      2|
|    0.0|     F|      3|
|    3.0|     M|      5|
+-------+------+-------+
```

Also, if you want to set default values for each column instead of removing the line data, you can use the fill method, passing a dictionary composed by the column name (as the dictionary key) and the default value to substitute missing data in that column (as the value of the key in the dictionary).

As an example, if you want to ensure that the variable balance, where missing, is set to 0, and the variable gender, where missing, is set to U, you can simply do the following:

```
In:df.na.fill({'gender': "U", 'balance': 0.0}).show()
```

```
Out:
+-------+------+-------+
|balance|gender|user_id|
+-------+------+-------+
|   10.0|     U|      0|
|    1.0|     M|      1|
|   -0.5|     F|      2|
|    0.0|     F|      3|
|    5.0|     U|      4|
|    3.0|     M|      5|
+-------+------+-------+
```

Grouping and creating tables in-memory

To have a function applied on a group of rows (exactly as in the case of SQL GROUP BY), you can use two similar methods. In the following example, we want to compute the average balance per gender:

```
In:(df.na.fill({'gender': "U", 'balance': 0.0})
    .groupBy("gender").avg('balance').show())
```

```
Out:
+------+------------+
|gender|avg(balance)|
+------+------------+
|     F|       -0.25|
|     M|         2.0|
|     U|         7.5|
+------+------------+
```

So far, we've worked with DataFrames but, as you've seen, the distance between DataFrame methods and SQL commands is minimal. Actually, using Spark, it is possible to register the DataFrame as a SQL table to fully enjoy the power of SQL. The table is saved in-memory and distributed in a way similar to an RDD.

To register the table, we need to provide a name, which will be used in future SQL commands. In this case, we decide to name it users:

```
In:df.registerTempTable("users")
```

By calling the sql method provided by the Spark sql context, we can run any SQL-compliant table:

```
In:sqlContext.sql("""
    SELECT gender, AVG(balance)
    FROM users
    WHERE gender IS NOT NULL
    GROUP BY gender""").show()
```

```
Out:
+------+-----+
|gender|  _c1|
+------+-----+
|     F|-0.25|
|     M|  2.0|
+------+-----+
```

Not surprisingly, the table outputted by the command (as well as the `users` table itself) is of the Spark DataFrame type:

```
In:type(sqlContext.table("users"))
```

```
Out:pyspark.sql.dataframe.DataFrame
```

DataFrames, tables, and RDDs are intimately connected, and RDD methods can be used on a DataFrame. Remember that each row of the DataFrame is an element of the RDD. Let's see this in detail and first collect the whole table:

```
In:sqlContext.table("users").collect()
Out:[Row(balance=10.0, gender=None, user_id=0),
 Row(balance=1.0, gender=u'M', user_id=1),
 Row(balance=-0.5, gender=u'F', user_id=2),
 Row(balance=0.0, gender=u'F', user_id=3),
 Row(balance=5.0, gender=None, user_id=4),
 Row(balance=3.0, gender=u'M', user_id=5)]

In:
a_row = sqlContext.sql("SELECT * FROM users").first()
a_row

Out:Row(balance=10.0, gender=None, user_id=0)
```

The output is a list of `Row` objects (they look like Python's `namedtuple`). Let's dig deeper into it: `Row` contains multiple attributes, and it's possible to access them as a property or dictionary key; that is, to have the balance out from the first row, we can choose between the two following ways:

```
In:print a_row['balance']
print a_row.balance

Out:10.0
10.0
```

Also, `Row` can be collected as a Python dictionary using the `asDict` method of `Row`. The result contains the property names as a key and property values as dictionary values:

```
In:a_row.asDict()

Out:{'balance': 10.0, 'gender': None, 'user_id': 0}
```

Writing the preprocessed DataFrame or RDD to disk

To write a DataFrame or RDD to disk, we can use the write method. We have a selection of formats; in this case, we will save it as a JSON file on the local machine:

```
In:(df.na.drop().write
    .save("file:///tmp/complete_users.json", format='json'))
```

Checking the output on the local filesystem, we immediately see that something is different from what we expected: this operation creates multiple files (part-r-...).

Each of them contains some rows serialized as JSON objects, and merging them together will create the comprehensive output. As Spark is made to process large and distributed files, the write operation is tuned for that and each node writes part of the full RDD:

```
In:!ls -als /tmp/complete_users.json

Out:total 28
4 drwxrwxr-x 2 vagrant vagrant 4096 Feb 25 22:54 .
4 drwxrwxrwt 9 root    root    4096 Feb 25 22:54 ..
4 -rw-r--r-- 1 vagrant vagrant   83 Feb 25 22:54 part-r-00000-...
4 -rw-rw-r-- 1 vagrant vagrant   12 Feb 25 22:54 .part-r-00000-...
4 -rw-r--r-- 1 vagrant vagrant   82 Feb 25 22:54 part-r-00001-...
4 -rw-rw-r-- 1 vagrant vagrant   12 Feb 25 22:54 .part-r-00001-...
0 -rw-r--r-- 1 vagrant vagrant    0 Feb 25 22:54 _SUCCESS
4 -rw-rw-r-- 1 vagrant vagrant    8 Feb 25 22:54 ._SUCCESS.crc
```

In order to read it back, we don't have to create a standalone file—even multiple pieces are fine in the read operation. A JSON file can also be read in the FROM clause of a SQL query. Let's now try to print the JSON that we've just written on disk without creating an intermediate DataFrame:

```
In:sqlContext.sql(
    "SELECT * FROM json.`file:///tmp/complete_users.json`").show()

Out:
+-------+------+-------+
|balance|gender|user_id|
+-------+------+-------+
|    1.0|     M|      1|
|   -0.5|     F|      2|
|    0.0|     F|      3|
|    3.0|     M|      5|
+-------+------+-------+
```

Beyond JSON, there is another format that's very popular when dealing with structured big datasets: Parquet format. Parquet is a columnar storage format that's available in the Hadoop ecosystem; it compresses and encodes the data and can work with nested structures: all such qualities make it very efficient.

Saving and loading is very similar to JSON and, even in this case, this operation produces multiple files written to disk:

```
In:df.na.drop().write.save(
    "file:///tmp/complete_users.parquet", format='parquet')

In:!ls -als /tmp/complete_users.parquet/

Out:total 44
4 drwxrwxr-x   2 vagrant vagrant 4096 Feb 25 22:54 .
4 drwxrwxrwt 10 root    root    4096 Feb 25 22:54 ..
4 -rw-r--r--   1 vagrant vagrant  376 Feb 25 22:54 _common_metadata
4 -rw-rw-r--   1 vagrant vagrant   12 Feb 25 22:54 ._common_metadata..
4 -rw-r--r--   1 vagrant vagrant 1082 Feb 25 22:54 _metadata
4 -rw-rw-r--   1 vagrant vagrant   20 Feb 25 22:54 ._metadata.crc
4 -rw-r--r--   1 vagrant vagrant  750 Feb 25 22:54 part-r-00000-...
4 -rw-rw-r--   1 vagrant vagrant   16 Feb 25 22:54 .part-r-00000-...
4 -rw-r--r--   1 vagrant vagrant  746 Feb 25 22:54 part-r-00001-...
4 -rw-rw-r--   1 vagrant vagrant   16 Feb 25 22:54 .part-r-00001-...
0 -rw-r--r--   1 vagrant vagrant    0 Feb 25 22:54 _SUCCESS
4 -rw-rw-r--   1 vagrant vagrant    8 Feb 25 22:54 ._SUCCESS.crc
```

Working with Spark DataFrames

So far, we've described how to load DataFrames from JSON and Parquet files, but not how to create them from an existing RDD. In order to do so, you just need to create one Row object for each record in the RDD and call the createDataFrame method of the SQL context. Finally, you can register it as a temp table to use the power of the SQL syntax fully:

```
In:from pyspark.sql import Row

rdd_gender = \
    sc.parallelize([Row(short_gender="M", long_gender="Male"),
                    Row(short_gender="F", long_gender="Female")])

(sqlContext.createDataFrame(rdd_gender)
```

```
        .registerTempTable("gender_maps"))

In:sqlContext.table("gender_maps").show()

Out:
+-----------+------------+
|long_gender|short_gender|
+-----------+------------+
|       Male|           M|
|     Female|           F|
+-----------+------------+
```

 This is also the preferred way to operate with CSV files. First, the file is read with `sc.textFile`; then with the `split` method, the `Row` constructor, and the `createDataFrame` method, the final DataFrame is created.

When you have multiple DataFrames in-memory, or that can be loaded from disk, you can join and use all the operations available in a classic RDBMS. In this example, we can join the DataFrame we've created from the RDD with the users dataset contained in the Parquet file that we've stored. The result is astonishing:

```
In:sqlContext.sql("""
    SELECT balance, long_gender, user_id
    FROM parquet.`file:///tmp/complete_users.parquet`
    JOIN gender_maps ON gender=short_gender""").show()

Out:
+-------+-----------+-------+
|balance|long_gender|user_id|
+-------+-----------+-------+
|    3.0|       Male|      5|
|    1.0|       Male|      1|
|    0.0|     Female|      3|
|   -0.5|     Female|      2|
+-------+-----------+-------+
```

In the web UI, each SQL query is mapped as a virtual **directed acyclic graph** (**DAG**) under the **SQL** tab. This is very nice to keep track of the progress of your job and understand the complexity of the query. While doing the preceding JOIN query, you can clearly see that two branches are entering the same `BroadcastHashJoin` block: the first one is from an RDD and the second one is from a Parquet file. Then, the following block is simply a projetion on the selected columns:

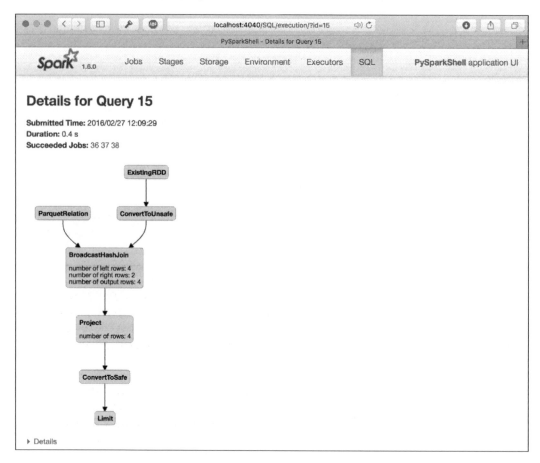

As the tables are in-memory, the last thing to do is to clean up releasing the memory used to keep them. By calling the `tableNames` method, provided by the `sqlContext`, we have the list of all the tables that we currently have in-memory. Then, to free them up, we can use `dropTempTable` with the name of the table as argument. Beyond this point, any further reference to these tables will return an error:

```
In:sqlContext.tableNames()

Out:[u'gender_maps', u'users']

In:
for table in sqlContext.tableNames():
    sqlContext.dropTempTable(table)
```

Since Spark 1.3, DataFrame is the preferred way to operate on a dataset when doing data science operations.

Machine learning with Spark

Here, we arrive at the main task of your job: creating a model to predict one or multiple attributes missing in the dataset. For this, we use some machine learning modeling, and Spark can provide us with a big hand in this context.

MLlib is the Spark machine learning library; although it is built in Scala and Java, its functions are also available in Python. It contains classification, regression, and recommendation learners, some routines for dimensionality reduction and feature selection, and has lots of functionalities for text processing. All of them are able to cope with huge datasets and use the power of all the nodes in the cluster to achieve the goal.

As of now (2016), it's composed of two main packages: `mllib`, which operates on RDDs, and `ml`, which operates on DataFrames. As the latter performs well and the most popular way to represent data in data science, developers have chosen to contribute and improve the `ml` branch, letting the former remain, but without further developments. MLlib seems a complete library at first sight but, after having started using Spark, you will notice that there's neither a statistic nor numerical library in the default package. Here, SciPy and NumPy come to your help, and once again, they're essential for data science!

In this section, we will try to explore the functionalities of the *new* `pyspark.ml` package; as of now, it's still in the early stages compared to the state-of-the-art Scikit-learn library, but it definitely has a lot of potential for the future.

Spark is a high-level, distributed, and complex software that should be used just on big data and with a cluster of multiple nodes; in fact, if the dataset can fit in-memory, it's more convenient to use other libraries such as Scikit-learn or similar, which focus just on the data science side of the problem. Running Spark on a single node on a small dataset can be five times slower than the Scikit-learn-equivalent algorithm.

Spark on the KDD99 dataset

Let's conduct this exploration using a real-world dataset: the KDD99 dataset. The goal of the competition was to create a network intrusion detection system able to recognize which network flow is malicious and which is not. Moreover, many different attacks are in the dataset; the goal is to accurately predict them using the features of the flow of packets contained in the dataset.

As a side node on the dataset, it has been extremely useful to develop great solutions for intrusion detection systems in the first few years after its release. Nowadays, as an outcome of this, all the attacks included in the dataset are very easy to detect and so it's not used in IDS development anymore.

The features are, for example, the protocol (tcp, icmp, and udp), service (http, smtp, and so on), size of the packets, flags active in the protocol, number of attempts to become root, and so on.

More information about the KDD99 challenge and datasets is available at `http://kdd.ics.uci.edu/databases/kddcup99/kddcup99.html`.

Although this is a classic multiclass classification problem, we will dig into it to show you how to perform this task in Spark. To keep things clean, we will use a new IPython Notebook.

Reading the dataset

First at all, let's download and decompress the dataset. We will be very conservative and use just 10% of the original training dataset (75MB, uncompressed) as all our analysis is run on a small virtual machine. If you want to give it a try, you can uncomment the lines in the following snippet of code and download the full training dataset (750MB uncompressed). We download the training dataset, testing (47MB), and feature names, using bash commands:

```
In:!rm -rf ../datasets/kdd*

# !wget -q -O ../datasets/kddtrain.gz \
# http://kdd.ics.uci.edu/databases/kddcup99/kddcup.data.gz

!wget -q -O ../datasets/kddtrain.gz \
http://kdd.ics.uci.edu/databases/kddcup99/kddcup.data_10_percent.gz

!wget -q -O ../datasets/kddtest.gz \
http://kdd.ics.uci.edu/databases/kddcup99/corrected.gz

!wget -q -O ../datasets/kddnames \
http://kdd.ics.uci.edu/databases/kddcup99/kddcup.names

!gunzip ../datasets/kdd*gz
```

Now, print the first few lines to have an understanding of the format. It is clear that it's a classic CSV without a header, containing a dot at the end of each line. Also, we can see that some fields are numeric but a few of them are textual, and the target variable is contained in the last field:

```
In:!head -3 ../datasets/kddtrain

Out:
0,tcp,http,SF,181,5450,0,0,0,0,0,1,0,0,0,0,0,0,0,0,0,0,8,8,0.00,0.00,
0.00,0.00,1.00,0.00,0.00,9,9,1.00,0.00,0.11,0.00,0.00,0.00,0.00,0.00,
normal.
0,tcp,http,SF,239,486,0,0,0,0,0,1,0,0,0,0,0,0,0,0,0,0,8,8,0.00,0.00,0
.00,0.00,1.00,0.00,0.00,19,19,1.00,0.00,0.05,0.00,0.00,0.00,0.00,0.00
,normal.
0,tcp,http,SF,235,1337,0,0,0,0,0,1,0,0,0,0,0,0,0,0,0,0,8,8,0.00,0.00,
0.00,0.00,1.00,0.00,0.00,29,29,1.00,0.00,0.03,0.00,0.00,0.00,0.00,0.0
0,normal.
```

To create a DataFrame with named fields, we should first read the header included in the kddnames file. The target field will be named simply target.

After having read and parsed the file, we print the number of features of our problem (remember that the target variable is not a feature) and their first 10 names:

```
In:
with open('../datasets/kddnames', 'r') as fh:
    header = [line.split(':')[0]
                for line in fh.read().splitlines()][1:]

header.append('target')

print "Num features:", len(header)-1
print "First 10:", header[:10]

Out:Num features: 41
First 10: ['duration', 'protocol_type', 'service', 'flag', 'src_
bytes', 'dst_bytes', 'land', 'wrong_fragment', 'urgent', 'hot']
```

Let's now create two separate RDDs—one for the training data and the other for the testing data:

```
In:
train_rdd = sc.textFile('file:///home/vagrant/datasets/kddtrain')
test_rdd = sc.textFile('file:///home/vagrant/datasets/kddtest')
```

Now, we need to parse each line of each file to create a DataFrame. First, we split each line of the CSV file into separate fields, and then we cast each numerical value to a floating point and each text value to a string. Finally, we remove the dot at the end of each line.

As the last step, using the `createDataFrame` method provided by `sqlContext`, we can create two Spark DataFrames with named columns for both training and testing datasets:

```
In:
def line_parser(line):

    def piece_parser(piece):
            if "." in piece or piece.isdigit():
                return float(piece)
            else:
                return piece

    return [piece_parser(piece) for piece in line[:-1].split(',')]

train_df = sqlContext.createDataFrame(
```

```
        train_rdd.map(line_parser), header)

    test_df = sqlContext.createDataFrame(
        test_rdd.map(line_parser), header)
```

So far we've written just RDD transformers; let's introduce an action to see how many observations we have in the datasets and, at the same time, check the correctness of the previous code.

```
In:print "Train observations:", train_df.count()
print "Test observations:", test_df.count()

Out:Train observations: 494021
Test observations: 311029
```

Although we're using a tenth of the full KDD99 dataset, we still work on half a million observations. Multiplied by the number of features, 41, we clearly see that we'll be training our classifier on an observation matrix containing more than 20 million values. This is not such a big dataset for Spark (and neither is the full KDD99); developers around the world are already using it on petabytes and billion records. Don't be scared if the numbers seem big: Spark is designed to cope with them!

Now, let's see how it looks on the schema of the DataFrame. Specifically, we want to identify which fields are numeric and which contain strings (note that the result has been truncated for brevity):

```
In:train_df.printSchema()

Out:root
  |-- duration: double (nullable = true)
  |-- protocol_type: string (nullable = true)
  |-- service: string (nullable = true)
  |-- flag: string (nullable = true)
  |-- src_bytes: double (nullable = true)
  |-- dst_bytes: double (nullable = true)
  |-- land: double (nullable = true)
  |-- wrong_fragment: double (nullable = true)
  |-- urgent: double (nullable = true)
  |-- hot: double (nullable = true)
...
...
...
  |-- target: string (nullable = true)
```

Feature engineering

From a visual analysis, only four fields are strings: `protocol_type`, `service`, `flag`, and `target` (which is the multiclass target label, as expected).

As we will use a tree-based classifier, we want to encode the text of each level to a number for each variable. With Scikit-learn, this operation can be done with a `sklearn.preprocessing.LabelEncoder` object. It's equivalent in Spark is `StringIndexer` of the `pyspark.ml.feature` package.

We need to encode four variables with Spark; then we have to chain four `StringIndexer` objects together in a cascade: each of them will operate on a specific column of the DataFrame, outputting a DataFrame with an additional column (similar to a map operation). The mapping is automatic, ordered by frequency: Spark ranks the count of each level in the selected column, mapping the most popular level to 0, the next to 1, and so on. Note that, with this operation, you will traverse the dataset once to count the occurrences of each level; if you already know the mapping, it would be more effective to broadcast it and use a `map` operation, as shown at the beginning of this chapter.

Similarly, we could have used a one-hot encoder to generate a numerical observation matrix. In case of a one-hot encoder, we would have had multiple output columns in the DataFrame, one for each level of each categorical feature. For this, Spark offers the `pyspark.ml.feature.OneHotEncoder` class.

 More generically, all the classes contained in the `pyspark.ml.feature` package are used to extract, transform, and select features from a DataFrame. All of them *read* some columns and *create* some other columns in the DataFrame.

As of Spark 1.6, the feature operations available in Python are contained in the following exhaustive list (all of them can be found in the `pyspark.ml.feature` package). Names should be intuitive, except for a couple of them that will be explained inline or later in the text:

- For text inputs (ideally):
    - HashingTF and IDF
    - Tokenizer and its regex-based implementation, RegexTokenizer
    - Word2vec
    - StopWordsRemover
    - Ngram

- For categorical features:
    - StringIndexer and it's inverse encoder, IndexToString
    - OneHotEncoder
    - VectorIndexer (out-of-the-box categorical to numerical indexer)

- For other inputs:
    - Binarizer
    - PCA
    - PolynomialExpansion
    - Normalizer, StandardScaler, and MinMaxScaler
    - Bucketizer (buckets the values of a feature)
    - ElementwiseProduct (multiplies columns together)

- Generic:
    - SQLTransformer (implements transformations defined by a SQL statement, referring to DataFrame as a table named __THIS__)
    - RFormula (selects columns using an R-style syntax)
    - VectorAssembler (creates a feature vector from multiple columns)

Going back to the example, we now want to encode the levels in each categorical variable as discrete numbers. As we've explained, for this, we will use a `StringIndexer` object for each variable. Moreover, we can use an ML Pipeline and set them as stages of it.

Then, to fit all the indexers, you just need to call the `fit` method of the pipeline. Internally, it will fit all the staged objects sequentially. When it's completed the fit operation, a new object is created and we can refer to it as the fitted pipeline. Calling the `transform` method of this new object will sequentially call all the staged elements (which are already fitted), each after the previous one is completed. In this snippet of code, you'll see the pipeline in action. Note that transformers compose the pipeline. Therefore, as no actions are present, nothing is actually executed. In the output DataFrame, you'll note four additional columns named the same as the original categorical ones, but with the _cat suffix:

```
In:from pyspark.ml import Pipeline
from pyspark.ml.feature import StringIndexer


cols_categorical = ["protocol_type", "service", "flag","target"]
```

```
preproc_stages = []

for col in cols_categorical:
    out_col = col + "_cat"
    preproc_stages.append(
        StringIndexer(
            inputCol=col, outputCol=out_col, handleInvalid="skip"))

pipeline = Pipeline(stages=preproc_stages)
indexer = pipeline.fit(train_df)

train_num_df = indexer.transform(train_df)
test_num_df = indexer.transform(test_df)
```

Let's investigate the pipeline a bit more. Here, we will see the stages in the pipeline: unfit pipeline and fitted pipeline. Note that there's a big difference between Spark and Scikit-learn: in Scikit-learn, `fit` and `transform` are called on the same object, and in Spark, the `fit` method produces a new object (typically, its name is added with a `Model` suffix, just as for `Pipeline` and `PipelineModel`), where you'll be able to call the `transform` method. This difference is derived from closures—a fitted object is easy to distribute across processes and the cluster:

```
In:print pipeline.getStages()
print
print pipeline
print indexer
```

```
Out:
[StringIndexer_432c8aca691aaee949b8, StringIndexer_4f10bbcde2452dd
1b771, StringIndexer_4aad99dc0a3ff831bea6, StringIndexer_4b369fea0787
3fc9c2a3]

Pipeline_48df9eed31c543ba5eba
PipelineModel_46b09251d9e4b117dc8d
```

Let's see how the first observation, that is, the first line in the CSV file, changes after passing through the pipeline. Note that we use an action here, therefore all the stages in the pipeline and in the pipeline model are executed:

```
In:print "First observation, after the 4 StringIndexers:\n"
print train_num_df.first()
```

```
Out:First observation, after the 4 StringIndexers:
```

```
Row(duration=0.0, protocol_type=u'tcp', service=u'http', flag=u'SF',
src_bytes=181.0, dst_bytes=5450.0, land=0.0, wrong_fragment=0.0,
urgent=0.0, hot=0.0, num_failed_logins=0.0, logged_in=1.0, num_
compromised=0.0, root_shell=0.0, su_attempted=0.0, num_root=0.0,
num_file_creations=0.0, num_shells=0.0, num_access_files=0.0, num_
outbound_cmds=0.0, is_host_login=0.0, is_guest_login=0.0, count=8.0,
srv_count=8.0, serror_rate=0.0, srv_serror_rate=0.0, rerror_rate=0.0,
srv_rerror_rate=0.0, same_srv_rate=1.0, diff_srv_rate=0.0, srv_diff_
host_rate=0.0, dst_host_count=9.0, dst_host_srv_count=9.0, dst_host_
same_srv_rate=1.0, dst_host_diff_srv_rate=0.0, dst_host_same_src_port_
rate=0.11, dst_host_srv_diff_host_rate=0.0, dst_host_serror_rate=0.0,
dst_host_srv_serror_rate=0.0, dst_host_rerror_rate=0.0, dst_host_srv_
rerror_rate=0.0, target=u'normal', protocol_type_cat=1.0, service_
cat=2.0, flag_cat=0.0, target_cat=2.0)
```

The resulting DataFrame looks very complete and easy to understand: all the variables have names and values. We immediately note that the categorical features are still there, for instance, we have both `protocol_type` (categorical) and `protocol_type_cat` (the numerical version of the variable mapped from categorical).

Extracting some columns from the DataFrame is as easy as using SELECT in a SQL query. Let's now build a list of names for all the numerical features: starting from the names found in the header, we remove the categorical ones and replace them with the numerically-derived. Finally, as we want just the features, we remove the target variable and its numerical-derived equivalent:

```
In:features_header = set(header) \
               - set(cols_categorical) \
               | set([c + "_cat" for c in cols_categorical]) \
               - set(["target", "target_cat"])
features_header = list(features_header)
print features_header
print "Total numerical features:", len(features_header)

Out:['num_access_files', 'src_bytes', 'srv_count', 'num_outbound_
cmds', 'rerror_rate', 'urgent', 'protocol_type_cat', 'dst_host_same_
srv_rate', 'duration', 'dst_host_diff_srv_rate', 'srv_serror_rate',
'is_host_login', 'wrong_fragment', 'serror_rate', 'num_compromised',
'is_guest_login', 'dst_host_rerror_rate', 'dst_host_srv_serror_rate',
'hot', 'dst_host_srv_count', 'logged_in', 'srv_rerror_rate', 'dst_
host_srv_diff_host_rate', 'srv_diff_host_rate', 'dst_host_same_src_
port_rate', 'root_shell', 'service_cat', 'su_attempted', 'dst_host_
count', 'num_file_creations', 'flag_cat', 'count', 'land', 'same_srv_
rate', 'dst_bytes', 'num_shells', 'dst_host_srv_rerror_rate', 'num_
root', 'diff_srv_rate', 'num_failed_logins', 'dst_host_serror_rate']
Total numerical features: 41
```

Here, the `VectorAssembler` class comes to our help to build the feature matrix. We just need to pass the columns to be selected as argument and the new column to be created in the DataFrame. We decide that the output column will be named simply `features`. We apply this transformation to both training and testing sets, and then we select just the two columns that we're interested in—`features` and `target_cat`:

```
In:from pyspark.ml.feature import VectorAssembler

assembler = VectorAssembler(
    inputCols=features_header,
    outputCol="features")

Xy_train = (assembler
                .transform(train_num_df)
                .select("features", "target_cat"))
Xy_test = (assembler
                .transform(test_num_df)
                .select("features", "target_cat"))
```

Also, the default behavior of `VectorAssembler` is to produce either `DenseVectors` or `SparseVectors`. In this case, as the vector of `features` contains many zeros, it returns a sparse vector. To see what's inside the output, we can print the first line. Note that this is an action. Consequently, the job is executed before getting a result printed:

```
In:Xy_train.first()

Out:Row(features=SparseVector(41, {1: 181.0, 2: 8.0, 6: 1.0, 7: 1.0,
20: 9.0, 21: 1.0, 25: 0.11, 27: 2.0, 29: 9.0, 31: 8.0, 33: 1.0, 39:
5450.0}), target_cat=2.0)
```

Training a learner

Finally, we're arrived at the hot piece of the task: training a classifier. Classifiers are contained in the `pyspark.ml.classification` package and, for this example, we're using a random forest.

As of Spark 1.6, the extensive list of classifiers using a Python interface are as follows:

- Classification (the `pyspark.ml.classification` package):
    - `LogisticRegression`
    - `DecisionTreeClassifier`
    - `GBTClassifier` (a Gradient Boosted implementation for classification based on decision trees)

- ○   `RandomForestClassifier`
- ○   `NaiveBayes`
- ○   `MultilayerPerceptronClassifier`

Note that not all of them are capable of operating on multiclass problems and may have different parameters; always check the documentation related to the version in use. Beyond classifiers, the other learners implemented in Spark 1.6 with a Python interface are as follows:

- Clustering (the `pyspark.ml.clustering` package):
    - ○   KMeans

- Regression (the `pyspark.ml.regression` package):
    - ○   AFTSurvivalRegression (Accelerated Failure Time Survival regression)
    - ○   DecisionTreeRegressor
    - ○   GBTRegressor (a Gradient Boosted implementation for regression based on regression trees)
    - ○   IsotonicRegression
    - ○   LinearRegression
    - ○   RandomForestRegressor

- Recommender (the `pyspark.ml.recommendation` package):
    - ○   ALS (collaborative filtering recommender, based on Alternating Least Squares)

Let's go back to the goal of the KDD99 challenge. Now it's time to instantiate a random forest classifier and set its parameters. The parameters to set are `featuresCol` (the column containing the feature matrix), `labelCol` (the column of the DataFrame containing the target label), seed (the random seed to make the experiment replicable), and `maxBins` (the maximum number of bins to use for the splitting point in each node of the tree). The default value for the number of trees in the forest is 20, and each tree is maximum five levels deep. Moreover, by default, this classifier creates three output columns in the DataFrame: `rawPrediction` (to store the prediction score for each possible label), `probability` (to store the likelihood of each label), and `prediction` (the most probable label):

```
In:from pyspark.ml.classification import RandomForestClassifier

clf = RandomForestClassifier(
    labelCol="target_cat", featuresCol="features",
    maxBins=100, seed=101)
fit_clf = clf.fit(Xy_train)
```

Even in this case, the trained classifier is a different object. Exactly as before, the trained classifier is named the same as the classifier with the `Model` suffix:

```
In:print clf
print fit_clf

Out:RandomForestClassifier_4797b2324bc30e97fe01
RandomForestClassificationModel (uid=rfc_44b551671c42) with 20 trees
```

On the trained classifier object, that is, `RandomForestClassificationModel`, it's possible to call the `transform` method. Now we predict the label on both the training and test datasets and print the first line of the test dataset; as set in the classifier, the predictions will be found in the column named `prediction`:

```
In:Xy_pred_train = fit_clf.transform(Xy_train)
Xy_pred_test = fit_clf.transform(Xy_test)

In:print "First observation after classification stage:"
print Xy_pred_test.first()

Out:First observation after classification stage:
Row(features=SparseVector(41, {1: 105.0, 2: 1.0, 6: 2.0, 7: 1.0, 20:
254.0, 27: 1.0, 29: 255.0, 31: 1.0, 33: 1.0, 35: 0.01, 39: 146.0}),
target_cat=2.0, rawPrediction=DenseVector([0.0109, 0.0224, 19.7655,
0.0123, 0.0099, 0.0157, 0.0035, 0.0841, 0.05, 0.0026, 0.007, 0.0052,
0.002, 0.0005, 0.0021, 0.0007, 0.0013, 0.001, 0.0007, 0.0006, 0.0011,
0.0004, 0.0005]), probability=DenseVector([0.0005, 0.0011, 0.9883,
0.0006, 0.0005, 0.0008, 0.0002, 0.0042, 0.0025, 0.0001, 0.0004,
0.0003, 0.0001, 0.0, 0.0001, 0.0, 0.0001, 0.0, 0.0, 0.0, 0.0001, 0.0,
0.0]), prediction=2.0)
```

Evaluating a learner's performance

The next step in any data science task is to check the performance of the learner on the training and testing sets. For this task, we will use the F1 score as it's a good metric that merges precision and recall performances.

Evaluation metrics are enclosed in the `pyspark.ml.evaluation` package; among the few choices, we're using the one to evaluate multiclass classifiers: `MulticlassClassificationEvaluator`. As parameters, we're providing the metric (precision, recall, accuracy, f1 score, and so on) and the name of the columns containing the true label and predicted label:

```
In:
from pyspark.ml.evaluation import MulticlassClassificationEvaluator

evaluator = MulticlassClassificationEvaluator(
    labelCol="target_cat", predictionCol="prediction",
    metricName="f1")

print "F1-score train set:", evaluator.evaluate(Xy_pred_train)
print "F1-score test set:", evaluator.evaluate(Xy_pred_test)

Out:F1-score train set: 0.992356962712
F1-score test set: 0.967512379842
```

Obtained values are pretty high, and there's a big difference between the performance on the training set and the testing set.

Beyond the evaluator for multiclass classifiers, an evaluator object for regressor (where the metric can be MSE, RMSE, R2, or MAE) and binary classifiers are available in the same package.

The power of the ML pipeline

So far, we've built and displayed the output piece by piece. It's also possible to put all the operations in cascade and set them as stages of a pipeline. In fact, we can chain together what we've seen so far (the four label encoders, vector builder, and classifier) in a standalone pipeline, fit it on the training dataset, and finally use it on the test dataset to obtain the predictions.

This way to operate is more effective, but you'll lose the exploratory power of the step-by-step analysis. Readers who are data scientists are advised to use end-to-end pipelines only when they are completely sure of what's going on inside and only to build production models.

To show that the pipeline is equivalent to what we've seen so far, we compute the F1 score on the test set and print it. Unsurprisingly, it's exactly the same value:

```
In:full_stages = preproc_stages + [assembler, clf]
full_pipeline = Pipeline(stages=full_stages)
full_model = full_pipeline.fit(train_df)
predictions = full_model.transform(test_df)
print "F1-score test set:", evaluator.evaluate(predictions)


Out:F1-score test set: 0.967512379842
```

On the driver node, the one running the IPython Notebook, we can also use the matplotlib library to visualize the results of our analysis. For example, to show a normalized confusion matrix of the classification results (normalized by the support of each class), we can create the following function:

```
In:import matplotlib.pyplot as plt
import numpy as np
%matplotlib inline

def plot_confusion_matrix(cm):
    cm_normalized = \
        cm.astype('float') / cm.sum(axis=1)[:, np.newaxis]
    plt.imshow(
        cm_normalized, interpolation='nearest', cmap=plt.cm.Blues)
    plt.title('Normalized Confusion matrix')
    plt.colorbar()
    plt.tight_layout()
    plt.ylabel('True label')
    plt.xlabel('Predicted label')
```

Spark is able to build a confusion matrix, but that method is in the pyspark.mllib package. In order to be able to use the methods in this package, we have to transform the DataFrame into an RDD using the .rdd method:

```
In:from pyspark.mllib.evaluation import MulticlassMetrics

metrics = MulticlassMetrics(
    predictions.select("prediction", "target_cat").rdd)
conf_matrix = metrics.confusionMatrix()toArray()
plot_confusion_matrix(conf_matrix)

Out:
```

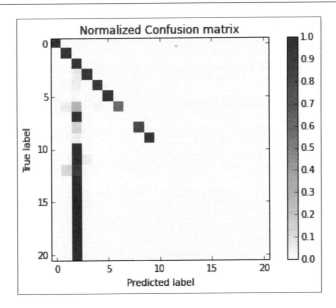

Manual tuning

Although the F1 score was close to 0.97, the normalized confusion matrix shows that the classes are strongly unbalanced and the classifier has just learned how to classify the most popular ones properly. To improve the results, we can resample each class, trying to balance the training dataset better.

First, let's count how many cases there are in the training dataset for each class:

```
In:
train_composition = train_df.groupBy("target").count().rdd.
collectAsMap()
train_composition

Out:
{u'back': 2203,
 u'buffer_overflow': 30,
 u'ftp_write': 8,
 u'guess_passwd': 53,
 u'neptune': 107201,
 u'nmap': 231,
 u'normal': 97278,
 u'perl': 3,
 ...
...
 u'warezmaster': 20}
```

This is clear evidence of a strong imbalance. We can try to improve the performance by oversampling *rare* classes and subsampling too *popular* classes.

In this example, we will create a training dataset, where each class is represented at least 1,000 times, but up to 25,000. For this, let's first create the subsampling/ oversampling rate and broadcast it throughout the cluster, and then flatMap each line of the training dataset to resample it properly:

```
In:
def set_sample_rate_between_vals(cnt, the_min, the_max):
    if the_min <= cnt <= the_max:
        # no sampling
        return 1

    elif cnt < the_min:
        # Oversampling: return many times the same observation
        return the_min/float(cnt)

    else:
        # Subsampling: sometime don't return it
        return the_max/float(cnt)

sample_rates = {k:set_sample_rate_between_vals(v, 1000, 25000)
                for k,v in train_composition.iteritems()}
sample_rates

Out:{u'back': 1,
 u'buffer_overflow': 33.333333333333336,
 u'ftp_write': 125.0,
 u'guess_passwd': 18.867924528301888,
 u'neptune': 0.23320677978750198,
 u'nmap': 4.329004329004329,
 u'normal': 0.2569954152017928,
 u'perl': 333.3333333333333,
 . . .
 . . .
 u'warezmaster': 50.0}

In:bc_sample_rates = sc.broadcast(sample_rates)

def map_and_sample(el, rates):
    rate = rates.value[el['target']]
    if rate > 1:
        return [el]*int(rate)
```

```
    else:
        import random
        return [el] if random.random() < rate else []

sampled_train_df = (train_df
                    .flatMap(
                      lambda x: map_and_sample(x, bc_sample_rates))
                    .toDF()
                    .cache())
```

The resampled dataset in the `sampled_train_df` DataFrame variable is also cached; we will use it many times during the hyperparameter optimization step. It should easily fit in-memory as the number of lines is lower than the original one:

```
In:sampled_train_df.count()
```

```
Out:97335
```

To get an idea of what's inside, we can print the first line. Pretty quick to print the value, isn't it? Of course, it's cached!

```
In:sampled_train_df.first()
```

```
Out:Row(duration=0.0, protocol_type=u'tcp', service=u'http',
flag=u'SF', src_bytes=217.0, dst_bytes=2032.0, land=0.0, wrong_
fragment=0.0, urgent=0.0, hot=0.0, num_failed_logins=0.0, logged_
in=1.0, num_compromised=0.0, root_shell=0.0, su_attempted=0.0,
num_root=0.0, num_file_creations=0.0, num_shells=0.0, num_access_
files=0.0, num_outbound_cmds=0.0, is_host_login=0.0, is_guest_
login=0.0, count=6.0, srv_count=6.0, serror_rate=0.0, srv_serror_
rate=0.0, rerror_rate=0.0, srv_rerror_rate=0.0, same_srv_rate=1.0,
diff_srv_rate=0.0, srv_diff_host_rate=0.0, dst_host_count=49.0, dst_
host_srv_count=49.0, dst_host_same_srv_rate=1.0, dst_host_diff_srv_
rate=0.0, dst_host_same_src_port_rate=0.02, dst_host_srv_diff_host_
rate=0.0, dst_host_serror_rate=0.0, dst_host_srv_serror_rate=0.0, dst_
host_rerror_rate=0.0, dst_host_srv_rerror_rate=0.0, target=u'normal')
```

Let's now use the pipeline that we created to make some predictions and print the F1 score of this new solution:

```
In:full_model = full_pipeline.fit(sampled_train_df)
predictions = full_model.transform(test_df)
print "F1-score test set:", evaluator.evaluate(predictions)
```

```
Out:F1-score test set: 0.967413322985
```

Test it on a classifier of 50 trees. To do so, we can build another pipeline (named refined_pipeline) and substitute the final stage with the new classifier. Performances seem the same even if the training set has been slashed in size:

```
In:clf = RandomForestClassifier(
    numTrees=50, maxBins=100, seed=101,
    labelCol="target_cat", featuresCol="features")

stages = full_pipeline.getStages()[:-1]
stages.append(clf)

refined_pipeline = Pipeline(stages=stages)

refined_model = refined_pipeline.fit(sampled_train_df)
predictions = refined_model.transform(test_df)
print "F1-score test set:", evaluator.evaluate(predictions)

Out:F1-score test set: 0.969943901769
```

Cross-validation

We can go forward with manual optimization and find the right model after having exhaustively tried many different configurations. Doing that, it would lead to both an immense waste of time (and reusability of the code) and will overfit the test dataset. Cross-validation is instead the correct key to run the hyperparameter optimization. Let's now see how Spark performs this crucial task.

First of all, as the training will be used many times, we can cache it. Let's therefore cache it after all the transformations:

```
In:pipeline_to_clf = Pipeline(
    stages=preproc_stages + [assembler]).fit(sampled_train_df)
train = pipeline_to_clf.transform(sampled_train_df).cache()
test = pipeline_to_clf.transform(test_df)
```

The useful classes for hyperparameter optimization with-cross validation are contained in the pyspark.ml.tuning package. Two elements are essential: a grid map of parameters (that can be built with ParamGridBuilder) and the actual cross-validation procedure (run by the CrossValidator class).

In the example, we want to set some parameters of our classifier that won't change throughout the cross-validation. Exactly as with Scikit-learn, they're set when the classification object is created (in this case, column names, seed, and maximum number of bins).

Then, thanks to the grid builder, we decide which arguments should be changed for each iteration of the cross-validation algorithm. In the example, we want to check the classification performance changing the maximum depth of each tree in the forest from 3 to 12 (incrementing by 3) and the number of trees in the forest to 20 or 50.

Finally, we launch the cross-validation (with the `fit` method) after having set the grid map, classifier that we want to test, and number of folds. The parameter evaluator is essential: it will tell us which is the best model to keep after the cross-validation. Note that this operation may take 15-20 minutes to run (under the hood, 4*2*3=24 models are trained and tested):

```
In:
from pyspark.ml.tuning import ParamGridBuilder, CrossValidator

rf = RandomForestClassifier(
    cacheNodeIds=True, seed=101, labelCol="target_cat",
    featuresCol="features", maxBins=100)

grid = (ParamGridBuilder()
        .addGrid(rf.maxDepth, [3, 6, 9, 12])
        .addGrid(rf.numTrees, [20, 50])
        .build())

cv = CrossValidator(
    estimator=rf, estimatorParamMaps=grid,
    evaluator=evaluator, numFolds=3)
cvModel = cv.fit(train)
```

Finally, we can predict the label using the cross-validated model as we're using a pipeline or classifier by itself. In this case, the performances of the classifier chosen with cross-validation are slightly better than in the previous case and allow us to beat the 0.97 barrier:

```
In:predictions = cvModel.transform(test)
print "F1-score test set:", evaluator.evaluate(predictions)

Out:F1-score test set: 0.97058134007
```

Furthermore, by plotting the normalized confusion matrix, you immediately realize that this solution is able to discover a wider variety of attacks, even the less popular ones:

```
In:metrics = MulticlassMetrics(predictions.select(
        "prediction", "target_cat").rdd)
conf_matrix = metrics.confusionMatr().toArray()
plot_confusion_matrix(conf_matrix)
```

Out:

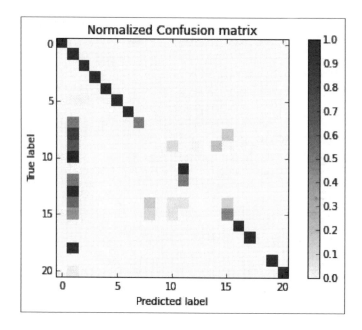

Final cleanup

Here, we are at the end of the classification task. Remember to remove all the variables that you've used and the temporary table that you've created from the cache:

```
In:bc_sample_rates.unpersist()
sampled_train_df.unpersist()
train.unpersist()
```

After the Spark memory is cleared, we can turn off the Notebook.

Summary

This is the final chapter of the book. We have seen how to do data science at scale on a cluster of machines. Spark is able to train and test machine learning algorithms using all the nodes in a cluster with a simple interface, very similar to Scikit-learn. It's proved that this solution is able to cope with petabytes of information, creating a valid alternative to observation subsampling and online learning.

To become an expert in Spark and streaming processing, we strongly advise you to read the book, *Mastering Apache Spark, Mike Frampton, Packt Publishing*.

If you're brave enough to switch to Scala, the main programming language for Spark, this book is the best for such a transition: *Scala for Data Science, Pascal Bugnion, Packt Publishing*.

Introduction to GPUs and Theano

Up until now we performed neural networks and deep learning tasks utilizing regular CPU's. Lately however, computational advantages of GPU's become widespread. This chapter dives in to the basics of GPU together with the Theano framework for deep learning.

GPU computing

When we use regular CPU computing packages for machine learning, such as Scikit-learn, the amount of parallelization is surprisingly limited because, by default, an algorithm utilizes only one core even when there are multiple cores available. In the chapter about **Classification and Regression Trees (CART)**, we will see some advanced examples of speeding up Scikit-learn algorithms.

Unlike CPU, GPU units are designed to work in parallel from the ground up. Imagine projecting an image on a screen through a graphical card; it will come as no surprise that the GPU unit has to be able to process and project a lot of information (motion, color, and spatiality) at the same time. CPUs on the other hand are designed for sequential processing suitable for tasks where more control is needed, such as branching and checking. In contrast to the CPU, GPUs are composed of lots of cores that can handle thousands of tasks simultaneously. The GPU can outperform a CPU 100-fold at a lower cost. Another advantage is that modern GPUs are relatively cheap compared to state-of-the-art CPUs.

So all this sounds great but remember that the GPU is only good at carrying out a certain type of task. A CPU consists of a few cores optimized for sequential serial processing while a GPU consists of thousands of smaller, more efficient cores designed to handle tasks simultaneously.

CPUs and GPUs have different architectures that make them better-suited to different tasks. There are still a lot of tasks such as checking, debugging, and switching that GPUs can't do effectively because of its architecture.

A simple way to understand the difference between a CPU and GPU is to compare how they process tasks. An analogy that is often made is that of the analytical and sequential left brain (CPU) and the holistic right brain (GPU). This is just an analogy and should not be taken too seriously.

GPU	CPU
Large number of cores (but slower than CPU cores)	Small number of cores, but much faster than GPU-cores
High memory bandwidth to control the cores	Lower memory bandwidth
Special purpose	General purpose
highly parallel processing	sequential processing

See more at the following links:

- http://www.nvidia.com/object/what-is-gpu-computing.html#sthash.c4R7eJ3s.dpuf
- http://www.nvidia.com/object/what-is-gpu-computing.html#sthash.c4R7eJ3s.dpuf

In order to utilize the GPU for machine learning, a specific platform is required. Unfortunately, as of yet, there are no stable GPU computation platforms other than CUDA; this means that you must have an NVIDIA graphical card installed on your computer. GPU computing will NOT work without an NVIDIA card. Yes, I know that this is bad news for most Mac users out there. I really wish it were different but it is a limitation that we have to live with. There are other projects such as OpenCL that provide GPU computation for other GPU brands through initiatives such as **BLAS** (https://github.com/clMathLibraries/clBLAS), but they are under heavy development and are not fully optimized for deep learning applications in Python. Another limitation of OpenCL is that only AMD is actively involved so that it will be beneficial to AMD GPUs. There is no hope for a hardware-independent GPU application for machine learning in the following years (decade even!). However, check out the news and developments of the OpenCL project (https://www.khronos.org/opencl/). Considering the widespread media attention that this limitation of GPU accessibility might be quite underwhelming. Only NVIDIA seems to put their research efforts in developing GPU platforms, and it is highly unlikely to see any new serious developments in that field in the years to come.

You will need the following things for the usage of CUDA.

You need to test if the graphical card on your computer is suitable for CUDA. It should at least be an NVIDIA card. You can test if your GPU is viable for CUDA with this line of code in the terminal:

```
$ su
```

Now type your password at the root:

```
$ lspci | grep -i nvidia
```

If you do have an NVIDIA-based GNU, you can download the NVIDIA CUDA Toolkit (`http://developer.nvidia.com/cuda-downloads`).

At the time of writing, NVIDIA is on the verge of releasing CUDA version 8, which will have different installation procedures, so we advice you to follow the directions on the CUDA website. For further installation procedures, consult the NVIDIA website:

```
http://docs.nvidia.com/cuda/cuda-getting-started-guide-for-
linux/#axzz3xBimv9ou
```

Theano – parallel computing on the GPU

Theano is a Python library originally developed by James Bergstra at the University of Montreal. It aims at providing more expressive ways to write mathematical functions with symbolic representations (F. Bastien, P. Lamblin, R. Pascanu, J. Bergstra, I. Goodfellow, A. Bergeron, N. Bouchard, D. Warde-Farley and Y. Bengio. *Theano: new features and speed improvements*. NIPS 2012 Deep Learning Workshop). Interestingly, Theano is named after the Greek mathematician, who may have been Pythagoras' wife. It's strongest points are fast c-compiled computations, symbolic expressions, and GPU computation, and Theano is under active development. Improvements are made regularly with new features. Theano's implementations are much wider than scalable machine learning so I will narrow down and use Theano for deep learning. Visit the Theano website for more information—`http://deeplearning.net/software/theano/`.

When we want to perform more complex computations on multidimensional matrices, basic NumPy will resort to costly loops and iterations driving up the CPU load as we have seen earlier. Theano aims to optimize these computations by compiling them into highly optimized C-code and, if possible, utilizing the GPU. For neural networks and deep learning, Theano has the useful capability to automatically differentiate mathematical functions, which is very convenient for calculation of the partial derivatives when using algorithms such as backpropagation.

Currently, Theano is used in all sorts of deep learning projects and has become the most used platform in this field. Lately, new packages have been built on top of Theano in order to make utilizing deep learning functionalities easier for us. Considering the steep learning curve of Theano, we will use packages built on Theano, such as theanets, pylearn2, and Lasagne.

Installing Theano

First, make sure that you install the development version from the Theano page. Note that if you do "$ pip install theano", you might end up with problems. Installing the development version from GitHub directly is a safer bet:

```
$ git clone git://github.com/Theano/Theano.git
$  pip install Theano
```

If you want to upgrade Theano, you can use the following command:

```
$ sudo pip install --upgrade theano
```

If you have questions and want to connect with the Theano community, you can refer to https://groups.google.com/forum/#!forum/theano-users.

That's it, we are ready to go!

To make sure that we set the directory path toward the Theano folder, we need to do the following:

```
#!/usr/bin/python
import cPickle as pickle
from six.moves import cPickle as pickle
import os


#set your path to the theano folder here
path = '/Users/Quandbee1/Desktop/pthw/Theano/'
```

Let's install all the packages that we need:

```
from theano import tensor
import theano.tensor as T
import theano.tensor.nnet as nnet
import numpy as np
import numpy
```

In order for Theano to work on the GPU (if you have an NVIDIA card + CUDA installed), we need to configure the Theano framework first.

Normally, NumPy and Theano use the double-precision floating-point format (`float64`). However, if we want to utilize the GPU for Theano, a 32-bit floating point is used. This means that we have to change the settings between 32- and 64-bits floating points depending on our needs. If you want to see which configuration is used by your system by default, type the following:

```
print(theano.config.floatX)
output: float64
```

You can to change your configuration to 32 bits for GPU computing as follows:

```
theano.config.floatX = 'float32'
```

Sometimes it is more practical to change the settings via the terminal.

For a 32-bit floating point, type as follows:

```
$ export THEANO_FLAGS=floatX=float32
```

For a 64-bit floating point, type as follows:

```
$ export THEANO_FLAGS=floatX=float64
```

If you want a certain setting attached to a specific Python script, you can do this:

```
$ THEANO_FLAGS=floatX=float32 python you_name_here.py
```

If you want to see which computational method your Theano system is using, type the following:

```
print(theano.config.device)
```

If you want to change all the settings, both bits floating point and computational method (GPU or CPU) of a specific piece of script, type as follows:

```
$ THEANO_FLAGS=device=gpu,floatX=float32 python your_script.py
```

This can be very handy for the testing and coding. You might not want to use the GPU all the time; sometimes it is better to use the CPU for the prototyping and sketching and run it on the GPU once your script is ready.

First, let's test if GPU works for your setup. You can skip this if you don't have an NVIDIA GPU card on your computer:

```
from theano import function, config, shared, sandbox
import theano.tensor as T
```

```
import numpy
import time

vlen = 10 * 30 * 768  # 10 x #cores x # threads per core
iters = 1000

rng = numpy.random.RandomState(22)
x = shared(numpy.asarray(rng.rand(vlen), config.floatX))
f = function([], T.exp(x))
print(f.maker.fgraph.toposort())
t0 = time.time()
for i in xrange(iters):
    r = f()
t1 = time.time()
print("Looping %d times took %f seconds" % (iters, t1 - t0))
print("Result is %s" % (r,))
if numpy.any([isinstance(x.op, T.Elemwise) for x in f.maker.fgraph.
toposort()]):
    print('Used the cpu')
else:
    print('Used the gpu')
```

Now that we know how to configure Theano, let's run through some simple examples to see how it works. Basically, every piece of Theano code is composed of the same structure:

1. The initialization part where the variables are declared in the class.
2. The compiling where the functions are formed.
3. The execution where the functions are applied to data types.

Let's use these principles in some basic examples of vector computations and mathematical expressions:

```
#Initialize a simple scalar
x = T.dscalar()


fx = T.exp(T.tan(x**2)) #initialize the function we want to use.

type(fx)                #just to show you that fx is a theano variable
type


#Compile create a tanh function
```

```
f = theano.function(inputs=[x], outputs=[fx])

#Execute the function on a number in this case

f(10)
```

As we mentioned before, we can use Theano for mathematical expressions. Look at this example where we use a powerful Theano feature called *autodifferentiation*, a feature that becomes highly useful for backpropagation:

```
fp = T.grad(fx, wrt=x)
fs= theano.function([x], fp)



fs(3)

output:] 4.59
```

Now that we understand the way in which we can use variables and functions, let's perform a simple logistic function:

```
#now we can apply this function to  matrices as well
x = T.dmatrix('x')
s = 1 / (1 + T.exp(-x))
logistic = theano.function([x], s)
logistic([[2, 3], [.7, -2],[1.5,2.3]])

output:
array([[ 0.88079708,  0.95257413],
       [ 0.66818777,  0.11920292],
       [ 0.81757448,  0.90887704]])
```

We can clearly see that Theano provides faster methods of applying functions to data objects than would be possible with NumPy.

Index

wide networks 148
WinPython
  about 15
  URL 15
word2vec 22

X

XGBoost
  about 7, 23, 24
  URL, for installing 23

Y

Yet Another Resource
        Negotiator (YARN) 8, 326

Z

zero-padding 202